956.   Perlmutter, Amos.
94   Israel, the
Per   partitioned state

DATE DUE			
FEB 2 7 1993			

ISRAEL
THE PARTITIONED STATE

Also by Amos Perlmutter

Modern Authoritarianism: A
Comparative Institutional Analysis
(1981)

Political Roles & Military Rulers (1981)

Politics & the Military in Israel,
1967–1977 (1978)

The Military & Politics in Modern
Times: Professionals, Praetorians &
Revolutionary Soldiers (1977)

Egypt: The Praetorian State (1974)

Military & Politics in Israel: Nation
Building & Role Expansion (1969)

ISRAEL
THE PARTITIONED STATE

A Political History Since 1900

Amos Perlmutter

Charles Scribner's Sons
New York

Library of Congress Cataloging-in-Publication Data

Perlmutter, Amos.
   Israel, the partitioned state.

   Bibliography: p.
   Includes index.
   1. Israel—Politics and government. I. Title.
DS126.5.P439   1985   956.94   85-14513
ISBN 0-684-18396-X

1 3 5 7 9 11 13 15 17 19   F/C   20 18 16 14 12 10 8 6 4 2

Printed in the United States of America.

   Acknowledgment is due to Martin Gilbert and George Weidenfeld &
Nicolson Limited for permission to reproduce the five maps taken from
The Arab-Israeli Conflict.

This book is dedicated with love to Ingeborg

Table of Contents

Foreword and
Acknowledgments

This book is, first and foremost, a political history of Israel.

As such, it centers on the domestic issues as they have influenced and modified the concepts of Israel's frontiers and security. Thus, much interesting diplomatic and military information and many developments have gone by the wayside, except as they pertain to the international, ideological and political arrangements and orientations of the Yishuv in Palestine and in the State of Israel.

This is not meant to be a detailed narrative of political and military events, nor even a purely analytical sociopolitical interpretation of Israel. Rather, it combines the two into one.

I have offered the concept of the partitioned state as the most efficient and in my view perceptive way of dealing with close to a century of a complex political movement and polity.

In order to remain loyal to the concept, some events and portraits of personages have been omitted with regret.

In writing and gathering material for this book I have been dependent on a multitude of original documentation, including a quite vast array of monographic and secondary literature in Hebrew, English, German, Yiddish and Arabic.

In gathering material for the first four chapters, I have greatly depended on the monographic and secondary literature which is even now growing by leaps and bounds. The remainder of the book relies heavily on my interpretation, which is based on original research, interviews, and my own personal and sometimes intimate acquaintance with practically all of the significant political and intellectual leaders of Israel since the 1960s.

This involves dealing with a two-edged sword. I like to think that personal contact has not influenced my interpretation, that objectivity has not been sacrificed.

I have had use of all the major contemporary Israeli periodicals without feeling the need to quote them extensively. However, a constant perusal of these papers, such as *Haaretz, Maariv, Yediot Aharonot,* and *Davar,* is absolutely necessary for the contemporary student of Israel.

This book had its beginning in a series of lectures for the Lehrman Institute, which provided intellectual and some financial support. Thanks go particularly to Nicolas Rizopolous, a scholar and a most severe critic who helped me shape the book in its early concepts. The number of critics the institute provided led to long and hairsplitting seminars which resulted in confronting me with the things I had not done and should have done. This may have been a painful process, but it was a necessary one and I am grateful.

I am particularly grateful to many friends and colleagues who read earlier drafts of the manuscript. I also wish to mention and thank the valuable people who helped in the structure and production of the book, in particular Gerhard (Gary) Tischler, a loyal, excellent and invaluable editor whose good humor helped keep things in perspective; my agent and critic, Leona Schechter, for all she did; and last but not least, Alex Holzman of Scribners for a wonderful job of trimming a heavy manuscript and putting it all in order.

This book is dedicated to someone I feel most intimate with who came in time to help and encourage and whose warmth softened the rough edges in myself and in the book.

THE ZIONIST STRUGGLE OVER TERRITORY AND PARTITION:

1917–1947

Preface

The war which Israel fought and pursued so successfully and tragically in Lebanon in 1982 was, on the surface, unlike any it had fought in its brief and often violent history. Technologically, it was very much a war of the latter part of the twentieth century, with Israel's thoroughly dominant and technologically sophisticated armed forces, combining tough and superbly equipped infantry with superior tanks and an array of electronically amazing air weaponry, battling a Soviet-equipped and highly professional Syrian army complete with missiles, and a Palestinian Liberation Army force that still called itself a guerrilla army but was about as far removed from a guerrilla army as Napoleon's forces were removed from a group of battling cavemen.

It was the first of Israel's wars fought exclusively in an Arab country, and technically a neutral country at that. For Israel and its Menachem Begin-led government, this caused considerable political, ideological, and emotional repercussions, both within Israel itself and on the international front. It was the first war in which large portions of the body politic within Israel seriously questioned both the aims and methods of the war being fought next door and protested loudly, thus making a political issue of a war which to many stretched the definition of "defensive" to its limits.

Even as the Falklands war was fought an ocean away in what amounted to a media blackout, the war in Lebanon may have been

3

the most heavily media-covered war not involving the United
States in the twentieth century, and the most controversial in the
images, information, and misinformation it brought to viewers and
readers throughout the world. Israel fought many wars: A war of
independence in 1948. A war in 1956 in collusion with Britain and
France against Egyptian-led fedayeen. A second war of liberation
in 1967, the famous Six-Day War against three Arab states, Egypt,
Syria, and Jordan. A war that began as a disaster and ended
triumphantly in 1973, the Yom Kippur war. But the war in
Lebanon was completely different from these. For the first time, as
the war dragged on with all its suffering, it seemed that Israel was
being held at great length under the scrutiny of world opinion, not
only for its military actions, but for its very structure, philosophy,
and leadership. It was as if Israel had for the first time been
recognized as something that existed in real time and space, not as
a heroic myth.

What was missing in all this scrutiny was perspective, both
historical and philosophical. It was easy to focus on Begin as a
master rhetorician, a stubborn, defiant autocrat, a former terrorist,
without understanding that he was not some simplistic ogre who
popped out of a political box several years ago, but rather
belonged to a tradition of dissent and conflict deep in the history
of Zionism and of Israeli politics. It was easy, in the United States,
to focus on Defense Minister Ariel Sharon as an overweight,
preening, Pattonlike villain conducting a vindictive war of conquest, and to forget the larger and complicated issues of the war,
which centered around perennial Israeli concerns of safety, borders, and security. It was easy to take heart in the dissent that the
war, especially the ugly Sabra-Shatila Christian Phalange massacre,
generated, and easy to see the burgeoning Israel Peace Movement
as a hopeful sign, without realizing that dissent, a peace movement, and political discord have been a part of the growth of Israel
since long before it became an official state.

Modern as the war was, as scrutinized and apparently controversial as Israel has become, there was nevertheless a ghostly
quality about the proceedings, as if Israel were still a nation trying
to become—a people and political entity still wrestling with old
issues and concerns. The political and economic realities of the
Middle East may be startlingly different today—there was no
OPEC when David Ben-Gurion, Chaim Weizmann, and Zionist
politicians and ideologues were fiercely debating the future fron-

tiers of the nation in the 1930s and 1940s, for instance. But the great debates that wrack contemporary Israel—borders and security, the nature of Eretz Israel, the Palestinian (read Arab) problem—reverberate throughout the political history of Israel in the twentieth century.

The great men who forged the modern state of Israel, either side by side or in bitter acrimony—Ben-Gurion, Weizmann, Jabotinsky, and others—may seem like dim memories today, but Begin was tied securely to their legacy, himself a vivid part of the struggle of creation. With the Egyptian-Israeli peace treaty already signed, with the Palestinians clamoring for a state of their own, the Balfour Declaration of 1917 seems to many people today as ancient and dusty as the Dead Sea scrolls, yet this flimsy, almost noncommittal piece of paper crafted by long-dead British imperialists remains at the heart of battles waged in the 1980s.

Modern as this last war was, and modern as Israel is, the principal issues of the war for Israel were issues that are almost as old as the first organized Jewish settlements. The principal issue of the Lebanese war was one of frontiers, borders, and security.

On a practical level, Israel accomplished what it set out to do in this war, and it would seem that Israel ought to feel satisfied with the practical results. Those results left the remaining combatants and major challengers to Israeli security in temporary disarray, their weapons blunted and no longer a serious threat. The Palestinian Liberation Organization, which had used Lebanon as a military haven from which to launch sporadic attacks against Israel, was militarily routed, chased from its sanctuaries, its military organization shattered, and its only remaining recourse to enter the diplomatic arena with very few cards left to play. Almost incidentally, the threat of Syrian missiles in the Bekaa Valley was also eliminated, and Syria's military forces suffered a chastening setback in brief, sharp, and costly encounters.

Despite a heavy diplomatic and political cost, Israel has managed to secure its northern borders. Coupled with the security afforded by the Egyptian-Israeli peace treaty, this makes Israel territorially secure for the first time in its struggle-filled history. Jordan has long since opted to stay away from military confrontation with Israel. Egypt will not challenge Israel's southern borders. With the PLO ejected from Lebanon, with Syria quiescent and the Golan Heights temporarily annexed, Israel has no serious, practical military challengers around its once insecure borders and frontiers.

Israel may be territorially secure, but old themes, voices, and faces still seem to echo from the past. The debate over autonomy, the Palestinians, settlements and the West Bank, and over secure boundaries is a variation on old debates that went by other names and were waged in World Zionist Congress meetings decades ago, in the political halls of the pre-state entity that was the Yishuv, in the first Knesset, and in the Knessets flush with undreamt-of military victories. To have heard Begin expound passionately on Eretz Israel, the old biblical lands of Israel, was to hear again the voice of Revisionist Zionism and its long-dead founder, Zeev Jabotinsky. When hearing the leader of the Labor Party, Prime Minister Shimon Peres, complain about Begin's autocratic ways, one must remember how fiercely Labor's founder and father, David Ben-Gurion, tried to stamp out the followers of Revisionist Zionism, and recall how deep the struggle really goes. Old themes, old fears, and old drives are still very much alive in today's Israel—frontiers, security, the Arab question, Palestine, Eretz Israel, internal political struggles, and the world at large.

Since its original establishment as a mandatory, Palestine has been actually partitioned three times—in 1947, in 1967, and again after 1973—and each time by the use of force. The focus of this book is the struggle between domestic, ideological, and political groups, and the dominant ideas and issues with which an extraordinary group of men and women struggled as they first tried to create and then to maintain a state. It is also about some highly individualistic people and their roles: Chaim Weizmann, Zeev Jabotinsky, David Ben-Gurion, Berl Katznelson, Yitzhak Tabenkin, Moshe Sharett, Moshe Dayan, Yigal Allon, Golda Meir, Menachem Begin, and Ariel Sharon. It is about these people, and it is about the political systems and arrangements inherent in the old Yishuv and in the contemporary state of Israel.

The political history of Israel often seems like a continuous rite of passage, from passionate, intellectual necessity to idealistic, almost revolutionary fervor, to a deadly struggle for survival, to the hard necessity of pragmatic politics, and the even more difficult role of a mini-superpower. The roots of Israel lie in Zionism, a movement expounded and developed by men who themselves had no affinity for the harsh soil of Palestine, but who called for an end to Jewish exile and diaspora as a solution to the dilemma of Jewish life in Europe, where assimilation and pogroms existed side by side. It was a movement which passionately called for return and regeneration, an irresistible drive for identity and safety to be found outside the confines of foreign states and countries. It focused, in deed and in theory, on issues of immigration, settlements, and frontiers, which all combined into a preoccupation with the issue of security, an issue that was to dominate the life of the Yishuv and of Israel.

The politics of prestate Israel—the Yishuv (meaning literally the Jewish Community in Palestine)—the social and political structures in Palestine built by Ben-Gurion, and what was eventually to become the Labor Party to function as a foundation and quasigoverning body, concentrated on the formation of the state and the defense of Israel's borders.

The proposed partitions of Palestine before 1949 were the works of foreign powers and the international community, not the work of Zionists, who had never planned for partition yet accepted them. These partitions served to reduce the territory that the Jews had claimed for themselves in 1922. The partitions since 1949, all of them the results of aggressive wars initiated by the Arabs against the Jews, reversed that trend, resulting in a protracted but continued enlargement of Israel's territory at the expense of the defeated Arabs.

The politics of the first partitioned state of 1947–1967 dealt with the agonizing and practical task of achieving independence and maintaining physical survival in a hostile Arab world. A marked change, however, occurred with the second partitioned state, which dates from the triumphant 1967 war. The problems after 1967 were still related to political legitimacy, frontiers, and settlements, but they were no longer connected with physical survival or political independence. They nevertheless resurrected with ever greater intensity several of the original problems that faced the Yishuv and the first partitioned state. This time in a different international environment and by a considerably different state of mind among the Israelis.

If the third partitioned state presided over by Begin—and now the National Unity government headed by Peres and Shamir—appeared to have settled the issue of frontiers, it did not settle the issue of the Arab question and the exact nature of Eretz Israel (complete Israeli domination of all western Palestine), which remains like a Gordian knot along Israel's eastern frontiers.

From the 1948 war for independence to roughly the mid-1970s, Israel enjoyed something it had not enjoyed in the days before independence: a national consensus on frontiers and the Palestine question. The debate over the nature of Eretz Israel, territory, and Palestine has now all but destroyed that consensus, propelled to a great degree by the implications of the war in Lebanon and the gradual annexation of the rest of the West Bank. The issue of Eretz Israel is old, and it again has deeply divided Israel ideologically and politically in a manner not seen since the early days of the Yishuv, when the issue of partition itself first arose.

That almost innocent consensus began to show cracks immediately after the 1967 war. Ironically, military victory brought an end to a kind of political simplicity within Israel and a simplistic vision of how Israel saw itself. The territories gained in the wake of the 1967 war were a mixed blessing, to say the least, in that they brought territorial safety but created new problems and serious schisms within the Israeli social and political fabric. They created a whole body of ideological movements which called for revision of the frontiers and of the first partitioned state. An almost bellicose, heroic posture emanated from a variety of factions and groups.

The Labor party took the lead with the creation of a string of military kibbutzim along the Jordan River and the implementation of Moshe Dayan's policy of "open bridges," meaning a way of keeping options open toward a Jordanian solution to the West Bank problem. As if on cue, a whole crop of political and ideological movements, either flush with victory or almost despairing over it, began to emerge. The movements were diverse and ran from the Land of Israel movement, which called for the total integration of the Sinai, the Golan Heights and the West Bank-Gaza into Eretz Israel, to its dovish counterpoint in the Peace Movement, which opposed settlements and wanted an Israeli-Jordanian-Palestinian compromise over the future of the West Bank.

These fissures were only the start. While Laborites, beginning to tire politically as their giant figures died one by one, sought a Jordanian solution on the West Bank, more radical forces saw the new boundaries as a mere correction of imperialistic errors. The rise of the Zionist orthodox Jewry and the growth of the usually moderate Religious Zionist parties into a fundamentalist, radical force widened the fissures still further. The Gush Emunim were in the forefront of the maximalists, expounding ideas and theses derived from the Old Testament Scriptures.

The elections of 1977, 1981, and 1984 bared the cracks that had begun to appear in the national consensus. The war in Lebanon added to the fissures when it lengthened and deepened into the drawn-out siege of West Beirut. The Sabra-Shatila massacre perpetrated by Phalangist forces, apparently with the implicit support of the Israeli Defense Force, ripped consensus apart as a commission of inquiry followed and debate raged while Israeli forces remained in southern Lebanon.

The question after the 1984 elections is not of one government or another's survival. Israel appears once again to be defining and redefining its territorial aspirations, which is the essence of the politics of security of the third partitioned state. As in the days before statehood, the same question is being asked and debated: What are the final boundaries of the state?

The answers to that question are, it is hoped, to be found in this book. Different men throughout Israel's history and prehistory have answered this question differently. For Theodore Herzl, there were no boundaries, no real country or state, only the passionate notion that the Jews must find a homeland of their own. For Chaim Weizmann, the Jewish state was indelibly tied to the British Mandatory, which existed like some protective umbrella overhead. For David Ben-Gurion, neither a fundamentalist nor a visionary, the boundaries of the state were flexible, never finally fixed, dependent on the nature and need of the historical moment. For Zeev Jabotinsky, who violently opposed the idea of any sort of partition, and even more so for Menachem Begin, the caretaker of Jabotinsky's ideas, the state meant unpartitioned Eretz Israel, Complete Israel, the old biblical lands of Judea and Samaria, in which there is no room for real Palestinian autonomy, let alone a Palestinian state.

Thus, the political history of Israel and its institutions becomes a description of a great debate over boundaries, argued by great men who then enacted imperfect resolutions of that debate. As we can see in Israel today, in Lebanon, and in the West Bank, the debate goes on.

CHAPTER 1

Why A Jewish State?
An Overview

Redemption, colonization, and statehood have been the permanent themes of the Jewish people's third attempt in two thousand years to bring an end to their great exile.[1] The Jewish return to Palestine did not spring miraculously out of a giant outpouring of post-Holocaust guilt. It was not an act of political trickery, nor was it entirely made possible by the courage and fighting spirit of the Jewish men and women who fought for independence. It was the culmination of a process and was made possible by men possessed of visionary, sometimes messianic idealism and a commitment to collectivism supported by stubborn individualism. The men who brought about the great return were a diverse lot, a group of highly committed, devoted, egocentric and diverse leaders, philosophers and ideologues, all of whom, in practice and spirit, were Zionists of one sort or another.

Today, we may feel that the language and rhetoric found in early Zionist letters and oratory contain strong strains of romantic visions and naivete. The early history of Zionism and pioneerism in Israel is replete with apocalyptic expectations, platitudes, and contradictions rooted in the pristine and uncomplicated early days of socialism and communism, and in the nationalist ideology of pre-World War I Eastern and Central Europe.

Naive, messianic, or even illogical as they may often sound, these pronouncements of the early visionaries of Zionism must be taken seriously and inspected closely if we are to understand the modern state of Israel. It is precisely the combination of hard-nosed, political pragmatism and passionate flights of ideological fancy that explains much about the formation of modern Israel and its political organization. The question, then, is this: Why the partitioned state? Here, we find the messianic dream coupling with the pragmatic.

To the practical Zionists who settled Palestine after 1917, partition was always a euphemism for eventual statehood. It was a vehicle to be used toward final achievement of Jewish sovereignty in historical Eretz Israel, never an end in itself. Soon after the first partition of mandated Palestine in 1922, however, it became painfully clear to the Zionists that the territory of Palestine would become divisible. With this realization came the knowledge that the intent of the mandatory—the supervisory British governing authority—was anything but to assist in the formation of a Jewish state. It would, in fact, impede that process. With some senior clerks in the British foreign and colonial offices advocating the eventual creation of an independent Arab state in Palestine, British antipathy would eventually turn into outright hostility in 1939 with the issuance of the Chamberlain government's famous White Paper, which forbade Jewish immigration to Palestine and land purchase in Palestine by Jews.

Israel's founding fathers and the early Zionists did not set out to create a divided, truncated and fragile state in Palestine. In fact, not until the middle 1930s, after decades of struggle, debate and bloodshed had already passed did the political leaders of Zionism (as personified by Chaim Weizmann and the leaders of the World Zionist Organization) and the leaders of what constituted the political entity of Palestine, known as the Yishuv, even begin to contemplate the possibility of a partitioned state.

Forced to confront such issues, the Zionists split into two camps. Socialist Zionists like David Ben-Gurion saw a partitioned Palestine as half a loaf, an initial and decisive step toward statehood, whatever the size of the original territory. Revisionist Zionists vehemently rejected any sort of partition. Under the leadership of Zeev Jabotinsky, they advocated establishing Jewish sovereignty and statehood over all of mandatory Palestine, including Transjordan.

When the issue of the partitioned state first began to be hotly debated, many more Zionist leaders than Zeev Jabotinsky looked at the idea with horror. The very idea and prospect of a partitioned state, which would by nature be initially weak, sparked a debate that was singularly heated and violent, leading to a political struggle that in some ways has never quite ended. Even Ben-Gurion, who eventually almost willed the partitioned state into being, was at first skeptical, but he saw its practical side, its wedgelike aspect that would eventually mean the possibility of a strong and independent Israel.

The early Zionists quite simply meant to establish an autonomous, undivided Jewish hegemony over the entire mandated territory of Palestine, despite the large Arab population in the same territory. The early Zionists were single-minded. Although they did not ignore the Arab problem entirely, they considered it a problem to be solved later, after their main objective was achieved—the creation of a Jewish state.

Zionist and Yishuv leaders alike wanted a Jewish state, but just what the borders of that state would be, none of them quite knew. Borders were not at first discussed in pragmatic, realistic terms. They grew not from preplanned maps, but from political and historical events and outside forces. From the Palestinian Arab and Pan-Arab nationalist movements which resulted in riots after 1920 to the British mandatory in Palestine after 1937 to the Arab-Israel wars of 1947–1949, 1956, 1967, 1973, and 1982, the actual borders of Israel changed with events. They will most likely change again in the wake of the war in Lebanon and certainly the ideas of boundaries will undergo yet another subtle transformation.

What is important to know about boundaries, and therefore partition, is that the changes in the borders—from the proposed British partition of Palestine in 1936–1937 to the actual United Nations resolution partitioning Palestine in 1947 and the re-shaped borders of the 1967 war (which amounted to another partition)—these changes have all resulted in a continuous debate and war over the ever-changing definitions and actual borders of the state. Outside influences—Anglo-Zionist diplomacy, Arab-Israeli wars, American-Israeli relations and negotiations culminating in the Camp David accords of 1979—have all tended to modify extreme Zionist aspirations to lay claim to the whole of British Palestine, which until 1922 included Transjordan as well.

The whole political history of Israel is the history and evolution of the partitioned state, including the challenge of the Arab and non-Arab international community. Before we examine such issues as the challenge of Arab nationalism and the relations between the Jews and the British mandatory, we must first look at the leaders whose names have become synonymous with the partitioned state, the Yishuv and Israel. We begin with Theodor Herzl, Chaim Weizmann, Zeev Jabotinsky, and that watershed historical figure, David Ben-Gurion.

Herzl, Weizmann, Jabotinsky, and Ben-Gurion

Men like Theodor Herzl, Chaim Weizmann, and Zeev Jabotinsky loomed large in the history of Zionism. All were pathfinders whose roots were in Europe, whose connections to Palestine were more cerebral or ethereally passionate than real. David Ben-Gurion, on the other hand, marked a radical turning point. He was different in nature, outlook, and especially in deeds. He was the man who literally brought forth the state. When all the arguments and differences, and there were many, were settled, his vision prevailed.

Herzl, Weizmann, and Jabotinsky were markedly different from Ben-Gurion: they were all fin-de-siècle Central and East European intellectuals. They were all dabblers and Renaissance men. Each spoke several European languages. Herzl was a journalist who sometimes wrote flimsy Austrian-style plays and comedies; Jabotinsky was a distinguished and prolific journalist who at one time or another wrote for many of the major and most influential Central European newspapers of the time; Weizmann, a chemist, was considered a distinguished scientist.

None of them particularly liked to rough it. They were men who called themselves, in true intellectual style, "modernists," admirers of the European and Jewish cultural renaissance. To varying degrees they all liked to partake of the good life, especially Weizmann, whose affinity for material pleasures might have stemmed from an impoverished early life. They were indelibly European in nature, steeped in European culture, diplomacy, and ideology. No wonder that Weizmann, a great admirer of Herzl, clung so long and so hopelessly to a British solution to Jewish sovereignty. He was the only Anglophile in the group, while Herzl, an Austrian Jew who never spoke Hebrew, and Jabotinsky, were classic assimilationists who nevertheless lost hope in assimilation as the answer to the Jewish problem.

All three men thought themselves to be highly cultivated, and accordingly dressed meticulously in the latest fashion. Weizmann was a warm, garrulous and sociable man, who, while he loved to spend hours with his friends and bask in their admiration, would often make pointed criticism of them once they were out of earshot. Herzl was more aloof, which, along with his Hungarian background, perhaps explains his admiration of German culture. Jabotinsky was less flamboyant and much less imposing, but he was the man who would cause serious dissension within the ruling body politic of Israel before it became a state. He also was the spiritual father of Menachem Begin. All three seemed to imitate and exude European statesmen and leaders of their day—they *looked* like natural leaders, distinguished and worldly. Small wonder that they were perceived by the Jewish masses as the uncrowned modern Jewish kings, recalling David and Solomon.[2]

For Herzl, Weizmann and Jabotinsky, Zionism, whatever form it eventually followed, was theoretical, an idea and a movement that was internationalist, liberal, and dedicated to the redemption of the Jewish idea. To them, the Jewish homeland was an idea, not necessarily a real place which would have to be fought over with blood and sweat. One could search for years and not find a man more different in both appearance and method from these three than David Ben-Gurion, who seemed so far removed from their backgrounds.

Ben-Gurion was an early Polish immigrant, self-educated, with no knowledge of Western European languages. He spoke mainly Hebrew and Yiddish-Polish. At first sight, he looked like a plodder. In his thirties, according to his biographer, he was "rough, stubborn, undelicate and unrefined. He was a short man, stocky, his face sunburned and determined. He looked energetic, powerful, and gave the impression of firmness. His articles and speeches were tedious and boring, and repetitious."[3]

While Weizmann, internationally famous by the 1920s, was pursuing his varied interests, of which Zionism was only one, Ben-Gurion was doing the dirty work of politics, the accumulative, tedious, and unexciting organization work for his party and trade union. He was tireless and single-minded. It was perhaps boring work, but it gave Ben-Gurion an enormous advantage in political experience at the lowest level, while Weizmann started at the top. For Ben-Gurion, politics was life itself. He was persistent and dogged, a politician who was elected to every office to which he aspired, often over the politically dead bodies of his rivals.

A self-educated intellectual, Ben-Gurion nevertheless admired both Weizmann and Jabotinsky. While his only medals and degrees came in the shape of sharp political scars, he was absolutely sure of his own worth, a confidence which he drew from himself, not his limited background.

If Herzl, and later Jabotinsky and Weizmann, were representative of Zionism in thought and spirit, then Ben-Gurion was the ultimate example of Zionism in action. Pragmatist and pioneer, he represented Zionism's fulfillment. His world was totally centered in Palestine, where, to put it in modern terms, the action was. Herzl visited Palestine once, and only once, and was appalled by its Ottoman-Arab backwardness. Jabotinsky eventually became an exile from Palestine. Weizmann, if he thought of Palestine at all, saw it from the vantage point of the great world of London, Geneva, or New York. In his own elegant way, Weizmann was still very much the wandering Jew. By contrast, Ben-Gurion's heart, his fists, his whole intellect were centered in dusty Palestine. He was home at last, he had sunk his roots deeply in Eretz Israel. Weizmann knew and enjoyed London society; Ben-Gurion knew the rough life of Zionist pioneers in Palestine.

Weizmann, Jabotinsky, and Ben-Gurion often seemed to grow from each other. With the exception of Herzl, who died young and was almost an icon to the other three, they crossed paths, worked together, and would eventually become involved in monumental political struggles with each other. There would come a struggle for leadership between Weizmann and Ben-Gurion in 1942 to 1949 over ideology and control of Zionist policy; a struggle between Ben-Gurion and his Mapai-Labor party over partition; and a struggle between Weizmann and Ben-Gurion against Jabotinsky and his Revisionist Zionist followers and terrorists. But they were, by any definition of the term, great men.

Yet a curious unfulfillment, a heavy strain of tragedy runs through all their lives, binding them together as surely as did their dreams, visions and deeds that centered around the Jewish homeland. Herzl, who sparked Zionism with his vision and ideas, died suddenly and young, without a profound idea of what passions and deeds he had stirred. Weizmann died a broken man, his Zionist leadership wrested from him by Ben-Gurion, his too-long-at-the-fair dance with the British discredited. Jabotinsky was exiled from Palestine and died in New York, his own Revisionist Zionist movement taken over by followers whose violent, radical tactics appalled him.

Even Ben-Gurion, without whom it can be safely said there would be no modern Israel, died in retirement and exile, touched by a certain amount of disillusionment, edged out of power by the very party he had nurtured and built in his own image.

Search for a Homeland: The Failure of Assimilation and the Coming of Theodor Herzl

In 1897, when Theodor Herzl, after issuing a plea for an unnamed Jewish homeland, became president of the World Zionist Organization, the land that would eventually become Israel had been a part of the Ottoman empire for some 400 years. What constituted Palestine, although it had no such name, was a barren land of some 27,000 square kilometers of no determinate boundaries, although it was bounded by the Jordan River. It included a thinly populated coastal line between Haifa and Jaffa (now Tel Aviv), both of which were port cities. There were few cities, and most of the population contented itself with agriculture. There was little else to do.

The population was predominantly Arab. Of the some 700,000 people residing in what constituted Palestine at the time, most were non-Jews, primarily Moslems, but also Christian Arabs. Most (some three-fourths) were peasants and 81 percent were illiterate. There were some 35,000 Jews, most of them residing in Jerusalem and the port cities, working primarily in commerce, banking, and the civil service. Except for a small foray by Russian anarchists and the Lovers of Zion movement in 1882, financed by Baron Rothschild, there had been no organized Jewish immigration of any sort in Palestine. That particular community of Russian Jews, which attempted to create an agricultural community while having absolutely no talent for it, was however the first fruit of a flowering Zionist movement all over Europe, and the first sign that many thinking Jews were beginning to despair of assimilation as an answer to their problems and to the virus of anti-Semitism.

The yearning to return to Zion, to the biblical lands of Israel, to Jerusalem, was nothing new, of course. The yearning, however, had always expressed itself as a surge of messianic movement, blazing briefly in various centuries, most recently in the 1870s. These earlier movements had seemed always to grow out of despair and yearning, and intense nostalgia, instead of from some practical vision. The Enlightenment and the French Revolution had in fact dimmed the fervor of Zionism briefly in Europe as Jews struggled to embrace assimilation as a way of finding themselves.

We are here talking about those Jews living in Western Europe—in France, England and especially Germany—not the Jews living along what is termed the Pale of Settlement in western Russia, eastern Poland, northeastern Austria, and Galicia. The most famous assimilationist was Moses Mendelssohn, a philosopher and teacher who translated the Bible into German and was a contemporary of Schiller (1759–1805) and Goethe (1749–1832) during the Weimar Renaissance in the middle eighteenth century. Mendelssohn, although often attacked by German anti-Semites, nevertheless concluded that the Jew neither had to live like a pariah among his neighbors, nor cling to his orthodoxy, that the Bible was not contradictory to modern life. There was a rush among the European Jews of the late eighteenth and early-to-middle nineteenth centuries to assimilate, to convert to Lutheranism, a rush that spilled over into the Russian Empire as restrictions against Jews everywhere were lifted. It was, as Jews ruefully learned, a false spring. Anti-Semitism persisted, a hurtful and dangerous clamor in the background. The gains—citizenship, participation in society and the political process, immersion into the cultural life of a nation—were not tantamount to acceptance and were achieved at the cost of self-identity.

Moses Hess, a German Jew and a forerunner of Karl Marx (who, incidentally, was contemptuous of Jewish attempts at assimilation), probably had it right all along. A leading intellectual and Socialist thinker and a student of Hegel, Hess was dubbed the Red Rabbi. He wrote in 1864 that Jews "were not German. Our noses are different. We have to go back to Jerusalem." Without anybody really noticing it, this was the first real call for practical Zionism.

The first flowering of Zionism came oddly enough in Russia, not in Germany of the Enlightenment. The ascension of Czar Alexander II (1855–1881) brought about the long-overdue freeing of serfs in 1861 and eased restrictions on Jews. Now Jews rushed to become journalists, poets, musicians, and writers in a frantic effort to show an unimpressed society that they had much to contribute to Mother Russia. This Russian spring ended quickly enough with the assassination of Alexander II in 1881 and the ascension of Alexander III (1881–1894), who did what European rulers have always done when disaster strikes: he blamed it on the Jews. The result was a massive series of pogroms which ended once and for all Jewish hopes for assimilation into the mainstream of Russian life.

The pogroms, violent and murderous, sent shock waves throughout the European community and sparked Leon Pinsker, a Russian Jew who previously had been an ardent assimilationist, to write a book called *Auto-Emancipation* (1882). Pinsker despaired of assimilation as the hope for the solution of the Jewish problem and called for the creation of a Jewish homeland. The pogroms also spurred the Lovers of Zion movement, which previously had been a scattered and half-hearted movement of intellectuals and students, to call for a return to the Jewish homeland in Zion. It was a contingent of Lovers of Zion members who in 1882 made up the first small trickle of Jewish immigrationists; the first Biln immigration.

It took somewhat longer for Theodor Herzl to become the father of Zionism. Born in 1860 in Budapest into the upper middle class, Herzl was almost the quintessential assimilated Jew. By 1895 he had become a journalist of some note and wrote for newspapers and journals all over Europe, including the *Neue Freie Presse* of Vienna. He was very much at home in the Hapsburg world of Vienna, a dilettante who might have been a character out of one of Schnitzler's light comedies and who, in fact, did himself write an occasional light play. Tall, more handsome than most, and sporting a typical Viennese beard, he had practically no sense of being a Jew. Although multilingual, he could not speak Hebrew.

The Dreyfus trial, which he took on as a journalistic assignment, penetrated to his very Jewish core. Dreyfus, a not entirely likable Jewish French officer, had been falsely accused of a treasonous act that had actually been committed by another, Gentile officer. The trial became a cause célèbre and a sensation; its obvious and patent railroading of the young Dreyfus attracted no less a personage than the novelist Emile Zola to rail against the French government with his famous pronouncement "J'accuse." More than that, however, it stirred the latent anti-Semitism in the French army and in French society and brought it to the surface, bubbling and out of control.

While covering the trial, Herzl had occasion to hear a rabid French crowd yell with unabashed fervor, "Death to the Jew." If there is such a thing as an instant conversion of the soul, if everyone has at one point or another a meeting on the road to Damascus, Herzl had his right then and there. He was still dapper, he was still handsome, but he had also become a Zionist, a messiah, as his later followers, which included the likes of Jabotinsky and Weizmann, called him.

This form of bearing witness, this living example of the failure of assimilation, seemed at once to mock his own existence and fire him with a sense of mission. An idea began to form within him, what he called "a work of infinite grandeur, a mighty dream"— Jews should have a homeland.

After taking his idea of Jews emigrating to some undefined promised land to various skeptical Jewish financiers, Herzl did what any writer would do: he set down his impassioned dream on paper. The result was a book published in 1896: *The Jew's State.* In it he decried the impossibility and failure of assimilation, recognizing that the Jew, no matter how German, how French, Russian or English he or she felt, would still be the stranger, the person apart. He felt that the Jews of the various nations of Europe were still reluctant visitors, and their hosts were still full of suspicion and deep-seated hatreds. The solution, he felt, was the creation of an independent Jewish state, in a location about which he was conspiciously unspecific.

Both the assimilated Jews of Europe, who converted in order to seek employment, education or position, and Orthodox Jews were hostile toward the idea. But the Lovers of Zion, a movement that at once believed in immigration and extolled the virtues of Jewish culture and the Hebrew and Yiddish languages, took up Herzl's battlecry with a passion. The movement, mostly centered in Russia and Poland, had been badly divided and faltering, but its members became Herzl's natural constituency and he was asked to lead them. Herzl, wandering about Europe, talking with assimilated Jews and with thousands upon thousands of the poor Jews of eastern Europe saw that the latter group was his mass following.

First, he sought influential support. He talked with the Grand Duke of Baden, a relative of Kaiser Wilhelm, and was received warmly if vaguely. He talked with the grand vizier of the Ottoman Empire in Constantinople, but was received cooly. At one point, in 1898, he found himself in Palestine, pondering the beauty of the land and the general squalor of Jerusalem. He also found himself in the presence of Kaiser Wilhlem himself in Jerusalem. Although the Kaiser agreed that the country or the land had something of a future, it was the last Herzl would hear of him and the last time the Kaiser showed any interest in Zionism or a Jewish homeland. Herzl traveled to London and although the general Jewish populace were enthusiastic, influential Jewish leaders were not so optimistic and refused to help.

All along, in all of his travels, Herzl discerned that it was the East Europeans who were sparked by the idea of a Jewish homeland, by the idea and vision of Zionism. Therefore, he decided that it was time to turn Zionism into a mass movement and to organize a mass gathering. In 1897, he called for a general Zionist congress in Basle, Switzerland. While Lovers of Zion delegates returned from their first congress to their homelands, Herzl prepared and began publishing a Zionist newspaper, which he used to publicize the upcoming World Zionist Congress and to spread the Zionist faith, for faith is what it had become to the now entirely committed Herzl.

The World Zionist Congress lasted for three days and had a tremendous turnout of delegates, whom Herzl had urged to dress in formal black dress. The Congress accomplished much: it established the first World Zionist Organization; it adopted a program for Zionism which was essentially Herzl's program; and it named Herzl president and chairman of the World Zionist Organization. Zionism had now become the chief nationalist political movement of the Jews. Among the attendees was Chaim Weizmann, who heard Herzl predict that there would be a Jewish state within fifty years, which turned out to be a remarkable feat of prognostication.

The East European poor and middle class were with him now and he could at least show the world that Zionism was a political movement of some force and pressure, a political lobby for nationalist Jews. But his progress with Jewish financiers and with European politicians was painfully slow. Long negotiations with British diplomats resulted in a British offer to give the Zionists Uganda (actually present-day Kenya), which the pessimistic Herzl dutifully presented to the 1903 meeting of the World Zionist

Congress. The result was probably more painful than even Herzl might have expected. The Congress was thrown into uproar, chaos, and confusion in a battle that nearly split the Zionist movement in two.

In the end, the delegates to the Congress wanted nothing to do with Uganda and rejected the whole idea. They would settle for nothing less than Palestine, which Zionists had already begun to settle, even though there had been attempts at establishing colonies in such distant places as Argentina, Australia, and even Petaluma, California.

The struggle was beginning to become a painful effort for Herzl, wandering all over Europe, meeting kings, diplomats, princes, bankers, and even the Pope. More than ever, he must have felt like the original Wandering Jew. Then, too, he was dismayed at the dissension that was beginning to wrack Zionism: pitched political battles among socialist Zionists, secular Zionists, religious Zionists. Praised in general and still looked upon as a sort of messiah and king, he was nevertheless attacked by the various groups on the specifics of his programs. In the end, he was not really a politician and did not have the strength of a king. He was a writer, a European who hoped that German would be the native language of Israel.

The various struggles, especially the Uganda uproar, very likely broke his zeal. In any case, on July 3, 1904, he died at age 44. The dream of Zionism had lost its king.

After Herzl: Different Roads by Different Men

The Emergence of Weizmann, Jabotinsky, and Ben-Gurion

The death of Theodor Herzl left the Zionist movement without its messianic figurehead. The gentle intellectual who had inspired the idea and the search for a Jewish homeland was gone, but there were others emerging who, although they would often clash in pursuit of their common goal, would make the idea a reality.

Chaim Weizmann, similar in background and cosmopolitan appearance, would come closest to emulating Herzl and wearing the mantle of successor. European to the core, he would pursue Zionism and a Jewish homeland through the diplomatic mazes created by the British Empire. To the end, when it was useless to do so, he clung to the British and would wrest from them early on the one piece of legitimacy that the builders of Israel would need.4

Zeev Jabotinsky would begin as the most assimilated of European Jews, an admirer and passionate follower of Herzl and of Great Britain and Weizmann's British solution. Yet, this Renaissance man of letters would abandon the mandatory to become near-prophet and messiah of a movement that would advocate opposition to Great Britain and the creation of an Israel that would encompass all the old biblical lands, including Judea and Samaria. He was principally a man of ideas, but his followers, romantic and more passionate than he, would take his movement (which would come to be called Revisionist Zionism) away from him. They would achieve a black fame as violent terrorists actively fighting the British. Ironically, the legacy of Jabotinsky, as embodied by former prime minister Menachem Begin, still lives in Israel today and still wreaks emotional havoc.

Finally, there was David Ben-Gurion, who was quite simply the doer, the engineer, the forger of the Yishuv, the founder of the state, the man on the scene. It was Ben-Gurion, at the head of the Socialist Zionist movement, who helped build the physical, social and political structures that encompass the modern state of Israel. Often fueled by sheer will power, stubbornness and doggedness, he had a natural gift for political manipulation and the game of politics.

In the early years of Zionism and the Yishuv, the paths of these three men would cross often. They were united in their love of Zionism and their admiration of Herzl, but often in little else. Over the years they would clash in heated battles. Weizmann, the acknowledged leader of World Zionism, would become locked in a political death struggle with Ben-Gurion for the hearts and minds of Zionism and of Israel. Jabotinsky, an early admirer of Weizmann, would eventually recoil at Weizmann's faithful and often unreasonable pursuit of the British. Ben-Gurion, watching the rise of Jabotinsky's Revisionist Zionist movement in the 1930s and its cadre of fanatical leaders, saw in the movement a threat both to the institutions he was building within Palestine and to his and his party's leadership. He would act ruthlessly and deviously to destroy that threat.

The earliest shaker and mover of the three was Weizmann, whose light shone among the old imperialists in England. The son of a teacher, Weizmann was raised in a small Polish shtetl called

Motale (population 1,000). An energetic youth, he was inspired by Herzl's vision of a Jewish homeland and was weaned on spiritual Zionism of the brand which swept across the Pale of Settlement in the middle and late nineteenth century. Weizmann was present at the first congress of the World Zionist Organization (WZO) in Switzerland, where Herzl made his impassioned plea for a Jewish homeland. Soon he became active in all the Zionist circles, rising in the ranks of the WZO hierarchy, even while he kept busy as a practicing chemist. He traveled all over Europe, carrying the Zionist message and making influential connections[5] with leading Jewish figures Martin Buber, David Wolfsohn, and Max Nordau.

In 1912, we find Weizmann in London, setting up the World Zionism office, working two jobs, as a chemist and as a Manchester University professor, and befriending Sir Lewis Namier, an influential historian, and C. P. Scott of the *Manchester Guardian,* whom many regarded as one of the greatest of Zionist editors. In London, Weizmann's circle of influential acquaintances widened to include three high-powered politicians, David Lloyd George, Winston Churchill, and Arthur Balfour. They seemed reasonable men to Weizmann, and as an admirer of British culture and British imperialism, he was comfortable with them. They in turn appeared sympathetic to the Jewish plight and to the Jewish commitment to the biblical homeland. They seemed dedicated to solving the so-called Jewish misery, and deep in their imperialist hearts they felt that there was no solving the Middle East situation vis-à-vis the Arabs without settling the Jews in Palestine, meaning the Jews had a political use.

During all these talks, some of which included the appearance of Joseph Chamberlain, an old-line imperialist, and Blanche Dougdale (Baffy),[6] a fanatic Zionist who was something of a spy within Britain's elite aristocracy, the idea of a Jewish homeland began to take root in the minds of British statesmen. Weizmann planted the seed, but the British meant to use it for their own ends, and not merely out of some liberal notion of humanity or pity.

By the time World War I was in full swing, the British began to look at Palestine, indeed at all of the old and crumbling Ottoman Empire, with renewed interest, and Weizmann's efforts began to bear fruit. He was always there as the British mulled over how they and the French could divide the Ottoman Empire. There were several schools of thought in the British foreign office; one favored an Egyptian solution, another a Mesopotamian approach, still another an Indian solution. The Hashemite Arabs of the Hejaz, working through Sir Arthur Henry MacMahon, the British governor of Egypt, offered to help the English against the Turks by sparking an Arab uprising. MacMahon indicated that the British might indeed do something for the Arabs in return for their help, a commitment the Arabs were later to interpret as a British promissory note on Palestine.

The British hoped to use the Jews in Palestine as a wedge in 1916–1917 against the French. In 1916 the French and British had signed a then-secret agreement—the Sykes-Picoc treaty—which was an attempt to divide up the Ottoman Empire between them. One of its provisions was that there would be an internationalized Palestine. Now the British wanted to violate the treaty by attempting to create a British mandatory in Palestine.

In February 1917, Sir Mark Sykes, head of the political section in the war cabinet, began negotiating with Weizmann and other Zionist leaders. To the British, the best and easiest way to secure the British mandatory seemed to be to reach an understanding with the Zionist leaders, who in turn appeared to prefer a single protecting power. There were several drafts of the resulting British pronouncement, the Balfour Declaration, but the final version is one of the more curious documents upon which the legitimacy of a nation was ever founded. It read in full:

> I have much pleasure in conveying to you, on behalf of his Majesty's Government, the following declaration of sympathy with Jewish Zionist aspirations which has been submitted to and approved by the Cabinet:
>
> His Majesty's Government view with favour the establishment in Palestine of a national home for the Jewish people, and will use their best endeavors to facilitate the achievement of this object, it being clearly understood that nothing shall be done which may prejudice the civil and religious rights of existing non-Jewish communities in Palestine, or the rights and political status enjoyed by Jews in any other country.
>
> I should be grateful if you would bring this declaration to knowledge of the Zionist Federation.[7]

It is worth taking a closer look at this document, from which so much strife resulted and from which so much hope was taken. In its own constrained, stuffy way, it is almost an informal document, sounding more like a letter of congratulation than an affirmation or commitment. Yet, this is the moral and political instrument, the cornerstone, upon which the Zionists of the Yishuv built the future Jewish state. For Weizmann, it was something of a crowning achievement, committed as he was to the British mandatory. For him, the sun never set on the British empire, and he hoped it would never set in Palestine. As he once said, "I want to turn the mandate of Eretz Israel to the Jews to make it as English as England." This probably would have made the more cynical statesmen of the mandate blanch in embarrassment. Certainly it would not have set well with the Socialist Zionists forging state, party and apparatus in Palestine itself.

The Zionists of the Yishuv knew very well what they had in the Balfour Declaration—a threadbare piece of legitimacy which they would ride and mold until it would seem holy writ chiseled in stone. They had no illusions about British intentions, but would use the Balfour Declaration for their own ends.

Analyzed closely, the Balfour Declaration does not hold up well as either a rallying point or a particularly odious act of imperialistic perfidy, as the Arabs have claimed ever since. The apparent intent is what is important in the Balfour Declaration: one can read "view with favour" and "facilitate the achievement of this object" as either fervent passion or lukewarm support. Likewise one can read "the establishment in Palestine of a national home for the Jewish people" to mean an independent state of Israel, which the Zionists chose it to mean, or something considerably less than that, just as today autonomy does not necessarily mean a future independent Palestinian state. In short, the Balfour Declaration was a classic old world European diplomatic document, something short of a commitment. It sought to please everyone and ended up pleasing no one, as the British, once they became anxious about relations with the Arabs, soon found out.

What was important to the British was that the Balfour Declaration was a document they could, and would, back away from and disown, at least in their minds. It was a cabinet declaration, not an executive decree which morally and politically obligated the mandatory to comply with it. On the surface it seems almost conversational, benign and majestically tolerant, fair to all sides, full of assurances and even a little warmth, encouraging the Zionists while protecting the Arabs with its clause stating "that nothing shall be done which may prejudice the civil and religious rights of existing non-Jewish communities in Palestine. . . ."

The Balfour Declaration as perceived by the Jews did have a prejudice in favor of the Jews, and both the Zionists and Arabs knew it. The Arabs saw in the Balfour Declaration official support for the Jews, and even a promise of an eventual Jewish state within their midst.[8] Indeed, publication of the declaration marked the moment that Palestinian Arab nationalism, quiescent but pregnant with possibility until then, took the offensive against the Zionists.

Weizmann, working patiently in London within the framework of the World Zionist Organization, probably did not see it that way, and if he had, would not have been particularly concerned about the Arabs. Jabotinsky remained at that time an ardent supporter of the British. But the Socialist Zionists in Palestine knew the Balfour Declaration for what it was: both a lifeline of legitimacy for the Jews and an endless and potentially murderous source of enmity between Arab and Jew.

While Weizmann toiled elegantly and effectively among the British aristocracy, the Jewish community in Palestine itself had grown considerably. After the long hiatus following the 1882 immigration of the small and basically ineffectual colony of Lovers of Zion, a new and much larger wave of Jewish immigrants arrived in Palestine in the wake of the horrific Russian pogroms of 1905. This group, most of them Russians or Poles, was not only larger (some 2,000) but also much more efficient, dedicated, and organized. They came to Palestine fired with a purpose, bent on creating a Jewish community, to establish a "Jewish renaissance," a society, an economy, a social structure, and somewhere in the distant future, a state. By the second decade of the twentieth century their number had swelled to some 20,000, a significant figure.

Among this wave of immigrants, most of them young bachelors, was David Ben-Gurion. Although today Ben-Gurion seems always to have been a short, human boulder with a patch of white hair, fierce and aggressive, one has to imagine him as a young man. Picture him as he saw himself: a boy fired with imagination and spirit in the small village of Plonsk in the middle of Poland. The scene seems always bleak, which perhaps accounts for the vivid imagination. In later years, and perhaps this is hindsight and mythmaking of the most majestic kind, he recalled that as a boy he literally saw visions of the old Jewish biblical leaders—Joshua, Saul, Solomon and, not surprisingly, David, who was also a king.

His father was the Jewish equivalent of a solicitor. According to Ben-Gurion himself, he became a political activist at the tender age of nine. As a teenager he joined the Workers of Zion movement and from there went on to become a secretary of the International Socialist Zionist movement. He had found a political and spiritual home equivalent to the emotional and physical home which he would later find in Palestine. In Warsaw, at age 17, he was editor of the Socialist Zionist newspaper *Poale Zion*. He was even then an activist, something of a revolutionary, imbued with the twin spirits of Marxism and Zionism. In 1904, he emigrated along with that illustrious group of 2,000.

The immigrants of this new wave were a different breed of Zionist, imbued with Marxist ideology, stemming mostly from Russia and Poland, foraging among the masses, advocating a leftist work ethic, creating a Leninist-elitist type of party machinery and political organization. These Socialist Zionists combined ideas with real actions, and Ben-Gurion was part of the first prototype kibbutz in the Galilee. They organized settlements and labor strikes against the settled Jewish landlords who ran cooperative settlements strongly based on Arab labor. To Ben-Gurion, still fired with Marxism, this took on aspects of a class struggle and involved a bitter political fight with the non-Socialist capitalist and farming Jews already in place. It also clearly indicated the somewhat divided and contradictory thinking of the Socialist Zionists about the Arab questions and their beloved vision of peaceful agricultural labor. Their thinking was complicated, but also important.[9]

It was from the ranks of Socialist Zionism that most of the leaders of the Yishuv and the state of Israel would come, the ideologues, writers, generals, and political leaders who would set the tone, structure and purpose of Zionist Jewish settlement in Palestine. In their ranks would be found Moshe Sharett, Levi Eshkol, Golda Meir, Yitzhak Tabenkin, the leader of the United Kibbutz Movement; Eliahu Golomb, the future head of the Haganah; the ideological saints of Socialist Zionism such as A. D. Gordon, Berl Katznelson and Y. C. Brenner; and Moshe Dayan, Yitzhak Rabin, Yigal Allon, Shimon Peres, and Teddy Kollek, the leading lights of Labor's second generation.

A Marxist orientation so dominated the early Socialist Zionists that the young Ben-Gurion would write that Arab hatred for Zionism was a combination of class antagonism to the modern Jewish pioneer linked to the Arab laborer's nascent but largely ignorant nationalism, an explanation that simply would not hold water for very long. By 1919, Ben-Gurion revised his thought, saying that the "hate of [an Arab worker] toward his Jewish equal is nationalistic, not class-oriented." That was true as far as it went, but Arab workers were reacting to potential Jewish nationalism and the effect of the "Jewish conquest of labor,"[10] which meant the creation of jobs for Jews and the autonomy of Jewish workers. The Socialist Zionists struggled mightily and hestitantly with their attitudes toward the Arab question, which was initially a labor question, often trying to wish it away with words and lofty idealism. They ignored the fact that the "Jewish conquest of labor" was directly at odds with the Arab population of Palestine and would lead to inevitable conflict. The Socialist Zionists had come to Palestine to establish Jewish hegemony, not an idealized and egalitarian Arab-Jewish state.

In practical terms, the Socialist Zionist "conquest of labor" began with the demand that the great influx of Socialist Zionist workers be employed in the Jewish *moshavot* (private agricultural settlements). The moshavot were operated by capitalists and farmers, Jews who were descendants of the 1882 influx of the Lovers of Zion movement, who had eventually prospered and were running vineyards and cooperatives employing large numbers of Arab workers. The Socialist challenge was mounted aggressively, as the very word *kibbush* (conquest) implies. Arab laborers were ousted from the moshavot. Small Jewish (Socialist Zionist) cooperative settlements were established all over Palestine, and Jews replaced the Arab watchmen who had formerly protected the moshavot from Bedouins and thieves. There was nothing subtle about this—most of the terms used by the Socialist Zionist settlers, such as "conquest," "labor battalion," and "watchman," were military in nature, reflecting the combat experience of the settlers who had fought against Arab marauders into Jewish settlements.

In the time leading up to World War I and beyond, Ben-Gurion was feverishly active. He had been called by the movement to edit the first Zionist paper in Jaffa, sent as a Zionist missionary and trainer to Poland, by 1909 found himself exiled by the Ottoman

Empire with all the Jewish elite of Palestine, and by 1915 had somehow found time to gain a law degree in Constantinople. Unable to return to Ottoman Palestine, he took up a self-imposed exile in America, where he recruited for immigration to Palestine among Socialist Zionist groups in New York. He then joined a quasi-Egyptian force of Jewish soldiers, Jabotinsky's organized Jewish Legions, who fought with the allies from 1916 to 1918, hoping now for British support of Jewish aspirations.

In late 1917, Ben-Gurion returned to Jerusalem for good. Immediately after the war he founded the United Labor party, which would eventually become Mapai (the Socialist Zionist political party), which in turn would evolve into the Labor party. He also organized the Histadrut, the trade union which would become the most powerful organization within the Zionist community in Palestine and the political base for the party. He also became first secretary general of the Histadrut.[11]

By the 1920s, Weizmann had become very much aware of Ben-Gurion, and initially the two admired each other. At first they seemed an unlikely pair—Weizmann, tall, urbane, mustachioed, the epitome of the worldly statesman, and Ben-Gurion, a five-foot-three-inch fire hydrant, with deeply tanned, leathery skin, always wearing ill-fitting clothes. There was a tacit understanding between the two that the World Zionist Organization, which Weizmann headed, would be in charge of overall Zionist affairs while Ben-Gurion and his Socialist Zionists would begin to take charge within Palestine. That understanding, which left the Yishuv and the Socialist Zionists in the background of the Zionist movement as a whole, would not evolve into conflict for years, even though Weizmann by this time was totally committed to the British as a vehicle to a Jewish state and the mandatory, while Ben-Gurion remained more skeptical of British intentions. For him, the mandatory was no more than a means toward the goal of a Jewish state.

Meanwhile, Ben-Gurion and the political leadership of the Yishuv faced a challenge from the powerful voice of Zeev Jabotinsky, who had had his own conversion on his own particular road to Damascus.[12] By the early 1930s, Jabotinsky, the former assimilationist who had translated Poe into Russian, the fervent admirer of Great Britain, had come full circle. He was the first to identify the British betrayal of the Balfour Declaration after 1922, when the Colonial Secretary, Winston Churchill, partitioned

Transjordan from Palestine. Jabotinsky showed open contempt for Weizmann's continued pursuit of the British and all but called for a declaration of war on the mandatory, at least in principle. It was a complete split from the Socialist Zionists, who were working gradually toward statehood.

The Socialist Zionists had come to Palestine to be redeemed—in spirit and in body. Taking much of their inspiration from the Bolsheviks and socialist democratic movements of Eastern and Central Europe, they sought in Zionism a social and intellectual revolution out of which would come a new kind of Jewish prototype, the pioneer. They would settle the desert and make it bloom, they would dry the marshes. The base and foundation of a society would be established first; the state would come later.

Jabotinsky, on the other hand, sought immediately to create state symbols and myths. He called for the immediate creation of a Jewish army and bureaucracy, and all the apparatus that goes into the formation of a state. Influenced, ironically enough, by the radical nationalism then rearing its head in Europe, Jabotinsky organized a Revisionist youth movement, Betar, that was highly organized, militant, and inclined toward uniforms and symbols.

Organized first in Poland, Jabotinsky and his Revisionist Zionists approached the anti-Semitic government there with a novel solution to the "Jewish problem." "Train us," they pleaded. "Help us organize. We'll help you get rid of us. Evacuate us." Indeed, Jabotinsky went so far as to advocate the immediate immigration of all diaspora Jews to Palestine.

For Ben-Gurion, a huge influx of Revisionist Zionists represented a real threat to Socialist Zionism and to his leadership. This influx would also mean trouble with the mandatory, since Revisionist Zionism's more radical leaders wanted all-out war against the mandatory and the British. The challenge to Socialist Zionism did emerge, as Betar grew by leaps and bounds in Poland during the late 1920s and early 1930s. Even as Jabotinsky was calling for a Jewish army to invade Palestine, Ben-Gurion was making his own plans to stem the tide. At a time when every Jew was needed in Palestine, he was taking every measure to assure that the Revisionist Zionists of Betar would be turned back at the point of immigration. That was not enough, however. Ben-Gurion, as he was to do again during the war for independence, needed to discredit the whole Revisionist Zionist movement in Palestine. In 1933, Chaim Arlozoroff, the foreign secretary of the Jewish

Agency and a Socialist Zionist, was assassinated in Tel Aviv. Quietly, Ben-Gurion and the Socialist Zionists spread the story that the atrocity was committed by radical Revisionist Zionists, possibly three young poets who were members of Betar arrested by the British but released for lack of evidence. The Revisionist Zionists never quite recovered or regained credibility in Palestine, although years later it would be ascertained with some solidity that the assassination was actually the work of an Arab hired by German Templars in Palestine.

By that time, Jabotinsky, never a violent militant, always a thinker, writer, and theorist, had lost direct control of his own movement, Betar, which was being taken over by radicals after his exile by the British from Palestine in 1928. In the late 1930s, Betar in Poland was already in other hands and the radicals in the movement—the Etzel and Lehi—had gone underground to commence a series of terrorist acts and bank robberies aimed at the British. Jabotinsky was aghast, but he was also out of the limelight, exiled from Palestine, living in the United States, where he finally died in 1940.[13]

Ben-Gurion's act of political expediency, committed to salvage Yishuv unity and his own leadership among the Jews within Palestine, was to be repeated in the war for independence, when he struck against Menachem Begin, who took up the mantle of the Revisionist movement's leadership in 1944. Meanwhile, the long and uneasy relationship between the Yishuv and the British mandatory[14] slowly began to bring forth the idea of a partitioned state.

The British, Weizmann, and English-Zionist Relations: Moving Toward Partition

The Zionists clung to the Balfour Declaration with both ferocity and suspicion, seeing in it the double mirror of legitimacy and potential for betrayal. It was the single most important achievement of Chaim Weizmann's close attachment to the British. World War I had made London the capital-in-exile for Zionism. Weizmann, with his special contacts among the luminaries of British statesmanship—Arthur Balfour, Joseph Chamberlain, Winston Churchill, Lloyd George, and Julian Amery—had emerged into the forefront of Zionist leadership. In the beginning, Anglo-Jewish relations in Palestine might in fact best be described as Anglo-Weizmann relations, for it was Weizmann more than anyone else who somehow managed to articulate both Zionist aspirations and the remnants of British imperialist design.

Weizmann felt at home with the British, more so than with the politically active Zionists who were beginning to lay the groundwork for the state of Israel in Palestine. He and many British statesmen shared similar views about the Arabs in Palestine, views which were not enlightened, to say the least. Weizmann saw the natives of Palestine with an imperialist's eye, which is to say that he tolerated but did not trust them. He felt, for instance, that Arabs and Jews must live separately, since the Arabs would only reduce the Jewish standard of living; Jewish settlements would lag if there was cooperation and fraternization among Jews and Arabs. Echoing typical British feeling, he doubted whether Arabs in Palestine had parochial or patriotic feelings; he saw them as nothing but backward fellahin, scheming, deceptive, and untrustworthy. He attributed Arab extremism to the British failure to persuade Arabs that Britain would firmly defend the Balfour Declaration. In turn, he saw this apparent British nonchalance as a product of ambivalence toward Zionism. In this, he was quite accurate. Yet doggedly, perhaps even knowing better, he insisted that Anglo-Zionist interests were axiomatically and politically identical. This belief sometimes led Weizmann into the back alley of imperial machinations under the blanket of furthering the Zionist cause.

More pragmatic politicians within the Yishuv were watching Weizmann's activities with a jaundiced eye. The military administration for Palestine (1918-1920) was unsympathetic to Jewish aspirations. These politicians were not surprised at the failure of Weizmann's talks in 1919 with the Arab leader, King Faisal of Syria, who also became king of Iraq in 1921. They were beginning to perceive correctly the nature and potential strength of Arab nationalism. Working with the British for them was a matter of dealing with the devil from need—not out of trust, but out of expediency. They knew in their hearts that although for the moment committed to the mandatory, British military authorities would not necessarily interpret the Balfour Declaration as Weizmann might want. The pragmatists also knew that in the long run the British were not truly committed to the Balfour Declaration, which, as their own creation, they could also eventually disown. They watched as the British worked closely with radical Arab leaders like Haj Amin al-Hussaini, whom the British supported as Mufti of Jerusalem while giving only lukewarm support to Arab moderates. From the viewpoint of the Socialist Zionists in Palestine, the British were practicing a two-faced policy in which London officials blamed local British officials for thwarting attempts to win over Arab moderates.[15]

None of this deterred Weizmann. Yet, as the middle 1930s approached, the British slowly began to disengage themselves from the Balfour Declaration, and developed a cooler attitude toward Zionism while seriously beginning to court the Arabs. As 1936 approached, it was becoming painfully obvious that the British were weighing Zionist aspirations against a new pro-Arab, regional and international policy of appeasement. The Palestinian problem had become a central concern for the foreign office, the chiefs of staff, and the cabinet itself, all of whom were weighing strategic interests, the prospects of war, and how Palestine might fit into the overall picture. The British, vulnerable in the Mediterranean, sought to meet the demands of Arab states and to maintain a close alliance with Transjordan, all at the expense of the Jewish portion of the Balfour Declaration's commitment.

By 1936 the British were faced with an Arab revolt led by the Grand Mufti of Jerusalem, Haj Amin al-Hussaini. In its wake, they decided that a partition plan for Palestine might be the only real alternative to riots between Arabs and Jews. Though quickly scrapped, this first partition proposal marked the beginning of the end of the British mandate in Palestine.[16]

Haj Amin al-Hussaini had, since the middle 1920s, become the central figure in the Arab shift to the radical extreme. Before becoming Grand Mufti of Jerusalem he had been the young scion of one of the leading families in Jerusalem. For years, Hussaini's family had alternated with the Nashashibi family in filling the position of Grand Mufti, a role of religious leadership which in theory had no political overtones.

In 1921, the position was scheduled to be filled by a member of the Nashashibi family, and failing that, an older member of the al-Hussaini clan. But, for reasons that to this day seem puzzling, Sir Herbert Samuel, a Jew and a Zionist who was British High Commissioner of Palestine, manipulated the appointive process to such an extent that Haj Amin al-Hussaini, then a tender but quite fanatical twenty-two years old, became Grand Mufti of Jerusalem. Samuel had accepted the advice of his assistant, Albert Haimson, an English Jew and a non-Zionist, to appoint a young Arab nationalist to appease the radical Jerusalemite Arabs. Whatever the reasons, the selection and support of Haj Amin proved to be a disaster, with tragic results for the British, the moderate Arab cause, and the Zionist cause. The ambitions of Haj Amin reverberated over the next three decades in a bloody and black montage.

Young, ambitious, totally ruthless, fanatic, and zealously and violently opposed to Zionism, Haj Amin al-Hussaini soon turned two institutions, one religious (the Higher Muslim Council) and one political (the Higher Arab Executive Committee), into personal instruments for Arab domination of Palestine. In his single-minded usurpation of Palestinian Arab leadership, this Moslem fundamentalist and extremist also managed to eliminate or cripple the more moderate Arab leadership, a result that later had dire consequences for the Arab nationalist movement as a whole.[17] He created an Arab paramilitary force to hold moderate Arabs at bay and to use as an eventual striking force against the Jews, for his eventual intent, which he proudly proclaimed, was annihilation of the Jewish community in Palestine.

By 1936, after years of harsh rule, manipulation, and agitation by Haj Amin, the Palestinian nationalist movement swung into major action, first with a violent and effective general strike, then by igniting bloody anti-Jewish riots in the major cities, especially in Jerusalem. In no time at all the conflict escalated from isolated local riots and incidents into what amounted to nearly a full-scale regional war, as the Arab states of Syria, Saudi Arabia, and Iraq joined forces with the Palestinian Arabs to pounce on the Jews, who fought back fiercely.[18] The British, skeptical at first about the strength of Arab opposition, did not interfere or help the Jews. But when the revolt widened into a general action against the British as well as the Zionists, the exasperated English efficiently and quickly doused the flames of revolt with a brutally effective military action.

On the whole, the revolt proved to be a major failure for the Arab cause. Haj Amin was forced to flee to Europe, where he schemed with Nazi Germany and where he remained an honored guest during World War II. His avowed intent to annihilate the Jewish community in Palestine served to trigger the effective reorganization of the Jewish self-defense league, the paramilitary force known as the Haganah, which would play a key role in thwarting Haj Amin once again during the war of independence.[19]

The most crucial immediate result of the revolt was that it ignited a fundamental change in the British attitude toward Zionism. The British now had a new goal: to stop the growth of a new Jewish national home and limit Jewish autonomy in Palestine. Their policy tilted unequivocally toward appeasement of the Arab states and away from the Balfour Declaration. There were two immediate consequences of this change. Beginning in 1936, Jewish immigration was suspended, and the Arab states became involved in British mediation efforts between Jews and Palestinian Arabs.

British policymakers had already toyed with the idea of introducing certain administrative changes in the mandatory during the 1930s, including a representative assembly which sought to alleviate rising Arab pressures while also taking into account the unprecedented growth of the Jewish community in Palestine. The eruption of the Arab revolt shelved that idea, but in 1937 a Royal Commission, after a year's study, recommended that Palestine be divided into two states, Jewish and Arab, with some territory to remain under British control.[20] Partition was not undertaken out of any sense of magnanimity or fairness, but out of real concern that with war imminent, British interests might otherwise be threatened. Partition was finally abandoned in 1938.

The result of the new policy was a disastrous 1939 conference aimed at a "comprehensive settlement." The Arabs insisted that they would not sit at the same table with the Jews and the prime minister, so the Arab and Jewish delegations met separately, like a husband and wife in a partitioned divorce court, with predictable results. The Jews, although unsure and divided, accepted the two-state "cantonization" plan, but to the surprise of the British, it was vehemently opposed by the Palestinian Arabs. The British, disturbed by the Arab rejection of the plan, now neatly shelved it, mainly at the behest of the foreign office's chief Arabist, George Rendell, who wrote that "Arab improvidence, disunity and indecision should not blind Great Britain to the growing influence of Arab nationalism. The creation of an insecure, expansionist Jewish state would ultimately involve the intervention of British troops." He was "greatly exercised by the hostile attitude of the Arabs and the consequent risk of alienating them."[21]

Unfortunately for the British, shelving the partition plan did not kill it. Without knowing it, they had opened up a Pandora's box, releasing forces that galvanized and traumatized the Yishuv, Zionism, and its leaders. It could be said that until 1936, the Yishuv and Zionism had been dreaming hazy dreams, that the movement had not coalesced into something that went beyond grand goals. The debate over partition finally forced them to face directly the great issues of sovereignty, territory, and regime. Partition set a fire in the heart of the Yishuv and ignited a debate that ran across the diverse ideological and political spectrum of Zionism.

CHAPTER 2

Battle Over Partition: The Arab Challenge and the Jewish Response

Prologue

By 1939, in the wake of the issuance of British restrictions on immigration and the Arab Revolt, which by then had begun to subside noticeably, the Jewish body politic stood poised on the brink of a great and fluctuating debate over partition. Until then, the various political Zionist leaders—Ben-Gurion, Weizmann, Jabotinsky, Tabenkin, Katznelson, and the like—had envisioned a Jewish state, or a Jewish entity, or a Jewish commonwealth in Palestine as being somewhere down the road. Their views and arguments at times seemed almost the writings and speeches of sleepwalkers because the final goal of statehood and commonwealth was still unreal and ill-defined in terms of means and methods, in terms of boundaries and actual physical territory, in terms of the international environment, and in terms of the Arab question.

Some, like Weizmann, would always cling to the mandatory and the promises inherent but not explicit in the Balfour Declaration as a means to achieve that nebulous goal. Others, like the pragmatically-minded Ben-Gurion, burrowing for political power in the fractious institutions of the Yishuv, would fluctuate, starting from an almost idealistic and doctrinaire Marxist approach and swinging to a steadfast clinging to the Balfour Declaration.

Jabotinsky's mushrooming Revisionist movement was calling for a complete break with the mandatory and outright war and resistance to it, while clamoring loudly for mass immigration and nothing less than the reclamation of Eretz Israel. Others, most notably Tabenkin and his powerful United Kibbutz movement, seemed to ignore boundaries and statehood altogether in their immediate push for more and more Jewish settlements.

The idea of partition was not new to any of them. The British vaguely suggested it in 1930, but the reality of the British proposals, mixed with England's obvious, slow and steady emasculation and disavowal of the Balfour Declaration, now made partition seem like a possible means toward the end they all sought. Ben-Gurion was to embrace partition, championing the idea and riding it like a political whirlwind to his personal political supremacy and to Israel's statehood.

The debate over partition was to shake the politics of the Yishuv and World Zionism and would involve all of its major figures. But it was part and parcel of, and had its roots in, another controversy we must first consider: the challenge of Palestinian Arab nationalist opposition.

Opposition to Zionism and Jewish Statehood[1]

The Zionist movement and its leaders did not ignore the Arab question, but actually debated various interpretations of it that stemmed from Zionism's multiple ideological orientations. However, Zionists, including the usually astute Ben-Gurion, did tend to underestimate the nature, power, vehemence, and strength of the Arab nationalist movement, particularly the strength of its opposition to Zionism and Zionist aspirations. At best, the Zionists unrealistically hoped that the mandatory would overcome unrelenting Arab opposition to their aspirations. No number of Zionist approaches to Arab leaders and no amount of appeasement, both of which were conducted with considerable ignorance and naivete, succeeded in alleviating Arab, and especially Palestinian, nationalist opposition to Jewish statehood.[2] This should not have come as a surprise since Arab and Palestinian opposition to Zionist aspirations dated to as far back as the 1880s, its roots lying in Ottoman and Moslem opposition.

The Ottoman government first announced its opposition to Jewish settlement in Palestine as early as 1881, two years after the first Zionist settlement (Mikve Yisrael) was established. This opposition continued under the anti-European policies of the Young Turks.[3] By the turn of the century, Arab notables in Jerusalem expressed their opposition to Zionist settlement on economic grounds. They feared an influx of Jewish and European finance and energy that could upset the status of the Arab elite in Palestine, especially in Jerusalem. A broader Arab anti-Zionism emerged between 1909 and 1914 on the grounds of Arab-Ottoman loyalism and sectional patriotism, not just the fear of economic competition and rivalry from the European Jewish settlers.

Before 1914 the Arabs were well aware of Zionist aims, and Arab nationalist writers clearly demonstrated their adamant opposition to twentieth century Jewish settlement. They did, however, tolerate prenationalistic and religious pilgrimages and the establishment of Old Jewish, non-Zionist settlements in Palestine. From the start, Arabs distinguished between "foreign Jews"—meaning Zionist-European—and "Ottoman Jews," meaning the inhabitants of the vilayet of Beirut and the Mutasarriflik of Jerusalem (as well as the two Ottoman provinces which later became the British Mandate of Palestine).

By the end of World War I, however, the main thrust of Arab opposition to Zionist aims was its adamant objection to the newly-organized political Zionist movement and to the Zionist plan to establish an independent Jewish state which lay at the heart of the Balfour Declaration. Opposition focused now on the Declaration as the chief legal document of the political Zionists led in London by Weizmann. As Professor Neville Mandel writes:

> The period before 1914 therefore takes on new importance in terms of the Arab-Zionist conflict. The roots of Arab antagonism, and perhaps the conflict itself, stretch back to it. . . . Indeed, it may even be argued that the Balfour Declaration was not so much the starting point of the conflict as a turning point which greatly aggravated an existing trend.[4]

Certainly, though, Palestinian nationalists recognized the danger of conflict inherent in the Balfour Declaration, even if Zionist leaders did not.

All Arab leaders clearly perceived that the political status of the Jewish community in Palestine had changed significantly as a result of the Balfour Declaration. They realized that the Jews in Palestine were going to play a new role and were going to share in the administration of the mandatory. Professor Yehoshua Porath's definitive study on the emergence of the Palestinian Arab nationalist movement demonstrates that the rejection of Zionism served as close to a unifying factor as Arab nationalism could possibly have.[5] "Above all," writes Porath, "the Palestinian Arab nationalists became convinced [as early as 1918] that they were facing the danger that stems from the [Balfour] Declaration; i.e., the threat of Jewish political domination over Palestine."[6] As a result, the Arabs made the military government, the provisional British administration, as well as the subsequent and permanent mandatory administration in Palestine, the target of their struggle against political Zionism.[7]

The fundamentalists led by Haj Amin al-Hussaini won. First, his appointment by Lord Samuel as Mufti of Jerusalem gave him hegemony over other Arab leaders. Second, while many Arab notables were pro-nationalists, al-Hussaini was both a fundamentalist and nationalist and was seemingly supported by the mandatory-led Arab opposition to political Zionism and the Declaration.

The Arab nationalists saw the Balfour Declaration as nothing less than a betrayal that, while promising to protect their rights, abrogated their nationalist claims to Palestine in favor of the Zionists. (In the 1930s, radical Jews would call the British pro-Arab policy a betrayal of the Declaration.) The Declaration thus became a symbol of British villainy and a principal target of Palestinian nationalists, whose ideology therefore had two goals: to justify the exclusive claim of the Palestinian Arabs to rule the independent state which was to be formed with the expiration of the British mandate,[8] and to repudiate the Balfour Declaration and any Zionist claims stemming from it. Their claims to Palestine were based on the contention that Moslems had the right to religious domination over Jerusalem and, more pragmatically, upon their numerical superiority and Wilsonian principles of majority rule and self-determination.[9]

At the outset, Jewish response to Arab opposition was pusillanimous. All Zionist leaders underestimated the strength and ferocity of Palestinian Arab nationalism. Psychologically, they were unwilling to accept the fact that Palestinian Arab nationalism had been captured and was dominated by radicals and extremists. They refused to believe that one could not make a deal with the more conservative Arabs who constituted the majority of Arab leadership at the time. As a result, the Zionist leaders unrealistically sought reconciliation with Arab and Palestinian moderates whose influence over the Arab nationalist movement was meager. Some, including Weizmann, even tried to appease Arab moderates by provisionally renouncing the claim to Jewish statehood. All found their approaches to Arab and Palestinian leaders ineffectual and frustrating.

Zionist Aims versus the Arab Challenge

The Zionist movement, as a nationalist movement, was uncompromisingly committed to four fundamental tenets:

1. Establishment of a Jewish state in Eretz Israel, "the historical land," as the territorial center of the Jewish nation. This was, after all, at the heart of Theodor Herzl's vision. A Jewish homeland in Palestine was a natural challenge, both in moderate and militant terms, to the Arab claim of exclusive ownership of Palestine.

2. Creation of a Jewish majority in Palestine. This was simply a logical consequence of creating and maintaining a Jewish state. If there was a single pragmatic foundation of Zionism, it was this: The bitter lessons of Jewish history showed that Jews could only survive in a Jewish commonwealth.

3. "Revolutionary constructivism" of the Jewish masses. This was fundamental as a philosophic base for Zionist aims. The transformation of a nation of agricultural workers called for Jewish "self-labor" in Palestine. The ideology of "the conquest of land and labor" implied that Jews would redeem and dominate Palestine's land. So-called revolutionary constructivism to a great degree cut across all the various political factions which were to make up the Yishuv, from the kibbutz movement, Mapai, and Labor to Marxists. Originated by Aaron David Gordon, it was promulgated most vehemently in practical form by Berl Katznelson, the leading ideologue-theoretician of the Mapai party, who sought to create new forms of settlement and to expand the working settlement movement into the empty spaces of Palestine.

4. Separation. In calling for Jewish statehood, in claiming the restoration of Jewish culture and the renaissance of Jewish nationalism, Zionists sought to establish a clear-cut position isolated from Arab and Muslim cultural values and social structures. The conscious aim of creating an independent and autonomous Jewish national culture and social system in Eretz Israel was to be fortified by erecting political, economic, social, and cultural walls to separate Jews from the Arab population.

The core of Zionist ideology—self-labor and the conquest of land and labor—so fervently adopted by the Labor party, by Mapai, by leaders as diverse as Katznelson, Ben-Gurion, Tabenkin, and Weizmann, by settlers, workers, ideologues, and hard-core politicians alike, stemmed from a most unpolitical thinker, Aaron David Gordon. A utopian and a mystic, Gordon's personal ethics system was to become the philosophical mainstay of the pioneer movement in Palestine and was to provide the philosophical underpinnings for Socialist Zionism, with its elements of modern Judaism, naturalism, humanitarianism, and the spirit of nature and labor.[10]

Gordon was born in 1856, in the small Russian village of Trayance. He left briefly to study in the Lithuanian city of Vilno, only to return and to work for fourteen years as a cashier in a small merchant store. Until 1903 he lived by all accounts a mundane life, marrying, raising a family, and making a living as best as he could. Then suddenly, like a philosophical Gauguin, Gordon took up his meager belongings and simply left his family to emigrate to Palestine, first settling in Tel Aviv, which he did not find to his liking, and finally founding the first genuine kibbutz (Dagania, where Moshe Dayan was born) in Galilee. Here he resumed his existence as a worker and cashier, and here he wrote and taught.

Gordon's cherished belief was that man "must be at one with nature," hardly original, but for the Jews of the diaspora, a fresh thought and a new belief system. "Man cannot live without nature," he wrote, "any more than a fish can live without water. A fish out of water misses the burden of water, the challenge of the pressure." Jews, Gordon wrote, had not been allowed to go back to nature and so had become historical pariahs. Like his protégé, Berl Katznelson, Gordon wanted the Jews of Palestine to be cut off from the city-concept of the diaspora. Jews must return to and work with nature.

Work and labor were the symbols with which Gordon addressed the Zionists of Palestine: "We must emancipate the land and create a new [Jewish] culture. Our structure is founded on labor and work. Labor is our national task." Gordon, something of a visionary and anarchist, saw a nation imbued with his "religion of labor." "We must work with our hands, in the crafts, trades, from the most skilled to the coarsest. Labor is one of the most fundamental elements of life."[11]

The Zionists, and especially the Socialist Zionists, took Gordon at his word long after his death in 1923, turning his words into practical actions whose consequences were more complicated than they could foresee. For one thing, Gordon's world did not take into account the Arabs or the outside world. The Zionist consensus on the future of the Jews in Palestine thus produced three major orientations relating to the Arab question: altruistic-integrative, isolationist-rejectionist, and socialist-constructivist. Put simply, they could just as well be called liberal, reactionary, and pragmatic. Each orientation stemmed from a Palestinian reality which existed at a particular moment and which in turn was interpreted by a Zionist political leader according to his own particular ideology.

The altruistic-integrative orientation quite simply saw the Jews and Arabs living together in peace in one Palestine. The proponents of this concept predated the politically organized and ideologically intensified Yishuv of the 1920s and 1930s. Intellectuals and writers in the main, men like the journalist Yitzhak Epstein and the writer Rabi Benyamin were responding to Arab anti-Zionism around the turn of the century. They considered the Arab question to be the most important problem facing Zionism, believing that the solution had to be found in Arab-Jewish integration and mutual aid. From this orientation came the binationalist theory of a Jewish-Arab state in Palestine, a theory which was to be rejected by the majority of Zionists but which persisted into the 1940s under the auspices of Brith Shalom (Unity of Peace, a Hebrew University Professors' group) and the left-wing Labor-Zionist Hashomer Hatzair kibbutz movement.[12] Rabi Benyamin's moderate Zionist thesis was that no fundamental or eternal separation need exist between the two peoples. He believed that frictions were only temporary and would be eliminated once the two nations united for "one goal and mutual aid."[13]

The militant nationalist rejectionists vehemently opposed this theory. Their approach was pessimistic and condescending. Professor Yoseph Klausner, a prominent historian of ancient Jewish history at the Hebrew University in Jerusalem and eventually a prominent revisionist scholar, argued that the Arabs and Jews were irreconcilable. He saw integration between the two as culturally dangerous, fearing that the Jews would "descend from their high culture into the semiprimitive Arab culture."[14] Moshe Smilansky, a farmer and author, saw the seeds of future Arab-Jewish conflict in integration. Zeev Jabotinsky, at the time second only to Weizmann in the World Zionist leadership, also saw the prospect of future conflict and struggle, although he, like many Zionist leaders, underestimated the strength and ferocity of Arab nationalism.[15]

Socialist and Labor Zionist attitudes toward the Arab question were the most complicated of the three, as well as the most significant, since the leadership and members of these factions would make up the component and driving forces of the Yishuv.[16] In the evolution of socialist-constructivist attitudes toward the Arab question we find serious contradictions, confusion, and wishful thinking mixed with realpolitik.

Initially, between 1905 and 1920, a Marxist orientation prevailed, powered by the leaders of Ahdut Haavoda and Poale Zion, the forerunners of the Mapai, which was formed in 1930.[17] Looking at the heated anti-Zionism of the Palestinians, the Marxist Zionists predictably saw elements of class struggle in the Arabs' antagonism. The conflict, they wrote with assurance, stemmed from the contradictions between landlords and fellahin, between fanatic Muslims and the ignorant and exploited peasants.

Both David Ben-Gurion and Yitzhak Ben-Zvi, who was to become the second president of Israel, blithely wrote that Arab hatred for Zionism was a combination of class antagonism to the modern Jewish pioneer worker linked to the Arab laborers' nascent but ignorant nationalism. That was in 1911. By 1913, Ben-Gurion was writing that the "hate of an Arab worker toward his Jewish equal was nationalistic, not class-oriented."[18] The Marxists discovered that the clash between Arab and Jewish workers was nationalistic and that the "class struggle" was a premature concept in the case of Arab workers lacking class consciousness but imbued with Islamic, not secular, concerns.

By this time, the Socialist Zionists began to discover the serious contradictions inherent in Gordon's romantic philosophy vis-à-vis the Arab question. The "conquering" of Palestine with Jewish labor—meaning the creation of jobs for Jews—propelled them to try and find a new and basically unrealistic explanation for the hatred which Arab workers and fellahin felt toward Zionists.[19]

The darker and, realistically speaking, more pragmatic side of Gordon's religion of labor was combative in its very language, specifically in "the conquest of labor and land." The phrase contains an aggressive word, *kibbush,* which literally means "conquest" in Hebrew. Translated into policy, it meant Jewish redemption and self-regeneration by demanding Jewish employment in the old Jewish moshavot, where capitalist farmers employed both Arab and non-Jewish labor.

The struggle which ensued between non-Zionist, capitalist-oriented Jews and Socialist Zionists very quickly escalated into Jewish-Arab economic warfare. Arab laborers were ousted from the moshavot, Jews replaced the Arab watchmen who had formerly protected the moshavot from Bedouins and thieves, and Jewish cooperative settlements were established in Palestine. The conquest of labor and land thus meant that Jewish workers replaced Arab workers and settled in formerly Arab-owned land. The combativeness that seemed to characterize the Socialist Zionist settlers seemed natural, both in terms of Gordon's ideology, with its vocabulary of "conquest," "labor battalion," and "watchmen," and from the fact that after 1918 most settlers were also veterans of the Jewish battalions that had fought with the allies in World War I, especially in the Dardanelles campaign.

For the some 8,000 Socialist immigrants to Palestine who made up the pioneer (Hehalutz) movement, the conquest of labor and land meant pioneer and collectivist Zionism. The pioneers, most of whom came from an East European environment, considered themselves to be elite, in the forefront of Zionism and socialism. To them, the non-Zionist Jewish farmers and Arab workers were nothing but the remnants of Ottoman feudalism and reaction. While "reactionary" Jewish farmers might describe their employment of Arab labor as the work of "good neighbors," Marxist Jewish workers considered it treachery against Jewish and Zionist nationalism. They viewed the employment of Arab labor from a traditional Marxist standpoint and saw it as colonialist exploitation of local natives by reactionary farmers. This viewpoint almost naturally, and also paradoxically, led to the demand and urge to separate the Jewish from the Arab community in Palestine.[20]

Some Marxist Jewish leaders, in spite of their strong nationalist commitments and sentiments, saw the contradictions inherent in the goal of achieving Jewish self-employment at the expense of the injustice to Arabs that the pursuit of their goal almost naturally engendered.[21] We should clearly remember that the Marxist Zionists were not grand theoreticians, but were influenced by Dov-Ber Borochov Marxist Zionism. For him, as for the socialist pioneers, the nationalist question loomed larger than the Marxist orientation. Only the Jewish Communists advocated Jewish-Arab worker alliance in Palestine. Yitzhak Tabenkin, the ideological leader of the aggressive kibbutz movement, saw the problem almost immediately, if not altogether clearly. He admitted in the 1920s that cooperation with Arab workers was actually governed by "political calculations [that] have obliged our leaders, both Socialist and Zionist, to mislead public opinion into the utopistic conviction that we can live in peace with the Arabs. As we consolidate our position here [in Palestine] we will encounter [in Arab workers] a hostile element."[22]

The demand for Jewish territorial concentration and Jewish hegemony, and the belief that Jews would eventually constitute the majority in Palestine, combined with the great influx of Jews between 1925 and 1929, intensified the struggle over land and labor. Oddly, this very struggle would sow the first seeds of eventual partition.

The concept of Jewish autonomy over uncultivated "empty spaces" was advocated by the most powerful leader of Socialist Zionism, David Ben-Gurion. He wrote in 1924:

> The growth of our national settlements in the city and in the countryside, their expansion, contiguity, and integration under autonomous Jewish activity. . .will also develop, fortify, and expand our national autonomy [from which] the Jewish State will be built.[23]

Ironically, the implementation of the ideology of Hebrew land and labor, which sprang forth from a desire to settle all of Eretz Israel, actually succeeded in bringing about the narrowing of the Jewish settlement of Palestine. The creation of a system of small, autonomous Jewish settlements in areas separated from each other and isolated from the Arab population formed the framework for an ipso facto sort of partition and later became the rationale for the eventual partition of Palestine—as proposed by Britain, not by the Zionists.

The consequences of this policy were obviously not immediately recognized by its founders, who had been counting on large-scale Jewish immigration to tip the balance in favor of a Jewish majority in Palestine.[24] They did not, and probably could not, realize that such a massive immigration would not be forthcoming, and therefore could not see that their policy would lead to the denial of Zionist hegemony over all of Palestine. As professor Anita Shapira writes:

> Thus we in fact can see that through the decision opting for an autonomous and separate Jewish community and economy. . .[they had] created the ideological and settlement foundations that in due course would justify [and eventually] fulfill the Partition Plan for Palestine.[25]

The victory of Hebrew labor ideology and the rise of the Socialist Zionists to a preeminent political position stemmed not so much from their moral and social protestations that Jewish settlements could not be established on "Arab sweat," nor from fear that Arab labor might grow into a competitive force, nor from concern that Jewish smallholders were exploiting Arabs, as it did from clear and practical political reality. It resulted from the conviction that Hebrew labor was a social, personal, and political act toward the settling of uprooted Jews in Palestine. In the end, the Socialist Zionists had to look at their aspirations realistically. In spite of their original and basically idealistic Marxist and humanist orientations, they had not come to Palestine to establish some wistful, utopian Arab-Jewish state, but a Jewish hegemony, although labor did seek to make it a socialist hegemony as well.

Furthermore, the Socialist Zionists were never quite able to reconcile "self-labor" with Arab nationalism. They did not consider Arab workers to be true participants in their struggle to establish the supremacy of the working class. Arab workers antagonistic to Zionism could hardly champion a Zionist aspiration to self-labor. This accounts for at least part of the reason why Socialist-Zionists and Zionist leaders of every stripe consistently underestimated Arab resistance and hostility, as well as Arab nationalism. Nor did they quite realize that there would be immediate and long-lasting consequences in their dogged and single-minded pursuit of "the conquest of labor and land." Certainly Gordon had given them no clues. As Ben-Gurion would ruefully admit in his declining years, in the early days Jews and Zionists were operating "under the illusion that Eretz Israel was an empty land and we could do all that we wanted to do in it, without taking into consideration the native inhabitants of that nation. That hurt us considerably."[26]

As we have seen, the problem was not that the Zionists ignored the Arab question, but that they misinterpreted it and were altogether much too sanguine about it for much too long. The response varied from the idealistic (the idea of binationalism persisted, after all, for decades) to the almost paternalistic, imperialistic rationales which both Weizmann, in his benign way, and Jabotinsky, in his more bellicose way, embraced. (Jabotinsky looked at the Palestinians in much the same way the British did—as "native habitants" who were incapable of the very idea of nationalism.) The problem was that the Zionist establishment, and here they were united in their misjudgment, refused to recognize that Arab nationalism was fueled by anti-Zionism.

In contrast, Ben-Gurion and the Socialist Zionists were very much aware of Arab nationalism, but thought of it as a nationalism that could be focused outside the confines of Palestine. They hoped that if they negotiated with Arab nationalist leaders of Syria and Iraq they could persuade the latter to absorb the Palestinian Arabs in their schemes such as Greater Syria and Iraq, and leave to the Jews an autonomous territory in West Palestine. Then, too, Ben-Gurion, and Weizmann for that matter, were quite willing to meet, negotiate and, to a degree, compromise. In the end, however, the Arab leadership which constituted Arab "moderation" undid both Ben-Gurion and Weizmann and sent them down the avenues of frustration. Ben-Gurion, after years of dealing with Arab leaders, eventually concluded that the situation was hopeless. Looking at the stature and array of that leadership, one might be tempted to agree.

If the Zionists had a blind spot, even a certain amount of contempt for Arab and Palestinian leadership, it can almost be understood, if not accepted, on the basis of the hopeless divisions among the Arab leadership, united only in their apparent hostility toward Zionism and the Jews in their midst. Although all Arabs seemed to want an eventual Palestinian state and still do, their territorial goals, then and now, have been colored by old enmities, religious splits and schisms, and imperialistic and dynastic designs and feuds.

Of all the Arab leaders, the Emir Abdullah, Hashemite ruler of Transjordan, was probably the most moderate and modern, but only in the sense that he saw the Jews as an inevitable reality, a presence to be tolerated and dealt with. Thus he was willing to negotiate, not merely out of some benign political pragmatism, but because like all Arab rulers of the time he had territorial designs of his own, which included the enlargement of his rule and of Transjordan.[27]

Ben-Gurion had occasion to meet either personally or through intermediaries from the Jewish Agency's intelligence network (the forerunner of Mossad) with all sorts of Arab leaders, including such Palestinian notables as Musa Alami, Abdullah of Transjordan, Nuri al-said, the nationalist leader of Iraq, the Arab intellectual-author-leader George Antoninus, and the leaders of the Syrian nationalist bloc Kutla Al-Wataniyah.[28] His experiences were unsettling. The Iraqis wanted West Palestine and Syria, the Jordanians wanted parts of Iraq and Saudi Arabia, the suddenly ambitious Saudis under Ibn Saud, working with British arabist and traveller Sir John Philby, were plotting to get parts of Iraq and Jordan. As one close associate of Ben-Gurion said, "They sign a rough draft of an agreement in Jerusalem one day, and the next day they're saying they never saw you."[29]

The British first considered partition at least partly because they saw it as a way of minimally satisfying Arab and Israeli aspirations simultaneously. They wanted to head off out-and-out conflict between the two opposing forces first and foremost because such a conflict would threaten the mandatory's status in Palestine and Great Britain's imperial claims and designs. They hoped that a conference among Arab and Zionist leaders would lead to acceptance of partition and at least a tentative rapprochement of some sort. As we have seen, they were to be deeply and sadly disappointed.

Prelude to Partition:
Ben-Gurion Takes the Middle Road[30]

Partition, by the time it became the focus of a passionate, drawn-out Zionist debate, was an issue that tended to arouse extremists on both wings of political thought in the Zionist movement. Ben-Gurion and the party he would lead always tended to take a course between the extremes.

The 1929 "Principles for the Formation of a National Government in Eretz Israel" was Ben-Gurion's first political program for Jewish statehood. He was at that time wedded to the idea that in essence Eretz Israel or Palestine (which included all of mandatory Palestine minus Transjordan) was destined for both the Jewish and Arab populations. Each political entity or national unit would be entitled to separate and full political development. While the mandatory would uphold essential functions of defense and central issues, the Arabs and Jews would develop self-government and autonomous institutions related to their particular interests and needs.[31]

Ben-Gurion's plan was to be followed in three stages. Stage One would lay the foundations in local matters (such as urban and rural problems) and in communal matters (religious and national). Stage Two, in which the mandatory would also play a key role, would tackle common national issues. Ben-Gurion was hoping that during the first stage the Jews, the Arabs, and the mandatory would plan for a second-stage ruling council, a national executive based on Arab-Jewish parity, with British participation. This council would deal with national functions such as justice, customs, taxation, transportation, health, commerce and trade, and would in effect be a shadow cabinet, a dual executive composed of Arabs and Jews. This second stage would begin after ten years of communal autonomy, extending into political and electoral districts.

Only in the third stage would work toward completion of an independent Jewish sovereignty begin. Two assemblies composed of Jewish and Arab representation would be established—the House of Nations and the People's House. The highest executive would be federal. The Jewish Yishuv and the Palestinian Arab entity would resemble separate states, such as North Dakota and Nebraska. Both would first function under a mandatory-run federal government, which would eventually be relinquished; in the end, an autonomous Arab-Jewish federal government and residual state governments made up of separate, autonomous Jewish and Arab states would reign. This would represent a compromise between United States and Swiss federalism, and it would always assure Jewish autonomy, independence, and limited sovereignty within a federal system.[32]

Ben-Gurion's plan prompted a political struggle within the fractious Mapai party, divided between advocates of "statism" (the third phase) and "autonomism" (the second phase). Those in favor of the latter argued that the mandatory would better protect Jewish autonomy, while the statists argued that autonomy was only a phase in the direction of some form of Jewish sovereignty. The autonomists also feared that the plan was premature, that it would not work until the Jewish community achieved its majority within Eretz Israel.[33] Chaim Arlozoroff, head of the Jewish Agency's political department and an influential rival of Ben-Gurion, argued for instance that autonomism would bring on a British-Arab coalition and would isolate the Jewish minority. In a modern state, argued Arlozoroff, the central authorities were dominant and their resources were such that the Jews would end up a permanent minority, just as they were in the diaspora. This, he said, was no Zionist solution.

Others, like Berl Katznelson, also distrustful of the British and the mandatory, rejected Ben-Gurion's concept of the "ruling executive" as another form of British rule without political advantage for the Jews.[34] In all these arguments, one can find fears, phrases, themes, and concerns which would be echoed in a much more detailed way and at much louder volume in the great debate over partition. But in Ben-Gurion's fledgling plan, however complicated and unrealistic it might appear on the surface, one also finds the constant, hard-core kernel of all his subsequent proposals: a way to establish a Jewish commonwealth as quickly as possible.

The issue of self-government preoccupied Mapai leaders between 1929 and 1936. The debate within Mapai and the Socialist Zionist movement derived from the mandatory's idea of establishing a legislative assembly for Palestine. But while moderate Jews were receptive, all the Arabs flatly rejected the concept. For them, it meant some kind of Jewish Zionist autonomy in Palestine, which they would never tolerate. Accepting a legislative assembly for Palestinian Arabs was tantamount to recognition of the Declaration that no Arab state except Egypt still recognizes today.

The British had hoped that in Palestine they could pay lip service to Wilsonian democratic ideas and also maintain their imperial interests. They sought at first to balance the demands of the Arab leaders for a free hand for themselves and their followers against the Zionist call for universal justice for Jews.[35] But as World War II approached, the British would turn their backs on the Balfour Declaration and call for political justice for the Arabs in Palestine.[36] The 1937 Peel Commission, coupled with the 1939 White Paper policy, marked a watershed in Palestine's history and "ended any Jewish hope that the British mandate would ever take Zionism back to its inheritance."[37]

Background to Partition[38]

Four events—the Arab Revolt of 1936–1939, the Peel Commission report, which first proposed partition, the British White Paper of 1939, and the war in Europe and the beginnings of the Holocaust—changed forever the Zionist search for statehood. All of these events shook Zionism, the Middle East, and the mandatory, and provoked a furious debate over partition.

The Arab Revolt of 1936–1939 we have described earlier. Ill-fated, badly and fanatically led, the revolt had two immediate and practical results. The first, the struggle against the mandatory, will be dealt with in chapter four. It is sufficient to say for now that it sparked a revived martial spirit within the Yishuv, a spirit that had its pragmatic result in the reorganization and strengthening of the Jewish Haganah, in thoroughly organizing Jewish defense capabilities, and in laying the groundwork for a future Jewish army.

The issuance of the 1939 British White Paper in the wake of the Arab Revolt was a clear sign that the mandatory was no longer making any pretense of supporting the Balfour Declaration, that it was clearly tilting toward the Arabs while abandoning and becoming hostile to Zionism and its aspirations, and was bent on curtailing any drive toward a Jewish commonwealth or Jewish statehood.

By restricting the immigration of European Jewish refugees to Palestine and by prohibiting Jewish land purchases, the White Paper crushed the hopes of those in Palestine who had advocated collaboration and even shook the pragmatic Ben-Gurion, who by this time had adopted partition as a vehicle for eventual statehood and still clung, however distastefully, to the Balfour Declaration for its legitimacy value. Britain's war against a Nazi Germany embarked on its "final solution" of the Jewish problem brought about a similar crisis of conscience within Ben-Gurion, prompting him to say that he would "treat the war as if there were no White Paper and treat the White Paper as if there were no war."

The British retreat from the Balfour Declaration and their pursuit of the Arabs as a means of protecting their own imperialist concerns had been a long time coming, and among Jewish leaders perhaps only the ardent Anglophile Chaim Weizmann failed to see it. The last official encouraging word from Great Britain had come in 1931, when Weizmann received a letter from then-Prime Minister Ramsay MacDonald expressly reaffirming both the article and the preamble of the League of Nations mandate and again recognizing that the mandate was undertaken on behalf of the Jewish people and not just the Jewish population of Palestine. In the intervening years there was silence or unsuccessful, half-hearted attempts at reconciling the aspirations of both the Jews and Arabs.[39]

The tide had obviously and slowly been turning within the top-hatted ranks of the colonial office. The turnabout was completed just prior to the start of the Arab Revolt, when the Peel Commission, investigating what Great Britain astutely perceived to be a mounting crisis in Palestine, issued a report on July 7, 1937, that was unequivocally pessimistic in tone and indicated a clear tilt toward the Arab position:

> Arab nationalism is as intense a force as Jewish. The Arab leaders' demand for national self-government and the shutting down of the Jewish National Home has remained unchanged since 1920. Like Jewish nationalism, Arab nationalism is stimulated by the educational system and by the growth of the Youth movement. It has also been greatly encouraged by the recent Anglo-Egyptian and Franco-Syrian treaties. The gulf between the races is thus already wide and will continue to widen if the present Mandate is maintained.[40]

The Commission concluded, somewhat halfheartedly, that Palestine should be partitioned into three sections, one comprising a Jewish state, one an Arab state, and one remaining under the authority of the mandatory. The proposed Jewish state was to encompass Galilee, the Jezreel Valley, and the coastal plain to a point midway between Gaza and Jaffa, or about one-fifth of the total mandate area.

While the report, and certainly the post-Arab Revolt White Paper, signalled Britain's disaffection with Zionists (eventually causing Ben-Gurion to split with the mandatory), it also forced the Zionists to consider partition seriously and to reevaluate the means and methods of eventually attaining a Jewish state.

The 1937 partition plan split the Zionist movement more than any previous issue. Should Jews fight for continuation of the mandate until they became a majority in Palestine, or should they accept the mini-state offered them? Those in favor of continuing the mandate believed that other Middle Eastern countries might be more willing to accept a Jewish state if Jews were in the majority. They also believed that the mini-state (its more vehement opponents derisively called it the Tel Aviv state), surrounded by a hostile Arab Palestinian state and a pro-Arab, British-controlled section of Palestine, would have doubtful viability and limited security.

Weizmann and the moderate wing of the Zionists in Palestine and in diaspora, and Ben-Gurion and the moderate left favored partition. They were prepared to exchange territorial claims and the uncertainties of continued and increasingly hostile mandatory administration for the benefits of early self-rule in an amputated Palestine.

The twentieth Zionist Congress, held in Zurich in 1937, regarded the Royal Commission report acceptable as a whole, voting 299 to 160 to endorse the attempts by the British to resolve the crisis. It did *not,* however, endorse the principle of partition. This ambivalent attitude was also reflected within the whole Labor party, the Histadrut, and the kibbutz movement. The controversy soon took the form of internal party conflicts and debate within Palestine. Nor did the controversy end when the British government finally shelved the partition plan. On the contrary, the British reversal exacerbated the debate. Suddenly, the Zionist and labor movements had to deal with the critical problems of Jewish statehood and its component parts: Jewish majoritarianism in Palestine; territorial boundaries; relations with Arab and Palestinian neighbors; and relations with the larger international community—especially those great powers with significant interests of their own. The irony in all this is that the

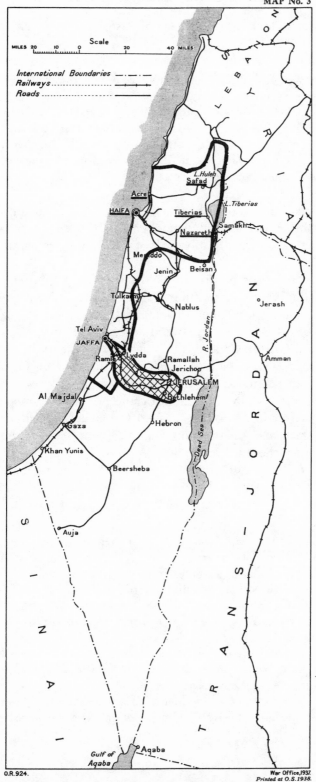

debate was so long in coming. As the historian Eli Sha'altiel points out:

> Despite severe and continuous pressure both within and without, the Zionist movement refrained for many years from defining its final goals. . . .Astonishing though this may seem today, the first time the need for a Jewish state was officially discussed by the Zionist movement was in 1937, twenty years after the Balfour Declaration, when an outside factor—the British Government which held the mandate over Palestine—forced them to do so.[41]

Now that the debate had begun, the attitude taken by the leaders of the Socialist Zionist movement "was a decisive factor in the crystallization of the position of the Zionist movement as a whole."

The debate over partition would eventually split Ben-Gurion from Chaim Weizmann; would weaken Weizmann's hold over the World Zionist movement; would sharpen the Weizmann–Jabotinsky–Ben-Gurion feuds and differences; and would deeply divide Ben-Gurion's Socialist Zionist movement itself.

The labor movement led by the Mapai and by Ben-Gurion was to rule the Yishuv and Israel for over four decades. Thus the debate within the Socialist Zionist camp not only illuminated the partition controversy, but continued to plague Zionist camps for years. In fact, many of the most salient current issues of the Israeli debate over the future boundaries of the state, the occupied territories, peace with the Arabs, and relations with the great powers first began to be discussed in the 1937 debate over partition.

> The attitude of the Zionist Labour movement towards the partition plan was a decisive factor in the crystallization of the position of the Zionist movement as a whole. From 1935 on the labour parties had constituted a clear and decisive majority in all the institutions of the movement, and the leaders of Mapai, especially David Ben-Gurion and Moshe Sharett, were among the chief architects of Zionist policies.
>
> The question of partition split all the camps. Political allies who had been in the same camp for years suddenly found themselves on opposite sides of the barricades. At the end of a lengthy and dramatic debate the Zionist Congress adopted a resolution empowering the Zionist Executive to enter into negotiations with the British govern-

ment on concrete proposals for partition. After violent disagreements in the Cabinet the British government decided, for extremely complex and intricate reasons, to reject the partition plan drawn up by the Commission it had appointed for this purpose. Despite the shelving of the 1937 partition plan, the idea of partition itself could not be ignored as a possible solution to the question of the Arab-Jewish conflict in Palestine.[42]

In the Yishuv, and in the Zionist movement worldwide, the partition debate quickly engaged the entire spectrum of thought and ideology. The battle lines were simultaneously clear-cut and fuzzy. Binationalists, the United Kibbutz movement, Revisionists, Labor's Socialist Zionists, and factions within Mapai battled one another. The central focus, for the most part, was the character of a Jewish state. Underneath, however, in this most politicized of movements another battle was waged: a struggle for political control which split factions from one another and saw old loyalties disintegrate and leaders rise and fall with remarkable rapidity. Eventually, the battle evolved into a struggle for control between the Yishuv in Palestine and the World Zionist Organization in London.

After 1937 two informal axes were established: the Weizmann–London axis and the Ben-Gurion–Jerusalem axis. So long as Jerusalem, the periphery, retained its faith in the partnership with the mandatory, Weizmann remained the undisputed chief negotiator in London. But during the critical period preceding World War II, the Jerusalem branch of the executive committee of the World Zionist Organization began to see its mission as a close surveillance of Weizmann in order to ensure his strict adherence to his commitment to the Balfour Declaration.

Eventually, the struggle between the WZO and the Yishuv for control of the Zionist movement was to personalize itself as a struggle between David Ben-Gurion and Chaim Weizmann. Much of the debate among Zionists over partition, which sprang naturally from the increasingly acrimonious ties between the mandate and the Zionists, was also personal in nature.

The old battlers and faces were very much in evidence: Ben-Gurion, single-minded in his commitment to partition as the fastest means to a Jewish state; Weizmann, the voice of moderation, haunting the halls of embassies and centers of power abroad; Jabotinsky, a strident voice of rejectionism, rallying Zionism to

rise up against the mandatory. But other voices and other personalities joined the fray, not the least of which were Yitzhak
Tabenkin and Berl Katznelson, both opposed to partition, but for
very different reasons.

The debate over partition raged in all the corners of the Zionist
movement—in London and Zurich, in the United States, and most
constantly and most vehemently within the Yishuv in Palestine.

When we look at the actual debate, its issues and viewpoints, we
will note that it appears to be mostly a battle of words. But the
words within the Yishuv were mighty, they constituted a veritable
avalanche and outlined the truly politicized and energetic nature
of the Yishuv. Daily newspapers came as close to resembling
out-and-out propaganda as a sheet pasted on a wall. Every day the
debate would be rolling in some corner of the Yishuv—in
meetings of a kibbutz here, a kibbutz there, out in the desert, in
hotels and at party meetings. Speeches by Tabenkin, or by some
minor Mapai functionary, or by Katznelson, would be published
verbatim, in the next day's newspaper along with the usual
obituaries, births and, predictably, announcements of more talks
and speeches and meetings. And always, whether you were at a
gathering in the United Kibbutz movement, which was usually
closed to outsiders, or at a meeting of Mapai party regulars, or at
a gathering on the fringes of the left or right, you would find
Katznelson, dressed in a suit, smiling, taking notes, adding an
opinion here and there, and always welcomed by all parties.

If the debate seems to be issue-oriented, full of rhetoric and
theory, it must always be remembered that it was consistently
conducted by the people, vibrantly so, passionately so, noisily so.
Partition, in the Yishuv, and within the Zionist movement, was
more than a word on paper, or lines on a map. Behind the debate
lurked the real political battle between the left and the right, and
particularly a struggle for power within the left.

Partition: The Debate[43]

The Nay-Sayers

Opposition to partition came from all quarters of the Zionist
movement: the liberal binationalists; the Jabotinsky-led Revision-

ist movement; the Tabenkin-led United Kibbutz movement; and, within Mapai itself, Katznelson.

There were, of course, splinters between and among these schools and orientations, as well as a central body of anti-Zionists, such as Orthodox Judaism, the Agudat Israel, and Jewish Communists—all without influence on mainstream Zionism in either its Socialist or Revisionist orientation. Within the mainstream, however, the opposing camps not only had different interpretations of Jewish sovereignty and its needs, but also different attitudes toward the mandatory and the Arabs.

The most militant opposition to partition was from the binationalists, whose most articulate spokesman was Shlomo Kaplansky. Binationalists perceived Zionism as an imperfect movement which would deprive the inhabitants of the country in order "to make room for the Jewish masses returning to their home." They argued that the new state must be established on the basis of political equality and cooperation between Jews and Arabs. The Jewish problem, wrote Kaplansky, "is a national problem. Eretz Israel is international." There was no chance that the Arabs would accept an arrangement under which Eretz Israel would be governed only by the Jews. An "agreement with the Arabs becomes an imperative condition for the realization of Zionism by 'peaceful' means."[44]

Here is how Kaplansky's plan would have worked, on the basis of two complementary arrangements for a binational state: The mandatory government would enter a transition stage in which two basic structural arrangements would emerge to serve as the basis for a binational entity. Under a federal council, two structures would converge—one national-ethnic, the other regional-federal. Each nationality (not religion, incidentally) centered within its territorial confines would serve as an autonomous entity in the federal council. (Ethnic federations would give greater autonomy to the local government of each nationality, and territorial federalism would confine each nationality within its geographic area—one with an Arab majority, the other Jewish.) The federal council would be presidential, elected in rotation—one Arab, one Jewish—every three or four years to maintain executive control in economic matters. Immigration would be the reserve of the ethnic national authority; and the federal council would base Jewish immigration on the principle of Arab and Jewish parity, a most touchy issue for Arabs: "Immigration will be arranged along rates, which is to say that Jewish immigration would not surpass Arab national growth." Purchase of land would also be restricted in relation to national capacity, to be decided by the federal council. But Britain, Kaplansky hoped, would continue its mandate until the binational state was stabilized.[45]

Working along similar lines in its opposition to partition was Hashomer Hatzair (Young Guard), a leftist kibbutz youth movement. Hashomer Hatzair called for a binational solution based on territorial aggrandizement for both Arabs and Jews at the expense of the mandatory. Its leader, Yaacov Chazan, wrote that "peace with the Arabs guarantees our existence in Eretz Israel. It is both a secular and a Zionist duty."[46] A Jewish minority in a Palestinian state, they contended, would be a disaster for Zionism. It would be abnormal. Peace, territory, socialism, and revolutionary Zionism could only be secured within a binationalist program.

Another Hashomer Hatzair leader wrote that "we have no doubt that the major aim of Zionism—concentration of the Jewish majority in Eretz Israel and its environment—could not be fulfilled with a small Jewish state." Bringing all the Jewish masses together to Eretz Israel could only be achieved with Arab-Jewish cooperation and only on the basis of a binational regime in Eretz Israel.[47] How naive to believe that Arabs would ever agree to a Jewish majority, even in a binational state.

Professor Y. L. Magnes, a liberal Zionist, a former leader of New York Jewish Kehila (community), rector of Hebrew University, and a member of Brith Shalom (Peace Movement), contended that the partition was a ruthless and cynical proposal demonstrating the failure of Arabs, Jews, and the British to achieve peace in the Holy Land. Dr. Magnes, and others like him, contended that partition would result in the Jews becoming foreign rulers in their homeland, ruling over an Arab majority population.[48] He rejected partition and the concept of Jewish statehood in order to allay Arab fears and establish closer cooperation with Palestinian leaders.

Revisionist Zionism's leader, Zeev Jabotinsky, was the labor movement's chief antagonist and one of the principal opponents of partition.[49] Jabotinsky believed that the Zionist goal must be to establish a Jewish state comprising all of pre-1922 Palestine, including Transjordan. He based the Revisionist program on three goals:

1. The gradual transformation of Palestine (Transjordan included) into a Jewish commonwealth; that is, into a self-governing commonwealth under the auspices of an established Jewish majority.
2. To create the tools for building this commonwealth, including a regular army, a system of state control over customs and taxation, and the nationalization of all land.
3. To harness the Balfour Declaration to Zionist aims through active political and diplomatic work.[50]

Jabotinsky opposed the concept of Jewish autarky and isolation from the rest of Palestine. He believed that the one national group—the Jews—would surpass the other—the Arabs—because their culture, values, and commitments were superior. A colonization movement, he believed, could not become a nation-state unless it was clearly committed to ultimate statehood, as opposed to a national home or a binational state.

Jabotinsky also challenged the labor movement's colonization concepts. It was imperative for Zionists to mobilize as many Jews as possible to relocate to Palestine, not just an elite of pioneers and colonizers. He even advocated evacuating all East European Jews, mainly the 3–4 million in Poland, for resettlement in Palestine. According to Jabotinsky, statehood could only be achieved by establishing a Jewish majority in Palestine.[51]

Most importantly, Jabotinsky vehemently opposed partition. The British must continue to govern Palestine until the Jews were ready to proclaim their statehood. On the surface, this opposition would seem to have contradicted his dedication to Jewish statehood, but he saw partition as a repudiation of the Revisionist Zionist political goal of creating a Jewish majority in all of Palestine.

The Revisionists expected that partition eventually would be abandoned and that Britain would ultimately realize that "the Arab nation" was a weak reed on which to establish a British imperial policy in the Middle East. But the Jewish state could not be established by a British diktat alone. Only when the Jews achieved a majority in Eretz Israel would they assume responsibility for national and political sovereignty. Thus the struggle was viewed as a conflict between Arabs and Jews. Etzel—the illegal Revisionist underground of this period—was designed to fight Arab terrorists and extremists, not the British government.[52]

Ben-Gurion and the proponents of partition principally encountered stiff challenges from within the labor movement itself, from Tabenkin and Katznelson.

The chief challenge came from Tabenkin, Ben-Gurion's old ideological and political rival who, like Katznelson, spoke as a Zionist constructivist, advocating the gradual socialization, collectivization, and Jewification of all of Eretz Israel. It was Tabenkin who jeeringly called the partition plan the "Tel Aviv state."

If the Zionist movement had what amounted to a battling sage, a rabbi-in-khaki, it was probably Yitzhak Tabenkin. A key member of the 1905-era immigration, Tabenkin came from an artisan family in eastern Poland. He was a thoroughgoing Marxist, an ardent admirer of Lenin, and a revolutionary in spirit and temperament. He was one of the founders of Socialist Zionism, a key leader of the United Labor party, an important member of the Histadrut, and a perpetual challenger to the power and machinations of Ben-Gurion. If Ben-Gurion battled Weizmann over the years for leadership of the Zionist movement as a whole, then Tabenkin was Ben-Gurion's chief rival for leadership within the Yishuv. His base of power was the United Kibbutz movement (UKM).

Tabenkin was single-minded in his approach to Jewish sovereignty in Palestine. That single-mindedness was also his weakness in the struggle with Ben-Gurion. His singular achievement was to keep the UKM a political force independent of the umbrella labor party, Mapai, and he was to prove an inspirational focal point for thousands of young pioneers born in Palestine. With all the strength of a visionary, he saw as his job, and indeed his duty, the need to transform the diaspora Jew into a pioneer. He saw absolutely no borders to a Jewish state. Jewish sovereignty, he felt, would be attained by perpetual and continual settlement, and he showed how by starting a kibbutz in the environs of the Jezreel Valley, which was to become a "Republic of Kibbutzim."[53]

In a way, Tabenkin was something of a passionate and spirited anachronism. Tall, imposing, he often seemed the quarrelsome rabbi, contentious and argumentative. Like a true revolutionary, he had no concept of the craft of diplomacy, no real idea about statehood and modern politics and statecraft. He was, in the end, the quintessential frontiersman, rough and charismatic.

If Tabenkin, like Jabotinsky and Ben-Gurion to a degree, was charismatic and at home with power, Berl Katznelson was Zionism's gentle ideologue. An ardent Labor Zionist, mostly loyal to Ben-Gurion, he nevertheless opposed partition for his own, carefully-thought-out reasons. For Tabenkin, the indivisibility of the land of Israel was paramount. Partition, he felt, was an imperialist plan designed to thwart the pioneer movement in Palestine. It meant forfeiting the Socialist Zionist ideology of Hebrew labor and betraying the precepts of A. D. Gordon. It meant giving up the Socialist Zionist vision of a new Jewish society based on creative labor.

Tabenkin believed that the nationalistic antagonism must be resolved. Otherwise, the state might be permanently limited in size to less than one-third the area of Palestine—the area the Jews occupied under the mandate—thereby limiting the number of pioneer Zionists who could settle in Israel. Under the mandate the borders were not yet defined and there was still room for expansion. Tabenkin argued prophetically that "the establishment of a Jewish state forthwith would mean the establishment of a militaristic society, which would have to send the best of its sons to serve in a professional army whose soldiers wore uniforms and devoted their lives to fighting."[54] He thus accurately foresaw the growth of the Israel Defense Force, but it was still a stunning argument coming from the mentor of the Palmach (the Haganah's shock troops) and the founder of the militant United Kibbutz movement.

Tabenkin believed in a last-frontier concept whereby the size of the future state of Israel would be determined entirely by the scope of a border settlement program, not by political bargaining, which he abhorred. At the United Kibbutz movement conference held at Beit-Hashita in July 1937, he declared war against partition, explaining that "the Jewish state will be attained through a large-scale colonization program of all parts of Eretz Israel. . .and also through the perpetual strength of the Jewish catastrophe [Polish and East European anti-Semitism] as an international political factor."[55]

The pillar of Mapai opposition to partition was Ben-Gurion's mentor and friend, Berl Katznelson. Short, quiet, unimposing, Katznelson was Mapai's ideologue, a party man with tremendous influence despite his never holding an official party office. Not surprisingly, considering his good nature and gentleness, he was profoundly influenced by Gordon's writings and was something of a protégé of the movement's eminent sage, though he recognized the gaps and flaws in Gordon's return-to-nature philosophy as it was translated into action. He was a man of the center and thus would always see both sides of a question—except when it came to the Revisionists, whom he consistently and passionately opposed. A prolific writer, his collected works of essays, speeches, letters and ruminations totalled twenty volumes. He was something of a puritan in his personal life, eclectic, and a man of the world who saw, for instance, Franklin D. Roosevelt's New Deal for what it was—a revolutionary process which would alter the political landscape of the United States, and portions of which could be applied in a socialist state.[56]

Katznelson thought that the mandatory's authority, even if it only existed on paper, should be maintained. Like Weizmann and Jabotinsky, Katznelson wanted to pressure the British into upholding their commitment to the Balfour Declaration. He believed that Arab intervention into Palestinian affairs would not end simply because an independent Arab Palestinian state was established. In his view, the Jewish Yishuv was unprepared for statehood, and he contended that the cooperative agricultural settlement would fare better under the mandatory because the League of Nations trusteeship assured the Jewish community of protection.

Katznelson was deeply troubled and fearful of a partitioned state's future. He opposed partition primarily because he feared the growing strength of the Arab nationalist movements, and thought that new political constellations in the Near East, based on growing sympathies between Nazis, Fascists, and some Arab nationalists, might threaten any independent state, small or large. He even suspected that pro-Arab elements in the British government favored partition only because it would leave the Jews to be strangled in an impossibly small territory, which would then fall into Arab hands.

Katznelson was in many ways Ben-Gurion's guru. His opposition to partition was of considerable concern to Ben-Gurion who, as an activist, could not see partition as Berl did from the vantage of an ideologue. Yet Katznelson was never rigid or doctrinaire, a characteristic also of Mapai, the party of compromise. In his role as a superb political analyst Katznelson opposed partition, but he never directed a political campaign against Ben-Gurion as Tabenkin did during the debate over partition.

Katznelson, although he disagreed with many people, including Ben-Gurion, was nevertheless universally regarded with affection by political friends and foes alike. He had the capacity to sympathize with his opponents, a quality the contentious Ben-Gurion saw as a weakness. But then, although they were personally close, the two men were always very different. Ben-Gurion, it has been said, always saw himself as the leader, the king, a historical figure twice removed, to the point that no one would dream of calling him by his first name. He was always Mr. Prime Minister, or at best, Ben-Gurion. The story goes that even Ben-Gurion's wife, through all their married life, either addressed him as Ben-Gurion or not at all. Katznelson, on the other hand, was never Katznelson, he was always Berl to everyone.

Ben-Gurion, of course, would always be the central figure in the debate over partition. Seeing more clearly than anyone that it would be the means and the vehicle to achieve Jewish statehood, he rode partition like a whirlwind and gambled his political future on it. Partition would catapult Ben-Gurion to the summit of World Zionism, and it would engage him in a bitter political struggle with both Weizmann and his own party.

The Yea-Sayer: Ben-Gurion and Partition

David Ben-Gurion, through all this, remained firmly committed to partition. He believed in the establishment of an independent Jewish commonwealth in part of Eretz Israel as quickly as possible. (Prophetically, he was never to define where and what the boundaries were to be.)

The opponents of partition, he argued, were attempting to see in it a solution to problems which the plan itself made no attempt to solve. The acceptance of partition stemmed from 'Zionist calculations'. He supported partition because it advanced the interests of Zionism and the Jewish people. The solution to the Arab-Jewish conflict—which was the necessary condition for the *complete* realization of Zionism—he postponed to other times and conditions. The adoption of partition would facilitate the creation of such conditions. Partition was the result of the interference of an outside power, whereas peace between the Arabs and Jews would be achieved only after the two *national movements,* Jewish and Arab, came to the conclusion that it served their common interests, without outside interference or great power pressure.[57]

Ben-Gurion proposed these options on the theme of partition:

1. That Eretz Israel "become completely Jewish."
2. That Eretz Israel be a unit in a large British commonwealth.
3. That Eretz Israel sign treaties with its neighbors.

The aim of Zionism is a Jewish state, he insisted, and it must be the basis for Jewish-Arab relations. The Jewish Yishuv is a force the Arabs will have to recognize when they are ready for a pan-Arab federation of their own outside of Palestine. "The Arab nations don't live in a diaspora. The Jews do. The problem is not an Arab Palestine state, but political states for Arab minorities in Palestine, where the Arabs have plenty of territory."[58]

Ben-Gurion all along aimed for an immediate Jewish Commonwealth and it was for reasons of expediency that he was willing to accept the idea of an amputated Palestine. His constant public plea was for a Jewish National Home as a "state on the way." He pounded on this theme constantly during the 1930s, before the Royal Commission, before Mapai party leaders, and in the Histadrut:

> Exile is complete dependence—in material things, in politics, in culture, in ethics, and in intellect. . .They who are dependent constitute an alien minority, they have no homeland and are separated from their origins, from the soil, from labor and from economic activity. So we must become the captains of our own fortunes. . . . We must become independent."[59]

Eloquently, and pragmatically, Ben-Gurion stated and restated his theme. He saw the state as a shelter for the organized community, an institution giving the community freedom of action and mobility: "We are a Jewish community which is in fact a Jewish Commonwealth in the making."

The urgency in his message arose from three factors: (1) the deterioration of the mandate; (2) the growth of Arab nationalism; and (3) the need for an open immigration policy in view of the increasing danger that was confronting European Jewry. He believed that a state, no matter what its size, would solve the compelling problems facing Zionism. The minuscule Royal Commission partition map did not discourage Ben-Gurion, for as he saw it, partition was the only way to gain initial independence from Britain and the Arab majority. The Arab Revolt, the rise of Hitler, and the withering away of the Balfour principles convinced him that independence had to come soon or that it might not come at all, and that a minimum solution should therefore be accepted.

Ben-Gurion's views proved crucial in the debate. He had been the leader of Mapai since 1935, the uncrowned leader of the Yishuv, and one of the three most important figures (along with Weizmann and Jabotinsky) of the World Zionist movement. An advocate of gradualism, Jewish majoritarianism in Israel, and Hebrew labor, he represented the mainstream of Zionism in the debate over partition. "The Zionist Verdict: A Jewish State Now" gives his sober and, as it turned out, prophetic assessment in 1936 of internal and international events.

> The rise of Hitler and Naziism, while threatening European Jewry's Zionist heartland, nonetheless promised to stimulate the immigration of Jews to Palestine. The immigration of such Jews, living under distressed conditions, circumvented the mandate's restrictions against unlimited immigration. . . . Partition, then, however repugnant, was preferable to full abandonment by Britain later in favor of pan-Arabism. The presence of the British gave the Jews time to consolidate their military power.[60]

Ben-Gurion also argued that the partitioned states stood a better chance of working in amity than they would as nations fighting over a single territory dominated by a foreign power. Furthermore, he advocated a new idea that became a cardinal tenet in his conception of Jewish-Arab relations: Arab-Jewish rapprochement would be achieved only *after* a Jewish state had been established. Once a Jewish state had consolidated Jewish economic and military power, one could expect the Arabs to realize that a strong Israel could benefit them directly. Ben-Gurion wrote a most revealing letter to Moshe Shertok (Sharett) in July 1937:

> If this plan of the Commission's is implemented—at the moment nothing is certain, for the difficulties and pitfalls are great and many— I am absolutely certain (to the extent that there can be any certainty in our thoughts about the future) that it will not be a final arrange-

ment. We will break through these boundaries—and not necessarily by the power of the sword. More than in other times I believe in an Arab-Jewish agreement in the forseeable future. And if we bring hundreds of thousands of Jews to our state and consolidate ourselves from the economic and military point of view, there will be a basis for a free agreement regarding the abolishment of frontiers between us and the Arab state. Not only the material benefits which would accrue to the Arab state—for these material benefits may not be sufficient to destroy patriotic Arab opposition to our immigration into their state—but their true national interests will impel the Arabs to compromise with us in exchange for mutual use and enjoyment of the areas of both our states.[61]

In defending his support of a partitioned state, Ben-Gurion argued that many aspects of the Peel plan favored the Zionists:

This report. . .gives us a wonderful strategic basis for our stand, for our fight. . .the first document since the Mandate which strengthens our moral and political status. . . .it gives us control over the coast of Palestine; large immigration; a Jewish army; systematic colonization under state control. . ."[62]

According to this argument, partition advanced the realization of Jewish statehood even though the time might not yet be ripe for securing the Jewish state. Cautiously, Ben-Gurion said, "No one without faith in the great Zionist vision would find the strength to reject a concrete offer to establish a Jewish State immediately in part of the country."[63] But what was still necessary was larger immigration and a better-trained Jewish army.

Ben-Gurion's concept of partition was, as he clearly said, tactical when "success is local and limited in time as an effort toward the final strategy." Partition is a tactic; the strategy—a Jewish independent and sovereign state. Borders are temporary. Immigration and settlement are the dynamic processes that will lead toward the state.

The Debate Over Partition: Final Phases

The debate over partition, when all was said and done, finally became a political battle royal, a struggle for power that caused a final duel between Ben-Gurion and Weizmann as well as deep splits within Labor itself.

Weizmann and Ben-Gurion had been trading increasingly bitter recriminations over the years, a process that started sometime in 1937 and was not to halt until 1947. Weizmann claimed correctly that Ben-Gurion wanted to replace him and that it was personal ambition which inspired his attacks. Yet the issues went beyond personalities. Weizmann clung to the mandatory and his British connections, still hoping against hope that there would be reconciliation between the Yishuv, Zionists, and Great Britain. He continued to try, through his friend Winston Churchill, to influence the British cabinet to reverse its policy. After much debate, the cabinet upheld the status quo.

Ben-Gurion, meanwhile, had come to believe that attention should be concentrated on the United States in the hope of inducing the American government to pressure Britain into rescinding the White Paper policy. And because he had cultivated good connections both within the American Jewish movement in general and with Jewish labor leaders in particular, the United States also offered Ben-Gurion a favorable arena for continuing his personal struggle with Weizmann. Although Weizmann also had serious allies in the United States, such as Rabbi Stephen Wise, Nahum Goldman, and Louis Lipsky, all moderate leaders of American Zionism, he could not hope to match Ben-Gurion's mass support from Jewish labor groups and Socialist Zionist organizations.[64]

The differences between the two men were illustrated by the tactical battle over statehood which took place during the American Zionist conference held at the Biltmore Hotel in New York in 1942. Ben-Gurion had gained the support of Rabbi Hillel Silver, an influential Zionist leader who had become frustrated with what he termed "Judenrat" leadership—the ghetto leadership that failed to resist the Nazis by force. Ben-Gurion and Silver proposed, and the Biltmore Conference agreed, that: (1) Palestine should be opened immediately to mass Jewish immigration; (2) authority over immigration and development of Palestine should be transferred to the Jewish Agency; and (3) a Jewish Commonwealth should be established in Palestine as an integral part of the new United Nations organization proposed in the Atlantic Charter. This third point was a first in the history of Zionist revolutionary activism, and the entire program represented a complete triumph over Weizmann's gradualist, pro-British approach.

Ben-Gurion's struggle was not restricted to the Zionist movement and Weizmann. The Biltmore controversy carried over into Palestine itself, where the differences between Weizmann, his supporters in the Mapai, Labor militants, and the Revisionists continued to grow.[65]

The Yishuv had been bitterly divided by the issuance of the White Paper. Etzel and Lehi, the militant Revisionist undergrounds, called for the ouster of the mandatory. The Lehi even wanted to declare open war against Britain, and their terrorist activities contributed to making British rule in Palestine intolerable.

Meanwhile, the Labor movement was divided over the strategic aspects of the coming struggle against the British. Three separate camps emerged: the activists; the left, essentially Hashomer Hatzair; and the mainstream led by Ben-Gurion. The activists, who led the United Kibbutz movement (UKM) and the Palmach, called for an unrelenting struggle against the British. Its leaders—Tabenkin, Galilee, and Allon—all split from the Mapai in 1942 and established a new labor party in 1944, assuming what had been the name of the very first labor party early in the 1900s, Ahdut Haavoda (United Labor). They were also known as Faction B.

Hashomer Hatzair, meanwhile, opposed the entire struggle against the British and continued to call for a binational state. So vehement were they that they too formed another party, which would become Mapam in 1948.

After the split of the UKM, Mapai was weakened and divided. In its May 1943 political committee conference, the collective leadership, by adopting a moderate stance on all issues, sought to regain its position as Zionism's centrist party and to distinguish itself from the UKM and the Revisionists.

Instead of taking an attitude of conciliation toward the leadership, Ben-Gurion called for the curtailment of Weizmann as the chief political and diplomatic authority of Zionism, limiting his political and diplomatic powers. Following up his triumph at the Biltmore Conference, Ben-Gurion sought to shift the movement's political-diplomatic struggle to Palestine and the United States. The result was one of the most heated political battles Mapai had ever seen. Opposition to Ben-Gurion was led by Katznelson and

Eliahu Golomb, head of the Haganah. The party called for discipline and for restraining Ben-Gurion, with the majority objecting to his high-handed tactics of confrontation with Britain and Weizmann. It insisted on the supremacy of its collective leadership, decried the "cult of personality," and called for "party discipline and obedience to the rule of the movement."

Ben-Gurion's setback was temporary. He finally won his personal battle against Weizmann during the Twenty-First Zionist Congress in 1946. Again allied with Silver, Ben-Gurion and the activists had an 80 percent majority in the Congress, at least partly because Weizmann's constituency, Eastern and Central European Jewry, had been decimated by Hitler. Even the divisions within the labor movement itself had left Weizmann at a disadvantage. Then seventy-two years old, he was left with only limited support from a small group drawn from the Mapai center and the Zionist left. He was defeated by the powerful American and Palestinian delegation led by Silver, Ben-Gurion, and the Ahdut Haavoda militants, and his post as president of the World Zionist Organization in London was left vacant. Ben-Gurion had won his personal battle.

The struggle for partition had been won by 1947, just as Weizmann became completely isolated. All along, it had also been a struggle against the British, who had originally proposed partition. The struggle constitutes the Jewish Revolt, a process that took heat from the British White Paper and continued up until the war of independence.[66]

CHAPTER 3

The Jewish Struggle Against the Mandatory[1]

The 1939 British White Paper: Watershed for the Yishuv and Zionism

The British White Paper of 1939 seems studiously long, languorous in its direction, an exercise in imperial fair-mindedness, almost sonorous in tone, like a letter from a latter-day Lord Chesterton to a rambunctious set of brothers. Written and promulgated by British Arabists and colonial civil servants in London and Jerusalem, different in outlook and attitude from the men who wrote the ambiguous Balfour Declaration, the White Paper seeks to reinterpret that declaration even while disowning it. Underneath the stately prose oozing reasonableness was a radical change in direction of British policy in Palestine—a distancing from the promise of a Jewish homeland and a turn toward accommodation of the Arabs.

The policy statement is a long diplomatic statement, but its salient features jump off the page in several sections, beginning with a hint of repudiation, a tipoff of the change of mind and direction, and ending with sharp and detailed statements of intent. Not an official policy, not even a formal declaration as such, it was repudiated by a League of Nations commission and had no official status. Yet it was a policy which the British were to pursue down to the last chaotic days of the mandatory. In its own way, the

White Paper contributed to the end of the mandatory in Palestine, reflecting as it did both British ignorance of the real situation in Palestine and British self-interest in terms of the future of imperialism in the Middle East. In its measured tone one finds an act of diplomatic self-deception.

For the Zionists, the White Paper was an eye-opener, as the British clearly were taking measures to divorce themselves from the Balfour Declaration, upon which rested Zionist claims for the legitimacy of a Jewish homeland and eventually a Jewish state. The intent of the British became clear in the constitution of the policy statement:

> Unauthorized statements have been made to the effect that the purpose in view is to create a wholly Jewish Palestine. Phrases have been used such as that "Palestine is to become as Jewish as England is English." His Majesty's Government regard any such expectation as impracticable and have no such aim in view. Nor have they at any time contemplated. . .the disappearance or the subordination of the Arab population, language or culture in Palestine. They would draw attention to the fact that the terms of the [Balfour] Declaration referred to do not contemplate that Palestine as a whole should be converted into a Jewish National Home, but that such a Home should be founded *in Palestine.* [Emphasis added.]
>
> But this statement has not removed doubts, and his Majesty's government therefore now declares unequivocally that it is not part of their policy that Palestine should become a Jewish State."

The total reinterpretation of the Balfour Declaration to suit British needs becomes much clearer in the later portions of the statement:

> The objective of his Majesty's Government is the establishment within ten years of an independent Palestine State. . . . The independent State should be one in which Arabs and Jews share in government in such a way as to ensure that the essential interests of each community are safeguarded.

This is a long way down the road from guaranteeing a Jewish homeland. The more specific portions of the White Paper in fact guarantee that no such thing will ever happen.

It has been urged that all further Jewish immigration into Palestine should be stopped forthwith. His Majesty's Government cannot accept such a proposal.

But:

Jewish immigration during the next five years will be at a rate which, if economic absorptive capacity permits, will bring the Jewish population up to approximately one-third of the total population of the country. . . . This would allow of the admission, as from the beginning of April this year [1939], of some 75,000 immigrants over the next five years. These immigrants would, subject to the criterion of economic absorptive capacity, be admitted as follows:
(a) For each of the next five years a quota of 10,000 Jewish immigrants will be allowed, on the understanding that a shortage in any one year may be added to the quotas for subsequent years, within the five-year period, if economic absorptive capacity permits.
After a period of five years, *no further Jewish immigration will be permitted unless the Arabs of Palestine are prepared to acquiesce in it.* [Emphasis added.]

This meant not only a restriction of Jewish immigration, but an eventual end to it. More than that, the British washed their hands of their promise to aid in the creation of a Jewish homeland:

His Majesty's Government are satisfied that when the immigration over five years which is now contemplated has taken place, they will not be justified in facilitating, nor will they be under any obligation to facilitate, the further development of the Jewish National Home by immigration regardless of the wishes of the Arab population.

Similarly, the British would apply restrictions on Jewish settlements and land purchases. And they would end the statement in a typically pious, tight-lipped vein which calls on some higher, nobler good:

The responsibility which falls on them [the Jews and Arabs], no less than upon His Majesty's Government, to cooperate together to ensure peace is all the more solemn because their country is revered by many millions of Moslems, Jews and Christians throughout the world who pray for peace in Palestine and for the happiness of her people.[2]

Reaction to the White Paper

For the people of the Yishuv in Palestine, 1939 was a tragic year, casting a traumatic pall of gloom over Zionism and all of its aspirations.

The White Paper disaster was heightened by events in Europe, when Hitler, bolstered by the successful conclusion of the Soviet-German pact and contemptuous of the British and French after the debacle over Czechoslovakia, invaded Poland, setting off World War II, a step that meant doom for millions of European Jews.

In August, less than a month before the war began, the World Zionist Organization met in Geneva in an atmosphere of deep depression. Chaim Weizmann, worn to the bone by months of emotional and bitter wrangling with Colonial Secretary Malcolm MacDonald over the White Paper and fearful over the Nazi cloud descending on European Jewry, gave an emotional closing speech in which he said, "It is with a heavy heart that I take my leave. . . . There is darkness all around us and we cannot see through the clouds."[3]

David Ben-Gurion, worried and bitter, was at the end of his emotional rope as far as the British were concerned. He was in a combative, defiant mood. "We have to demonstrate skills and the ability for real resistance," he told a Mapai gathering. "Words are not meaningful anymore. Words will not arrest the White Paper policy."[4]

Many of those attending the WZO congress in Switzerland would disappear in Europe, killed in the Holocaust. Meanwhile, MacDonald's insistent pursuit and implementation of the White Paper, which cost Great Britain dearly in political divisiveness, hit even such ardent supporters of Great Britain as Weizmann like a slap in the face.

From the start, the White Paper pleased no one. In addition to limiting and eventually ending immigration, it called for prohibitions or restrictions on land sales to Jews in all but a small portion of the Tel Aviv-Haifa area. For the Arabs, it proposed the slow construction of self-governing institutions which aimed squarely at a Palestinian state to be created at the end of ten years, subject to the consent of the Jewish community.

This double approval or veto power for the Jews and Arabs would, MacDonald hoped, somehow bring the two communities together in mutual acts of cooperation. Unfortunately—and predictably—the reactions were just the opposite. The Zionists were appalled and stunned, so much so that when the White Paper's stipulations were announced openly in May of that year, there were heated demonstrations of protest throughout the Yishuv. The Arabs, although many of them privately saw it correctly as a sign of progress and a tilt in the British position toward the Arabs, nevertheless refused to accept the White Paper, held back by the radical representatives of the Mufti, who demanded establishment of an Arab Palestine.

The closeness between Weizmann and the thirty-seven-year-old Malcolm MacDonald, son of the pro-Zionist former prime minister Ramsay MacDonald, was shattered, much to Weizmann's chagrin. Great Britain was also lambasted in the United States, where reactions ranged from President Franklin Roosevelt's unveiled disapproval to attacks in the press. To make matters worse, the White Paper was declared illegal by the League of Nations, a fact the Zionists would return to again and again during the course of World War II.

For the British, it was another tried and true matter of practical politics from the appeasement-oriented Chamberlain government. They got short-term results while hoping to please everyone in some wishful long run. The Arab revolt had subsided, at least partly because the Arabs saw that the British were trying to throttle the Zionist aspirations for a Jewish homeland in Palestine. The British also felt that they could still rely on Zionist cooperation simply because the Yishuv and World Zionism had nowhere else to go. In this, they were only partly right in the short term, and fatefully wrong in the long run.

For the Zionists, who over the years had harbored varying degrees of doubt about the British, it was a time of near-total disillusionment. It was obvious that the British were making an abrupt turn in policy, that they were abandoning partition and the Balfour Declaration, that they were trying to nip the promised future Jewish homeland in the bud. Even Weizmann felt betrayed, and Ben-Gurion, long an advocate of working with the mandatory, felt that the time had come for some sort of resistance. Revisionist Zionists, especially Betar-Etzel, cried, "I told you so!" and by 1940 prepared to battle the British openly.

What hurt the Zionist leaders more than anything was restricting immigration. It seemed to men like Ben-Gurion and Weizmann an appalling, cynical, and ruthless policy at a time when European Jewry was threatend by Hitler and Nazism. None of the Zionist leaders, whether in the Yishuv, or in the World Zionist Organization, or in the United States, could accept it. As the war progressed, as news of the plight of the Jews in Europe became more vivid and Hitler's Final Solution could no longer be ignored, Zionists came to see the White Paper as something akin to the Devil's Manifesto. If their aim had been to create an independent Jewish state, the Zionists saw secondly that their aspiration was also a means of saving Europe's Jews. They were outraged at Great Britain's continued support of its White Paper policy, at the sight of British troops in Palestine turning back ships filled with Jewish refugees, and of the American and British refusal to do anything to help the Jews in Europe, such as bombing the rail centers near concentration camps or rescuing Jews.

Except for a brief period of cooperation in the early stages of the war, when German forces threatened Great Britain's very existence in the Middle East, the empire never really wavered from the White Paper, even though Prime Minister Winston Churchill was purported to be an avid Zionist supporter, a champion of partition and a Jewish homeland.[5] The White Paper, more than any other event, therefore provided the spark for what was to become the Jewish struggle against the mandatory, a struggle which would be waged first on diplomatic fronts as a subversion of the White Paper policy restrictions against immigration and land purchases, and finally as out-and-out guerrilla war against the British.

Yishuv's focus from 1939 to 1948 would shift away from the Arabs and onto the British, engaging the passions of all the various Yishuv factions and of World Zionism. The armed struggle would take on something of the nature of a political debate, with a variety of military factions emerging. The Haganah represented the forces of Socialist Zionism, meaning Labor, Mapai, and Ben-Gurion; the Etzel and Lehi sprang from the womb of Revisionist Zionism, including Betar and the Biryonim (the renegade militant faction of Betar).[6] The debate also involved the Palmach, the elite shock troops of the Haganah, representing the continued infiltration of Labor by the United Kibbutz movement and its chief ideologue and leader, Yitzhak Tabenkin.[7]

At the center of the struggle stood Ben-Gurion, who always looked a little further down the road than anyone else, whose goals were to create an instrument of political power, build a Jewish state, and preside over the triumph of his Socialist Zionist cause, the triumph of Labor. Ben-Gurion would oppose the mandatory, but he would also ruthlessly opt for unity within the Yishuv, at the cost of purging or rendering powerless potentially dissident forces such as Begin's Etzel, the Palmach elite, and the radical terrorist Lehi group.

The various military or defense factions such as the Haganah, Palmach, Etzel, and Lehi did not spring up overnight with the issuance of the White Paper. The idea of Jewish defense forces stretched as far back as the guard units of Poale Zion (diaspora forerunner of Socialist Zionism), units that protected the Jewish community in the Ukraine in the 1880s. Within Palestine various factions had been created, discarded, reorganized, and changed over the years, and we must now review the development of these armed groups.

The Haganah and Its Forerunners[8]

There had always been different options for the creation of an autonomous Jewish military force in the Yishuv, the question was one of control and domination. Ben-Gurion and Mapai wanted to control any Jewish military force. Weizmann and Jabotinsky advocated a military force totally subordinated to Yishuv-Zionist authorities. Etzel-Lehi sought to create an autonomous military organization independent of all Zionist parties, including Revisionism and Betar.

The idea of a Jewish military force was transferred to Palestine first with the creation of a self-defense society called Hashomer (the Watchman), which literally provided watchmen or guards for Jewish settlements. Imbued with the spirit of the "tough" Jew, Hashomer members were dedicated and revolutionary-minded Socialist Zionists who sought to set up fortified Jewish collectives. Hashomer's ideas were clearly set forth as early as 1912, in its "Proposal on the Protection of the Yishuv":

1. Hashomer would not limit its role to physical protection of Jewish settlements, but would strive to inculcate a consciousness into the settlers that they must protect themselves.
2. Hashomer would provide the nucleus for a widening of the defensive functions of the Jewish community.
3. Hashomer would serve as the professional armed force of the Yishuv.

Hashomer would adhere to those basic tenets right through the 1920s, and its effectiveness was notable when Jews in Jerusalem, Tel Aviv, and other cities were made vulnerable in the Arab riots of 1920. Although settlement Jews defended themselves successfully with the help of the Hashomer group, it still represented more of a militia than a professional military group.[9]

Meanwhile, under the leadership of Berl Katznelson, the various organizational groups within the Socialist Zionist movement were coming together under one umbrella with the establishment of the United Labor party (Ahdut Haavoda) in 1919, and the Histadrut in 1920. The United Labor party would become Mapai by 1930 and would dominate the Yishuv and Israel in years to come. The Arab riots of 1920 moved the Labor leadership, which until then had allowed Hashomer almost exclusive control of defense, to appoint a committee headed by Eliahu Golomb and Dov Hoz for the express purpose of creating a defense society. Hashomer opposition to the committee was broken after Hashomer declared strong Leninist leanings, and the Golomb-Hoz committee recommendation to organize the Haganah, the first Jewish underground in Palestine, was accepted on June 25, 1921. Hashomer continued to exist as a defense force independent from Labor's influence.

The Haganah was a creation of Socialist Zionism and was to be tightly controlled by and allied with Mapai and Ben-Gurion. More than a military force, it became a political institution of the established Yishuv. Critics even called it a state within a state.

The organizing of the Haganah was slow and difficult, but Ben-Gurion, prescient as ever, knew it was important, predicting that "the Jerusalem riots of 1920 and the Jaffa massacre of 1921 would be as nothing compared to what we would face in the future." Yet, an appeal by Golomb to the World Zionist Congress in 1930 failed to raise special funds for it, and for a long time Haganah failed to attract very many quality recruits. The most seasoned candidates remained with Hashomer, which still opposed the very idea of the Haganah and was jealous of its defense prerogatives. By the late 1920s Hashomer ceased to exist as a military organization. The Haganah was now the single Yishuv military force.

The 1936–1939 Arab Revolt changed the situation. The Jews saw that the British were reluctant to protect Jewish settlements from Arab attacks and therefore began to build the Haganah in order to defend themselves. In 1936 Ben-Gurion and the Yishuv decided to reorganize the Haganah under the auspices of the Histadrut, and began paying full-time salaries to Haganah leaders. Operating out of Histadrut headquarters in Tel Aviv, the Haganah became an embryonic ministry of defense. Working with the British, who now had their hands full with the Arabs, Ben-Gurion and the Socialist Zionist moderates were able to build up a clandestine Jewish army at once protected by the British army, even partially armed by it, but not responsible to it.

With the Arab Revolt in full swing in 1937, Haganah, under the leadership of Yitzhak Sadeh (later founder of the Palmach), adopted a more aggressive fighting position. Sadeh created the first patrol, a military unit composed of collective youth, which raided centers of Arab terrorism repeatedly. As he put it: "Don't wait for the Arab marauder. Don't wait to defend the kibbutz. Go after him, move on to the offensive."[10] This battle cry attracted the outdoor-hardened youth of the kibbutzim and greatly swelled the ranks of the Haganah. By 1937, it was revitalized and in full bloom. Thus, it could be said that the Arab Revolt backfired on the Arabs vis-à-vis the Jews by providing the excuse to undertake the groundwork that led to the very military apparatus used to sustain the Jews in the war of independence.

The Haganah organization operated as a general staff for a large-scale unofficial army recruited from the kibbutzim, the privately owned and operated cooperatives, and in the cities from the children of Mapai bureaucrats. It organized centers for officer training, modernized the kibbutz communications systems, and poured out military publications. The Haganah organized a huge clandestine arms-purchasing operation, established a thriving but minuscule small arms industry, and even created the beginnings of an air force and navy. In addition, the Haganah conducted national fund-raising campaigns, distributed literature for members and set up an intelligence network. It also attracted the admiration and help of Captain Orde Wingate, a quixotic British officer.

Stationed in Palestine, Wingate practically became a convert to Zionism, even though his ultimate loyalties lay with the Empire. He vehemently opposed the pro-Arab mandatory authorities, and approached Haganah intelligence officers with the idea of forming night squads which would raid Arab positions. These night squads were manned by young kibbutz members who later would become some of the most illustrious leaders of Israel—Moshe Dayan and Yigal Allon were among the first members.[11]

Publication of the White Paper in 1939 momentarily ended British-Haganah cooperation, driving the Haganah into a semiunderground. This was a position already occupied by the militant forces of Revisionist Zionism.

The Forces of Revisionist Zionism: Etzel and Lehi[12]

The Haganah and its elite corps, the Palmach (see page 88), operated within the framework of the Yishuv, Socialist Zionism, and the United Kibbutz Movement, threatened by "the Arab problem" and the Yishuv's tenuous, complex relationship with the mandatory. By and large, the Haganah was a politically and militarily moderate force. Although only semilegal, it was hardly a truly underground force. Not so the forces that emerged from Revisionist Zionism and that stood outside the Yishuv institutionalized system. The Revisionists refused to recognize the legitimacy of the Jewish Agency and its military arm.

Zeev Jabotinsky first toyed with the idea of forming Jewish legions as early as 1914. Jabotinsky, Weizmann, and Yoseph Trumpeldor, a Socialist Zionist radical and veteran of the Russo-Japanese War, decided that a Jewish legion fighting on the side of the allies in World War I would be a useful lever for favorable British concessions in the Middle East. Jabotinsky also saw a Jewish legion as the first stage of the development of a Jewish force as part of the British army in Palestine. In 1915, two Jewish legions, composed of volunteers from the United States, Great Britain, and Palestine, were actually formed, but they served mainly as transport units and in 1918 were disbanded.

To Jabotinsky, the Jewish legions of World War I would become the models for Betar and the Etzel. Betar was Jabotinsky's original youth movement, established in Latvia in 1924. It was to become the nucleus of a mini-legion, a militant, military-trained Zionist political organization. In the 1930s Betar was radicalized by Palestinian militants. They organized within Betar secret military cells which eventually became the Etzel underground.

Betar would eventually become the chief reservoir for the recruits of Etzel, which sprang from a National Haganah splinter group in 1931. But neither Jabotinsky nor Begin, the Betar leader in Poland, could accept Betar's evolution into the radical Etzel-Lehi in 1939. Here Avraham Stern would play a key role.

When Betar first took over Etzel from the original Haganah splinter group in Palestine, it was then headed by Moshe Rozenberg. David Raziel, who followed in 1938, was a loyal Jabotinsky adherent, and despite his militant tone was essentially a firm believer in legal action. Raziel saw Etzel as the military instrument of Betar, not as a policy-making instrument. Jabotinsky would be Etzel's Supreme Commander.

Avraham Stern, an enigmatic, ascetic convert, saw things differently. Never a Revisionist or a Betar member, he challenged Jabotinsky's Palestine Revisionist authority and politics, calling instead for a total war against the British Empire. He called for a war on metropolitan England as well as the Empire itself, which he called "that foreign occupier." This wounded Jabotinsky deeply: his sympathies for the British had not entirely faded, and Stern's rebukes and challenges were a direct attack on Jabotinsky's authority.

Stern first recruited members from Hebrew University intellectuals of the 1930s and formed a splinter group of Etzel, which would be known as Lehi, or, following a series of bank robberies, assassinations and murders, the Stern Gang. His main reservoir of recruits proved to be the Betarim of Poland. In 1937, Stern went to Poland and organized secret cells of Etzel within Betar, thus challenging Betar's rising star and rhetorician, Menachem Begin.[13]

By 1940, a group of moderate Revisionist and United Kibbutz movement activists called for the formation of a united Jewish underground front of all persuasions. Dr. Eliav-Lubotsky and Eliahu Lankin of Betar-Etzel called for Haganah-Etzel-Lehi cooperation and the creation of a new political movement, *Am Lochem* (Fighting Nation). The idea was to establish Jewish cadres, to militarize Zionist Jewry, to pierce through the White Paper and establish an independent Jewish army autonomous from the British and the allies.

Am Lochem was not the last effort to politically unite all military activists in Palestine.[14] The White Paper, so naked in its determination to deny Jewish statehood and its desertion of the Zionist cause, had galvanized all of the various factions. There was no longer a question of resistance and struggle, but only a question of how much and what kind.

The Zionist Response and Debate: Restraint, Cooperation, or Defiance and Resistance?

The twin calamities of 1939—the issuance of the White Paper and the start of World War II—presented the Zionist leadership with a dilemma. They knew at once that relations with Great Britain could no longer be business as usual, but they were also faced with the problem of the agony of the Jews in Europe. Nazi Germany was the common enemy of both Great Britain and the Jews and must be fought together. As the catastrophe of the Holocaust became more and more evident in early 1942, the dilemma faced by the Jews became incrementally more agonizing, so that every action by the British which prevented immigration and settlement seemed to the Jews to be an act that at worst aided and abetted the destruction of the Jews and at best callously ignored it.

All of the various factions of Zionism—Socialist Zionists, Revisionists, the United Kibbutz movement—knew that some form of resistance to the British White Paper with all its implications must be established. The debate that arose focused on means and degrees.

Ben-Gurion and the Socialist Zionists saw the problem in almost Solomonlike terms. They wanted to resist the White Paper primarily on a political level, employing military resistance only as an adjunct. "We cannot fight against England," Ben-Gurion said at one point, "but we must fight England's policy." He put it even more succinctly later, saying that "we shall fight against the White Paper as if there were no war, and we shall fight Hitler as if there were no White Paper."[15]

Basically, Ben-Gurion was telling the Yishuv that the connection and concord with Great Britain and the mandatory still existed, especially in light of the common fight against Nazism, but that British policy, while it would have to be resisted politically and militarily, would also be resisted dispassionately, not out of some burning hatred for England. The Yishuv would use the Haganah only to subvert the British restrictions on immigration and settlements.

Ben-Gurion knew that in the long run Great Britain would not be able to establish its rule at the point of a bayonet, that it was not a monolithic, totalitarian state like the Soviet Union or Nazi Germany, that in the end, faced with Jewish resistance and opposition, and finally with Jewish military strength, it would relent. Thus, the Jews would continue to build up military arms, would subvert the White Paper's immigration policy, and would continue both to fortify the settlements they already had and to open new settlements in new areas, regardless of land restrictions. It would be an open, direct defiance of the White Paper, but without the spilling of Jewish or British blood.

For the forces of Revisionism—or more accurately, the militant and increasingly aberrant Stern group—this was entirely too tame an approach to the British. They wanted all-out war against the British Empire and pursued it with assassination, robberies, and repeated acts of sabotage which taunted and outraged the British forces in Palestine.

The Betar radical approach was often simplistic and the Sternists (Lehi) even sought alliances and assistance from the Fascists.[16] Jabotinsky himself flirted with the idea of approaching Mussolini to discuss a possible alliance against England sometime in 1936–1937. He and his followers wanted an immediate, massive influx of Europe's Jews into Palestine. Jabotinsky's followers, Raziel, Stern, and the activist members of Betar, were in a combative mood and their rhetoric reflected their attitude. As early as 1927, Jabotinsky, mocking Labor, had said that "Zionism must come riding into Palestine on a tank, not a donkey." Now their ideology and rhetoric quoted the bloodier, fiery passages of the Bible, recalling great warrior deeds and battles. They also imitated the nationalistic fervor that was rampant in Poland between the wars. They insisted there would be no peace for the Hebrews as long as the British were in Zion.

The immediate problem for the Socialist Zionists was to regroup the forces of the Haganah into a professionally functioning organization. In this, they no longer enjoyed British cooperation. The British had begun to crack down on the Haganah after the Arab Revolt subsided, and viewed any Jewish armed forces with suspicion and alarm. Fearing that the Haganah could become a future vehicle for resistance to the mandatory, Colonial Secretary Malcolm MacDonald told the mandatory forces in no uncertain terms that they should take "the firmest possible measures to suppress this illegal Jewish organization."

The British showed that they meant business in October 1939 when they arrested a force of forty-two Haganah men, fully uniformed and armed. Among them was Moshe Dayan, who later said he had been threatened with the death penalty and that some members of his unit were beaten severely. They were all sentenced to long terms at Acre prison, a result they all wore like a badge of honor. Weizmann and other Zionist leaders were shocked and outraged. "Men who have done distingushed service with the British forces in Palestine," he wrote in a seething letter of complaint to Lord Halifax, "are now lying in prison in rags, half-starved and treated as criminals."[17]

Nevertheless, by the end of 1940 some 30,000 Jews had volunteered to serve with the Allied forces against Nazi Germany, prompting a further need to strengthen the Haganah. As Yigal Allon noted: "A force protecting the Jewish community in Palestine is necessary. The Jewish community's best men are fighting on a variety of fronts far from home and protection of the Yishuv may not be forthcoming since the mandatory has not relinquished its White Paper policy." The first and most urgent need was for the creation of an armed infantry and a regular force autonomous from Great Britain. As a result, a committee of Haganah leadership, including Allon, created the Palmach, a commando and field force, in May 1941.[18] It would become a permanent and independent Jewish professional elite corps around which a future permanent and independent army could be built. Yitzhak Sadeh was appointed to the general staff for Palmach at Haganah headquarters.

Although it drew its members from the United Kibbutz movement, the Palmach was designed as a professional corps. It became the first full-time professional military cadre of the Haganah, which had relied primarily on part-time volunteers. Its importance to the future of Israel cannot be overemphasized. Of the twelve general staff officers during the War of Independence, three were from the Palmach—Allon, Dayan and Sadeh. Out of some forty colonels of that time, half would come from the ranks of the Palmach. Four former Palmach officers—Dayan, Yitzhak Rabin, Chaim Bar-Lev, and David Elazar—later became IDF Chiefs of Staff, and Rabin went on to become prime minister.

The Palmach was composed of Jews who were either born or grew up in Palestine and its members were followers of the doctrines of pioneer Zionism. Their ideology can be summed up in six major points: (1) pride in the nation; (2) devotion to the principles of socialism and the kibbutz movement; (3) self-discipline; (4) egalitarianism; (5) leadership; and (6) devotion to intellectual pursuits and culture.[19] They were highly motivated and their ideology was largely to become that of the modern Israeli army even though the Palmach membership never exceeded 2,000.

The Early War Years:
A Short Honeymoon of Cooperation[20]

The early years of World War II proved to be disastrous for the British and forced them to soften their attitudes toward the Jews, particularly toward arming Jews. They discovered that the Arabs upon whom they had pegged their White Paper policy were unreliable allies. At the center of their repeated problems with the Arabs was the Grand Mufti of Jerusalem, who was openly flirting with the Nazis and formenting trouble in Iraq. In a letter to Hitler in 1941 he prophesied the defeat of "the Jewish-Anglo coalition" and proposed a German-Arab alliance that would aim for Arab independence, destroy the prospects of a Jewish national home and, in words echoing Himmler, solve the Jewish question. While Rommel was cavorting with his seemingly invincible tanks in the Libyan desert, Iraq, under Prime Minister Rashid al-Kilani, was secretly dealing with Germany and Italy, and thereby provoked a full-scale battle with the British. Although the Arabists in the British foreign office were nervous and advised British withdrawal, Churchill was of a different mind. The British converged on Baghdad in May 1942, driving out Rashid and the Mufti, who fled to Europe and went to work with the Nazi SS in the Balkans.

Later in the war, the British faced similar problems with Syria and its nationalist radicals and with Egypt, where in 1942 a group of army officers (including Anwar al-Sadat) organized an abortive attempt to join up with Rommel's forces. But always, they were reminded just how implacable a foe the Mufti could be. In 1942, he arrived in Berlin and was greeted cordially by Hitler, for whom he promised to recruit an Arab Legion which would fight for the Nazis.

All of this, of course, made the British more amenable toward accepting the Zionists, whom they now perceived as reliable allies. Against the advice of the Palestine mandatory, the British government in 1941–1942 decided to train and help arm the Haganah, knowing full well that it might be honing to a fine edge a force that could later be used against it.

The training was done through the auspices of the Special Operations Executive (SOE), an intelligence unit taking its orders from London, not the mandatory. These particular British intelligence-commando units were totally impervious to British policy in Palestine vis-à-vis the Jews or Arabs and saw only the need to defeat the Germans. Even as local authorities in Palestine persisted in viewing the Haganah as an illegal unit and continued to hunt down its members, SOE personnel began to arm the Jewish force. They trained Haganah members in kibbutzim throughout Palestine, setting up courses in explosives, mines, and artillery, and began to use Haganah units in operations against Italians, Germans, and opposition Arabs. They even gave the Haganah three small ships which could theoretically raid the Lebanese and Italian coasts, and thereby laid the groundwork for the future Israeli navy.

The Jews were not receiving charity. They helped, fought, and carried out intelligence operations eagerly and enthusiastically, and paid a price in blood. Particularly effective in intelligence matters, the Haganah provided scores of maps, documents, postcards, and verbal testimony culled from the still horrified new arrivals in Palestine—those European Jews who had managed to escape. Soldiers of the Palmach also infiltrated Syria, blew up installations, and came back with valuable intelligence.

Although valuable, the experience of cooperation was costly. Dayan lost an eye in one of the Lebanese raids. There was an ill-fated attempt by a British officer commanding twenty-three Jewish sailors to blow up oil refineries in Tripoli in Lebanon. The unit set out in a single boat and never came back. And David Raziel, who had assumed leadership of the Etzel in 1938–1939, lost his life in a British skirmish against Iraq.

Raziel had been asked by the British to mount an operation against Iraqi supply dumps, and after consulting with his deputy, Yaacov Meridor, he agreed to lead the attack, which would include gathering intelligence, destroying Baghdad's oil supplies, and perhaps even capturing the elusive Mufti.[21] Raziel and Meridor flew to Habbaniya, but en route from there to Baghdad a lone German plane strafed their transportation vehicle, killing Raziel and effectively ending the operation.

The Rise and Fall of Stern and the British Retreat from Cooperation[22]

Raziel's death was another blow to the moderate forces of Revisionism. Coupled with the death of Jabotinsky in the United States in 1940, it paved the way for Israel's most militant political terrorist, Avraham Stern. By any stretch of the imagination, Stern was probably the most bizarre and enigmatic figure in the ranks of Zionism. Not until his death did he gain a measure of respectability, and that was of the variety usually attained by dubious martyrs. By 1940, the split between Raziel's Etzel forces and Stern and his Lehi forces was irrevocable and complete. Stern was organizing commandos, building up arms caches, and using his blazing rhetoric and totally committed passion to recruit furiously among incoming Betarim from Poland.

The base of Stern's rhetoric—and it was rhetoric, not ideology—came from his own little book of Maolike sayings, which he composed with one of his operation officers, Hanoch Strelitz. Called *The Principles of Renaissance,* it was a melange of religious mysticism mixed with militant nationalistic orientations. It talked of "The Jewish Nation—the creator of monotheism," and "care for zealot loyalties," and "Israel's eternal aspirations," which included the formation of the Third Temple. It planned a transfer of the Arab Palestinian population and, addressing itself to the British, promised "the conquest of the Jewish fatherland from its foreign occupiers." It envisioned a "Jewish fatherland and the borders of Israel according to the Torah, from the Nile to the Euphrates," all to be achieved by the creation of a Jewish army in the underground, in the diaspora, and everywhere.[23]

Stern's "national liberation army" would sign treaties with all those who would render it direct aid, and thus his group dealt with Polish anti-Semites, Italian Fascists, and even Hitlerian Nazis. He saw Eretz Israel becoming the key military, political and major force in the eastern Mediterranean. The Marxists and Socialist Zionists in the Yishuv were "traitors," especially Weizmann, Ben-Gurion, and Shertok.[24]

Although he was never a follower of Jabotinsky's Revisionist Zionism, Stern also was not really a Zionist ideologue with clear-cut ideas. He was a zealot in the worst sense of the word, a crusader and hollow-eyed poet of blood. He was never *for* any particular brand of Zionism; rather, he was against the British, against imperialism, and against the Arabs. He went to absurd, ridiculous, and horrifying ends in his fight to oust the British from Palestine.

Stern saw not Germany or Italy, but Great Britain as the archenemy, the ultimate hated one. He even sent one of his representatives, Naftali Lubentchik, to Beirut with a plan to send scores of Jews from Italy to Palestine. This, he thought, would appeal to the Germans by helping them with their Jewish "problem" while being able to strike at the British at the same time. Stern probably had no idea what the logical conclusion of Germany's Jewish problem actually was, and in that he retained a fanatic's brand of innocence and blindness. He would have had Jews side with Germans to fight the English.[25]

This was too much for the Haganah, for the Yishuv, and even for Etzel. To many of them, Stern's group was nothing more than a particularly murderous group of gangsters with a burning brand of motivation that justified anything, and many Jewish policemen cooperated with the British in rounding up members of Lehi, or the Stern Gang. In 1942, the *Palestine Post* called for the "whole population to put a stop to such unprecedented crimes," meaning the murder of Jewish policemen by Lehi killers. Shortly thereafter, a reward of 1,000 pounds was put on Stern's head. He became a hunted man, his ascetic face peering from wanted posters. He wandered through the streets of Tel Aviv, sleeping in alleys and alcoves, avoiding kibbutzim. On June 27, 1942, agents of the British Criminal Intelligence Division surrounded Stern in the house of friends in Tel Aviv. What happened then is a matter of some controversy. A British CID senior detective named Colonel Morton recalls that Stern tried to run and was shot. Others say he was discovered hiding in a closet and was shot. No one is sure just how the British were tipped-off to his presence, or even if they were. But it has been established that CID undercover agents discovered letters between Lehi members which led to the discovery of Stern's last hideout. One fact is undeniable. Stern was shot while in police custody, and was thereby transformed from a bizarre outcast into a martyr in some quarters. If Stern had a legacy, it was to give the British a foretaste of things to come. Outcast that he was, Stern was also a symbol of the brewing revolt that Menachem Begin would come to embody.

With Rommel at the gates of Cairo in 1942, British-Jewish cooperation reached its zenith. It was Britain's, and potentially Palestine's, darkest hour, as they faced the prospect of a Middle East dominated by Germany and supported by the Arab population. Therefore they continued to train the Haganah, and Haganah units disguised as Arabs operated underground as resistance fighters in Palestine and Syria. Yigal Allon, commanding a Palmach unit, recalls: "We were disguised as Arabs, boys and girls. We lived as families and we got jobs as shopkeepers, clerks or craftsmen. But we were trained snipers, saboteurs, intelligence operators and wireless operators."[26]

As soon as Montgomery stopped Rommel at El Alamein, the British once again reversed themselves. With the ultimate disaster averted, the need to train the Haganah was gone. Once again the British began to arrest Haganah men found with arms. But the genie was out of the bottle; Palmach and Haganah regulars refused to disarm and in fact engaged in a lively traffic in arms.

The British stepped up the tempo of their drive against the Haganah, in part to appease potential Arab reaction, and went so far as to try four men accused of carrying illegal arms in 1943. The trial, inconsequential in and of itself, was used as a stage by the British to attack the Haganah. Calling them "thieves," the prosecutor linked the Haganah with Stern and Lehi, and failed to distinguish between the groups, a not uncommon British shortcoming. He said that there was in Palestine "the existence of gangsters of the worst sort, terrorists who prevented witnesses from coming forward."[27]

Zionists were outraged by this attack on the Haganah, especially since it took place against the background of the growing holocaust in Europe. Ben-Gurion remarked glumly that: "Helpless Jews were slaughtered under the eyes of the British authorities in Hebron and Safed in 1929 because they had not got a Haganah."

A revolt was brewing among the Jews, but the British failed to gauge its intent, its passions, and its strength. That failure of attitude was typical of the mandatory's actions in dealing with Jewish resistance. Right down to the day when mandatory forces left Palestine in full military regalia, the British in Palestine seemed never to lose their state of confusion and their lack of clear intent about their own policy and about the Yishuv.

The British on the Eve of the Revolt

Millions of Jews were trapped in Hitler's Europe but unable to go to Palestine. Between rescue and annihilation the wall of the White Paper stood high. To the Jews, the British seemed remarkably callous, not necessarily in their brutality, but in their efforts to ignore totally the Jewish catastrophe in Europe. Thus when British authorities would turn back boatloads of Jewish refugees, the Zionist authorities were shocked. This was the case of the *Atlantic* in 1940, a ship which carried some 1,500 Jews from Cyprus. The British transferred the refugees to a boat named the *Patria,* which exploded, killing 200 Jews. Another disaster occurred with the *Struma,* which carried Jews escaping from Rumania in 1941. It never reached Palestine and ended up in Istanbul, its passengers suffering for want of water and food. Eventually, the Turks set the *Struma* adrift. On Feb. 24, 1942, there was an explosion that quickly sank the ship, drowning 767 Jews.[28]

It has not been determined who or what sank the *Struma,* but the Jews on board could have been saved had the British Minister Resident in Egypt, Lord Moyne, not defeated Churchill's call to free illegals (stateless refugees) and detain them. A similar incident occurred with another ship, the *Darien,* which was first interned in the Atlit port by Haifa in Palestine and then sent back to the high seas with its load of refugees. His Majesty's Government's implacable attitude in the last years of the war created an irreparable hostility to Britain in the Yishuv.

The British failed to perceive that the Jews were not simple natives in some colonial outback but a nation of long historical tradition. Yet the British war against the Jews went beyond the limits of a colonial struggle. In a vicious and ruthless manner, the British government, amidst a Jewish war for survival against Hitler, relentlessly pursued the Jewish refugees who had escaped to Palestine illegally. Even after liberating the death camps in Europe, the British continued to discriminate against Jews, so much so that those rescued fled to American-run camps, where General Eisenhower treated them in a much more humane manner. The record of the British campaign against Jewish refugees remains one of the ugliest chapters of World War II.

The British attitude toward immigration and the tragic results of that attitude enraged the forces of Zionism, something the British never quite understood. Neither did they understand the nature of the costly and frustrating war they were fighting. Field Marshal Montgomery, Chief of the Imperial Staff, visiting Palestine in 1947 in the wake of the kidnapping of a British ex-army officer and a British judge, could not fathom what was happening: "I'm absolutely horrified at what is being allowed to go on in Palestine," he wrote General Dempsey, Commander in Chief of the British Middle East Forces, "and have given my views to the Colonial Secretary in no uncertain voice. . . . I'm all in favour of a firm policy but have never seen one yet. . . . We have been led into the present situation by a policy of weakness and of weak will-power and by the futile and ineffective methods . . . and we have only ourselves to blame for what is now going on."[29] Montgomery wanted an all-out war and scoffed at the civil authorities' attempts to negotiate. "It is quite monstrous," he wrote, "to negotiate with illegal organizations or to say that unless they do this, then we do that."[30]

Montgomery was rightly infuriated and at least half right in observing that the British had only themselves to blame. Throughout the revolt they failed to distinguish among the various military forces of Zionism, and thus were never in possession of real intelligence about the forces they opposed, even when the Haganah, for instance, collaborated with them to quell the excesses of Lehi or Etzel. Fighting what amounted to an urban guerrilla war, they nevertheless tended to raid kibbutzim in the countryside.

Even the most successful operation mounted by the British against Jewish resistance—Operation Agatha in June 1946—failed to put a serious dent into the opposition forces, in spite of the extravagant claims made for it. The operation commenced in the wake of the kidnapping of six British officers by Etzel, a flamboyant operation that incensed the British. With 100,000 troops and 10,000 policemen, the British raided the Jewish Agency headquarters in Jerusalem, occupied various other Jewish official buildings, including Histadrut headquarters, and descended on twenty-five Jewish settlements, netting close to 3,000 suspected resistance personnel in the process, including Moshe Shertok and David Ha-Cohen. The British soldiers were not in the least subtle. Facing widespread passive resistance, they looted and shouted Nazi slogans. Prime Minister Clement Attlee, describing the purpose of the operation, wrote that "It is proposed to raid the Jewish Agency and to occupy it for a period necessary to search for incriminating evidence."[31] Indeed, a great volume of paper and documents was taken from the Jewish Agency headquarters, but to little avail, because the British used Jewish policemen to assist in translation. Typically, the policemen were also Haganah men and flushed incriminating material down the lavatory.

British observers claimed the operation was a hugh success, which was nowhere near the truth. Major Haganah leaders like Moshe Sneh, Israel Galilee, and Yitzhak Sadeh slipped through the net; David Ben-Gurion was in Paris; and most of the Haganah's arsenals remained intact. If anything, the operation, known to the Jews as Black Saturday, deepened the spirit of resistance, spread and fanned its flames. Golda Meir, who to her considerable embarrassment was not arrested, describes the reaction this way: "We all felt that something had to be done. Thousands of Jews had been picked up. The Haganah had ordered them to refuse to give fingerprints and many of our men were beaten up when they refused. I told Weizmann the Yishuv would not just pass it over. I suggested a campaign of disobedience. I told him that if we did nothing, the Irgun and Lehi would do something, something far more serious."

As a matter of fact, Irgun (Etzel) and Lehi had been doing far more serious things all along, and would do so again.

Menachem Begin: Etzel Resurrected

Until his election as prime minister, Menachem Begin always operated on the stage of history in the shadow of giants like Jabotinsky and Ben-Gurion. The charisma which makes him the focus of heated debates in today's Israel was not always part of the Begin image. His primary skills lay in organization, in dogged perseverance, and in politics. Begin was the colorless loyalist par excellence, a party organizer, apparatchik, and leader of the Polish Betar. But his persistence and loyalty served him well as a leader. He was considered to be a trustworthy person, a reliable colleague, and a true comrade. He lacked the charisma, eloquence, ideological abilities and penchant for original thought, and European worldliness of Jabotinsky. Begin was and for that matter, in spite of his later blazing rhetoric, still is basically a cautious, highly disciplined, self-conscious person.[32] These qualities made him the savior of Etzel, the man who resurrected the moribund and scattered forces of Revisionist Zionism.

By mid-1942, Etzel, Lehi, and the forces of Revisionist Zionism were in shambles. Jabotinsky had died in the United States, Raziel had been killed in a joint British operation, and Stern's almost suicidal tendencies finally had caught up with him. Revisionist Zionism as a political force was in total disarray.

In April 1942, Begin had arrived in Palestine as a member of the Andres Free Polish Army. Etzel members, led by Arieh Ben-Eliezer, asked Begin to take over their group's leadership, which he accepted while somewhat strangely refusing to defect from the Andres army. For several months, Revisionist Palestinians had to engage in tortuous negotiations with the Polish army to acquire Begin's release.[33]

Finally, in 1943 Begin was released from his Andres army duties and was appointed commander in chief of the shambles that were Etzel. By 1944 he began to emerge from the shadow of Jabotinsky. Slight, bespectacled, the undiluted Eastern European Jewish intellectual and nationalist, as meticulous in dress as in speech, Begin had never fired a pistol while serving in the Andres Polish army, nor would he as head of the underground between 1944 and 1948. He did, however, give the orders which resulted in the bombing of the King David Hotel and the controversial execution of two British sergeants in retaliation for the execution of captured Etzel members.[34]

Long before Castro, Begin was one of the leaders of a modern national liberation force, turning a group of so-called bandits and gangsters into an efficient political and military underground organization. As leader of Etzel, Begin's primary gifts came into play: his gifts as mediator, conciliator, organizer, and leader, as well as his stoic patience. He sought to turn Etzel into a militarily active successor to Revisionism of which he would be leader.

He first set out on a course with two paths. On the one hand, signaling the start of what he termed the Revolt, he called for action and a fierce guerrilla struggle against Great Britain, blowing up the King David Hotel, raiding police stations, hanging the British sergeants. On the other hand, he advocated conciliation with the forces of the Haganah and even Lehi. He was even willing to reconcile with the British mandatory, but only if that would lead to the evacuation of the British from Palestine.[35]

By attacking the British in Palestine, Begin was appealing to the people of Great Britain, playing on their sense of justice, liberalism, and fairness. He hoped that the country as a whole would become thoroughly sick of the continued British presence in Palestine with its ugliness, its cost in lives, and its brutality. His strategy was to embarrass liberal England by advertising its mandatory government rule as brutal and oppressive.[36] His support of an alliance of all three military undergrounds in Palestine—Etzel, Lehi, and Haganah—was bitterly opposed by Ben-Gurion. It came about even after forces led by Ben-Gurion, Sharett, Allon, and the Palmach very nearly tore Zionism apart, cooperating with the British in the arrest of Etzel members and other guerrillas during an operation known as the Sezon.

Sezon: Civil War in the Resistance[37]

For the Zionist forces, the struggle against the British was often like a roller-coaster ride. There were periods of cooperation with the British—the early part of World War II—and periods of calm and unity when the Haganah, Etzel, and Lehi would fight, each in their own way, side by side, especially after the massive Operation Agatha, or Black Saturday, in 1946. But the struggle also came close to inciting a Jewish civil war in the wake of a particularly destructive operation by Lehi forces—the assassination of Lord Moyne in October 1944.

At the time of his assassination by Lehi (Begin's Etzel was opposed to personal terror) Lord Moyne (Walter Edward Guinness 1880–1944) was British Minister Resident in the Middle East, headquartered in Cairo. A former conservative M.P., he had served in several conservative cabinets. In his capacity as minister resident Lord Moyne wielded considerable influence over Palestine policy. He was an anti-Zionist and was opposed to Jewish refugee settlement in Palestine, doubting its capacity to absorb the refugees. Under the veneer of gentility he was a rabid pro-Arabist and vigorously defended the White Paper against Churchill, against whom he prevailed with arguments of Arab hostility, and shortages of housing and food in Palestine. He was an "ideal" target for the Sternists of Lehi.

The immediate effect of the assassination was to chill Winston Churchill's pro-Zionist fervor, since Lord Moyne was a close friend of his. But so strong was the shock and reaction on the part of the British and within the Jewish community, that Yishuv leaders, with Ben-Gurion in the forefront, decided it was time to curb the forces of Etzel and Lehi. Using the Haganah as the operating tool, they launched the Sezon—a term from French: the hunting season. In Palestine it was a period of several months in which the Haganah and the British cooperated in arresting Etzel soldiers and leaders and in general brutally cracking down on the radical (Etzel) and fanatical (Lehi) renegade forces of Revisionist Zionism.

The operation had the firm approval of Zionist moderates, including Weizmann, who wrote in a letter to the Yishuv Executive Committee in Palestine: "I warn you that I shall not be able to continue with my political work if terrorism is not suppressed."[38] Rabbi Stephen Wise in the United States said, "It was better to destroy the assassins and have done with it."

The Haganah gave every semblance of stamping out Etzel but not Lehi, who were too small to attack and who, after the Moyne killing, suspended terror. Even so, 119 suspected terrorists were immediately arrested. Within three months of the assassination Haganah and the Jewish Agency had supplied the British CID with the names of 561 suspects, which resulted in an additional 284 arrests. Haganah and Palmach men also led the British to

Etzel arms caches. This appeared to satisfy Weizmann, who reported to Churchill, "Our cooperation with the authorities in stamping out terrorism is proceeding satisfactorily. . . . The assassination of Lord Moyne has caused abhorrence and violent resentment amongst all sections of the Jewish public, which is helping in tracing suspects, resisting extortions, and morally isolating the terrorist group."[39]

Ironically, although the Sezon was prompted by a Lehi murder, the assassination of Lord Moyne, the Sezon itself concentrated mainly on the forces of Begin's Etzel. Even today the Sezon is an unpleasant affair in Israel, where many see it as a period of shame when Jew fought Jew. Yigal Allon, one of the Palmach men who helped round up terrorists, recalls it as "a painful, difficult and thankless task."

Begin was bitter about the Sezon. In 1944, he railed against Jews fighting Jews, drawing from the Bible for his pained rhetoric: "You are raging mad, Cain. Thousands of your agents throng the streets of Jerusalem and Tel Aviv, the towns and the settlements, brought there to denounce, not to protect; to spy, not to work; for fratricidal war, not for any war of liberation. . . ."

But in terms of action, Begin remained passive throughout. "I will not fight Jews," he insisted.[40] His attitude toward the Sezon helped preserve the beleaguered forces of Etzel and paved the way for his claim to legitimacy as a political leader, not merely as an undisciplined guerrilla. He preserved his fragile little military organization and launched a campaign against the British that satisfied the militants while cooperating with the resistance movement as a whole. In all of this he demonstrated a political shrewdness for which he has not been credited.

The Sezon was a difficult period for the resistance, yet Etzel emerged cleaner and stronger. Neither Haganah nor the CID succeeded in crushing Etzel, and Begin was never arrested. The Sezon added to the making of the myth of Begin.

For the moment, the ultra-radicals, Lehi, had been stopped if not destroyed. For Ben-Gurion it was yet another example of squashing incipient rival forces, a matter of preserving the unity of the Yishuv and keeping its political and military structures under one umbrella, the umbrella of Socialist Zionism, Labor, and Mapai. Time and again, he would quell forces that he perceived to be threatening that unity and his own power. He attacked Etzel again, after the King David affair and the hanging of the British sergeants, and during the war for independence he ordered the Haganah to blow up the *Altalena,* a ship carrying arms for the use of Begin's Etzel forces. These arms would have allowed Etzel in effect to become an army in its own right, which Ben-Gurion would not and could not countenance. Here again, Begin, so often described as rash, radical and irrational, stood aside, displaying his virtue of loyalty to Eretz Israel, his refusal to clash with fellow Jews.

The Revolt and Etzel: King David and the British Sergeants—The Radicalization of Jewish Resistance[41]

When Menachem Begin took over the leadership of the fragmented Etzel organization, he resolved that the fight would be a war against the British in Palestine. He saw the British as the main obstacle to Jewish aspirations, clinging to empire and, if not exactly helping to doom Europe's Jews, at least being cynically complacent about the Holocaust. "One cannot say that those who shaped British policy at that time did not want to save the Jews," he later wrote. "It would be more correct to say that they very eagerly wanted the Jews not to be saved. . . . They were highly interested in achieving the maximum reduction in the number of Jews liable to seek to enter the land of Israel."

Accordingly, Begin officially launched his Revolt on February 1, 1944. It was a declaration of war against the British.

"The time has come to strike against Britain," he wrote. "She herself has written the bloody chapters in the history of Jewish repatriation. Her agents murdered in the towns and in the country. Her judges slandered evilly and went out of their way to dishonour the Jews of the world. . . . There is no longer an armistice between Jewish youth and the British administration in the Land of Israel, which hands our brothers over to Hitler."[42]

Begin's declaration had some teeth, beginning with a series of bomb attacks on police stations, immigration offices, and tax offices in Jerusalem, Haifa, and Tel Aviv.

It is not our purpose here to detail the number and types of operations and raids carried out by Etzel. What is important is that Begin sincerely believed that open warfare against the British would make ripples and waves in England itself, where self-disgust, shock, horror and loathing would eventually force the British to get out of Palestine. It has been fashionable over the last two decades to view some of Etzel's major operations as random and particularly vicious acts of murder and terrorism by Lehi-Stern which, if anything, harmed the cause of Zionism. By Begin's definition, however, another interpretation is just as plausible, and this is especially true of two of the most controversial acts perpetrated by Etzel—the bombing of the King David Hotel and the execution of two captured British sergeants in retaliation for the hanging of captured Etzel soldiers.

The King David Hotel in Jerusalem was a natural target. The headquarters and symbol of the mandatory in Palestine, it was a constant reminder of the British presence. It was here where Begin and Etzel, with the connivance and prodding of the Haganah, focused one of their major efforts. Begin insists that one of the primary purposes of the bombing was to destroy documents that reportedly detailed Haganah-Etzel-Lehi connections. Actually, the documents were in another building used by the British CID. Even so, the rationale was very much like using a machine gun to kill an ant. Whatever the reason, the action was loosely coordinated with the Haganah, who would later try to distance themselves from it, placing the blame entirely on Etzel.[43]

Begin was very much aware of Etzel's plight: its absence of leaders, its shortage of weapons, and Ben-Gurion's adamant opposition to fighting against the British. He made tentative moves to achieve some collaboration with the other underground groups, something not done since the days of cooperating with the British before El Alamein. By 1946, the British government of Clement Attlee's Labor party was recognizably tilting toward total abandonment of the mandatory and the establishment of an Arab Palestine, a position which left even the moderate Zionists at the mercy of the activists, who no longer could defend the British.

Ben-Gurion had written a letter from Paris to Moshe Sneh, commander of the Haganah, after the disastrous Black Saturday operation, in which he indicated he would support a demonstration of revolt, but only if it came under the auspices of some higher authority, including the Jewish Agency. Sneh and his deputy Yitzhak Sadeh, Palmach commander, managed to gain an agreement on the division and coordination of Etzel-Haganah-Lehi activities against Great Britain.[44]

The Jewish Resistance Movement: 1946

A committee of six, called the "X Committee," was formed along political party coalition lines ranging from Labor to Revisionists, but not Begin, to supervise the military activities of *Tnuat Hameri Haivrit*, the Jewish Resistance Movement.

In mid-1946 the X Committee vetoed (by a 3-2 vote) the plan to attack the King David Hotel, succumbing to pressure from Weizmann. Sneh, one of the dissenters on the vote, resigned as Haganah commander and planned to fly to Paris to consult with Ben-Gurion. Before leaving, he instructed Palmach to cancel the operation but neglected to tell Begin, Etzel, or Lehi forces about the political maneuverings, including Weizmann's ultimatum and the "X" decision. He informed them only that the operation should be "postponed." The Sneh strategy was to gain the support of Ben-Gurion, then reassume command of Haganah and unleash Begin.

Thus, he left Galilee, met with Begin on July 17, 1946, and asked Begin and Lehi to postpone the operation for an unspecified period of time. Begin was skeptical but reluctantly agreed to delay, assuming that it was tactical, not political. He originally planned the operation for July 19, but canceled it until three days after Sneh went to Paris. Then, on July 22, 1946, Begin ordered the attack on the King David Hotel.

Near noon, when the hotel was at its busiest, the King David was rocked by a huge explosion, which was soon followed by another. Three warnings had been issued prior to the explosions, but apparently they had been ignored. As a result, over 80 people were killed—25 British, 40 Arabs, and 17 Jews. Begin saw the operation as a success, but the Jewish community, as well as the world at large, was shocked at the carnage. The effect was to make pariahs again of Etzel and rip the resistance movement apart. In a meeting between Etzel and Haganah leaders after the operation, Galilee, Sadeh, Begin and Sneh shouted recriminations at each other, Sneh claiming that Etzel began the operation before the group had agreed on the best time to avoid casualties.

If the unity of the resistance movement began to fall apart in the wake of the King David attack, and if Etzel, with Ben-Gurion leading the attack, was being shunted into the nether world of pariah status, then both of these trends were aggravated severely by the British sergeants affair. It was, with the exception of the Dir

Yassin massacre during the war for independence, probably the most horrifying deed perpetrated by Etzel, but in retrospect it may also have been one of its most dramatic and effective deeds.

Begin's Etzel forces had kidnapped two young British sergeants, conscripts with no particular animosity toward the Jews, in retaliation for the capture of three Etzel men. In effect, the British were being held hostage. Then, on July 29, 1947, the Etzel men were hanged by the British in Acre prison.

The drama that had been played out for months was coming to a grisly climax. Parents of the sergeants had pleaded for their lives. British officials called the "hostage" system heinous. In many ways, this was another misperception on the part of the British. The mandatory viewed Etzel and the underground groups as terrorists fighting an illegal war. Begin saw it as a real war and viewed their fighters as legitimate soldiers. Etzel Chief of Staff Amichal Paglin said that "we had nothing against the two boys personally. We just wanted to stop the hangings."[45]

After the Etzel fighters were hanged, even Zionist supporters pleaded with Etzel to spare the two British soldiers. The plea fell on deaf ears. Immediately upon hearing the news of the hangings, the two sergeants, hooded, were placed on chairs and a noose was put around their necks. Etzel men kicked the chairs away. The bodies were transported to a eucalyptus grove nearby and hung upside down from a tree for the British to find. The area around the bodies was booby-trapped and mined.

The latter touches, in particular, were grisly beyond the comprehension of moderate Yishuv forces, and constituted brutality, not an act of national responsibility. Once again Etzel was assailed from all sides. But Begin justified the action: "We repaid our enemy in kind. We had warned him again and again. He had callously disregarded our warnings. He forced us to answer gallows with gallows."

The British, however outraged they were by the brutality of the hangings, got the message. The hangings of Etzel and Lehi soldiers stopped. "I think that by what we did, we must have saved the lives of several dozens of Underground men. It was a cruel deed to hang the two sergeants, but it was inescapable," Begin wrote in *The Revolt*.[46]

Etzel, often confused with Lehi, of course performed numerous acts of violence against the British, not all of them as grisly or horrifying as the King David bombing or the hanging of the

British sergeants. These included a daring raid on the supposedly impregnable Acre prison to release Lehi and Etzel prisoners. What was most important was that the acts were played out to the world, and it would not be wrong to say that they played as key a role in pushing the hamstrung, weary, frustrated British out of Palestine as did the combined efforts of the Haganah and Palmach, and the political tenacity of Ben-Gurion and Weizmann.

Looking back at the struggle against the mandatory from the standpoint of modern times, there is no denying the importance of both the more moderate forces of Ben-Gurion and the terrorist forces of Etzel and Begin. Begin provided the often horrific spark which would stir and incite the British to the point where they were ready to leave Palestine. Ben-Gurion, often in politically ruthless ways, kept the forces of resistance together, and molded the state-in-being that was to become Israel.

CHAPTER 4

Anglo-American Rivalry and the Final Partition of Palestine

British Policy in Palestine 1944–1947

Self-delusion, false expectations, and bad intelligence guided the Zionist and Yishuv establishment between 1944 and 1947. Mapai was shocked to discover that a Labor government formed in mid-1945 would refuse to get out of Palestine and would firmly adhere to the White Paper policy, not as a tactical move but as a major doctrine.

Partition was dead. In fact, Britain proposed to circumvent American pressure for solving the problem of European displaced persons in a disguised plan for self-autonomy for Jews and Arabs in Palestine. The Americans perceived the plan for self-autonomy as another foreign office machination to help establish an Arab Palestine.

Ben-Gurion retreated then from the Biltmore Resolution back to partition, while vehemently rejecting the autonomy plan. The debacle for Weizmannist Zionism was complete; Britain was going to turn Palestine into an Arab state.

The arena of struggle for the activists became clear: Both Begin's Etzel and UKM's Palmach and even David Ben-Gurion turned toward resistance, now regrettably linked to a bankrupt Zionist diplomacy.

The major figures of the Jewish Agency retreated both from the

Biltmore Resolution and from partition. In 1946 the Jewish Agency led by Nahum Goldman and Rabbi Stephen Wise, the American representative of the Jewish Agency, accepted the Anglo-American Morrison-Grady autonomy proposal.

The Zionist policy was based on two linked demands: (1) Jewish statehood (partition), and (2) a solution for the Hitler refugees immigrating to Palestine.

In its effort to debunk Jewish demands, British policy was arrogantly indifferent to the American competition that emerged at this time, while simultaneously hoping for support from the American president—a hope that utterly failed. President Truman, committed to solving the Jewish refugee problem in Europe but never to Jewish statehood, unwittingly paved the way once again for partition.

British Foreign Minister Bevin, and especially his Palestine advisors led by the Arabist Sir Harold Beeley, completely misread President Truman. To Bevin's advisors the American concern for settling refugees was perceived as interfering with Britain's renewed interest in retaining its power in the Middle East. Lack of clarity and wrong readings of American intentions in the end ousted the British from Palestine and eventually from the whole Middle East.

The British debacle was not so much the result of Zionist policy, Etzel, and Jewish resistance movement operations. It was a consequence of the totally unrealistic self-image of the British Labor government in believing that it could simultaneously advance socialism at home and imperialism abroad and in hoping that America would continue to support this policy. British diplomacy failed to estimate properly the United States' not unfounded suspicions of the British desire to sustain its imperial role in the Middle East, and failed to become aware of America's rising competing interest and power. America's realistic aspirations in the Middle East were clearly to replace Britain—not to give it a helping hand, but to shove it from the area.

The British, the Americans, and the Zionists on the Eve of the British Departure from Palestine

Historians, political analysts, and even the participants themselves have never been able to reach a consensus on what finally propelled the British into leaving Palestine. Some have argued that the Nazi Holocaust, and the moral pall it cast over all of British policy, severely hamstrung English efforts to deal with the Jews in Palestine. Others argue that Zionist diplomacy, sometimes frenetic, always many-sided, and more often than not effective, finally forced the British to leave. Another group holds that the efforts of the more or less legitimate Jewish underground, as exemplified by the Haganah and Palmach, was the final prod. Still others, and former Israeli Prime Minister Menachem Begin is very much among them, insist that the ruthless but effective Etzel military activities proved to be too bitter a pill to swallow. Finally, there are those who suggest that the role of the United States, as it became increasingly involved in the situation in Palestine, was decisive.[1]

There is of course the apologist notion that the British had been prepared to leave all along and were just waiting for the most auspicious moment.[2] Elizabeth Monroe, a chief foreign office Arabist, advances this rather silly argument; it is simplified, and I think inaccurate. More to the point is the Zionist anti-British view that England was prepared to maintain its hold on Palestine and its influence in the Middle East as long as it could. The British, from their own standpoint, were certainly in an agonizing dilemma in the Middle East because they had opted for a policy of cooperation with the Arabs. The fact of the matter is that the orientation of the British Foreign Office, a divided department dominated by Foreign Minister Ernest Bevin, was to establish an Arab Palestine under the guise of a bi-national state, while extending a minority autonomous status to the Jews. This policy had been set in motion by the White Paper and continued right up until the moment that British troops departed Palestine.

Nevertheless, the policy was a failure and, again, one can cite a number of factors which went into that failure—Jewish opposition and terrorism, the Holocaust, the diplomatic pressures of American Zionists, the uncompromising attitude of the Arab League and its political impotence, Etzel-Lehi activities, and misperceptions of American aspirations and goals in the area.

Yet, by 1946 the British were facing pressures that worked against their pro-Arab policy. They were trying to mesh two cardinal interests. One was the maintenance of their imperial goal, which involved a pro-Arab policy and a continuing British presence in the Middle East; the other was a pro-American policy

which during the war sought successfully to involve America in
England's fight against Nazism, and after the war sought to present
a common front against the new foe, the Soviet Union. The two
policies—imperialism in the Middle East and a common fight
against the Soviets—were irreconcilable.

The Americans were very much the Cold War warriors, as
history shows, but they were also hostile to the continued
maintenance of British imperialism, not only in the Middle East
but elsewhere. If anything, they sought indirectly to replace the
British in the Middle East, where economic and strategic concerns
were beginning to make themselves felt.[3]

For England, the cost of maintaining a military presence in
Palestine was proving to be costly, especially for a postwar
economy that was very nearly bankrupt. The military, especially
Field Marshal Bernard Montgomery, at the head of some 100,000
troops, saw only one solution: a full-scale campaign to eliminate
Jewish terrorism no matter what the cost in blood or diplomatic
coin. This the British government refused to sanction, not so
much out of a new-found morality, but because of the political and
economic cost. To keep troops overseas was becoming impossibly
expensive; to strike at the survivors of the Holocaust was morally—thus politically—impossible. Instead, they pursued a somewhat half-hearted policy which failed in all of its aims.

In Palestine, the British were not prepared to propose or
impose a compromise solution on both the Zionists and the Arabs.
They chose to impose a solution on the Zionists and were
expecting some sort of help from the Americans.[4] But by putting
immense pressure on the Zionists in the Yishuv they managed to
deepen an incipient rivalry and conflict with the United States, to
which the Zionists had transferred their political, moral, diplomatic and propaganda efforts, trying to stir the president, Congress and public opinion. The shift of Zionist diplomatic efforts
had come about after 1942, as partition began to become a key
issue.

The November 1947 United Nations resolution that created a
partitioned Palestine was in the end a victory for the pragmatic
Zionists, especially David Ben-Gurion. But Zionist diplomacy
had by no means been steady and single-minded about partition or
how to achieve it. In fact, between 1942 and 1947 Zionist
diplomacy took an up-and-down, zigzag course which was initially

propelled by opposition to the White Paper, and not some firm, clear-sighted policy about partition.[5]

Ben-Gurion's emphatic declaration for the establishment of a Jewish commonwealth at the 1942 Biltmore Hotel conference in New York seemed at the time to circumvent the very idea of partition. It must be remembered that the declaration was made in a political vacuum, when Great Britain was still dangerously beleaguered by the forces of Fascism, was on the run in the Middle East and Africa, and needed the forces of Zionism, who were their only reliable allies, while the Arabs as a rule flocked to the enemy.[6] At the time, there was no real British, let alone American, policy toward Palestine. Thus, the Biltmore conference was a challenge to the hated White Paper policy and not a call for partition.

Yet, if the Biltmore decision to establish a Jewish commonwealth on the surface seemed extravagantly ambitious in its aims, it did not entirely negate the idea of partition, especially after the turn of the tide at Stalingrad and El Alamein. Ben-Gurion, and to some extent Weizmann, was emotionally ready for partition, if only as a means of circumventing the White Paper.

The activists in Mapai, the United Kibbutz movement, and, naturally, Etzel-Lehi, already fighting the British, had never accepted the idea of partition, not in 1936 when the notion first surfaced, and not in the 1940s. But the hope that the new British Labor government under Clement Attlee would reverse the White Paper policy, a not unreasonable expectation considering its leftist orientation, was quickly dashed as British policy veered more than ever to a pro-Arab course. The Zionists began to move toward partition because there seemed nothing else left to do.

By August 5, 1946, the Executive Board of the Jewish Agency (with non-Zionist and American participation) met in Paris and by a decisive majority adopted the concept of partition as the official policy of the Zionist movement (Weizmann was not present). It seemed that the Zionist movement was at something of an impasse, deeply divided among individual proponents of accommodation with Great Britain like Weizmann, Nahum Goldman, among American Zionists like Stephen Wise and Louis Lipski, among the Palestine Zionist establishment, among moderates like Shertok (Sharett), Eliezer Kaplan, and Bel Locker, and among the pragmatists like Ben-Gurion, Sneh, the UKM, and Palmach.[7]

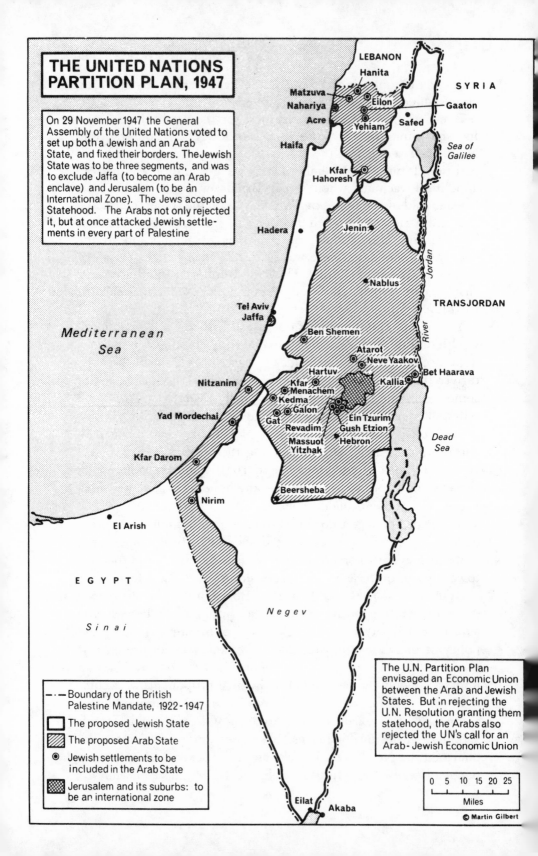

THE UNITED NATIONS PARTITION PLAN, 1947

On 29 November 1947 the General Assembly of the United Nations voted to set up both a Jewish and an Arab State, and fixed their borders. The Jewish State was to be three segments, and was to exclude Jaffa (to become an Arab enclave) and Jerusalem (to be an International Zone). The Jews accepted Statehood. The Arabs not only rejected it, but at once attacked Jewish settlements in every part of Palestine

LEBANON
Hanita
SYRIA
Matzuva
Nahariya
Eilon
Gaaton
Acre
Yehiam
Safed
Haifa
Sea of Galilee
Kfar Hahoresh
Jenin
Hadera
Nablus
TRANSJORDAN
Mediterranean Sea
Tel Aviv
Jaffa
Ben Shemen
Atarot
Neve Yaakov
Hartuv
Kallia
Bet Haarava
Nitzanim
Kfar Menachem
Kedma
Galon
Ein Tzurim
Gat
Revadim
Gush Etzion
Yad Mordechai
Massuot Yitzhak
Hebron
Dead Sea
Kfar Darom
Beersheba
Nirim
El Arish

EGYPT

Sinai

Negev

The U.N. Partition Plan envisaged an Economic Union between the Arab and Jewish States. But in rejecting the U.N. Resolution granting them statehood, the Arabs also rejected the UN's call for an Arab-Jewish Economic Union

- – - Boundary of the British Palestine Mandate, 1922-1947

The proposed Jewish State

The proposed Arab State

⊙ Jewish settlements to be included in the Arab State

Jerusalem and its suburbs: to be an international zone

0 5 10 15 20 25
Miles

Eilat
Akaba

© Martin Gilbert

Partition was now policy, but the question was how to achieve it. Ben-Gurion knew the United States was crucial to all this, that the Zionists had absolutely no chance of obtaining their goals from Britain without American help and pressure. He also knew that Truman was opposed to partition and would not accept the Biltmore program.

Ben-Gurion and the Zionists then decided to combine the Holocaust and independence, the plight of Jewish displaced persons and survivors of the camps with the concept of partition. Even for the Zionists this was something of a departure, for they had come late to the issue of the plight of the victims of the Holocaust. The pursuit of a displaced persons policy had not been one of the Zionists' major goals (no matter how much some historians like to insist it was.)[8] Now, in 1946, the plight of the displaced persons in British camps coincided with pragmatic politics on several levels. On the most immediate front, immigration to Eretz Israel was always a major Zionist concern, and the survivors of European Jewry represented hundreds of thousands of potential Jewish settlers who had nowhere else to go since the gates of most countries, including the United States, were closed to them. The displaced persons therefore also represented a practical way to mix humanitarian concerns with pragmatic politics. This was especially true in finding a way to get the United States involved in the Palestine problem. The British, without meaning to, were eminently cooperative.

Ben-Gurion knew that Truman was opposed to partition and to the creation of a Jewish commonwealth. By no stretch of the imagination could Truman be described as sympathetic to Zionist aims. In fact, as late as 1946 he was heard to say, as pressures for a Palestinian solution increased, "The Jews aren't going to write the history of the United States or *my* history."[9]

Truman was, however, interested in the plight of the displaced persons and he was known to be in sympathy with the idea of releasing 100,000 Jewish refugees freed from the Nazi camps to emigrate to Palestine. The crux of the problem for Zionists was turning Truman's sympathy into political action and leverage.

The British were doing all they could to help these aims, propelled by their own anti-Zionist paranoia. The British, who ran the majority of the displaced persons camps, viewed the human refuse in the camps from a viewpoint diametrically opposed to that of the Zionists. While the latter saw a human reservoir for a

Palestinian-Jewish state, the British saw potential Zionist terrorists and acted accordingly. They tended to mistreat those in the camps, and zealously pursued Jewish immigrant ships in the Mediterranean.[10]

The Americans, on the other hand, were clearly touched by the plight of the displaced persons, whom they viewed solely as victims. American soldiers had been horrified by what they saw when they liberated camps like Belsen in the spring of 1945, so there was already a reservoir of sympathy and empathy in the United States.[11]

Earl G. Harrison, a presidential representative sent in 1946 to Europe to inspect refugee camps, send back a shocking report stating that British troops treated the displaced persons in a manner which was not all that dissimilar to the treatment the Jews received at the hands of the Nazis, except that there was no extermination process. The report stunned the American populace and spurred Truman into action. Harrison's report included an appeal for the immediate admission of 100,000 displaced persons into Palestine and Truman officially adopted this recommendation as a part of U.S. policy.[12]

Pragmatic Zionists like Ben-Gurion realized immediately that this was a wedge to get the United States further involved in Palestine, where it might yet prove to be an insurmountable barrier for British Palestinian policy.

Slowly but steadily, pressure from both the British and the Zionists was mounting on Truman to become involved in Palestine. Britain expected the United States to pay for the defense of the Middle East and for British troops "protecting" the Middle East from the Soviets. This policy was unrealistic, but was pursued with vigor by the foreign office, Bevin, and Lord Halifax, the U.K. ambassador to the United States. Zionists tried everything to get the U.S. involved, including getting displaced persons in British camps to flee to American camps, thus making them an American responsibility. The British, through commission reports and delaying tactics, were also trying to involve the U.S., with some results.[13]

The British tried many ways to thwart partition and maintain their colonial aspirations and Arab ties. Their first attempt was the creation in 1946 of a joint Anglo-American commission, a move designed to halt Jewish political and propaganda efforts in the United States while wedding the U.S. to British policies in

Palestine. Ostensibly the commission was supposed to deal with the displaced person and immigration problem, but for the British its actual purpose was to undo partition, bury the displaced person problem, and deflate Zionist influence in the United States.[14]

This first attempt turned out to be a disaster for the British. Instead of gaining United States military and economic support for their efforts in Palestine and the Middle East to "keep out the Communists," the commission turned sharply toward the Zionists. It recommended the issuance of immediate certification papers for 100,000 displaced persons to emigrate to Palestine, and the replacement of the land regulation portion of the White Paper with a policy of "freedom of sale, lease or use of land, irrespective of race, community or creed."

Bevin correctly saw this as a mortal blow to the British White Paper policy. Nevertheless, he persisted in his attempt to thwart Zionist aspirations, and this time he achieved some results. Still another Anglo-American commission was appointed, and it issued the Morrison-Grady report on July 30, 1946. Though seemingly a compromise, its results were devastating to Zionists. The plan, organized by Bevin's chief of the Middle East Department on Palestine, Sir Harold Beeley, while supposedly meant to implement the recommendations of the previous Anglo-American commission, actually circumvented them.

The Morrison-Grady report recommended the division of the Palestine territory into three provinces: 30 percent British, 40 percent Arab, 30 percent Jewish. The major functions of government—defense and foreign affairs—would remain in the hands of a central authority headed by the British Commissioner. As if this did not obviously work against any sort of Jewish autonomy, let alone partition, the next provision was perceived as a death blow by the Zionists. Rather than implementing the first commission's recommendation that 100,000 displaced persons emigrate to Palestine, the report instead recommended that the immigration be conditioned on joint Jewish and Arab consent.[15] Since the Arabs were hardly likely to consent, this meant an end to immigration. The report also effectively curtailed partition; it meant there would neither be a Jewish entity or an Arab entity, but rather a provincial setup with Arab and Jewish autonomy under British governance.

The report was a defiant retreat from partition and a naked slap in the face of Zionism. This time, all the forces of Zionism were united. From here on Weizmann and Goldman were the only Zionist leaders willing to espouse any sort of cooperation with the British. Zionist forces were electrified and illegal immigration and terrorist activities against the British surged. By antagonizing the Zionist forces in general, the British also showered credibility on the aims and tactics of Etzel-Lehi, who now joined with the more legitimate forces of Haganah and Palmach in an all-out effort against the British. Jewish terror increased, climaxing in the bombing of the King David Hotel. In the United States, Rabbi Abba Hillel Silver summed up feelings when he wrote that "the Jews are not African natives who need time to develop politically."[16]

It was to be expected that the Zionists would totally and vehemently reject the report and its recommendations. What was not expected by the British, who should have known better by now, was that the idea of provincial autonomy would be rejected just as vehemently by the Arabs. The report, while seeking to circumvent the aspiration of Zionists, completely backfired on the British.

Perhaps even more important, the results pried open the Zionists' access to the United States and fueled their efforts to get the Americans involved in Palestine. In Washington, President Truman was, if not insulted, highly irritated by the report's recommendations. Even though he was still no champion of partition, Truman wanted the displaced person problem settled, and on this he remained adamant. After seeing the report and listening to his advisors, he was convinced that the British were stalling and were attempting to embroil him in their Palestinian problem.[17]

While the Zionists stepped up their terrorist activities, they also saw that the main effort must be to obtain American support. It was obvious that Truman was committed to solving the displaced persons problem. It was equally obvious that he was opposed to the Biltmore program which called for a Jewish commonwealth. To accomplish this meant compromise and unity, and so the Zionists adopted partition as the only alternative to the Morrison-Grady report. This was no longer just a policy of the pragmatists like Ben-Gurion, but also of the radicals like Begin, who had once opposed it vehemently. It was the way to get the British out of Palestine.

Now, in another great meeting in Paris, the Zionists pondered just how to gain American support for partition as a means of getting the British out of Palestine. Many of the representatives at the Paris meeting of 1946 decided that what was important was to ignore the more reprehensible parts of the Morrison-Grady report and push for a solution to the displaced person question, thus prying open the door toward partition. Goldman and Weizmann in fact called for rejection of the Morrison-Grady report on moral grounds, not necessarily in terms of a political claim for independence. The voices of moderation and despair were in the air.[18]

Let there be no confusion here. The options on partition seemed to be closed and thus Weizmann and Goldman decided to circumvent Morrison-Grady by rejecting the report, but used it as the Zionists' last claim for eventual independence. The Zionist leaders unfortunately were working in the fog. They could not accept the British pro-Arab policy and tried to use the Americans to bend it. They failed because they were actually operating in a political vacuum, failing—as the British did—to understand what was America's real purpose. Thus they oscillated and zigzagged between partition and other schemes they hoped to harness eventually for their political purpose—independence.

Goldman and Weizmann were both pushing for diplomacy, not resistance. Ben-Gurion, however, still insisted on a complete break with England even as he was being told by people like Goldman that "the King David way must end." Ben-Gurion, fearing British overreaction and worldwide reaction, finally gave in, and pushed for partition instead of activism as a compromise solution.[19]

In the United States, Truman was under a great deal of pressure from his advisors in the White House, David Niles and Clark Clifford, and apparently was leaning toward compromise. Goldman persuaded then-Deputy Secretary of State Dean Acheson that the figure of 100,000 displaced persons would not suffice, that more were needed. He suggested an amendment to the Morrison-Grady report which would make Jewish immigration a Jewish responsibility, grant full administrative autonomy, and provide for a Jewish state which would include those areas recommended by the Peel Commission (1937) and the Negev as well. In addition, Goldman suggested full economic autonomy. These changes were bound to subvert the aims of the original Morrision-Grady report. Acheson agreed to present the case to Truman, who was being buffetted and pressured by his advisors, by the Zionists, and by the British, whom he mistrusted.[20]

Truman finally came to a decision, and it amounted to a Zionist victory. On October 4, 1946, he made his now-famous Yom Kippur speech in which he called for a compromise between the British and Zionist plans. While the word compromise was used, in essence this amounted to a British defeat because the United States was now involved in Palestine with a president who was committed to Zionist compromises.

This perhaps should not have come as a surprise to the British, who were slowly passing from the stage of power in the Middle East to be replaced by the United States, the emerging super-power along with the Soviet Union. Aspects of this trend had been appearing throughout World War II under Roosevelt, who, although he personally admired his ally Winston Churchill, had every intention of seeing the British Empire dismantled piece by piece at the conclusion of the war; Palestine, as his successor saw it, was another part of the old empire.

Relations between the two powers deteriorated with the death of Roosevelt and the defeat of Churchill. The Truman-Attlee relationship was not close and not particularly cordial. Britain's postwar bankruptcy could not sustain its aspirations to remain a great power. And "the efforts throughout 1946 to promote Anglo-American cooperation and collaboration in political and strategic fields ran afoul of difficulties in. . .the seemingly insoluble dilemma of Palestine. The issue of Palestine overshadowed all others in relations between Great Britain and the United States during these months, generating ill feeling and hostility."[21]

Truman's reactions to the various commission reports on Palestine are typical of his cool attitude toward cooperation with Great Britain. It was obvious that Truman did not particularly want to create a common position with Great Britain in the Middle East, nor did he want the United States to accept a large share of the burden in Palestine by stationing troops there or pouring money into the country. Truman was at once concerned with Jewish terror in the Middle East and Jewish voters in New York. Although he dispatched Grady to act as a roving ambassador, he ignored Grady's commission reports or looked at them skeptically. "I was unable," he recalled, "to say that [the recommendations] could cause anything except more unrest."[22]

Thrust into the arena by Zionist pressure, the United States under Truman and thereafter did not intend to become a mere silent spectator as its cultural, strategic, and economic interests grew in the Middle East. The preservation of its existing missionary and educational institutions in the area now converged with its commercial and strategic interests. The United States wanted to replace Great Britain as the major power in the Middle East while keeping her strong enough to play a subordinate role. It would not follow Great Britain in the Palestinian quagmire, but would go its own way, much to the dismay of the British, who felt betrayed.[23]

Although United States involvement in the Palestinian issue all but assured that the Zionist cause would win, it was not by any means pro-Zionist as later events and policies would demonstrate repeatedly. The whole administration—State Department, Defense Department, Joint Chiefs of Staff—except for the president and a few White House advisors, was pro-Arab, anti-Imperialist, and anti-Zionist.[24] Hostility to the British and ulterior political motives spurred United States policy rather than sympathy for Zionism. If anything, the policy was and would remain basically hostile to Zionism. America's policy, in fact, was not nearly as much affected by the Jewish vote as has been assumed. Rather, it was initially spurred by the refugee question, from which long-range design sprang. In later years, as in 1946 and 1947, the United States would try to mollify Arab hostility by means of economic aid, military assistance, and support for their claims in conflicts that did not directly affect Israel or American interests.

The great British failure in the Middle East was that they never came to terms with America on a Palestine policy. The Zionists on the other hand, in spite of the basically anti-Zionist attitude in Washington, were remarkably successful in manipulating American action. The rivalry between the British and the Zionists over Palestine became a fight for, if not the hearts, certainly the minds of the American government. It was a rivalry played against the background of dramatic events, and as such, little publicized. But it was a deep, serious and acrimonious rivalry with far-reaching consequences for both Great Britain and Zionism. For Britain, it accelerated the pace of its disappearance as a major factor in the Middle East and certainly it propelled them out of Palestine much sooner than planned. For Ben-Gurion and the forces of Zionism, winning the duel meant statehood and legitimacy, recognition, and a continued relationship with the United States, for better or worse, over the next several decades.

As stated earlier, history is composed of a multitude of factors. Certainly Jewish resistance, Arab intransigence, the economic state of Great Britain, and the refugee issue all contributed to the resolution of the key issues in Palestine through the establishment of the partitioned state and the departure of the British. But it is not too presumptuous to say that the emergence of the United States as the superpower that replaced Great Britain in the Middle East was a crucial factor in deciding the issue in Palestine.

THE FIRST PARTITIONED STATE

STATE

1948–1967

Preface

The political battle was no longer over the future of the security of the Zionist Yishuv. The 1948–1949 war of liberation achieved that goal. The diplomacy of Zionism, whose major purpose was achieving an international and legal recognition, ended with the United Nations partition. The battle now was over the nature and structure of the state, its orientation, not over legal recognition of the boundaries settled by the war of liberation and the fragile armistice agreements.

The Zionist political parties were ideological in orientation. They now had to make the transition from narrow ideological orientations. That meant to set the constitutional and institutional arrangements and procedures required of a modern state.

In retrospect the parties, both the left and right, were unable, not cognizant, and some even unwilling to accept the historical verdict that henceforth they must become creators and protectors, setting the legal and constitutional rules and procedures of the new state. The political struggle centered in two domains: one, hegemony over the new state—a struggle between Mapai and the left and right oppositions; the second, the need to become secular so as to turn the Yishuv community into the State of Israel.

As in the Yishuv era, the direction, purpose and orientation were once again dictated and determined by Labor. Thus the struggle over the secularization and de-ideologization of the

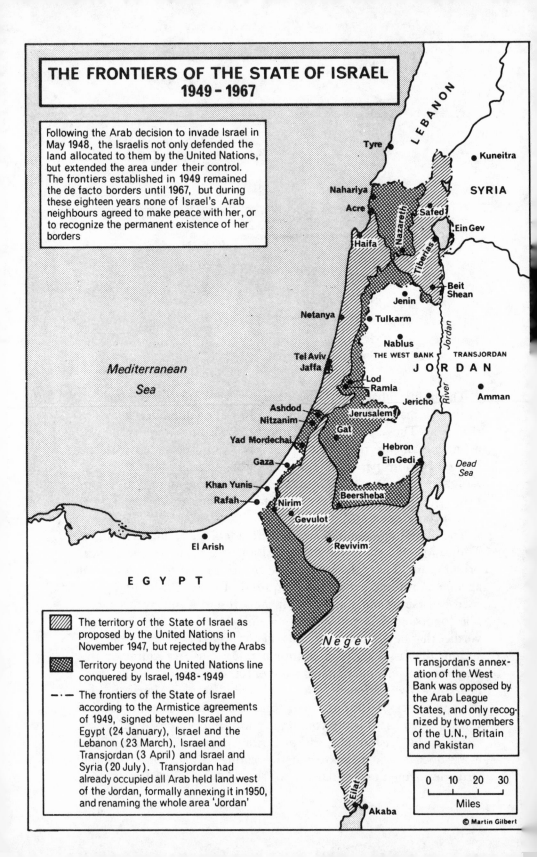

THE FRONTIERS OF THE STATE OF ISRAEL
1949 - 1967

Following the Arab decision to invade Israel in May 1948, the Israelis not only defended the land allocated to them by the United Nations, but extended the area under their control. The frontiers established in 1949 remained the de facto borders until 1967, but during these eighteen years none of Israel's Arab neighbours agreed to make peace with her, or to recognize the permanent existence of her borders

LEBANON

Tyre

• Kuneitra

SYRIA

Nahariya

Acre

Safed

• Ein Gev

Haifa

Nazareth

Tiberias

Beit Shean

Jenin

Netanya

Tulkarm

Nablus

THE WEST BANK

TRANSJORDAN

Tel Aviv
Jaffa

JORDAN

Lod
Ramla

Jericho

River

Amman

Ashdod
Nitzanim

Jerusalem

Gat

Yad Mordechai

Hebron

Gaza

Ein Gedi

Dead
Sea

Khan Yunis

Rafah

Beersheba

Nirim

Gevulot

El Arish

Revivim

E G Y P T

Mediterranean
Sea

Negev

The territory of the State of Israel as proposed by the United Nations in November 1947, but rejected by the Arabs

Territory beyond the United Nations line conquered by Israel, 1948-1949

—·— The frontiers of the State of Israel according to the Armistice agreements of 1949, signed between Israel and Egypt (24 January), Israel and the Lebanon (23 March), Israel and Transjordan (3 April) and Israel and Syria (20 July). Transjordan had already occupied all Arab held land west of the Jordan, formally annexing it in 1950, and renaming the whole area 'Jordan'

Transjordan's annexation of the West Bank was opposed by the Arab League States, and only recognized by two members of the U.N., Britain and Pakistan

0   10   20   30

Miles

Eilat

Akaba

© Martin Gilbert

parties was conducted within the ruling party of Socialist Zionism, Mapai. The majority of the party's leadership considered the function of the party in the newly established state to be the handmaiden and guide for the new state institutions and structures, once again guided by the ideological norms of the past.

The state was to become democratic and socialist. The minority, David Ben-Gurion, the single voice in the senior leadership that sought a revolutionary role for Mapai, was to secularize and dissolve its ideological underpinning. Thus, to undermine in fact the foundations of the Yishuv's Zionist parties and institutions.

A trumpet was sounded in the political desert. Ben-Gurion was calling for a revolutionary departure from Yishuv's partyism. Mapai had changed from a party of class to a party of the nation in 1930; it was now to become the mailed fist of the secularized state. The struggle between Ben-Gurion and Mapai's majority is the theme of the first partitioned state.

The State of Israel is a direct descendant of the Yishuv. The same parties, the same styles of rivalry and ideological battles, as well as the highly personal battles that characterized the Yishuv carried over to the state itself. The Labor movement, which had dominated the Yishuv and turned the Revisionist Zionism movement into a pariah, continued to dominate. Revisionist Zionism had been moribund after the exile and death of Zeev Jabotinsky. The three successors to the movement—the Palestine Revisionist movement, Etzel, and the Lehi underground—never had mainstream support; the only claimant to the Jabotinsky mantle was Menachem Begin, who created the fledgling Herut party which swallowed Revisionism. Especially in the wake of the *Altalena* affair, Ben-Gurion succeeded in making a political mockery of Herut, which captured only a minuscule 10–12 percent of the vote in the 1949 elections.

By that time the Labor party's domination of the state already had become total. The civil service was almost exclusively managed by Mapai-Histadrut-Hityashvut personnel. Although Ben-Gurion called for its depoliticalization, the Israel Defense Forces (IDF) nevertheless did not appoint or advance personnel of Etzel-Lehi-Herut loyalties above the rank of major, a policy that continued well into the 1960s. The first IDF chiefs of staffs were all Haganah-Mapai loyalists such as Yaacov Dori, Moshe Dayan, Mordechai Makleff, and Yigael Yadin. The defense ministry was a virtual Ben-Gurion fiefdom, the foreign office a Sharett barony.

Mapai-Labor-Histadrut controlled all the key ministries from prime minister to foreign, defense, treasury, labor, agriculture, and trade and commerce. The system was for all practical purposes democratic-socialist in style, structure, and political orientation.

Social scientists, particularly S. N. Eisenstadt, who have argued that Israel moved from the "voluntarism" of the Yishuv political procedures and institutions to the rational bureaucratization of the state were wrong. The Yishuv noncoercive style was never far removed from the coercive bureaucratic style; this was a dichotomy that marked both the Yishuv and the state.

The Mapai party, the Histadrut, and the cooperative/collective agricultural system were all bureaucratic in both the Yishuv period and in the State of Israel. Their ethos propagated voluntarism, but their structure mitigated against it. There was confusion between the concept of virtue, the Renaissance citizen-soldier values, and the political voluntarism advocated by the Hehalutz pioneer movement. The political structures of the Yishuv and the Yishuv's political parties were well institutionalized and highly bureaucratic. But they were not prepared to establish the secular arrangements of a modern state. The Yishuv was no state.

In fact, with the exception of the IDF (on the whole), the state buttressed the political domination of Mapai-Histadrut over the society and economy, and further politicized the polity. The domination of the Socialists and the center was complete. All Israeli governments until 1967 followed Ben-Gurion's dictum of a "coalition government without the extremes," meaning without Herut on the right or the Communists on the left.

The Labor movement dominated agriculture, industry, the major health services, and the largest education systems. The state budget favored Labor-Histadrut sectors, industries, and distribution organizations. The nascent defense industry and industrial concerns were Labor-dominated as was Israel's major financial institution, Bank Hapoalim.

Although some scholars have argued that a process of depoliticization and structural institutionalization marked the difference between the Yishuv and the state, the distinction blurred. The state structures, although not in the "voluntaristic" mold of the Yishuv, were Mapai-dominated and highly politicized. And although Ben-Gurion sincerely tried to divorce the military from politics, he nevertheless preferred to appoint nonleftist Palmach veterans and Mapai loyalists to elite military positions. In short,

Ben-Gurion equated nonideological officers with military professionals.

The struggles for power therefore centered within the Mapai-Histadrut as well as against the left, rather than becoming a matter of the left against a weak center-right (General Zionists) and a right (Herut) which remained almost insignificant in its influence on Israeli politics and policies until 1967. The small orthodox religious parties consistently supported Mapai and the center.

The struggles within Mapai were over the relationship between party and state, the direction and orientation of foreign policy, the structure of IDF and national security, and attitudes and policies toward Israel's Arab antagonists. Neither the Zionist left nor the conservative right succeeded much in influencing the course of Israel's foreign policy between 1947 and 1967.

CHAPTER 5

Partyism vs. Statism

The Locus of Authority: David Ben-Gurion and Mamlachtiout

The Zionist institutions of the Yishuv in Palestine were elitist and particularistic, i.e., ideological, structures. The "heroic age" of Zionism and the Yishuv clearly encouraged the operation of personalities more than collective elites. The emergence of the Yishuv brought its central structures and personalities into the Israeli state. But the transformation of the "voluntaristic" and elitist Zionist and Yishuv political movements and parties into the political structure of the State of Israel was not as smooth or as fast as most authors writing on the subject assumed at the time.[1] The new state acquired formal bureaucracies and institutions, including a legislature, cabinet, civil service, and judiciary, but except in the case of the IDF replacement of the Haganah and Etzel, the political, social and bureaucratic structures of the Yishuv and Zionism continued to exist. The Histadrut, the cooperative and kibbutz movements, the political parties (especially Mapai), and the socioeconomic and corporate structures affiliated with the Histadrut Workers Society system all remained intact after the formation of the new state.[2]

The only transformation the creation of the new state effected instantly was the resolution of the demographic problem: after partition, a Jewish majority finally dominated a truncated Palestine. The War of Independence of 1947–1949 modified this. Once the war was over, the major crisis was perceived as transforming the existing particularist political institutions to universalist ones. The presumption was that decision-making on crucial issues, especially in matters of defense and foreign affairs, would now shift from party to state. But it did not. The Israeli political system continued to be characterized by a multiplicity of more or less autonomous parties and factions, with the Labor-dominated Histadrut, Hityashvut, and Kupat Holim (Workers Health Fund) behaving with particular independence. Although the coalition government was led by a plurality party, Mapai (later Labor-Maarach alignment), that party never received more than 40 percent of the vote (and between 1947 and 1977 the percentage, never greater than 37.5, sank as low as 32.5). As a result, rationalization of authority never occurred. Instead, appointment and promotion were not based on merit but on the "party key system," which distributed appointments to all offices among the parties according to their electoral strength (which augmented the power of Mapai-Histadrut parties).[3] Thus an apolitical civil service never emerged in the earlier decades. Mapai "contributed" its talents to the state by dominating the state's fledgling bureaucracies. In fact, some of the bureaucracies of the "voluntary" structures were directly transferred to the state, changing their name and title but not their provincial practices.

The struggle over the establishment of the formal institutions of the State of Israel, centered around the labor movement and its most powerful instruments, the Histadrut and Mapai, was fierce. In fact the first decade of the State of Israel does not demonstrate an evolution (the IDF is the only exception) from voluntaristic to formalized structures nor the transferring of power from the Yishuv-Labor structure to the state. Instead, the drive toward formalization enhanced the political structures of the labor movement at the *expense* of the newly formed state structures. It became more powerful, but it failed to secularize the state. Because the state machinery and the civil service were dominated by a government coalition led by Mapai, they could not hope to gain economic and political autonomy in the face of the established partisan power of the Histadrut, the cooperative/collective movements, and Mapai itself.[4] The relationships among Israel's power structures in the first decade resembled the early days of the

Soviet Union before Stalin, more than Western parliamentary democracies. They were centrist, elitist, intolerant of opposition, and interventionist in socioeconomic structures and the life of the society. (Obviously, of course, there were also substantial departures from the Soviet model and experience—including the existence of competing parties and structures and the pluralistic nature of the labor movement and of Zionism.)

The Mapai and Histadrut were to set the style and structure of Israeli politics in their attempt to infiltrate and dominate every political, social, and economic institution in Israel. This effort included a monumental but ultimately unsuccessful effort by the labor movement—the center left—and Mapai to dominate Zahal, the Israel Defense Forces. Thus to call the Yishuv Zionist political structures "voluntaristic" is a misnomer. They demonstrated every requirement of institutionalization: complexity, cohesiveness, adaptability, and resilience.[5] Although not formal representatives of a state in Israel's first two decades, they were clearly more efficient and powerful than any of the state's institutions. The "voluntary" institutions of the Yishuv and Labor in essence acted in a tutorial role vis-à-vis the state bureaucracies and the military. Seeking autonomy from the mandatory, the Zionist parties had developed a highly institutionalized posture in the Yishuv. The labor movement maintained its hold over the newly established state machinery by using its own autonomous structures to control functions formally assigned to the state bureaucracies, including labor relations, health, education, and even integration of some 600,000 new immigrants. Thus centralization of the state ipso facto meant more power for the labor movement.

David Ben-Gurion opposed these tendencies almost singlehandedly. For Ben-Gurion, the establishment of the State of Israel signaled the end of the diaspora and of the Yishuv's particularist, personal, and elitist collective practices. Ben-Gurion's conceptions were paradoxical. He was an elitist, statist, and anti-populist nationalist. To him, the Labor collective (especially its left-wing Ahdut Haavoda advocates) was reminiscent of the Leninist conception of a *Partiestaat* (party-state), a state system dominated by a single party. He was dedicated to modifying the linkage between party and state.

Above all, Ben-Gurion set himself the task of diminishing the role of the Histadrut-Hityashvut practices and collectivist, nonstatist orientations. A nationalist before he was a socialist,

Ben-Gurion became a statist par excellence. And as a formalist, he believed in the government of laws and procedures, not of personalities and collective action. In fact he hoped to use the party's political power to strengthen the secular institutions of the State of Israel.

Ben-Gurion's orientations and politics provide the crucial explanation of the play and balance of forces in Israel. His cardinal concept of state and society relations in Israel was *mamlachtiout*, a term whose literal translation is as complex as its connotations. In Hebrew, *mamlacha* literally means kingdom; mamlachtiout means kingship. The concept derives from the Jewish kingdoms of the Old Testament, in which the political meaning of kingdom had a universalistic, nonparticularistic overlay. It is possible to translate mamlachtiout as statism (not a very successful translation), but the term is better understood as an operative political concept that connotes a set of intellectual and political aspirations. In fact mamlachtiout is not a traditional personalist authority kingship structure. Instead, in its pure form, mamlachtiout is a legal, rational and secular form of authority. As such, it supersedes the patrimonial, prebureaucratic "voluntaristic" Yishuv Zionist concept of relationship between state and society. Since the most exalted Jewish historical political entities were the kingdoms of David and Solomon, mamlachtiout means the creation of a *political order* in the third Jewish Commonwealth in Eretz Israel. Except for the Marxists, Zionists had not developed a political philosophy and provided only a rudimentary sketch of political theory on the relationship between state and society. A. D. Gordon's religion of labor and Jabotinsky's formalist concept of statehood were relegated to the status of political ritualism once political power was consolidated.

Mamlachtiout was an aspiration, a Ben-Gurion brainchild. It was a serious effort to turn away from the life of the ghetto, from the ideological communalism of the Yishuv's parties. For Ben-Gurion the Jewish State was the greatest creation of Judaism in modern times. The state was to be fitted to a greater task than socialism or other Zionist ideologies. Ben-Gurion wanted to create citizens, not pioneers. The state was to provide new symbols, new holidays, new uniforms (IDF), even a new history derived from archaeological digs rather than Rabbinical-Talmudic Judaism. The new beliefs and rites, the new institutions, procedures and structures of the state would become a kind of new civic religion. The effort was to place the Zionist enterprise in the context of a certain Jewish historical period that was anchored in the kingdoms of David and Solomon.

For Ben-Gurion the new civic religion was to become the central integrative social and political process to mobilize the nation. Here he was bitterly opposed and finally defeated by the socialist Mapai-Histadrut-kibbutz political power.[6]

As we have seen, until partition the Zionists hardly articulated the idea of Jewish statehood other than in vague messianic terms. The partitioned state was not a political philosophical concept; it was a realistic and pragmatic response to events. Similarly, the formation of the state preceded any clear definition of the relationship between state and society. The Zionist ideologues founded their theories long before the state was critical and the tenuous partition became a necessity. Because the pragmatists of the labor movement were engaged in nation-building, state-making, and Arab-fighting, they failed to create any clear political theory, even after the state was formed. Thus powerful political forces in Israel continued to be preoccupied with the concerns of the prestate era, the gathering of Jews into Israel, and the creation of a Jewish commonwealth protected by internationally partitioned and guaranteed borders and defended by its own military forces.

David Ben-Gurion was no exception. Although he had some pretensions to being a political philosopher, he never worked out a clearly stated theory of mamlachtiout. However, his concern for establishing it was expressed in his writing, his speeches, and his actions. Ben-Gurion perceived that despite its protestations, the labor movement, Mapai, and its leaders were mainly preoccupied with dominating the state and society rather than in providing the definition for the boundaries between them. Ben-Gurion sought to prevent the state from becoming the pawn of a parochial labor Zioinism. Aware that political power stems from organization, Ben-Gurion became Israel's top leader by using the political organization—the accumulation of social and economic power—as a vehicle to achieve a political order. He believed that political order (the state, maintenance of security) should subordinate—sometimes even replace—political organizations (party, Histadrut, Health Fund, etc.).

Mapai, the Histadrut, and Mamlachtiout

The labor movement saw itself as the quintessence of pragmatic Zionism, the tutor of society and state in Palestine and Israel. Its leaders never contemplated the surrender of party organization and institutions, either to the Jewish Agency for Palestine during the mandate or to the government of Israel. Mapai upheld the ideology of the first Ahdut Haavoda party (1919–1930). In the words of Berl Katznelson, "Since its creation Ahdut Haavoda carried the flag of political Zionism, mass immigration and independent existence."[7] Ahdut Haavoda identified socialism with Zionism and the creation of a national economy. Although a Socialist Zionist party, it was also conceived as an overarching political organization of the Yishuv. The antecedents for Ben-Gurion's concept of mamlachtiout can be identified as early as 1920, when he said, "The life and problems of the worker and the nation are convergent."[8] By the 1930s he had developed the first pillar of mamlachtiout, the concept of "from class to nation." According to this concept, the labor movement, particularly Mapai, was not a *class* party but a *service* party for nation building.[9] Mapai was thus destined to become the instrument for revolutionary constructivism—to consolidate socioeconomic and political power and to establish not a trade union workers party but a labor hegemony. Political organization was Mapai's paramount aspiration. It had begun during the struggle over the independence of the Ahdut Haavoda party (forerunner of Mapai) that in 1920 had created the Histadrut. The intended function of the Histadrut was to consolidate and politically centralize the work of the pioneers. It was not a simple labor union, but an instrument of labor organized by a party (Ahdut Haavoda) to fulfill the works of Zionism in Palestine. Like Histadrut in 1920, mamlachtiout now was also designed to overcome "partyism," i.e., the ideological and party schisms among the Socialist Zionists that had occurred first between 1904 and 1919. Thus the basic Histadrut-Ahdut Haavoda debate surfaced again in Israel thirty years later, even though the establishment of the Histadrut was supposed to have ended party politics and ideological schisms and instead mobilize and rationalize the forces of labor in the direction of Zionism's supreme goal, Jewish national liberation. Ben-Gurion, who began as the strongest advocate of the formation of Histadrut and asserted its priority over the Ahdut Haavoda party, ended by advocating the primacy of the State of Israel over the Mapai party. The tensions Ben-Gurion created in Mapai and in the labor movement's institutional pillars, the Histadrut and the Hityashvut (settlement) systems, represented another phase in the evolution of his concept. The extreme advocates of Histadrut like Berl Katznelson called for abolition of the Ahdut Haavoda party in 1920.[10] At the time, Ben-Gurion did not go that far. In his view, the Ahdut Haavoda party was necessary to embody the ideology of Socialist Zionism and to represent class democracy while the Histadrut represented the worker's state.[11] According to Ben-Gurion the Ahdut Haavoda could continue to represent workers in the institutions of the Yishuv and Zionism and would be dominant in the Histadrut and give it direction.

Ben-Gurion's antagonists in Israel's first decade continued to hold this view, but Ben-Gurion now called upon Mapai to act as the service elite for the *state,* as Ahdut Haavoda had done in the past for the Histadrut. We must review mamlachtiout in the context of the evolution of Ben-Gurion's concept of Zionism. Even though Ben-Gurion had called for statism over partyism as early as the 1920s, he was still reconciled to the autonomous integrative role played by the Ahdut Haavoda party in the Histadrut. He did not view Ahdut Haavoda as just another social democratic party fighting for political power, but as a party using Histadrut for the accumulation of socioeconomic power. This concept was rather strange to Central European (even British) social democracies, which were mainly electorate parties. The Histadrut concept advocated a democratic-pluralist framework but sought to allow labor to act as the hegemonial party dedicated to organizing and financing immigration and settlement in Palestine. Ben-Gurion's antagonists, who represented the majority in Mapai's elite and rank and file, opposed this view, while Ben-Gurion sought to employ Mapai's hegemonial role for statist purposes. The Commonwealth of Israel is the state, not the Histadrut or the Commonwealth of Labor, argued Ben-Gurion.

In the 1920s Ben-Gurion was willing to grant Ahdut Haavoda, not an electoral party, an autonomous role within the Histadrut to establish contacts with Jewish masses in diaspora, with international labor, with the mandatory, and with opposition Zionist and Yishuv parties and movements. In fact, Histadrut was to become a purely Labor Zionist Yishuv structure while Ahdut Haavoda would function as liaison with the Socialist Zionist parties, movements, and international labor. Histadrut, then, was seen as the instrument of labor; Ahdut Haavoda, as the educator and source of service elite for the Histadrut. It is clear that Ben-Gurion was not advocating the dissolution of Mapai or the end of its role as a service elite party, nor did he challenge its political hegemony. However, he firmly called for the party and its elite to serve the state and for the Histadrut to reject its economic particularism in favor of statism. Opposition to Ben-Gurion came from the Histadrut section of Mapai, or Mapai leaders in the Histadrut. Although Ben-Gurion felt Mapai should remain intact as a political force, an electoral vehicle, and a source of power, he did seek to divest the party and the Histadrut of their historical responsibilities and to eliminate their functions as a state within a state. The Health Fund, which was a source of economic and political power for the Histadrut, was to be nationalized and the Histadrut was to surrender control of education, agricultural settlements, and labor relations to the state on a gradual basis. The Histadrut, argued Ben-Gurion, "was the consolidation of redemption process of the Jewish nation."[12] And the State of Israel had a mission to free Israel from the last vestiges of diaspora (i.e., a Community without a state), even if it meant changing the role of the mighty Histadrut. The fact that Ben-Gurion opted for Histadrut power and Ahdut Haavoda as a service party in the 1920s was tied to his concept of mamlachtiout. In the era of the mandatory it referred to the consolidation of Jewish sovereign power over Palestine, now it was the State of Israel. The party and Histadrut must become subordinate and service the goals of Jewish statehood—sovereign, universal and nonideological.[13]

Ben-Gurion and Tabenkin on Territory and the Concept of the Jewish State

David Ben-Gurion and Yitzhak Tabenkin, the two charismatic leaders of Mapai and Ahdut Haavoda, played a tremendous role in influencing generations of Labor leaders. The differences between the two—their concepts of state and society—are also symbolic of the deeper cleavages of Labor and Socialist Zionism.

For Tabenkin, Eretz Israel must be complete. Israel must be the Jewish Republic of Kibbutzim; it could not rest in a small partitioned territory. Eretz Israel was necessary for the growth of constructivism, which was far from the Jabotinsky-Begin legalistic concept of Jewish political sovereignty and from Ben-Gurion's pragmatic partition ideas. For Tabenkin, Eretz Israel was agricultural-industrial living space for Jewish constructive kibbutzim communism. Partition must therefore be rejected. No finite, legal boundaries could be established unless and until Eretz Israel was completely and fully settled by Jews.

Tabenkin hated and feared the very concept of state, which he saw as an oppressive, anti-revolutionary instrument. He saw that a partitioned state would be small and overly dependent on a large military establishment, instead of reliant on Jewish manpower from the agricultural and industrial sector. A Jewish state, he felt, could only be achieved at the expense of a divided Eretz Israel, but that would deny the most important (to him) goal of Jewish majoritarianism. He would rather have settled a complete Eretz Israel than define unrealistic borders and a state that was not capable of protecting its own populace.

On the other hand, Ben-Gurion saw the state created by partition as an instrument to fulfill the territorial Zionist goal of a Jewish majority within a majoritarian Jewish state. Borders, he thought, were temporary and political. The burden of the 1930s Zionist leadership was to fulfill immigration to Eretz Israel. The borders themselves would be defined by future generations of Jews. Borders were absolutely necessary on a political level, for without secure borders, the Arabs would never recognize an Israeli state. But their exact definition could come only when a Jewish state was established. Ben-Gurion further thought that a partitioned state whose boundaries were not permanently defined would eventually guarantee Jewish strength and Arab respect for the strength, no matter how long the process might take.

The divided and conflicting conceptions of state and territory expressed by Ben-Gurion and Tabenkin are representative of the struggle within Mapai between 1942 and 1944 (which ended with Tabenkin's UKM-Ahdut Haavoda party splitting from Mapai) and the debate over state, society, party, and kibbutz socialism that took place between 1946 and 1950.

The Challenge: Party and State

The history of Socialist Zionist parties in Palestine-Israel is one of fission and fusion, split and unification. As Professor Michael Aronoff has identified it in *Power and Ritual in the Israel Labor*

Party, factionalism is one-issue orientation of a faction in Mapai or Labor.[14] In the history of Israeli labor parties, factionalism was based on both ideology and personality. But democratic centralism also sustained Mapai against its factions. Both the struggle for power under the guise of ideology and the ritualization of power in the name of special interests represented conflicts of ideological and personal differences. Mapai was notoriously intolerant of factionalism. A centralist party, Mapai emphasized the role of party discipline, sometimes at the expense of its ideology.

The first serious split from Mapai occurred when Ahdut Haavoda broke away in 1942,[15] taking a substantial number of supporters of the United Kibbutz movement and most of its youth cadre. In this case the center won at the expense of such Palestine-born labor leaders as Israel Galilee and Yigal Allon. The emergence of Hamishmere Hatzeira (Youth Guard), better known as the *Zeirim* (youth), in the early 1950s gave the party a new crop of young leaders to replace the Ahdut Haavoda rebels. On the whole, these leaders did not come from the kibbutz movement, but rather were young urban activists of Mapai, and its security force-IDF elite. This was the first generation to develop a political career in the state of Israel and they represented its first elite. Mapai totally dominated the senior and middle echelons of the civil service and governmental bureaucracies, and until 1956 the party made sure that senior army officers were either former Mapai members or sympathetic to the party. In fact, between 1949 and 1952, Ben-Gurion himself ousted some thirty former Palmach and Zahal (IDF) senior officers suspected of Ahdut Haavoda affiliations (including Yigal Allon, Yitzhak Rabin, Chaim Bar-Lev, and David Elazar—the last three eventually became IDF Chiefs of Staff), although some eventually returned as apolitical professional officers.

The figure who rose most conspicuously in the Zeirim (Youth) leadership was General Moshe Dayan. He retired as the hero of the 1956 Sinai campaign and moved into politics, establishing a pattern followed by more than one senior officer. Similarly, Shimon Peres, former head of Hanoar Ha'oved, the Mapai working youth movement, eventually became director general of the Ministry of Defense. The other Mapai youth movement, Hatnua Hameuchedet (United Movement) was composed of high school graduates led by Avraham Offer, Asher Yadlin, and Aharon Yadlin. These young Mapai apparatchiks became Israel's leading technocrats; the last two eventually were ministers in Golda Meir's and Yitzhak Rabin's cabinets.

The next members of the Zeirim to follow Dayan by entering politics were Abba Eban, after he served as Israel's ambassador to the United States and the United Nations, and Dr. Giora Yosephtal, Secretary General of Mapai. In the 1950s the Zeirim began making public statements about the lack of party democracy and organized a movement for party regeneration which unsuccessfully challenged Mapai's most powerful institution, the Tel Aviv *Gush* (bloc), dominated by Ben-Gurion antagonists. Although the Zeirim succeeded in imposing a constitutional amendment to party rule, expanding the Mapai central committee dominated by senior leaders, this victory was short-lived. The amendment was defeated and replaced on the floor of the eighth party conference in 1956.[16] "Although there were several important ideological differences which differentiated the older generation of the Gush from the Zeirim, *their struggle became primarily a contest for the control of the party and succession to the top leadership.*"[17] (Emphasis added.)

Having failed to serve the apprenticeship required of Mapai's bureaucrats, the Zeirim lost any chance of ruling the party's most important organizational structures, the nominating and standing committees, and the secretariat. The Socialist Zionist parties, which had had the organizational genius of twentieth-century Marxist parties, became probably the only Menshivik-style parties in modern times, elitist and oligarchical to the top, hierarchical and corporate in structure. From 1925 on, only tenured and dedicated party professionals and apparatchiks were allowed to maneuver for top positions.[18] With the establishment of the state the party apparatus became one of the most highly institutionalized political structures in the country, far surpassing in political influence such executive institutions as the cabinet and major ministries. The party apparatus was responsible for appointment and promotion of *all* the senior civil service in *all* the ministries dominated by Mapai, the leading party in the coalition. (Less important ministries were dominated by Mapai's coalition partners, the apparatchiks of the National Religious party, the Liberals, and later the Mapam party.) Mapai's control extended over the prime minister's office, and over the ministries of defense, foreign affairs, treasury, commerce, labor, transportation, and housing. In other words, it had total domination of national security, foreign relations and socioeconomic bureaucratic structure. In that sense, between 1947 and the early 1960s, Israel was a party-state dominating a pluralistic parliamentary political system.

To combat this structure of control, Ben-Gurion led the revolt of mamlachtiout. He knew he needed allies to succeed. Despite his past roles as secretary general of Mapai and Histadrut, he had no friends within his own party, so he sought the help of the "children" of the state. These were people who were engaged in *bitzuism* (actionism). They were not the old ideologues who established the party, but the pragmatic technocrats of the state: Dayan, Peres, Eban and Yosephtal. Once Ben-Gurion and his allies had succeeded in subordinating IDF and the defense structure to the state[19] and in integrating the school system (1953) and the employment bureaus (1958), they launched their most aggressive attack, stunningly defeating the Health Fund and establishing a national health insurance plan[20] which they later lost to the Histadrut, unwilling to surrender a powerful social and financial instrument like medical care insurance. However, the real test of Ben-Gurion's power of mamlachtiout and of the power of the Zeirim took place in the most sensitive area of national security and defense. The foreign policy Ben-Gurion and his colleagues sought was designed to achieve both a military superiority for Israel and a position of power for the Zeirim, especially for Dayan and Peres, the leading contenders for party leadership between 1957 and 1967. In 1942 the party had split over ideology, personalities, and the issues of struggle against Britain. Now the political struggle over Israel's security, its role in international politics, and its attitudes toward the Arab states and the Palestine problem would actually be waged within the confines of the Mapai party collective elite and the party executive, even if publicly the arena appeared to be the cabinet, the IDF high command, and the ministries of defense and foreign affairs. Ben-Gurion's mamlachtiout would finally be defeated in the monumental battle against the party over the Health Fund, health insurance, labor relations, integration of new immigrants, and the cooperative/collective agricultural pressure groups. This complicated struggle pitted party against state, bitzuistim against apparatchiks, and generation against generation. In addition, it constituted a strategic and foreign policy debate and a struggle for control of Mapai between Ben-Gurion's Zeirim and the ultimate winners, the party "collective," who finally broke Ben-Gurion and ousted the Zeirim.

The battle raged against the background of several significant events between 1953 and 1965: the affairs of 1954 (*haparasha*); the raids that culminated in the Sinai war of 1956; the resignation of Ben-Gurion in 1953; his return in 1955; the decline and departure of Sharett in 1955–1956; and the Lavon affair of 1961–1962. Despite the drama of these events, the nature of the Israeli political system requires that we stop for a moment to clarify the role of Ben-Gurion.

David Ben-Gurion was a founding father of Histadrut and Mapai. During the debate over the formation of the Histadrut, neither he nor his colleagues showed any willingness to dissolve the Ahdut Haavoda party, Mapai's forerunner. Ben-Gurion understood and used the elements of political power very well, which often contradicted his belief in mamlachtiout. Even though he was totally committed to establishing an apolitical government of laws and perfect justice, he knew he could not achieve his political aspirations through utopian and nonpolitical behavior. He knew that without the Ahdut Haavoda party, there would be no Histadrut; without commitment to partition, no Jewish state; and without Mapai, no mamlachtiout. But means can also be used to justify ends. Statism, Ben-Gurion believed, would be achieved only if he and the statist-oriented Zeirim could dominate Mapai. In other words, to eliminate partyism they sought to achieve political supremacy over the party, which was where the raw political power was located at that time.

It was obvious even then that Ben-Gurion, Dayan, and Peres intended to use the instruments of the state, i.e., the Ministry of Defense and the IDF, to fulfill their personal and political ambitions. Ben-Gurion realized that to gain victory for the concept of statism he had to fight the party oligarchy called the "collective" by all possible political means including, if necessary, reciting Socialist Zionist ritualistic incantations. Ben-Gurion had been a minority in his party in his struggle with Weizmann over partition.[21] Even after the death of Katznelson and Golomb, neither the party nor its collective rejected the idea that the party should be supreme in the making of the state. Nor did the center change its nonmilitant and gradualist orientation. The institutionalization of political power therefore took two forms, one in the state and the other in the party, although both were linked. The

Zeirim used its political instruments to support Dayan, Peres, the Ministry of Defense, and Zahal. Thus the struggle between the party and the state was complicated by the conflict of personalities, orientations, and political structures seeking control over the destiny of the newly established state. Each actor used the political weapons at his disposal to contend sometimes with the party, sometimes with the state—and sometimes with both.

The Unsettled Partition: Borders, Security and Legitimacy, 1947–1956

Ben-Gurion

The 1947 United Nations partition plan was accepted by the Jews and vehemently rejected by the Arabs.[22] It resulted in the first Arab-Israeli war, which ended in armistice in 1949 after Britain, France, and the United States intervened.[23] The war nullified the partition boundaries, with some portions of what was intended to become Arab Palestine going to Israel and other portions to the Arab states. Israel expanded its northern, eastern, and southern borders. Transjordan occupied the heart of Arab Palestine on the West Bank and became the Kingdom of Jordan; Egypt occupied the Gaza Strip district. Lebanon and Syria also modified the partition's borders, but the territories of the partitioned states were now dominated by Israel, Jordan, and Egypt. Although the armistice was never transformed into a peace treaty, its terms have continued to govern the disputed borders and boundaries between Israel, Jordan, Syria, Lebanon, and Egypt ever since. (There is one exception—the Egypt-Israel boundaries were renegotiated between 1977 and 1982. But even in this case the status of the Gaza and Arab Palestine remain in doubt.) The precarious nature of the post-1949 modified borders left the partitioned territories in an uneasy state that was neither war nor peace. The neighboring Arab states were united by their desire to abolish partition and its consequence—Jewish statehood in Palestine.

Undefined borders, the precarious state of the armistice, and the Arab rejection of Jewish sovereignty and of Israel's right to exist politically all produced a garrison mentality in both Israel's political-military elite and its citizenry.[24] Ben-Gurion, the first prime minister and defense minister, grasped these objective geographic conditions as well as the lessons of the war of independence, and created a new set of political and strategic doctrines with the aid of his disciples in the Mapai, Moshe Dayan and Shimon Peres, the leading figures of the Zeirim. Eventually other Mapai colleagues joined Ben-Gurion, including the brilliant leader-orator Pinhas Lavon, and Shaul Avigur. Security became the primary concern of Israel's political elite, and all aspects of foreign policy were strongly influenced by this concern. But to understand and explain security and foreign policies in the Ben-Gurion era (1947–1963), we must also analyze them with reference to the domestic scene, including Ben-Gurion's struggle against his opponents in the party's elite and in the labor movement.[25]

Ben-Gurion's conception of the Zahal (IDF) is especially revealing of his concern with security; his desire to forge the IDF as an apolitical, professional army provides a key to understanding his foreign policy. Under Ben-Gurion, this military body was the first prestate structure (it began as the Haganah) to become routinized and professionalized. As such, it was the first instrument of mamlachtiout, the first fulfillment of statism. After 1947, Zahal became Ben-Gurion's foremost preoccupation and he took care to establish a personal domination over it. His total dedication to Zahal's welfare, growth, development and organizational morale meant that it was formed very much in his image. For Ben-Gurion, Zahal was not a simple military force, but the essence of the nation, the carrier of Zionist morality and pragmatism, and the defender and legitimizing force of the state.[26] All the major battles he fought within the Mapai and even against his closest comrades and collaborators were over Zahal's function and structure, although many of these quarrels stemmed from the political and foreign policy implications and complications of his personal control over Zahal. Even the struggle for succession within Mapai was tightly linked to Ben-Gurion's concepts of security and foreign policies, compromising the integrity and role of the Zahal officer corps. The implications of this commitment to Zahal are evident in all of his actions between 1947 and 1963 and many paradoxes and contradictions—personal, intellectual, political, and conceptual—stem from just these orientations. But even though he was a dedicated statist committed to national authority, he institutionalized Zahal in personal terms rather than on the foundation of rational authority. He sometimes vindictively purged high-level professional officers whom he suspected of membership in the opposition left Ahdut Haavoda-Mapam parties, and his appointments after 1952 were clearly political; for example, Moshe Dayan rapidly advanced from colonel to chief of staff in 1953.

Ben-Gurion's national security cadre was composed of active Mapai centralists like Shaul Avigour, Iser Arel, and Ehud Avriel. In the party, he still maintained a close relationship with his partisans—which was, of course, in contradiction to mamlachtiout. No sympathizer or member of Herut, Mapam, or Communist opposition party was permitted to assume an important position and none was allowed to be part of the Zahal high command. Not one senior officer was appointed without the open or tacit approval of the Mapai central committee between 1947 and 1957. And Ben-Gurion had carefully checked the past of any officer before he even proposed the name to the committee. Furthermore, no officer was promoted above lieutenant colonel without the approval of Ben-Gurion, his close associates, and sometimes Mapai's collective. Ben-Gurion even told Yitzhak Rabin, who was one of Israel's most brilliant officers but was suspected of Ahdut Haavoda leanings, that as long as Ben-Gurion was defense minister Rabin would never become chief of staff.[27] In the name of mamlachtiout Ben-Gurion used his domination over Zahal as a political weapon to preserve the influence of the centrist Mapai against the leftist Ahdut Haavoda and Mapam. In addition, he felt that the battle over Zahal was also over the Labor Zionist youth movement. He therefore chose Peres, the leader of Mapai's youth movements, to head the ministry of defense, which was composed of purely Mapai and Haganah centrists.[28] In the name of mamlachtiout he destroyed the Etzel (Begin's underground) ship *Altalena* after it had already surrendered to Zahal, thus politically annihilating his anti-labor foe Begin and abolishing Etzel.[29] Ben-Gurion used all the power at his disposal, including his charisma and his political and institutional power both inside and outside the party, to create an apolitical and professional military loyal to the state and, of course, to Ben-Gurion. He rationalized his stand by insisting that the IDF must be formally dominated by the cabinet, through the defense minister, and thus succeeded in deflecting unacceptable partisan influence in IDF. Yet Ben-Gurion did not find it difficult to practice his own variety of partisanship in the defense ministry, where he replaced all the Ahdut Haavoda bureaucrats with Mapai centrists. (The first three directors general of the ministry, Levi Eshkol, Pinhas Sapir, and Shimon Peres, had similar partisan loyalties.) Ben-Gurion's aggressive drive for IDF independence, however tainted by his own domination of it, was necessary and had a deep impact on governmental authority in Israel. Although he deradicalized Zahal's senior command, he failed to establish the formal structural and procedural arrangements necessary for orderly civil-military relations in Israel's unique political situation. In Israel, dedicated to civilian supremacy over the military, the boundaries between authorities in the area of national security should have been clear and rational. Ben-Gurion's failure to establish such boundaries had severe consequences, ultimately resulting in two of the most traumatic experiences in Israel's history, in 1973 and in Lebanon in 1982.

Ultimately, after achieving legendary and almost mythical stature, Ben-Gurion failed—a politician who stayed at the game too long. Like Weizmann, he found himself in the political desert, ignored by friend and foe, dying unfulfilled. As he said in an interview in 1969:

> This is not a nation, not yet. It is an exiled people still in the desert longing for the flesh of Egypt. It cannot be considered a nation until the Negev and Galilee are settled; until millions of Jews immigrate to Israel; and until moral standards necessary to the ethical practice of politics and the high values of Zionism are sustained. This is neither a mob nor a nation. It is a people still chained to their exilic past. Redeemed but not fulfilled.

David Ben-Gurion and Moshe Sharett

Zionism was a movement of individuals. So was the labor movement. Yet as a party Mapai could also impose party discipline on radical and highly individualistic orientations. The party was generally moderate on defense and foreign policy. Although Moshe Sharett was a Weizmannist, Ben-Gurion's conflict with him was different from the one he had conducted with Weizmann. Much has been written in Hebrew blaming the conflict between Ben-Gurion and Sharett on personality differences, but I believe that their personalities are certainly not a sufficient explanation.

Moshe Sharett (born Shertok), Israel's Foreign Minister, 1947–1954, and Prime Minister in 1953–1954, the successor of Chaim Arlozoroff in 1933 as head of the Jewish Agency's Political Department, lived all his political life under the shadow of the two great men, David Ben-Gurion and Chaim Weizmann. A leader of Mapai since the 1930s, one of Zionism's finest diplomats, Shertok-Sharett, a graduate of the London School of Economics influenced by Harold Lasky, the Labor left ideologue, was a Weizmannist in orientation but was personally dedicated to Ben-Gurion. Throughout his career this sensitive intellectual was torn between his dedication to Weizmannist diplomacy and blind admiration and almost subservience to Ben-Gurion, although he often quarreled with Ben-Gurion with little or no success. Sharett for our purposes represents the political orientation of Mapai's center and its majority in the 1950s. Although his power was derived from the latter, they never actually supported him in his battles against Ben-Gurion. Yet it was Sharett that represented Mapai, Israel and the Zionist center against Ben-Gurion. I chose Sharett not because he was Ben-Gurion's equal, but because after Weizmann he was the most articulate spokesman for the Zionist centrist policy, and even if he was unsuccessful, he effectively articulated an alternative Israeli foreign and security policy.

The literature on the relationship between Ben-Gurion and Sharett is growing. Although Ben-Gurion, whose output was voluminous, wrote very little on this subject, his biographer, Michael Bar Zohar, succeeded in distilling Ben-Gurion's views after he gained sole and privileged access to Ben-Gurion's archives, including many unpublished writings. Dayan, Eban, Meir, and others have also commented on the Ben-Gurion-Sharett relationship. All this has meant that Ben-Gurion's views are the ones that have been transmitted to scholars and the public.

Until recently, Sharett's position has been eclipsed. His disciples in the party and in the foreign office failed to publicize his side of the issue. Thus, until the publication of Sharett's *Personal Diary* in 1978, his viewpoint was treated much less seriously than Ben-Gurion's. Ben-Gurion was portrayed the more powerful of the two, a visionary, crafty, resourceful, childishly charming person. He had all the intellectual virtues—he was portrayed as an omnivorous reader, essayist, scholar of Greek and Biblical literature. The myth of Ben-Gurion as *yachid bedoro* (the one and only in his generation, the unique one)[30] was perpetuated by Bar Zohar, Peres, and other disciples in all media.

Sharett was cast as the anti-hero. Although, like Ben-Gurion, he left a considerable written legacy, including a five-volume (to date) *Political Diary* (one of the best sources on the diplomacy of Zionism before 1945), he had no advocates. In fact, until 1978 he was treated as a political nonperson, even though he was better educated than Ben-Gurion and a far more eloquent writer. Much of this neglect has to do with the man himself. A nervous, pedantic scribe, he was seemingly more concerned with the niceties of Hebrew grammar than with the political content of his writings and speeches. Sharett was relegated to obscurity after his final defeat by Ben-Gurion in November 1955, betrayed by those who exploited his quarrel with Ben-Gurion to enhance their own careers. Sharett worshipped the statesman Ben-Gurion even though he deeply resented his expressions of contempt. Sharett's view of their relationship emerges from the pathetic and apologetic tone of the *Personal Diary* and his correspondence with Ben-Gurion.

The history of the *Personal Diary* as well as its contents is worth some explanation here. Sharett also wrote a political diary of which five volumes have been published so far (1985). He also wrote in *Davar,* the Labor party paper, and his writings go back to the first publications of Labor Zionism in Israel. His speeches and statements, although not yet collected, are multitudinous. Yet no diary written by a Zionist or Israeli in contemporary times equals Sharett's. Nor does any political leader's in this century. The *Personal Diary* was not written for publication. Sharett sent the diary to his son Yaakov and left for him and the family to decide on publication. The family approved the publication and Yaakov Sharett (Koby) worked over five years on the organizing and editing of the diary. Published with the help of *Maariv* in 1978, there are eight volumes totaling over 3,000 pages. These volumes contain Sharett's innermost thoughts. It is a monument to his achievements and failures; there is no better psychohistorical work I know of written by the subject himself. It is well-written, interesting, agonizing, sad, and sometimes pathetic, especially in his pleas to Ben-Gurion. It is a Renaissance document, a martyr's document, a tribute to the post-Freudian era in its agony, its penetrating judgments of persons and events, foreign and domestic.

The *Personal Diary* will revise much of Israel's political history, not only in the crucial 1953–1957 years, but the entire period covered. It certainly will serve as a challenge to the Ben-Gurion mythmakers and resurrect the much-maligned Sharett from political and historical oblivion. Yet I must admit—despite my considerable admiration for Sharett's eloquence, style, perserverance and candor, for his personal, moral and political integrity and courage in bearing the burden of the outcast—I remain convinced that in the end the radical, aggressive Ben-Gurion's vision and strength proved him to be correct in his making momentous decisions. Yet I also think that some of the post-1977 political history of the conflict will vindicate Sharett's perceptions. He was a first-rate political analyst (B.Sc., London School of Economics). He might have done better as a scholar; as a columnist, political analyst, and linguist he deserves recognition. The *Diary* stands as a monument despite his detractors.

• • •

Sharett writes with sad eloquence; although tinged with bitterness, the writing is analytical, perceptive, inquiring. Ben-Gurion's answers are curt, formal, but inherently insulting. He seems to raise questions largely to demonstrate Sharett's misperceptions. Ben-Gurion's correspondence takes the self-righteous tone of a heroic martyr, while Sharett portrays the sacrificial lamb. These love-hate, master-student, hero-antihero dichotomies marked a political partnership that lasted over twenty-five years and ended with total estrangement. If the two were divergent personalities, so were their politics. In fact, this relationship was a symbiosis between vigor and rigor, pathos and rationality, thoughtlessness and thoughtfulness. Like Herzel-Nordau and Weizmann-Jabotinsky, their names were household words in the Yishuv and Israel and they were friends who complemented each other even though their search for Jewish independence took different paths.

The Ben-Gurion–Sharett Conflict

The 1950s, especially 1953–1956, were the formative years of the Jewish state, and much that took place then became the political and behavioral model for later years. The conflict between Ben-Gurion and Sharett most clearly represents the political issues, orientations, motivations, and perceptions of Israel's political leaders at the time. It also represents the struggle for power between activists and moderates within Mapai.

The struggle for power was carried on in several areas:

(a) *The international arena,* including the great world powers and regional issues. Above all, the concern was with the perception of and reaction to United States actions and with the nature of the Israel-United States relationship. Other concerns were the alternative if a United States relationship could not be developed—closer relations with France and Germany—and the frustrating relationships with the United Nations, especially the armistice commissions.

(b) *Relations with Arabs,* perceptions on the Arab question, the role of force and diplomacy, and the reaction to perceived Arab antagonism and rejectionism. Here the role of Zahal and Ben-Gurion's activist policy eventually became the source of deepest conflict with the moderate Sharett, especially in the struggle over Ben-Gurion's concept of the IDF and its role in the strategy of deterrence. The relationship between security and foreign policies, the effectiveness and wisdom of the policy of military retaliation and the policy of committing the United Nations to become a more effective buffer instrument between Israel and the Arab states also came into play.

(c) *The internal party struggle* between Ben-Gurion and the Zeirim and the role of the party in security, Zahal, and foreign policy.

The Ben-Gurion and Sharett views represented the contradictory positions they held over six decades of Yishuv-Israel politics, originating during the early 1920s, before either rose to political power. At that time Ben-Gurion was a relative optimist hoping to settle relations with the Arabs through political compromise. He ended in the early 1950s as a cynic and pessimist who believed a peaceful settlement of conflict with the Arabs was unlikely. He consistently suggested that the solution of the Jewish problem might be at the expense of the Palestinian Arabs. At the same time, however, he wrote to uphold the principle of nonexploitation of Arab workers and fellahin by Jews.[31] His schemes, "solutions," and programs were all connected first, however, with the campaign to establish the Jewish state in Palestine, not with directly solving the Arab problem. During Ben-Gurion's career we find a consistent trend despite his intellectual acrobatics. As Gabriel Sheffer writes:

Ben-Gurion refrained from taking a stance that would be a cate-gorical and irrevocable departure from the position he had taken previously. He changed his views while meticulously diagnosing the condition of the solution to the conflict from the vantage point of his general beliefs. Thus each phase incorporated elements from its predecessor. Next, Ben-Gurion refused to abandon his socialist orientations, which dictated much of his writing on the conflict. But more than any member of his generation he tried to include the *nationalist elements* in the party's platform and in day-to-day politics even when the place of socialist principles in the relationship of Arab and Jews in Palestine became secondary in importance.[32]

Ben-Gurion was a pragmatic socialist and nationalist. He changed his views on solution of the conflict as the Israeli and international environment changed, thus differing from most of his contempo-raries, who were chained by socialist dogma. He believed that he could pierce the Arab wall of antagonism, but he also believed in using violence when all (in his view) peaceful means were ex-hausted. Ben-Gurion thus waited for a "historical opportunity" to help settle the conflict. However, in the interest of gaining that opportunity, he also provoked several actions ultimately culmi-nating in the Kadesh Sinai war of 1956.

Compared with Ben-Gurion, Sharett was much more pessimis-tic, and in fact more realistic. Sharett's traumatic experience of returning from his service with the Ottoman Army in 1916 to find that the Ottomans had exiled the Yishuv influenced his orienta-tion on the Arab question.[33] Sharett realized that negotiation with the Arabs depended on their acceptance of a national Jewish home in Palestine, but acceptance, he soon realized, was a chimera. The Arab riots of 1920–1921, a prelude to the 1936–1939 Arab revolt, only strengthened his pessimism. As a result, he opposed Ben-Gurion's schemes for Arab-Jewish workers' organizations and cooperation. Sharett perceived that the two communities were irreparably separated and he correctly predicted the violent reaction of the Arabs to Zionism, which Ben-Gurion played down. Sharett's practical credo was this: "All the declaration of powers on our behalf will not suppress the power of the Arabs. On the contrary, these (declarations) will encourage the Arabs to prepare for a serious war against us."[34] Sharett subscribed to a defensive concept of redemption and statehood: "Immigration (Aliyah), fortification (Hitbatzrut), and Haganah (defense).

Haganah, fortification and Aliyah."[35] Ben-Gurion, in contrast, optimistically sought to take the offensive to pierce the walls of Arab hatred.

In Profesor Michael Brecher's view, the contradictions between Ben-Gurion and Sharett stemmed from their different perceptions of Jewish history. Ben-Gurion believed in physical stubbornness and flexible militancy, while Sharett's evolutionary persistence always took the international environment into account.[36] In that sense Sharett was a true disciple of Weizmann. Ben-Gurion belonged to the zealot tradition; he persistently pursued a dialectical policy of alternating force and moderation. Sharett was a leader who believed in revolutionary constructivism; that is, he felt immigration and settlement were the foundations of Zionism and Israel. Ben-Gurion felt that Israel had to be protected by force, even if that meant alienating its friends in the international community at times. The confrontation between Sharett and Ben-Gurion was thus inevitable in view of Israel's growing isolation, its neglect by the great powers, and the rising role of Arab nationalism in international and regional politics. In the 1950s Ben-Gurion managed to maintain two orientations that were contradictory by advocating a two-stage policy. He believed that an overall solution of the conflict could be reached; however, because he felt such a solution was not possible in the near future, he advocated reliance on force in the interim.[37] While Sharett recognized Arab intransigence, he was the one who wanted to avoid force.

In 1947, Ben-Gurion wrote: "We will determine the faith of this land. We have laid the foundation for a Jewish state and we will keep it. We have never had a conflict with the Arab nation [he did not include the Palestinians] and if the Arabs seek peace, the hand of the Jewish state is extended to them. Our political plan is now as in the past: security, a Jewish state and an Arab-Jewish alliance."[38] Sharett advocated conflict reduction if conflict resolution was not immediately attainable. Between 1953 and 1956, Israel's most turbulent years, the mounting conflict between Ben-Gurion and Sharett was apparent on numerous issues, including all aspects of international relations and diplomacy. Principally, Ben-Gurion advocated an offensive strategy. In order to solve the conflict, he believed, a resort to violence could be justified, and he preferred a mixture of political and military activism. In contrast, Sharett rejected the concept of an overall solution. His pessimism led him to prefer diplomacy to force, and he felt Israel's moral position was an instrument of foreign policy because it would lead the great powers to defend her. Western and Third World public opinion would preserve Israel's right to exist and would serve as a political and diplomatic counterweight to Arab rejection. Unlike Sharett, Ben-Gurion preferred confrontation with the mountain of Arab hatred even at the expense of Israel's moral stature in the eyes of world public opinion.

During the 1953–1956 period Ben-Gurion grew to believe that each diplomatic mission in search of peace cost Israel territorial concessions to the Arabs. Not only did he refuse to retreat from the 1949 partition boundaries, he even believed that partition was only an interim solution to Israel's final borders. For Sharett, United Nations safeguarding of partition was all-important. For that purpose (and in this he resembled Weizmann's insisting on Britain's responsibility for the Balfour Declaration), he wanted to secure the commitment of the great powers, the international community, and eventually the Third World, to partition. Ben-Gurion felt these borders were still unsettled. Not until the Arab world learned to live with the State of Israel—taught by force if necessary—would they be fixed and secure. Ben-Gurion often closed the doors to diplomatic conciliation, while Sharett attempted to keep them open. The price Ben-Gurion and Israel paid was changing the world's image of Israel. Once thought a weak but "perfectly" just state, it is now viewed as a militant state that lives by the sword. Although Sharett staked his political career on attempting to protect Israel's moral stature, Ben-Gurion prevailed, largely because of Egyptian leader Gamal Abdul Nasser, pan-Arabism, and shifts in United States and British foreign policies.

Ben-Gurion and Sharett and their respective allies differed on matters of foreign policy and national security,[39] Israel's attitude toward the United States, military alliance with the French, the policy of nationalization, of Mapai-Histadrut enterprises, and the role of the IDF. The specific issues upon which they disagreed were related to the complicated negotiations with the United States over arms supply, and the diversion of the Jordan River waters for Israeli irrigation. Sharett was apprehensive about implications of the Eisenhower-Dulles "even-handed" policy, which restricted arms supplies to Israel, the American power to deny weapons and money to Israel, and Israel's isolation. Like

Weizmann, he conducted a policy that hoped to harness both the United States and the United Nations armistice machinery as an alternative to Ben-Gurion's policy of force. Sharett hoped to use Eisenhower's dedication to the United Nations to serve Israel's purpose in establishing firmer relations with the United States. Sharett's policy toward the great world powers was based on his unreasonable hope that Israel could remain neutral in the East-West conflict.[40] (This noble idea turned out to be the destiny of Egypt, instead, as a result of the USSR's drastic change in policy from support for partition to support for the Arabs.)

Sharett adopted his policies because he believed that Israel alone could not resolve the conflict with the Arabs, that it needed a friendly international atmosphere to build up support in favor of its independence. He thus pursued a policy of moderation, ready to make concessions when necessary. (He had even been ready to suggest a postponement of the proclamation of independence in 1948.)[41] Sharrett believed in incremental political solutions if they would strengthen Israeli-United States-United Nations relations and contribute to a reduction of conflict. A highly analytical, logical, and rational man, Sharett opted for diplomacy over violence, for reasonable concessions over the use of force. Whenever he could, Sharett attempted to prevent Israel from adopting the revanchist policies of Ben-Gurion and Moshe Dayan and to guard against their "adventurism" and violence. Sharett was committed to the 1949 partition and he wished to commit the United States and the United Nations to it as well. He felt the deployment of international forces to enforce the 1949 boundaries would legitimize the Jewish state and force the Arabs to come to terms with it. He pinned his hopes on an international commitment, because he believed Israel could never accomplish it alone, even through force. Sharett's "testament" is found in his *Personal Diary,* in the entry of March 29, 1955:

What we have succeeded in achieving in these twilight years [1937–1947] and during the great tumultuous years [World War II] and 1948 [the War of Independence] could not be repeated at our will [a reference to Ben-Gurion's call for the occupation of Gaza in the same cabinet meeting to which this testament refers]. New and revolutionary opportunities still lay on the far horizon. In this era it *has been decreed that we accept our present borders* and that we strive to reduce tensions with our neighbors in order to prepare the ground for peace and to strengthen our relations with the powers. [We must do this] in order to increase our security and also to cultivate a deeper international sympathy, which will also enhance our security. Yet, sometimes, to protect our security we must act in ways which damage our relations with the powers. This diminishes world sympathy for us and increases tensions with our Arab neighbors. In such cases we must reduce [justified and measured retaliation] as much as possible rather than increase it.[42]

For Sharett, international legitimacy superceded the lure of military and political activism.

Was Sharett a Real Alternative?

Since the publication of Sharett's personal diary after the Camp David accords of March 1979, and the release of Israel foreign office documents for the years 1949–1953, some historians and political scientists have been toying with a tantalizing What If: What would have happened if Sharett's orientation, not Ben-Gurion's, had prevailed and become Israeli policy?

Before we answer that question, it is pertinent to note from the outset that while Sharett did indeed have personal inclinations, orientations, and a style different from Ben-Gurion, he actually had no independent or alternative *policy*. He was personally a liberal humanitarian trapped in the web of Israeli power politics. Sharett himself admitted that he could not handle an aggressive policy when necessary. Instead, he preferred to modify policy, to make Ben-Gurion's and Israel's besiegement more palatable. Personally, Sharett was better acquainted with and intellectually more sympathetic toward Arab nationalism than Ben-Gurion. Ben-Gurion was a hardened person without much human empathy for friend or foe, a man who sternly realized the nature and challenge of the force that Arab nationalism presented to the Zionists.

There was a difference of personal tastes and styles, but not of policy. Although he tried unsuccessfully to articulate what seemed an alternative foreign policy, Sharett not only accepted Ben-Gurion's authority, but loyally executed his own functions as foreign minister no matter how much his personal and psychological inclinations might have differed from Ben-Gurion's.

Along with Ben-Gurion, Sharett in 1954 was aware of the extreme fragility of the Jewish state and its armed forces. It was a country that in five years had doubled its population but still had only a ramshackle and exhausted IDF to protect it. The rate of Arab infiltration and harassment of Jewish settlements had grown exponentially between 1949 and 1956, while at the same time the IDF was composed of a few rather poorly organized divisions. The Arab threat loomed large with the rise of Egypt's Free Officers to power and the emergence of a nascent but growing pan-Arab Nasserism in Egypt, Baathism in Syria, and the continued radicalization of national and political forces throughout the Arab world. All these circumstances imposed on the Israeli political leadership actions they might have avoided in other circumstances.

The question remains: Did Sharett really offer alternatives to the Israeli policies that emerged? Certainly Sharett reacted to Ben-Gurion and the IDF's actions. But did he identify different problems, offer a consistently different solution? Did he offer alternatives to Ben-Gurion's basic positions and assumptions? The answer is no. Always he offered positive criticism and searched for reexamination of the political consequences that resulted from Ben-Gurion's policies, but he never went too far. He never, for instance, offered or threatened to resign, or even considered resignation while he served Ben-Gurion between 1948 and 1953. He contemplated resignation only during his tenure as prime minister. Sharett never wrote to Ben-Gurion suggesting alternative policies or direction. Neither did he do so in his intimate diary, which would have been the most appropriate place to express one's innermost doubts and thoughts.

Sharett and Ben-Gurion shared similar opinions, especially when it came to the United States, Europe, and the Soviet Union. Sharett distrusted the great powers as much as Ben-Gurion. His *Personal Diary* is replete with such concerns and conclusions. For example, in Geneva, in 1954, after Sharett had met Dulles, Molotov, and the British and French foreign ministers, he wrote Ben-Gurion a letter that, had it not borne Sharett's signature, could have passed for one of Ben-Gurion's letters to Sharett, so remarkably similar were the opinions and observations expressed.

However, even here there are differences, and they are the crucial differences of style. Sharett was more reflective, private, a man who often looked inward. Ben-Gurion's diaries are impersonal, blunt. They deal with politics, action, personalities in politics, and contain no-nonsense analyses of events, issues and persons. Sharett's diaries mix the substantial and serious with the trivial. For instance, in one paragraph he analyzes Molotov's adamancy while in the next he writes at length about a United Jewish Appeal contributor who is a relative of a former Labor party member who had immigrated to the United States in 1925. Ben-Gurion occasionally can be trivial, too, but his diaries are mostly full of action and reaction.

In the end, Ben-Gurion was a supreme political innovator while Sharett was always a student and disciple, either of Ben-Gurion or of Weizmann. The ideas concerning Histadrut, Mapai, partition, state, the settlement of the Negev, the Arab confederation, the role of the IDF, all originated with Ben-Gurion. Sharett's only real passion was for India and Asian-Israeli relations. He simply was not an innovator or a leader but a fine and intelligent person, one of Israel's best diplomats, a talented writer, one of the most distinguished editors of the Labor daily *Davar* and the Labor publishing house Am Oved, and a supreme linguist who commanded close to ten European and Semitic languages. Where Ben-Gurion was worshipped by his followers and hated by his rivals, Sharett was essentially colorless and did not arouse deep passions.

Sharett would not have had a better chance than Ben-Gurion to achieve peace between the Arabs and Israel during the 1950s. Both he and Ben-Gurion accepted these basic premises:

- A Jewish state in a territory composed of a Jewish majority.
- No extended Jewish state in heavily populated Arab territory in Palestine.
- The divisibility of Eretz Israel.
- Rejection of binationalism and complete Eretz Israel ideologies and orientations.
- The mixture of diplomacy and military action to protect Jewish sovereignty and independence.
- The pro-Western orientation of Israel.
- The primacy of the United States in Israeli foreign relations.
- Israel's efforts to leapfrog and overcome Arab animosity and establish relations with the Third World.
- The need to seek peace only through strength with the Arabs.

The differences between Sharett and Ben-Gurion were over the priorities, level, scope, degree, style and timing of these policies. Sharett the diplomat emphasized negotiation over military retaliatory action, although he never opposed retaliation when diplomacy and negotiation had failed. With his Asian orientation, he emphasized the priority of establishing relations with the Third World. Although Sharett was a great supporter of the IDF, he emphasized the need to achieve the strength to deter Arab aggression through the political and diplomatic accumulation of influence, in addition to military means. In short, Sharett was committed to a different style but not substantively different policies from Ben-Gurion's.

To argue that Sharett presented an alternative to Ben-Gurion misinterprets the two key leaders of Israel in the 1950s. Sharett's orientation and style could not have changed Arab and Egyptian views; his nuances and modifications could not have changed the course of Arab nationalism, Baathism, Nasserism, and radicalism that characterized the tide of Arab nationalism, pan-Arabism and unionism between 1950 and 1967.

Not that there were no alternative policies, ideologies and orientations opposed to Ben-Gurion and Mapai. There were essentially two-and-a-half. One the binationalism of Hashomer-Hatzair, and Brith Shalom, a Hebrew University professors' group which espoused the idea of no independent Jewish state. This binationalism surrendered the concept of Jewish sovereignty, territorial majoritarianism and the divisibility of Eretz Israel. The second was the Jabotinsky-Revisionist, Begin-Herut Complete Eretz Israel concept based on the historical mandate's having included both sides of the Jordan River. This included Jewish sovereignty and domination of all the pre-1922 British Mandate over Palestine and Transjordan. The "half" was the Tabenkin-Ahdut Haavoda-UKM concept of a socialist nation of workers and peasants dominating Complete Israel, i.e., Western Palestine, a republic of kibbutzim and moshavim.

It is significant that Sharett never subscribed to any of these alternatives. He was supremely and unalteringly grounded in the Zionist mainstream represented by Weizmann, Ben-Gurion and Mapai. His personal standards, his ethos, and the essential humility of his character are clearly evident in an entry in his *Political Diary*:

I realize that it is not possible to run the State of Israel in our generation [the 1950's] without lies and adventurism. . .these are unchanged historical facts. I have no control over them. I have control only over myself. I don't believe in self-righteousness. I am even ready to suppose that in the end history will also justify the tactics of lying and the will of adventurism. I thus certainly know only one thing, that I, Moshe Sharett, am not fit for such acts and therefore it is out of the question for me to run the state.[43]

This was written in 1956, at the time he resigned as prime minister and retired from government.

David Ben-Gurion's Zahal Strategy: The Politics of the "Mailed Fist"

Ben-Gurion's perceptions on the legitimization of the partitioned state are best recorded in Sharett's *Personal Diary,* in a passage summarizing Ben-Gurion's position in a critical cabinet meeting on the issue of Gaza and Egypt: Ben-Gurion says, "Only the most daring of the Jews created this state and not the decisions of *UM-Shmumm.*" (*UM* is "United Nations" in Hebrew; *shmumm* is a pejorative word that rhymes with UM. Shmumm also rhymes with *klum* which means "nothing" in Hebrew.) During the debate over the language of the Israeli Declaration of Independence in 1947 Ben-Gurion deleted this phrase of Sharett's: "Israel was born at the behest of the UN."[44] Ben-Gurion continues, again in Sharett's paraphrase: "The UN partition decision was important but the Jewish people would have achieved independence without the UN and partition; American public opinion will not give us security; if Great Britain were to invade the Negev [a reference to Eden's 1955 Whitehall speech calling for a road from Egypt to Jordan through the Negev as a solution to the conflict], we shall fight them, defeat them, and oust them ingloriously from the Middle East. Our power is in our deeds, not in our words. Only in the use of force shall we make ourselves a serious force in the region. We must challenge Nasser's Egypt when the Arabs are divided [Nasser was opposed to Nuri al-Said over the Baghdad Pact] before Egypt reestablishes a security treaty with Britain and the U.S."[45] To repeat, for Ben-Gurion the 1949 revised partition was only an interim solution until the IDF could pierce the wall of Arab hatred. As one of the most-quoted (but possibly apocryphal) of Ben-Gurion's sayings goes: "It is what the Jews will do that counts, not what the Gentiles will say."

Although Ben-Gurion reached the zenith of his power from 1953 to 1957, these troublesome years also sowed the seeds of his decline. Disgusted with the United Nations' impotence, frustrated by America's rejection, immensely suspicious of Britain's aspirations to reestablishing its hegemony in the Middle East, and by Nasser's junta, by 1953 Ben-Gurion had clearly opted for a military solution to the Arab conflict. As a result, he devoted far more time to his role as minister of war than to his duties as prime minister. The IDF, said Ben-Gurion in 1947, would be Israel's "mailed fist." From 1947 to his retirement, Ben-Gurion devoted more time to building and developing the strategic conceptions of Zahal than to any other political or organizational issue. In the 1920s Ben-Gurion helped build the Histadrut; in the 1930s Mapai; and in the 1940s, the concept of statehood. Now Zahal became his major political and organizational occupation. For Ben-Gurion, Zahal was to be the quintessence of Israel, the school for its young leaders, the molder of the new generation. Zahal was to play a key role in Israel's nation-building; it was to legitimize the state; and its distinctive elite would inculcate the values of the state into the next generation of native-born Israelis.[46]

Ben-Gurion's concept of Zahal's role is illustrated by the following:

> One of the reasons I believe in the policy of retaliation is that it will deter the enemy. But there is another reason, educational and moral. Look at these Jews. They come from Iraq, from Kurdistan, from North Africa. They come from countries where shedding Jewish blood was cheap, where others had the legitimate right to torture and beat them. . .they are used to being helpless victims of the Gentiles. Here [in Israel] we must show them that their blood is not cheap; that there is a Jewish State and Army that will not permit [their oppressors] to do with them as they please; that their lives and properties have value; that they must walk erect and with pride. We must demonstrate to them that whoever assaults them will be punished; that they are now citizens of a sovereign state that is responsible for their lives and their security.[47]

Zahal was thus conceived by Ben-Gurion as the major instrument of mamlachtiout. To understand Ben-Gurion's domestic and foreign policies it is imperative to analyze his strategic conceptions of the role of Zahal in security.

Ben-Gurion set himself the goal of nationalizing, formalizing, and depoliticizing Zahal. But to him depoliticization meant deradicalization. Deradicalization, in turn, meant elimination of his (and Mapai's) opponents from the IDF, including Ahdut Haavoda, the radical left Mapam party, and the Hashomer Hatzair movement, the pro-Soviet, left-wing kibbutzim. Civilian control to Ben-Gurion, however, meant elimination of party influence, which in turn implied that no political force or individual would be allowed to interfere with Ben-Gurion's domination of Zahal. The authority relationships Ben-Gurion established caused serious political and constitutional problems between 1953 and 1955.[48] Ben-Gurion was personally involved in supervising the integrity, morale, and professional standards of Zahal's officer corps and he had a hand in the career of every senior officer. In addition, Ben-Gurion centralized decision-making by delegating considerable power to the chief of staff. Nevertheless, he retained control over appointments and dismissals. When chiefs of staff Yigael Yadin and Mordechai Makleff, the second and third IDF commanders (1951–1953), disagreed, they were summarily dismissed.

Ben-Gurion developed a strategic concept which I call the theory of encirclement, similar to the Soviet conception of an imperialist conspiracy.[49] Ben-Gurion saw the challenge as breaking the hangman's noose by developing an offensive strategy of striking the enemy on his own territory.[50] "What we need," said Ben-Gurion in a speech to a settlement hit by Egyptian fedayeen in 1955, "is a hammer. Not only here [the name of the settlement was Patish Hammer]. We need hammers sown all over Israel. Here [southern border with Egypt] we need a mighty hammer, that will destroy the enemy's back. Zahal has a supreme mission to protect the whole state."[51] This doctrine, although successful in 1956 and 1967, damaged Israel's image beyond reckoning, contributed to the estrangement with the United States, and alienated other international supporters, ultimately leading to the fiascos of 1953–1955.

The chosen Zahal senior elite corps were spoiled by Ben-Gurion, who related to them as patrimon. However, this coddling also produced some of the most brilliant victories, military officers, and fighting forces of modern times.[52]

The doctrine of transferring the war to the enemy territory, the policy of retaliation, was remarkably successful between 1953 and 1967, but it had grave political consequences. This "heroic" era produced Israel's most shameful politico-military disasters, forcing a wedge between civilian and military authorities and creating Israel's most severe crisis of political authority. The policy of retaliation led to cover-ups, intrigue, and personality assassination. It also resulted in a battle of the titans between Ben-Gurion's successor, Pinhas Lavon, and his colleagues, Moshe Dayan and Shimon Peres.

CHAPTER 6

The Lavon Affair and Its Consequences

Prologue

Pinhas Lavon, once something of a golden boy in Israeli politics, had been eased out of the defense ministry and had been kicked upstairs in the wake of a major intelligence fiasco that had resulted in the demise of a poorly-organized Israeli spy ring in Egypt in the mid-1950s, just prior to the outbreak of the Sinai war. Although still influential within Mapai party circles, still surrounded by influential political friends, his meteoric star within the Israeli body politic had lost its potential for the kind of illustrious fulfillment that was destined for younger men like Moshe Dayan, Yigal Allon, or Shimon Peres.

In the summer of 1961 he was still seeking exoneration. This time, however, he was doing it loudly and in public. The Lavon affair, hitherto something of a secret cause célèbre whose details had been kept from the Israeli public at large, would now be aired in public, in the newspapers, in the halls of the Histadrut and the Knesset. The outcome would be confusing and inconclusive, and the details would probably remain as muddled as before, but Israel, its government, and its politics would never quite be the same again.

Lavon's relentless drive for vindication would eventually spill over into other, larger areas and would become a prime example of the bitter battle between party and state, as personified by Mapai and David Ben-Gurion, who, in many eyes, *was* the state. There would be a battle for a redefinition of what constituted the state and a battle for control of the state and the party, and which served which. For David Ben-Gurion it was nothing less than a fight for supremacy.

In the process, all of the key figures who defined and shaped the budding state of Israel in the years following the war of independence would emerge again, some to become stronger, others to become diminished. The Lavon affair was more than merely a matter of a botched intelligence operation, or even a matter of affixing responsibility for that operation. The Lavon affair opened a Pandora's box and publicly exposed the political life-and-death issue of the succession for leadership and all the philosophical, political, and ideological machinations involved in that battle.

During the course of that controversy over the Lavon affair and the battle for succession, Moshe Sharett, the short-lived prime minister and foreign minister, that perhaps too-gentle and intro-spective personification of the virtues of diplomacy, would play out his last act, almost regretfully but most assuredly decisively. On and off again the storm raged from 1961 to 1965, and when it was over, Ben-Gurion, Israel's philosophical and pragmatic leader, would be diminished and sent bitterly on the first step toward political decline. But it would take another decade to end Labor's supremacy. The new allies that he had acquired in the early 1950s—the young men of Zeirim like Dayan, Peres, and others—would also be temporarily diminished, although for them, unlike Ben-Gurion, the setbacks would not be permanent.

If the Shatila massacre by the Christian Phalangists in West Beirut and the Israeli special commission of inquiry that followed seems often to be highly reminiscent of America's agony over Viet Nam and the Mai Lai massacre, then the Lavon affair seems to predate America's Watergate. This parallel is not because Israel's leaders were like all the president's men, nor did the IDF massacre the Palestinians; the Phalange did. Rather, the whole affair with its revelations of power struggles, lies and mysteries involved a loss of innocence, a besmirching of Israel's moral political standing, as perceived by the Israeli general public.

The political fracas, actually the denouement of a long-brewing storm, brought into focus the very nature of the state of Israel, of what the Yishuv had become, of the struggle between party and state, of Mapai and Ben-Gurion, and of the struggle between one pragmatic-aggressive approach to the Arab world (as personified by Ben-Gurion) and a gradualist, diplomatic approach (as personified by Sharett). The Lavon affair, in fact, was not so much a giant scandal as it was a fuse for an explosion that rearranged all the particles in the Israeli political firmament, a small, irritating blaze that turned into something of a supernova.

By 1949, the Labor party—principally Mapai—had begun what amounted to nearly total domination of the state. Mapai, Histadrut, and Hityashvut personnel permeated the civil service. As we have seen, while Ben-Gurion struggled to depoliticize the Israel Defense Forces (IDF), it was nevertheless no coincidence that no non-Mapai, Labor movement personnel managed to rise above the rank of major, a stifling policy that continued well into the 1960s, and it might be supposed is still something of a political irritant to Menachem Begin and company. The defense ministry was a Ben-Gurion fiefdom and the fiercely loyal Sharett controlled the foreign office like a barony. The triad of Mapai-Labor-Histadrut controlled all the key ministries from prime minister down to agriculture and trade.

The Labor movement dominated agriculture, industry, the major health services, and the largest education systems. The state budget favored Labor-Histadrut sectors, industries, and distribution organizations. The nascent defense industry and industrial concerns were all Labor-dominated, as was Israel's major bank, Bank Hapoalim.

This is not to say there were no differences or that political struggles were stilled. The struggles were now *within* Mapai and were fought over the relationship between party and state, as well as over the direction and orientation of foreign policy, the structure of the IDF and national security, and the attitude and policies toward Israel's Arab antagonists. Much of the struggle was between the party itself and its key personalities, especially party and state leader David Ben-Gurion.

The Lavon Affair (1953–1954)

A series of military adventures, intelligence mishaps, and political fiascos in the years 1953–1956 were committed clandestinely.

The conspiratorial elite responsible for these misadventures was not publicly identified until 1960, and the Israeli people were unaware of what had happened until that time. The public was shocked to find that its political leaders were not paragons of integrity and unselfishness but quarreling power-seekers. Their exhalted military heroes were revealed to be a group of intriguing colonels, not entirely unlike the officers across the borders in Syria, Egypt, Iraq, and Jordan. The disillusionment extended to no less revered a figure than Chief of Staff Moshe Dayan.

Ha-Parasha, the affair, became a code word for all the Byzantine intrigue and military adventurism that had been concealed from the Israeli people for so long. The Lavon affair, the culmination of a series of military fiascos with major political consequences, also represented a serious challenge to mamlachtiout. It was the shame of a whole nation and no senior Mapai political leader emerged unscathed.

In 1960–1961 the Israeli body politic was also rocked by the battle over Ben-Gurion's successor. Although the obvious successor was Sharett, Ben-Gurion refused to confirm him, and Minister of Finance Levi Eshkol, a leading Mapai figure, refused to acquiesce. Ben-Gurion was left with a choice he knew was dangerous—Pinhas Lavon as defense minister. In the 1950s, the party-state conflict over succession in Israel was a most brutal political event. It rocked the party from its elite to its cadres and Mapai never recovered. There were no formal rules for succession in Mapai; it was simply accepted that one of the two or three most prominent party leaders would be the successor. The struggle, however, started long before Ben-Gurion's retirement; it began with the intelligence fiasco. The new defense minister, Pinhas Lavon, and Prime Minister Moshe Sharett were unable to impose their will on the ambitious Moshe Dayan, a man who, Sharett said, "would serve both God and Satan."[1] Sharett had no support from his party collective and colleagues and he was ignored by Ben-Gurion, who watched the system he had left to collapse from his desert Sdeh Boker observation point. Ben-Gurion was convinced that Sharett's incumbency would be temporary, and he was right. Sharett failed to manage the government. He could not tame Lavon or fire him until Ben-Gurion agreed to return as defense minister in February 1955. He was also unable to discipline Chief of Staff Moshe Dayan or to challenge Shimon Peres, Director

General of the Defense Ministry, whom Sharett suspected of intriguing against him.

Ben-Gurion, who never bestowed his mantle on Sharett, nevertheless did his best to formalize the system, but his dedication to his party prevented him from depoliticizing the ministry of defense or Zahal. Mapai partisanship in the government, in the ministry of foreign affairs, and Zahal then undermined Sharett's efforts to establish his own authority. Clearly Eshkol, Meir, and Sapir, his supposed allies, preferred to watch from the wings rather than help their party leader rationalize the system. Sharett was no more their candidate for succession than Lavon. Thus the intelligence fiascos and later political misdeeds that encompass the Lavon affair took place in an environment of undefined and nonformalized authorities, roles and structures, politics and personalities. Because the boundaries of party, state, and army were permeable, the resulting turbulence finally grew too severe to contain and broke into public view in 1960. Before we discuss the intelligence fiasco of 1953–1954 and the affair of 1960–1961, we must explain the relationship between Mapai and Zahal, because that relationship is a crucial element in the events of the early 1950s.

Ben-Gurion and the Israeli Defense Forces: Civil-Military Relations and the Role of Partisanship

The IDF was a true successor to the Haganah, and in fact the IDF high command actually evolved from the Haganah high command.[2] The Haganah was the product of the labor movement and during the Yishuv years it was a labor's political-military instrument. Opposition to Haganah domination by Mapai came from both the right and left. The right tried to "nationalize" the Haganah, that is, to establish a party system for their participation. One branch of the left, the United Kibbutz Movement (UKM) or Ahdut Haavoda, called for total labor domination over the Haganah and for militant activism. The Marxist-left Hashomer Hatzair movement and Mapam party also called for labor domination of the Haganah, but they sought to direct it toward rapprochement with the Arabs. The struggle for control was technically resolved in 1936 when the Haganah was subordinated to the Jewish Agency for Palestine, but the strife continued and eventually intensified. The 1948 war catapulted the Palmach, the

Haganah's elite force, into prominence because the Palmach command played such a major role in the Southern Command and the war against Egypt. A creation of young kibbutz activists, the Palmach was oriented toward Ahdut Haavoda. The most distinguished Palmach commanders of 1948–1949, Yigal Allon, Yitzhak Sadeh, Yitzhak Rabin, Shimon Avidan, and Israel Galilee were members of the United Kibbutz Movement, which had split from Mapai in 1942 and became the Ahdut Haavoda party in 1944. Ben-Gurion set himself the task of destroying Palmach independence by abolishing its Southern Command in 1949 and by purging Palmach officers between 1949 and 1950.[3]

The toughest battle between Ben-Gurion and UKM-Palmach, however, concerned the organization of Zahal and the creation of the defense ministry. It was conducted on two planes, one professional-military, the other political. The leaders of the two camps, Ben-Gurion, Tabenkin, and Israel Galilee, argued for professionalizing and depoliticizing the IDF; only the rhetoric differed. Ben-Gurion called "for the army and all of its parts to be subordinated to the people's authority and only to the people's authority."[4] Galilee sought "a people's army imbued with the élan of Palmach."[5] It was obvious that the struggle over professionalizing the military bore directly on other issues—the authority of the ministry of defense, the relationship of the chief of staff to the high command, and their relationship to the government and the people.

A five-member government committee recommended that authority be divided. This plan removed Zahal from the direct control of the ministry of defense. It also created two directors general, one for the administration of defense economy and the other in charge of the IDF (such an office, the *Rama,* had existed in the Haganah). Israel Galilee of the UKM was clearly intended for this role, which meant that Ben-Gurion would no longer be the IDF chief. Although this action took place in the midst of the war of independence, Ben-Gurion resigned in protest from all his offices.[6] He then returned to the defense post, purging all prominent Palmach generals and colonels and eliminating Galilee's office. He began to organize Zahal with the twofold purpose of strengthening his political hold over it and making it more professional now that Ahdut Haavoda activists were eliminated. To ensure Zahal's aggressiveness, he appointed militant Mapai-oriented officers to the high command. To enhance the

IDF's professionalism, on the other hand, he appointed former graduates of the Jewish Brigade and the British Army from World War II. He believed these men, because they had received British training, were more professional than the Palmach "partisan warriors." The war of independence proved him wrong, however. Most of the British-trained officers did not distinguish themselves, while the Palmach officers who originated the innovative Israeli military doctrines did so. (Five of the IDF chiefs of staff between 1947 and 1980 came from the Palmach.)

To assure Ben-Gurion's personal domination, to balance professionalism with aggressive leadership, to free Zahal from the United Kibbutz movement-Palmach-Ahdut Haavoda politics, there was no better candidate for chief of staff than General Moshe Dayan. Dayan was born in Degania, the son of a Mapai cooperative leader, Shmuel Dayan. Not a product of the Palmach (although one of its first volunteers), he was fierce and charismatic, an adventurer and a born leader of men. He had, in short, the qualities Ben-Gurion was looking for, a combination of pragmatism and imagination, independence and loyalty. Dayan had been a junior Mapai politico and he had some experience in diplomacy (Ben-Gurion had sent him to negotiate with King Abdullah of Jordan and other Jordanian officers in 1950). As such, he was Ben-Gurion's ideal choice for the chief of staff who would prepare Zahal for the second round of war and challenge the 1949 partition. Ben-Gurion's decision was clearly partisan and personal. He wanted to ensure IDF professionalism and daring, but above all he wanted the loyalty of Zahal senior officers. In December 1953, having failed to persuade Sharett, his foreign minister, and the majority of the cabinet to pursue an aggressive policy, Ben-Gurion decided to retire.

After extensive research, I have concluded that Ben-Gurion had no intention of retiring permanently. He had a habit of resigning or threatening to do so (in the battle with Weizmann in 1944, for example, and in the controversy over the reorganization of Zahal with Galilee in 1949–1950). The threat of his resignation was designed to frighten his party colleagues because they believed that his retirement would weaken the party's power. As a result, the elite would pay his price—the elimination of his opponents or acceptance of his dictates on crucial issues—to entice him to return. Nevertheless, Ben-Gurion never successfully used his resignation threat to achieve his aims except in his battle against Israel Galilee, when Mapai united behind its leader against the left. On other occasions, Ben-Gurion's colleagues united to defeat him, as when he failed to topple Weizmann in 1944. In 1953–1954 Ben-Gurion's hope was that his retirement would signal the party to eliminate Sharett. However, as the party's number two leader, Sharett had a considerable following among the party elite and apparat. He also was the unofficial leader of its moderates, who in fact were the majority in the party. The more hawkish leaders, like Golda Meir and Levi Eshkol, joined with the dovish Pinhas Sapir and Zalman Arran in support-ing Sharett for prime minister because they suspected, not without reason, that Ben-Gurion was preparing for a comeback. Although the Mapai collective leadership refused to allow the departing Ben-Gurion his wish to block Sharett's appointment, it did accept three appointments he had recommended just before his retire-ment. (The fact that he made these appointments signified that his resignation was not intended to be permanent.) Pinhas Lavon became defense minister; Moshe Dayan was appointed IDF chief of staff; and Shimon Peres became director general of the defense ministry. As a result, Sharett would now be surrounded by three Ben-Gurion disciples, all of them activists and hawks. Thus when Ben-Gurion left office at the most critical juncture in Israel's history he also left a legacy. And the battle over succession stemmed directly from the politics of security, expanding its impact to encompass the defense ministry, its senior officials Lavon and Peres, and Zahal's new chief of staff, Dayan, as well as IDF senior officers in the intelligence and special operations divisions.

The Spectre of Nasserism and the Role of the United States in the Middle East, 1952–1954: The Israeli Perception

The roots of the explosion of 1960–1961 can be traced to the fiascos of the 1953–1954 period, but the context is all-important. The events of 1960–1961 cannot be understood apart from the struggle for succession in Mapai, the blurring of authorities and roles within the cabinet and between the ministries of defense and foreign affairs, and the role overlap of the leaders of the IDF. Yet the public saw the crisis as a series of concrete and serious events. Like any other country, Israel has a foreign policy anchored in its political culture—in its decision-makers' perceptions of the motivations, intentions, and goals of Israel's chief ideological and political rivals.

The 1947 partition, even after it had been altered by war, did not give Israel peace, legitimacy, or acceptance by the Arabs. Frontiers were insecure and the armistice was clearly unsatisfactory. The resolution of both problems was dependent on two external groups—the great powers, mainly the United States and Britain, and the Arabs. The United States and Egypt played the most significant roles. Despite President Truman's support for partition and recognition of Israel, the more pessimistic Israeli decision-makers felt that the American foreign policy and national security bureaucracy as a whole opposed the idea of an independent Israel.[7] Optimists hoped that United Nations intervention would coerce the United States into adopting a more favorable attitude toward Israel, and eventually move the Arabs to modify their stance toward Israel, but Ben-Gurion was less sanguine.

American policy in the early 1950s and the rise of Nasserism after 1952 provided the raw data to support the Ben-Gurion view. When President Eisenhower and Secretary of State John Foster Dulles adopted an "even-handed" policy toward the Middle East, Israelis saw it as proof of an anti-Israeli coalition between the great powers and the Arabs. The British evacuation from Egypt in 1954 was perceived as only opening the way for the Americans to replace the British and America's refusal to provide Israel with new weapons seemed to corroborate the belief that Dulles favored the Arabs. These perceptions were on the whole reasonably accurate.[8] Further evidence that the noose was tightening around Israel's neck included American military aid to the Baghdad Pact countries and United States failure to guarantee Israeli shipping and navigation in the Suez after Britain withdrew. (The Baghdad Pact, established by Britain in 1954 with American support, involved Iran, Iraq, Turkey, and Pakistan as a northern tier shield against the USSR.) The sharp rise in border infiltration from Gaza and the inability of the United Nations armistice structure to restrain these incidents were further clues that all was not well. When Eisenhower shifted to oppose the USSR, Assistant Secretary of State Henry Byroade's speech on an "even-handed" American policy haunted all Israeli decision-makers, hawks and doves, throughout the decade of the 1950s. American Middle East policy was couched in national, imperial, and moral terms, and its consequences were perceived by the Israelis as detrimental to their national interest. This convergence of events—the creation of the Baghdad Pact,[9] the British evacuation of Suez, and the Eden-Dulles rivalry over who would assume imperialist leadership in the area (Eden favored the Hashemites; Dulles the Egyptians)—only bolstered Israeli suspicions.[10]

The frustrations and fears were clearly related to the growing imbalance of military force between Israel and the Arabs that resulted after Iraq received American weapons denied to Israel. The early 1950s thus saw the emergence of a garrison mentality, a state of mind that continues to grip Israel to some extent in the 1980s. The decision-makers, especially those responsible for security and military affairs, identified the source of trouble as Nasser's Egypt. When asked why Israel must establish a hammer—a mailed fist—in the south rather than the north, Ben-Gurion answered by retelling an old fable. When a snake lies next to your legs, he said, and a fly is over your head, you hit the snake first.[11] The literature on Nasser and Nasserism in English, Arabic and Hebrew is already considerable, although no final assessment can yet be made.[12] I wholeheartedly concur with Professor P. J. Vatikiotis's view that Nasser's perception of the challenge of Israel was anchored in his perception of pan-Arabism and anti-imperialism. "It is futile to try to establish whether or not Nasser believed in a political doctrine of Arab nationalism," Vatikiotis writes, "[It] is his vision of its instrumentality and how close Egypt, under his rule, came to using it [the "Arab Circle" of Nasser's *Philosophy of the Revolution*] successfully for her own ends."[13] According to Vatikiotis, "A combination of circumstances and coincidence of events pushed Nasser toward Arabism and the adoption of Arab nationalism and unity both as means and as end simultaneously."[14] Events like the Evacuation Agreement with Britain in 1954, the 1955 Bandung Neutralist Conference, and the Soviet arms deal of 1955 encouraged Nasser to seek the role he did. His rejection of the West, imperialism, and the anti-Soviet Baghdad Pact were his major motivations in choosing the pan-Arabist course, although no Israeli decision-maker, including Sharett, accepted this. But Israel's overreaction to Nasser increased the lure of Arab nationalism in Egypt. Ben-Gurion's Gaza raids policy of 1954–1955 did not push Nasser into the Arab belligerent camp, as some authors claim. He was already there. It only cemented his resolve to head an Arab coalition against Israel. "Nasser's attitude toward Israel," writes Vatikiotis, "evolved with his Arab policy, or his struggle for Arab leadership, and his adoption of an anti-Western policy at home and in the Middle East region as a whole."[15]

Egypt was always perceived by the Israelis as the Arabs' most significant and powerful state. It was the intellectual, educational, and literary center of the Arab and Islamic world. The Israeli perception of Nasserism was exaggerated, however, at least partly because Israel and Egypt had little contact after 1947 except for limited Armistice Commission meetings. In the minds of the Israelis, the revolution in Egypt evolved from "Egyptianhood" in 1952 to "metaphysical Nasserism" in 1955, and they insisted on treating Nasserism according to metaphysical explanations. Israeli intelligence analysts, Arabists, and scholars spent hours on Nasserite literature, with the result that the study of Nasserism became a kind of demonology and Nasserite Egyptianhood was even compared to the Nazi concept of *Deutschtum* (Germanhood). The other side replied in kind. Israel was identified with imperialism and branded *al-Isti'mar,* the imperialist devil, in the Nasserite literature and press.[16] As Vatikiotis put it in 1978, "To combat imperialism inevitably entailed fighting Israel, until fighting Israel replaced the struggle against imperialism. . . ."[17] This attitude was well understood by Ben-Gurion, Dayan and the Israeli intelligence community in 1953–1955. They felt they were victims of Anglo-American anti-Communism. The Israeli-Egyptian perceptions of each other's actions and reactions led to a self-fulfilling prophecy of war.

Israelis feared appeasement, and it is for this reason that Ben-Gurion and his followers condemned Sharett and his allies. Sharett, in turn, considered his Israeli adversaries dangerous adventurers, especially Pinhas Lavon. "Lavon," he wrote, "shows satanical influence both in his character and his intellect. He concocted atrocious operations and was ready for the most adventurous acts."[18]

Ha-Essek Ha-Bish, *The Intelligence Fiasco— The Rise and Fall of Lavon*

Ben-Gurion clearly set himself the task of challenging Nasserism and Egypt. He sought to call the strategic importance of Israel to the attention of the United States, to defeat the Dulles-Byroade "even-handed" American policy, and to check the British neoimperialism of the Baghdad Pact. To these ends, Ben-Gurion advocated extraordinary policies and approved unconventional military operations. This implicit, and often explicit imprimatur led some of his hand-picked followers to take unconventional action that severely shook the government and even more severely shook the Israeli national self-image.

Three events collectively became known as the Lavon affair: the intelligence fiasco of 1953, the Cairo trials of 1954, and the political struggle in Mapai over succession of 1960–1961, which ended in 1965 with Ben-Gurion's ouster.

In 1953 a vaguely worded and certainly not clearly authorized order by defense minister Pinhas Lavon was given to burn American and British political centers, including the USIA library in Cairo. Later, the order for this operation, put into motion by dedicated young Egyptian Zionists who were members of an Israeli intelligence network, was discovered by the Egyptian authorities, who turned it into a fiasco. The Israeli officer responsible for the operation escaped, while the Egyptian Jews were arrested, put on trial in December 1954, and convicted in January 1955. Two were executed, the rest were sentenced to spend twelve years in Egyptian prisons. A second Israeli intelligence agent committed suicide in an Egyptian prison during the trials.

The Egyptian ring was organized by Unit 131, a special operations commando unit of the IDF designated for service only in time of war. The identity of the person who gave the order to activate Unit 131, the means by which Israeli commandos escaped from Egypt, and the reasons for the mission's failure—all were subject of inquiry for several blue-ribbon Knesset and cabinet special committees in 1953–1954 and in 1960–1961. As the trial of the Zionists took place in Egypt, the Lavon affair began in Israel. The authorization for the Egyptian operation became the crux of the affair. "Who gave the order?" was the question that rocked Mapai in 1960–1961 when Lavon's role was exposed, generating fratricidal conflict within the party itself.[19] The Dori-Olshan Committee, formed by Sharett to investigate, did not reach a definitive verdict. They concluded their report:

> We deeply regret that we are unable to answer all the questions posed to us by the Prime Minister Sharett. We cannot say that we are convinced beyond reasonable doubt that Aman's [the intelligence service] chief [Colonel Benyamin Jibly] did not receive the order [for

Unit 131's operation in Egypt] from the Defense Minister [Lavon]. At the same time we are not sure that the Defense Minister actually gave the order that is attributed to him.[20]

Despite the committee's knowledge of the close relationship that Lavon and Jibly had at the time of the operation, this judgment was rendered because there was no clear evidence. If the committee had been able to give a decisive verdict (and we know now without a doubt from evidence provided by Haggai Eshed and the "third man" that Lavon gave the order for the Egyptian operation) there might have not been a Lavon affair.[21]

Israeli fears and apprehensions concerning the role of the great powers after the British evacuation from the Suez contributed a great deal to the fiasco. Lavon and the intelligence department overreacted. The Essek Bish, the fiasco, resulted from accumulation of military and political miscalculations. The Egyptian Jews recruited by Israeli intelligence were military amateurs; the Israeli commander, an exception to his fellows in the highly disciplined IDF, was irresponsible. Intelligence and internecine rivalries between Dayan, Lavon, and Sharett did take place. In his efforts to weaken and oust Dayan, Lavon tried to ally with Jibly, who betrayed him, and failed to accept the authority of Sharett, who "eventually" deserted him. In the end Dayan and Peres benefitted from Lavon's unsavory character and lack of authority. Although they were not involved in the affair, it helped them get rid of Lavon. But their names are connected in the minds of the public and of historians with the affair.[22]

. . .

A few points should be made concerning Unit 131 and the ambiguity of authority in Israeli military intelligence. The function of intelligence in the Haganah was never subordinated to its military authorities. Intelligence was created by the Arab department of the Jewish Agency between 1930 and 1937. By 1939 *Sherut Yidiot (Shay)*, the forerunner of *Mosad,* was subordinated to the agency's political department, headed by Moshe Shertok (Sharett). Between 1939 and 1947 the Shay was organized as counterintelligence and the Mosad was in charge of illegal immigration and purchase of weapons for the Haganah. In 1947 the foreign ministry and Mosad under Ben-Gurion had control of Shay, and in 1948 it was abolished. Mosad became the chief counterintelligence agency, headed by another Ben-Gurion loyalist, Iser Arel. Mosad, which spied on Etzel and later on the labor left, was a quasipolitical agency that was never under the authority of either Haganah or Zahal's high command. Between 1947 and 1951, IDF military intelligence was controlled by the deputy chief of staff, Makleff, and Reuven Shiloah (Zaslany) of the foreign office. Unit 131 was under a combined civil-military authority. Arel, an empire builder, wanted to dominate all IDF and ministry of defense intelligence activities and eyed the integration of Unit 131 with Mosad. In 1954 Dayan made 131 into a purely military unit, part of the IDF. Arel, who replaced Zaslany, resented the change and sought to bring 131 under Sharett-Lavon "codominion." He proposed to act as "liaison" for 131, with the ultimate intent of changing it into a counterintelligence unit once more. Lavon went over Dayan's head to establish this liaison, an action that ultimately brought about his own downfall; in this way he became involved in the affair.[23]

· · ·

To return to the politics of the fiasco: We must point out that the "Egyptian operation" was inspired by Lavon, who, though formerly a centrist, was now the most militant person in the defense establishment. Lavon was convinced that Israel's security would be strengthened if the British-American plans for withdrawal from the Suez were upset. Ben-Gurion liked Lavon's wit, sharp tongue, brilliant oratory, and maverick parliamentarianism, but Lavon had not been his first choice for defense minister. Although he had been a leader of the Mapai youth movement Gordonia, Lavon had had no experience in national security and foreign affairs. He was Mapai's most brilliant orator and parliamentarian and Ben-Gurion felt that Dayan and Peres could work with him. Because Lavon was an intellectual, Ben-Gurion assumed he would be a quick learner.

Once in office, Lavon impatiently sought to establish his own authority in isolation from Dayan and Peres. Like Sharett, Lavon suspected that Ben-Gurion intended to return from retirement but to give the Zeirim their political chance in his absence. To differentiate himself from Dayan and Peres, to establish his authority, to weaken Sharett, and above all to outdo Ben-Gurion, Lavon now became a cabinet superhawk. In order to dominate the IDF and the ministry of defense (MOD) Lavon set about curtailing the bureaucratic and political powers of Dayan and Peres. He deliberately kept Sharett ignorant of the politics and actions of the MOD and IDF, and in an attempt to isolate Dayan and keep Peres from running the MOD independently, went over Dayan's head to establish contact with senior officers of the high command, especially in intelligence.

This action was in the Ben-Gurion tradition, of course. Ben-Gurion had had a hand in every detail of the organization of IDF and had even taken a role in military operations during the war of independence. Dayan, however, could not tolerate the novice Lavon's meddling in his realm and he certainly could not stomach interference in military operations. As the first IDF chief to successfully formalize, professionalize and institutionalize the military,[24] Dayan objected strongly to outside interference.

Lavon went to extremes in his duties as defense minister, escalating raids and retaliatory activities and encouraging the intelligence division to put some of Israel's most drastic contingency plans into operation. The triple external threats of Baghdad, Suez and Nasserism, combined with Lavon's volatile and ambitious character, led him to adventurism and drama. He never perceived the dire political consequences inherent in his actions, and neither Dayan nor Peres helped to curb his erratic tendencies. They left him to endure the consequences of his errors alone.

During this period, Moshe Dayan advocated a policy that combined military activism and diplomacy. The complex Dayan was a nonideological political pragmatist and the only political figure in Mapai who remained relatively isolated from internal labor politics. The uncrowned head of Zeirim, Dayan let others in the party fight his political battles. But even though he ignored inner party struggles, Dayan was highly political, using his power as chief of staff to influence Israel's military and foreign policies. Over the years he went through several transformations that mirrored the kaleidoscopic panorama of Middle Eastern politics; it is not surprising that he was the only labor leader to defect to the opposition, becoming Foreign Minister for Likud in 1977. Dayan could be a hawk or a dove, depending on the circumstances. A champion of close Israeli-United States relations, the "American man" in the Likud government, Dayan did not hesitate in 1954 to challenge United States diplomacy in the Middle East because he felt that the United States, Britain, and other powers leaned toward Nasser's Egypt. In fact, he and Ben-Gurion were the architects of the Kadesh-Sinai war of 1956. Yet, in 1978, when he realized that Sadat meant to disengage, Dayan supported the Camp David diplomacy with Begin. In 1967 he both opposed the war in the Golan Heights and tried to dissuade Jordan's King Hussein from entering the war.

To return to the situation in the mid-1950s, where Lavon represented Israel's isolation-interventionists and Sharett its internationalists. Dayan doubted both. He felt Sharett's diplomacy was futile, that neither the armistice system nor the Third World would save Israel. Dayan also set himself against what he called "excessive political activism," such as sending an Israeli ship into the Suez Canal to test Egyptian and world reaction to a United Nations resolution on free navigation in 1955. His experience with the United Nations' armistice system had shown him that the organization had little political clout. Any effort to cross the canal "diplomatically" might only serve to expose Israel's political weakness. Dayan also opposed Lavon's adventurism as reckless. The only alternative was to challenge Nasser by military means to open the canal, and this was the task Dayan set himself. Between 1953 and 1956, Ben-Gurion and Dayan relentlessly pursued the politics of force.

The Road to Kadesh: Sinai, 1956

Sharett, Lavon, and the Mapai leadership were right—Ben-Gurion did not retire for good and had never intended to. His goal was Sharett's dismissal, which he achieved only by deserting the ship of state at a most inopportune time. As events in the Middle East unfolded, Sharett was deposed but Ben-Gurion would ultimately have to face the struggle in Mapai. This struggle was postponed until after the Sinai campaign. In fact, the seeds of the 1960–1961 *parasha* (affair) were sown in 1953–1954, when Ben-Gurion was out of power. Nevertheless he later shared the fate of those who were directly in command of Israeli policy in 1953–1955.

Sharett, as he tells in diaries, admitted that he no longer had the stomach for the IDF-MOD-cabinet-party intrigues. He "voluntarily" resigned, explaining in his diary that he did so because Ben-Gurion and his disciples, Dayan and Peres, intrigued to topple him, which in fact the latter two did. Upon finding that Lavon was dishonest and uncooperative, Sharett decided to invite Ben-Gurion back, but only as defense minister; this he did in February 1954. It was a way of "deposing" Lavon (in Sharett's mind) without great injury to him, and of bringing Ben-Gurion back so that the MOD-IDF intrigues would come to an end. By the end of 1955, Sharett gave up and asked Ben-Gurion to become his successor. The party, however concerned with Ben-Gurion's aggressive military policies, accepted this judgment in the hope of party unity and their sincere concern with Nasser's new ambitions.

By 1955 Ben-Gurion had become convinced that the 1949 borders and the political status quo would eventually force Israel to return to the original 1947 United Nations partition boundaries. He felt that London and Washington were sending a clear message: if Israel wanted their support, it should make compromises with Egypt and Jordan and surrender some territory.

The Israeli crisis of confidence in the great powers was reflected in Sharett's desperate efforts as prime minister and then as foreign minister under Ben-Gurion to alter the harsh attitudes toward Israel expressed by the representatives of the four major powers—Dulles, Molotov, Eden, and Bidault—at the Geneva Conference of October 1955.[25] A Czech-Egyptian arms deal announced early in 1955 convinced Israeli decision-makers that Nasser had to be challenged before the Egyptian army could make these weapons operational. At Geneva, Sharett organized a conspicuous public relations campaign with Britain, France, and the United States for weapons to counter the Soviet intervention through their Czech surrogate. He achieved little. Secretary of State Dulles candidly rejected the proposal to supply Israel with defensive weapons, while British Prime Minister Harold Macmillan cavalierly dismissed him. Dulles insisted that Israel must agree to "an overall settlement with the Arabs,"[26] rejecting the idea of Abba Eban, ambassador to the United States, for an Israeli-American alliance, which had Ben-Gurion's support. Even though Egyptian fedayeen increased their activities in the Gaza-Negev area and clearly had gone on the offensive, Soviet Foreign Minister Molotov rejected Sharett's pleas. "The Arabs are afraid of you. There is no reason you should fear them. If you do, why don't you ask the help of your allies: Britain and the US?"[27] Sharett wrote to Ben-Gurion: "The Westerners [United States,

Britain] are not ready for a security treaty [with Israel]. The U.S. has refrained, in order not to demonstrate total indifference to us but *at the same time to harness us*—they think of a stronger tripartite guarantee. . . . Dulles will pressure for a 'solution' which means concessions from us."[28]

One month after he took office as defense minister in March 1955, Ben-Gurion had placed before the cabinet the startling resolution that Israel should occupy Gaza.[29] Sharett, who remained prime minister in title if not in fact, led the opposition, and the proposal was rejected. Ben-Gurion, however, refused to give up. After the failure at Geneva, he instructed Dayan—who was now in Paris to forge a military alliance and obtain aid from a France that had fought the Algerian rebels supported by Nasser—to prepare an operational plan for conquering the Straits of Tiran and breaking the Egyptian blockade that had existed since 1949.[30] The last effort to salvage deteriorating Israeli-American relations and to prevent an Egyptian-Israeli war was the secret mission of Robert Anderson, Eisenhower's special envoy to the Middle East, who tried to act as a go-between to Ben-Gurion and Nasser.[31] "I want to talk shop," Ben-Gurion writes in his diary about his comments to American Ambassador Edward Lawson. "Three things are very close to my heart: Israeli security, peace in the Middle East, and Israeli-American friendship. The U.S. can accomplish the three in one operation: a security treaty between Israel and the U.S. . . .when the U.S. will sign such a treaty with us the Arabs will realize that their dream of annihilating us will wither away and then they will come to terms with us in time."[32] These comments had inspired the Anderson mission. At first Nasser seemed ready to meet with Ben-Gurion. Then, however, he began to make conditions. Ben-Gurion interpreted these conditions as the equivalent of Nasser's old demands for border rectification and return of Palestinian refugees. The mission finally failed when Nasser rejected a personal meeting with Ben-Gurion.[33] The die was cast.

Israel was desperately in need of weapons and they now came from an unexpected source. Although at war in Algeria, the French government responded cautiously but favorably to Israel's request. The Israeli-French connection, which began in 1953 and culminated in a secret alliance, was a crucial step in the journey that ended in the Sinai war.[34] It is significant not only as an issue of foreign and security policy but also because it played a key role in the struggle within Mapai and the cabinet. The architect of the alliance, Shimon Peres, was elevated to director general of the ministry of defense, and Dayan's autonomy increased as he became more deeply involved in French domestic and military affairs. Negotiations with the French were almost totally in the hands of Ben-Gurion, Peres, and Dayan, leaving Sharett, both as prime minister and later as foreign minister (in the Ben-Gurion government established in November 1955) almost totally out of the picture.[35] Peres all but established a political headquarters in Paris. The defense ministry mobilized to close Israel's first significant arms deal and Dayan organized the IDF to absorb the influx of weapons and prepare for its largest military operation since the war of independence. The alliance was clandestine. In the cabinets of both countries, only the prime minister, defense minister, and director general were involved in the secret entente.

Sharett's opposition to the French connection, to the border raid policy, and to the autonomy of Peres and Dayan in dealing with France grew firmer as his power declined.[36] He had reached the height of his power when he dominated the armistice machinery that made the United Nations guardian of the borders. Realizing now that he no longer had the support of Ben-Gurion and that Ben-Gurion, Dayan, and Peres would lead the country to war, Sharett resigned as prime minister in November 1955. The end of three decades of cooperation with Ben-Gurion came when Sharett also resigned as foreign minister in June 1956, after Ben-Gurion shifted the armistice division from the foreign ministry to the defense department. Brooding and hurt, Sharett nevertheless did not retire from politics. His continuing role in Mapai, especially during the Lavon affair, was to provide him with a measure of revenge against Ben-Gurion and his cabal.

Denouement: The Lavon Affair of 1960–1961 and the Victory of the Collective against Ben-Gurion (1960–1965)

The battles over security and foreign policy and between personalities in the mid-1950s were in fact largely about succession, involving a fundamental battle over the survival of the party, which was threatened by the statist onslaught of Ben-Gurion and his allies. A coalition of Lavon, Sharett, Mapai leader Levi Eshkol (Ben-Gurion's successor in 1963), Golda Meir (Eshkol's successor in 1969), chief Mapai ideologue and Minister of Education Zalman Arran, and chief party apparatchik Pinhas Sapir, struggled against the Ben-Gurion group over nothing less than the integrity of the party. Mapai was the collective instrument that had organized and defended the state and society. To Mapai's elite the loss of the party meant political anarchy, and they were unwilling to allow the triumph of Ben-Gurion's statism. They united in the name of ideology, using party procedure and personal power to defeat Ben-Gurion.

Party warfare opened with Lavon's cry for exoneration and rehabilitation. Lavon was not going to forgive and forget, and his personal campaign began soon after his resignation in February 1955. It evolved into a struggle between the Histadrut and the State,[37] ending only when Sharett was forced by party pressure to defend Lavon (whom he characterized in his *Personal Diary* as an unsavory, dishonest, irresponsible character).[38] The Lavon affair of 1960–1961 helped consolidate an alternative party leadership dedicated to saving the party (if necessary, from Ben-Gurion himself) and to reestablishing supremacy by eventually merging with the leftist parties, Ahdut Haavoda and Mapam.

The Sinai war in 1956, which "interrupted" resolution of the party-versus-state struggle, was a temporary victory for Ben-Gurion and his allies. The Kadesh operation, the apex of the policy of deterrence and retaliation, ended in a decisive military victory over Egypt, but isolated Israel politically. Nasser and Nasserism became the chief beneficiaries of the "imperialist war" conducted by Israel, France and Britain, for it strengthened Nasser's power at home, in the Arab world, and in the Third World. It also convinced Nasser that Israel's designs were aggressive and prompted him to build Arab, Moslem, and Third World coalitions around Egypt. Israeli-American relations were deeply strained after Sinai and Ben-Gurion's withdrawal of Israeli forces from Gaza in February 1957 once again showed the "futility" of military operations not backed up by foreign policy.

. . .

Some comment is in order here. Obviously, Ben-Gurion's supporters believe that the 1956 Sinai action coerced the United States into organizing and in fact guaranteed free navigation in the Straits of Tiran. When Nasser again challenged Israel in May 1967, Abba Eban returned home with a 1957 Dulles-Hammerskjold-Eban (i.e., United States-United Nations-Israel) agreement on free navigation, Israel's only legitimate document for a *causus belli*. In fact, Ben-Gurion's supporters argue that in 1967 Israel went to war to defend the freedom of navigation legitimized by the United States a decade earlier. Thus Israel could hold the territories it captured in 1967 as bargaining leverage to achieve peace. Once more one can argue two ways. One, if Israel had immediately withdrawn in 1967, the war of attrition and the 1973 war would not have occurred. Two, the position upheld by all governments of Israel since 1967, that the Arabs would come to terms only with a powerful Israel. Events since 1977 tend to support the second argument. Ben-Gurionites still claim that his perception of a strong Israel and peace with the Arabs is the essence of Israeli realpolitik and that in the end, with the Camp David accords, it worked.

. . .

The debate over diplomacy versus retaliation now clearly became part of the larger debate over Mapai's future role and leadership, and this crucial battle was waged in three theatres.

The first theatre involved opposition to the Ben-Gurion–Peres "European" orientation—the special relationship with France and especially a new military relationship with West Germany. Ben-Gurion wanted a balance to Israel's American orientation in the wake of America's rejection of a security alliance and its refusal to supply arms to Zahal. But anything German was anathema to many Israelis, and opposition to Israeli-German rapprochement came quickly from Eshkol and Meir, from Ahdut Haavoda, and most vehemently from the Herut-Begin party.

The second theatre of the struggle was the integration of Ben-Gurion's favorites, the Zeirim, into the party elite and the cabinet. In the 1959 election, when Mapai won its largest and last major electoral victory (47 members in the Knesset) Ben-Gurion, the victor of Sinai, appointed four members of the Zeirim to cabinet positions—Dayan, Eban, Peres, and Yosephtal. They were balanced, however, by Mapai elite and centrists, including Eshkol, Meir, Arran, and Sapir, the group that would eventually depose Ben-Gurion in 1965. As Arran, one of Mapai's oldest apparatchik-leaders proclaimed, "We are not old Eskimos. We have teeth."[39]

The third theatre, closely connected to the second, was the renewal of the Lavon affair. Helped by Ephraim (Eppi) Evron, his chief of cabinet in the Histadrut, and by Y. L. Hayerushalmi, a Mapai public relations officer, Lavon organized a brilliant campaign for his rehabilitation. He used half-truths and biased witnesses to paint himself as a victim of conniving intelligence officers, and was well served by the fact that the defense and Zahal establishments had long been sealed off from public scrutiny; a public gradually becoming acquainted with the 1953–1954 chicaneries now heard Lavon's version of events first. Eventually, a formidable coalition formed in defense of Lavon, including old Ben-Gurion victims from past political wars, the anti-Zeirim ruling elite of Mapai, party moderates and liberals simply disgusted with the 1953–1954 fiascoes, and opponents of the "European orientation."[40]

Ben-Gurion, who traditionally had been unsuccessful in working with coalitions, was not prepared to undertake a counteroffensive. Convinced of Lavon's guilt, but unwilling to succumb to public and party demands to punish intelligence officers who, though they were guilty of lying, were not guilty of giving the order for the Cairo fiasco, he preferred state-appointed committees of inquiry, not party internal committees. He called on Lavon to state his complaints before a court of law, urging him to stop pandering to public opinion, the press, or the liberals. True to his concept of mamlachtiout as a government of laws, Ben-Gurion refused to exonerate Lavon either personally or via the machinery of the party and the cabinet, claiming that the party elite was pressuring the party coalition, now led by Levi Eshkol (soon to become Ben-Gurion's successor), to exonerate Lavon. The party was not forced to decide on its political responsibility to the state; instead, the issue of exoneration was channeled through the party. Eshkol appointed a seven-member cabinet committee to inquire only into the guilt of Colonel Benyamin Jibly, implicated with Lavon, since Lavon was not considered a defendant. There supposedly was no incriminating evidence against him after all. Although he "gave the order," it was not explicitly established that it was the particular order that led to the Egyptian fiasco. The committee's purpose was to defend Zahal and its reputation. The political implications were quite apparent, however: if Jibly were to be found guilty, Lavon would be politically exonerated, even though he was certainly responsible for the Cairo fiasco.

In the end, the committee found Jibly guilty only of falsifying documents unconnected with the 1953 fiasco. With someone else guilty of something, the Israeli public now saw Lavon as a victim of irresponsible liars and forgers in the IDF. Editors, university professors, and intellectuals joined the Lavon campaign. The issue of Lavon's guilt or innocence was submerged by public indignation at discovering what they had believed impossible—low moral standards among senior Zahal officers. To the public, the guilt of Jibly proved the innocence of Lavon. They fastened on the committee statement: "We clearly determined that Lavon never gave the order on which 'the senior officer' [Jibly] relied. The 'fiasco' was executed without Lavon's knowledge." But the public failed to understand that the statement referred not to the Cairo operation, but to another intelligence fiasco in which Jibly supposedly attempted to implicate Lavon by falsifying documents.

Ben-Gurion had made his decision not to become part of the Lavon exoneration procedure. Writing to Sharett on October 28, 1960, before the committee began its hearings, he said: "I am determined not to participate in this government and Knesset, this after I have made it clear to the government that only a legal authority should handle the matter."[41] The opinion of Haggai Eshed is that the elite of Mapai, Eshkol, Sapir, Meir, Arran, Sharett and their supporters, had decided in October 1960 to oust Ben-Gurion or to create conditions leading to his forced resignation from the leadership of the party and the state.[42] Events lend considerable support to Eshed's claims. Ben-Gurion rejected the conclusions of the Committee of Seven, and Golda Meir, a Ben-Gurion ally for over three decades, resigned in protest. Meir, who played a key role in the affair, wanted the party and the Histadrut to be preserved and retain hegemony and the Zeirim, especially Peres and Dayan, to be subordinated. She firmly believed in the party's moral supremacy, political integrity and vanguard role in developing the Jewish state, and was ready to fight rather than surrender to Ben-Gurion or his allies on these commitments. Thus Ben-Gurion must go. So must Lavon. On February 2, 1961, Mapai's secretariat called for dismissal of Lavon as the party's representative to the Histadrut executive committee.[43] Lavon was then ousted from his post as Histadrut secretary general, and a February 4 party conference appointed Israel Becker to replace him. Thus, although Lavon had been politically exonerated, the party elite saw to it that his mecurial political career was over.

It is interesting to observe that Ben-Gurion not only refused to lend a hand in Lavon's ouster from the party, but even demanded that the party convene a special inquiry into Lavon's future in it. He clearly distinguished Lavon's party responsibilities from his earlier responsibilities to the state as defense minister. Ben-Gurion felt the state had punished Lavon by dismissing him from Sharett's cabinet, but the party should not punish him for his mismanagement of his defense post. Ben-Gurion did feel that the party had a responsibility to review the acts of its public servants, but was not a court of law. It could neither prosecute nor exonerate alleged crimes; only the state could do that.

The inner party struggle continued. Weakened by the affair, Ben-Gurion failed to form a cabinet coalition acceptable to Mapai; Ahdut Haavoda and Mapam refused to join it. Ben-Gurion resigned on January 31, 1961, so that he would not have to form a new government. Now Golda Meir came to Ben-Gurion's support rather than allowing other parties to oust a Mapai leader, saying, "Let the struggle over succession not weaken the party."[4] The new government was joined by Ahdut Haavoda, a move intended to strengthen Levi Eshkol, who organized the coalition. Ben-Gurion became prime minister once again, but he no longer negotiated the frontiers of government and he would not give up his demand that the Lavon affair be submitted to the courts. He became obsessed with statist justice, even though the party, led by Eshkol, decided to end the affair. Eshkol called for alliance with Ahdut Haavoda after twenty years, thus bringing the "lost children" back into the party fold. His intent was clear. He sought to infuse the party with its "old" new youth—Israel Galilee, Yigal Allon, and Yitzhak Ben-Aharon—to replace Ben-Gurion's Zeirim.

Eshkol-Meir-Sapir now set about to strengthen the party and to defeat Ben-Gurion, who, they said, still "unreasonably" sought "justice" in the case of Lavon. In addition, they intended to push his allies to the fringes of power. Under pressure from the Lavonites, Eshkol canceled the party's decision to oust Lavon from the Histadrut. In February 1965 the party conference met to end the Lavon affair. It symbolically reinstated Lavon (but he did not regain the office of secretary general), a clear sign that Ben-Gurion and Mapai had come to a parting. And they defied Ben-Gurion's demand to resolve the Lavon affair in a state-appointed committee of inquiry. The price of this resolution was the final official ouster of Ben-Gurion by a Mapai internal party tribunal, and the resulting creation of the Rafi party, a Ben-Gurion group whose real spirit was Shimon Peres. Thus the Ben-Gurion era ended much as Weizmann's did: with defeat, isolation, and separation from the party he had helped establish and the political system he had helped design.

The heir to the greatest military victory of Israel, the 1967 war, was Levi Eshkol, who built on foundations unquestionably laid by Ben-Gurion. Nasser's challenge to the first partition state once more legitimized Ben-Gurion's military policies. It also convinced the nation's political and military elites, as well as the public, that the first state that emerged from partition was only an interim solution.

THE SECOND PARTITIONED STATE:
1967–1973

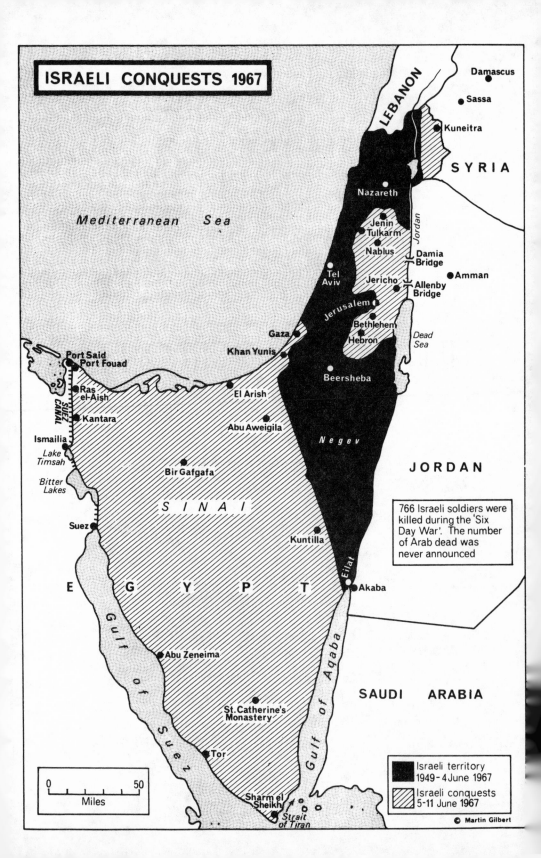

Preface: Consolidation and Fragmentation

The 1967 war brought to the surface the frustration of a beleaguered people and the repressed anxiety of the survivors of the Holocaust. Regardless of whether Nasser really intended to go to war in June 1967, he unquestionably provoked Israeli fears of attack. So this time, perhaps subconciously recalling Hitler's final solution, the Israelis launched a preemptive strike.

By June 10, after the swiftest six days in Israeli history, the Israeli Defense Forces found themselves on the banks of the Suez Canal in the south, on the Golan Heights in the north, and on the Jordan River in the east. These enormous conquests had not been planned; there had been no Israeli annexation policy before 1967. Now, although the IDF had moved to destroy the Arab armies in self-defense, it had suddenly quadrupled the country's territory. Dayan stated that the new boundaries were ideal as defensible borders, and soon the conquered territory was viewed as having value far beyond that of a bargaining point in future negotiations. The 1967 war demonstrated to even the most moderate Israelis that the prewar boundaries had been inadequate.

In their desire for secure borders, the Israeli political elite and the public misperceived the stubbornness of the Arab refusal to accept the situation the 1967 war created. As a consequence of the continuing Arab-Israeli deadlock, Israel, at the same time that Egypt and Syria grew closer together, experienced its first political fragmentation since 1935. Although both hawks and doves still claimed membership in the Labor party, the ideological divisions cut deeply into the traditional consensus, leading to an impasse in foreign policy.

The disagreement was symbolized by two minority groups: the Eretz Israel movement, which advocated total annexation of all occupied territories, and the new left, which advocated the creation of a Palestinian state confederated with Jordan on the West Bank of the Jordan River to pacify the Palestinians and Arabs. Although they constituted only small coteries of intellectuals, these two groups dictated a new ideological frame of reference in Israeli politics between 1967 and 1973, disrupting historical friendships and traditional political alliances. No longer did the Revisionists monopolize militant Zionist ideology or the Mapai the middle of the road. Both the Labor party and the Labor alignment were split internally along ideological lines.

Paradoxically, this fragmentation and the spreading of the ideological divisions took place during the climax of Labor's march toward hegemony. In 1969, the Ahdut Haavoda (split from Mapai in 1942) and Rafi (split from Mapai in 1965) parties had reunited with the mainstream Mapai, which was integrated into the Labor party. The alignment, Maarach, an electoral coalition between Labor and the left Mapam party, had been created in 1968. At the same time, further political consolidation was achieved by the opposition. The religious parties united in a bloc known as the United Religious Bloc and the revisionist and Liberal Zionists (General Zionists in the past) united with the Herut party in the Gahal bloc, which became the Likud party in April 1973. No longer did a dominant Mapai confront a weak and fragmented opposition. After 1967, the three powerful electoral blocs of Labor, Likud, and the URB characterized the nation's political life.

This spectacular consolidation did not reflect the actual breakdown of consensus in both foreign security and domestic policies. Cleavages within the parties and blocs were related to two issues:

1. The nature and structure of Arab-Israeli peace negotiations. The hawks—Likud, the Rafi faction of Labor, radical NRP, the State party (L'Am), and militants of Ahdut Haavoda—without exception advocated direct Arab-Israeli negotiations with little or no interference by outside powers, especially the great powers. They believed that the United States would seek to impose an unwanted solution on Israel and that the Soviet Union, as sole

supporter of the Arabs, would prejudice the negotiations. But the doves—moderate Mapai, Mapam, and independent liberals—advocated great-power intervention, believing that the United States could curtail the aspirations of Israel's hawks. Fiercely anti-Soviet, the moderates sought a mediatory role for the United States as the only hope for peace in the Middle East.

2. Believing in an Arab conspiracy to annihilate Israel, the hawks argued that the security of Israel depended upon territorial acquisition and some degree of annexation. Some members of the radical NRP and of Ahdut Haavoda even argued that the newly acquired territories were more than a security guarantee—they were Israel's historical possessions and had religious significance. The doves were divided. Most did not accept the annihilation thesis and felt that the impasse in peace negotiations could only be broken through reasonable and incremental Israeli territorial concession and withdrawal. Extreme radical doves advocated a return to the 1967 borders and the establishment of a Palestinian state led by the PLO, the Palestine Liberation Organization.

Of the various partition plans put forward by the British and the United Nations during the prestate period, none had ever been implemented; the partition eventually effected had been "negotiated" by force of arms in the Arab-Israeli war of 1948–1949. The Israel which resulted—the first partitioned state—existed until 1967; its failure to gain Arab acceptance resulted in a new round of "negotiations," the war of June 1967. The outcome of that conflict went far beyond the conquest of new territories; the very existence of Israel had been renegotiated and its conception of itself had been altered. A new state, the second partitioned state, had emerged.

Immediately after 1967 the people of Israel felt relieved and fulfilled: relieved in believing that they had fought the last Arab-Israel war, and fulfilled finally to have achieved some protective territorial space. Sinai, the Golan Heights, and the West Bank separated Israel from direct invasion of Arab armies into the Israel of the first partition state. This also meant that the IDF would no longer have to maneuver Israel's military forces within the boundaries of the first partition; the newly acquired territories changed the strategic doctrines of Zahal. The territories and the expected new borders thus created new concepts of security and political legitimacy as well as new political movements and ideologies. The second partition state soon became imbued with several infallible doctrines mainly conceiving the boundaries seemingly imposed by the second partition as a new buffer zone, the "Maginot Line" to which Israel aspired.

In the middle 1960s the feeling among the Labor elite and others had been that the Zionist elan was on the decline and that partyism and political opportunism had taken over at the expense of the pristine nationalist and socialist ideologies and structures. The repartition of Palestine now gave rise to new ideologies on the left and the right. At the very moment when the "End of Ideology" epitaph was being proclaimed by political and intellectual elites in Israel, two extraparliamentary political and ideological movements appeared. One was committed to the permanent annexation of all the conquered territories and thus the establishment of Israel's final boundaries; the other sought to restore the first partition state and make it permanent so that Israel could live in peace. The first, the Land of Israel movement, was established by political and nonpolitical figures representing the old spectrum of political parties from left to right. Former and present leaders and ideologues of Mapai, Herut, Rafi and Ahdut Haavoda joined. The second movement, the peace movement, sprang mainly from the left kibbutz movement, but drew on other historical peace movements as well. While the Land of Israel movement concentrated on settling occupied territories and establishing the newly acquired territories as the final boundaries of Israel, the peace movement concentrated on restoring the borders of the first partition state and on the future of an independent Arab Palestine; in fact, the peace movement was to become the first Israeli political movement to identify Israeli security with the establishment of a Palestinian Arab state. The two movements, especially the Land of Israel movement, gained momentum at the expense of Israel's traditional and secular political parties, especially Herut, Ahdut Haavoda, and Rafi (Ben-Gurion's party). But virtually all the major parties—Mapai, Herut, General Zionists—eventually adopted different aspects of the Land of Israel movement's ideology, concepts and even rhetoric. It became the movement par excellence of the second partition state.

The influence of the peace movement was restricted to the left wing kibbutz movement and Mapam party, not because a majority within the parties or in the general public were maximalists who wanted to retain all the new territories permanently, but because the peace movement's championing of the formation of a Palestinian state restricted and curtailed its momentum and political appeal. It enjoyed its greatest influence between 1973 and 1977, but the more militant stance eventually prevailed politically in post-1967 Israel. The Land of Israel movement did not succeed in replacing any party, or even in taking over the hawkish Herut and Rafi, but it did create a psychological and political veto over diplomatic efforts to return to the borders of the first partition state, even if such a return might mean peace and security for Israel. The influence of the Land of Israel movement went beyond its miniscule electoral capabilities. The 1967 victory, with its territorial conquests that brought a new concept of space, resurrected old 1930s' debates. Land of Israel was reminiscent of Tabenkin's Complete Israel and Jabotinsky's Revisionism, while the peace movement recalled the binationalism and pacifism of Hashomer Hatzair and Brith Shalom. The debate over the new partition became as fierce between 1967 and 1973 as it had been in the 1930s.

CHAPTER 7

Neo-Zionism: The Land of Israel Movement and the Rise of Political and Territorial Militancy

The Land of Israel movement (Hatnua Le-Maan Eretz Yisrael Hashlema—LIM) was the product of the 1967 victory and change of boundaries, but its ideology had roots in Ahdut Haavoda's Herzelian Zionism, specifically in its contention that the territorial solution of the Jewish problem superseded the notion of *Juden-not*—Jewish misery. For Eretz Israel had not only been established to relieve Jewish misery by providing a haven for Jews (after all, the first partition state could have fulfilled this function), but also as a return to the historical Jewish homeland: only within its *historical* boundaries, some early Zionists argued, could the Jewish people be redeemed and fulfilled. Similarly, LIM's manifesto clearly states:

> The whole of Eretz Israel is now in the hands of the Jewish people, and just as we are not allowed to give up the *State of Israel,* so we are ordered to keep what we received there from Eretz Israel. We are bound to be loyal to the entirety of our country—for the sake of the people's past as well as' its future, and no government in Israel is entitled to give up this country.[1]

As Rael Jean Isaac notes in quoting of the above, "Implicit here is the notion that a power higher than state sovereignty limits the power of the state, and that the land belongs not to the citizens of Israel, but the entire Jewish people, which are not represented in its government, and which can therefore not act in its name."

The movement was ideological, political, and elitist. Never intended to become a mass movement, it became instead a vehicle for neo-Zionism, composed of frustrated individuals within different Israeli political parties as well as scholars, writers, and ideologues. It was not just a movement of politically frustrated members of Rafi, Mapai, Ahdut Haavoda, and Gahal (the Herut-General Zionist electoral bloc formed in the 1965 elections) but a vehicle for a nationalist regeneration. The LIM took its ideas from the Zionist and pioneering past, the Scriptural heritage, and the historical museum. It succeeded in regenerating territorial and maximalist Zionism in its most pristine, prestate, prepartition, even pre-Yishuv forms. It penetrated Jewish secular and orthodox establishments, the parties (especially their radical fringes), and the defense department bureaucracy, and the established youth movements and several elite high schools in Israel's major cities. It made inroads into the inner sanctums of the labor and kibbutz movements. Because it had wide, though not deep support, LIM political influence was disproportionate to its political or electoral strength. LIM set itself to create a new political consensus in Israel and above all to de-legitimize and discredit within the political establishment, the government, the opposition and other parties, the historical political leadership (young and old), and the historical consensus that partition was the only reasonable solution for a stable and peaceful Jewish state. LIM felt deeply that the concept of partition was unworkable, unrealistic, and detrimental to Israel. Eretz Israel was to be complete, the integrity of its boundaries sacred and inviolable.

Partition, LIM argued, was a foreign concept, imposed on Israel by the British and the United Nations. The movement insisted on the legitimacy of Israel's claims over the territories taken in the 1967 war. "Territories for peace," the government's slogan, was seen as a betrayal of Zionism because it apparently accepted the idea that the territories were "Arab." LIM members argued that partition was no longer the basis for contention, separation, and conflict, and that territories could no longer be bargained for as they had been in 1937, 1947, and 1956. LIM confidence stemmed from the stunning victory of Zahal. Yitzhak Tabenkin, the founder of the United Kibbutz movement and an ardent LIM member, stated:

> The choice is not really in our hands; there is no alternative of going back to the old boundaries. We are condemned to be strong. . . .One thing all members of the Movement have in common is a sense of strength, and this is not chauvinism or overbearing pride, but comes from a feeling *that either the State of Israel will be strong or it will not exist.*[2] (Emphasis added.)

R. J. Isaac has summarized the LIM world view this way:

> In the perspective of the Land of Israel movement, Zionism's goal was indeed statehood and normalization of the Jewish condition, but these goals had not yet been achieved. Zionism had as its goal the ingathering of all the Jews of the world, with the exception of a small number who would be assimilated and lose their identity in their countries of origin, and this goal had clearly not been realized, Israel having little more than a fifth of the world's Jews living within her borders. Zionist faith was thus the answer to the "demographer-Zionists" as they were scornfully called by movement members, for the movement, in its official position, advocated granting full rights to the Arabs of the new territories once they were absorbed into Israel. But all the world's Jews could only be ingathered within an "undivided Land of Israel." The twin goals of Zionism were thus inextricably connected: the settlement of the "entire land" required the "aliya" of world Jewry and needed the entire land to provide them with the conditions making settlement of millions of additional immigrants possible.[3]

The movement did not exceed the aspired goals of historical Zionism. It called for basic Zionist aims—a Jewish majority in all of Palestine, a Jewish sovereign state within its historical boundaries, and territorial space for those Jews who were to return from the diaspora. Historical Zionism did not have to prescribe the boundaries of the Jewish state precisely, nor its role in the area. LIM embodied certain pristine Zionist, and especially Labor-kibbutz-activist aspirations: a modern, productive and secure state not limited territorially by partitions. It drew from Ben-Gurion, Tabenkin, Jabotinsky, Herzl, and Nordau to challenge the Israeli establishment, especially the Labor party. LIM's leading ideologues and organizers were largely former leaders of the Labor movement, which indicates that LIM's ideology was not marginal, although its electoral strength was. Its influence over power at the center of Israel's political establishment was considerable. No Labor minister or major Labor party leader joined LIM, even if Moshe Dayan and Israel Galilee were sometimes considered to be close to the LIM camp. Menachem Begin's militant Herut was no partner of LIM, although some of its most conspicuous dissidents were LIM's founding fathers. The real spirit of the movement came from former UKM militants whose spiritual father and a leading LIM member was Ahdut Haavoda's Yitzhak Tabenkin. A month after the Six-Day War, Tabenkin wrote:

> From my point of view, to the superpowers we are nothing but a function of power politics. The rules of international politics dictate that they aspire to leaving us to the oil frontiers. . . .We cannot depend on the great powers. They are seeking a compromise by exerting pressure on us for their own benefit, depriving us of the achievements that guarantee our place [the territories]. . .our security will grow only if the great powers will have to recognize our political independence and make compromises only among each other. We will not compromise our settlements and pioneer achievements which represent Jewish history.[4]

LIM attacked the government and the opposition parties as an old partition-oriented establishment whose ideological and political usefulness had come to an end. But membership in LIM was voluntary and people were not prohibited from staying with or joining political parties. Among LIM members some divisions from the "old politics" remained. In particular, two fundamentally different orientations prevailed to justify the movement and set its further goals; these were clearly divided between the former adherents of Socialist and Revisionist Zionism. The basic premise for the territorial integration sought by the Labor-oriented members of LIM was territorial security. The premise of the former Revisionists was metaphysical and existential. Writes Zvi Shiloah, a Rafi party member and Ben-Gurion disciple:

> I have not based my views on a historical conception of borders, because there have been many boundaries and all of them are historical. We need a geopolitical conception. We need a conception of "greatest Israel" extending from the Mediterranean to the Persian Gulf. . . . The concept of space has not been grasped yet in

Israel. . . .We must develop the geopolitical vision to recognize that it is essential to control large spaces, so that people cannot talk of Israel as a small obstacle in the Near East. The unity of Arab states is in any case a fiction, but once Israel becomes a big wedge between them, even the fiction disappears.[5]

A leading LIM member, a former Lehi commander, probably Revisionism's most fanatic militant, who in an interview proudly proclaimed himself a Jewish Fascist, is Dr. Israel Eldad, a brilliant journalist and psychologist. His view of the purpose of LIM holds that:

The existence of the partition of the country is a function of the division of the existential soul of Zionism in its different layers. In these layers, from the beginning, there was a deep fragmentation, with guilt feelings towards the cosmopolitan ideals of socialism and liberalism, which were to liberate the world from nationalism—maybe even from the plague of the nation-states—and which would liberate the Jews entirely from their separate unique existence. . . .This is a typical schizophrenia. We have guilt feelings that we presumably have betrayed these universal ideals by turning to Zionism, which is of necessity "reactionary" for it is a return to sometimes irrational roots. . . .Had it only at least been possible to implement "utopian Zionism" in "ways of peace" through convincing the Arabs that we bring blessings to them too, and socialist liberation and progress! But in vain! To go on with psychological language, what is left is frustration—the feeling that perhaps Zionism is after all a reactionary movement.[6]

LIM confronted the government on all the issues of Zionism—territory, international power politics, the Arab question, the future of the Jewish state. The challenge would turn out to be more real than was perceived by the political establishment between 1967 and 1973. Let us now examine the attitude of the ruling Labor party to the 1967 events and its consequences.

The Golden Era of Labor's Collective, 1967–1973

The 1967 victory created conditions for political consolidation and integration in Israel. As the Ben-Gurion era faded, Levi

Eshkol's short-lived leadership formed. The military victory, the occupied territories, the perceived helplessness of Arab military power, the absence of serious American pressure on Israel to relinquish the territories without negotiations (as had been the case in 1956), and the rise in immigration, productivity, and per capita income created almost ideal conditions for political consolidation. And the parties and factions of left and right moved in this direction. The natural locus for political consolidation was of course Mapai, by far the largest party at the time. The victory was Labor's. Although the national unity cabinet formed just before the war included all factions except the Communists, the Socialist Zionist camp reaped the greatest share of the spoils of victory. The post-1967 euphoria created an era of good feeling, of hope and optimism as well as complacency. "The Affair," the Ben-Gurion split, the pre-1967 fractricide were dissolved in the chemistry of victory and success. The idea of a political merger of all Socialist Zionist parties and kibbutz and cooperative movements was the goal of the Mapai collective but the real motor was the Alignment (Maarach), labor's most corporate group, its best organized, most comprehensive and thoroughly autonomous Ahdut Haavoda party.[7]

For its leaders, Yigal Allon, Israel Galilee, and Yitzhak Ben-Aharon, a Socialist Zionist merger would mean their final ascendancy to power. It was this trio that had linked the Ahdut Haavoda party with Mapai into an electoral bloc, the Maarach, in 1965, and it was this group that now moved to consummate the 1967 achievement into a Labor merger dominated, they hoped, by themselves in alliance with Mapai. The Mapai collective, especially its leading trio of Levi Eshkol, Golda Meir, and Pinhas Sapir, felt after defeating Ben-Gurion and his allies that the golden opportunity had arrived. Close to four decades after the formation of Mapai all the House of Labor corporate structures, parties, kibbutz, cooperative movements, and the Histadrut were finally to merge into an all-inclusive, most awesome Labor Party.

Thus, on January 21, 1968, some seven months after the guns were silenced and a little before the start of a war of attrition at the Suez Canal, the three former Labor parties, Mapai, Ahdut Haavoda, and Rafi joined to create the Israel Labor Party (ILP), which soon established an electoral bloc with the left-Zionist party Mapam to form a new Maarach. The union took place despite serious divisions over it within Mapai and Rafi. Mapai middle-echelon groups had feared the infiltration of Ahdut Haavoda in 1965, and correctly perceived the latter's ambition to coalesce with Mapai's top group to achieve domination with the party.[8] The Labor merger was a pure act of political power for Mapai-Ahdut Haavoda elites. The collective struggle was no longer ideological but organizational; it was concerned with power and control of the party and the state. The Labor party no longer generated ideology, it ritualized ideology and imposed its political culture on the political system.[9] The power ratio in the newly established Israel Labor Party central committee after Sapir's successful organizational campaign in 1969 represented an alliance between Eshkol-Meir of Mapai and Galilee–Ben-Aharon of Ahdut Haavoda. For the 1969 elections, the ILP presented a cohesive political elite and a collective of Mapai-Ahdut Haavoda not known since the rupture in 1944.[10]

The merger had tremendous implications for foreign and security policies. The Mapai-Ahdut Haavoda combination brought together the most determined and most hawkish political group since the formation of the Yishuv in Palestine. Prime Minister Levi Eshkol was himself something of a pragmatist and activist, but Golda Meir, the woman who replaced him after his death in 1970, was a tough product of Labor Zionism and trade unionism long experienced in Zionist diplomacy. Like Ben-Gurion before her, and like Rabin and Begin after her, she saw her role as foreign minister as being preeminent. The key office after hers was that of defense minister, held by former Rafi leader Moshe Dayan, a leading hawk. Yigal Allon, the minister of labor (later education minister and deputy prime minister) was an Ahdut Haavoda-Palmach activist, and Israel Galilee, the merger's linchpin and a protégé of Tabenkin, was an advocate of dynamic pioneer Zionism. He was put in charge of settling (selectively) Golan, Sinai, and the West Bank. Pinhas Sapir, the powerful finance minister, and Abba Eban, the nominal foreign minister, were leading doves of this cabinet of hawks. Sapir was never involved in security and foreign affairs issues, and Eban had had no serious political constituency in the party; his political views hardly modified those of Mrs. Meir, who, when prime minister, ran foreign affairs herself while leaving Dayan in charge of security and the occupied territories. Another hawk who entered the new Labor politics was former chief of staff, now ambassador to the United States, General Yitzhak Rabin, an Ahdut Haavoda-Palmach activist.

Rabin wielded more influence than Eban and, significantly, re-ported directly to Mrs. Meir rather than to the foreign minister.

The apparent victory of partyism over Ben-Gurion's mamlach-tiout curiously served to strengthen the state. Now it was no longer Ben-Gurion and his protégés who were running defense, Zahal, and the machinery of armistice, but a Mapai-Ahdut Haavoda collective group that achieved a clear and most effective division of labor. This actually *enhanced* statism and made foreign and security policies the autonomous discretion of senior minis-ters. The state was in place.

Labor's Doctrines of Settlement and Relations with the Palestinians

A new doctrine concerning the conquered territories evolved during Golda Meir's tenure as prime minister. A true Ben-Gurionite when it came to ruling the cabinet, the country, the party, and her Labor ministers, her world was narrow and simple, set in the early 1920s when she consistently opposed partition. The Jews would no longer tolerate the great power partition of their land. The next partition must be made only with negotiating and cooperating Arabs. Until such negotiations emerged (Meir did not especially seek them out, and even discouraged serious diplomatic opportunities which contradicted her unchanging views) Israel would remain in the occupied territories, settling them and creating its own de facto partition.

The individual in charge of settlement in the newly acquired territories was Israel Galilee of the United Kibbutz movement, an old Haganah fighter and Ben-Gurion antagonist not particularly dedicated to the first partition's boundaries. Galilee's mentor was Yitzhak Tabenkin, the LIM member for whom the settlement of the entire Eretz Israel remained an active concern. Said Galilee:

> From the beginnings of Zionism to our own days [1978], we oscillate between our deepest quest to settle *all* of Eretz Israel [including the West Bank of the Jordan River] and the necessity to recognize outside constraints and accept reality which contradicts our quest for settle-ment.[11]

Galilee, as a minister without portfolio in the Eshkol, Meir, and Rabin governments (1967–1977), became the chief architect of government settlement policy in occupied territory. The concept was anchored in the doctrines of pioneer Socialist Zionism that went back to Hehalutz and the Labor Legion, the founding structures for the United Kibbutz movement. A realist and a pragmatist, Galilee sought a compromise between Ben-Gurion's and Tabenkin's concepts of settlement. Aware that Israel had now replaced the mandatory in the West Bank, but that it also held Egyptian and Syrian territories, he devised a settlement policy designed to integrate both national security and dynamic Zionism. This was to be achieved by extending the borders to create enough territorial and strategic depth to defend successfully the territory of the first partition state and especially areas of concentrated Jewish population. The borders of the first partition state were to be modified for Zahal purpose's, creating enough strategic depth so that it would not be totally dependent on intelligence and other alert systems, or on continuous and costly military mobilization. As much unpopulated Arab territory as possible was to be converted into an Israeli defensive and military ground. Sinai, Golan, and the West Bank would serve as military corridors to deter Arab aggression and facilitate Zahal preventative and mobility advantages.

The first partition state's geographical configuration was to be radically and drastically altered by Israel's new defense posture. Zahal was given better training facilities (especially air space) and better deployment policy, moving the battlefield from Israel's urban centers. The military settlements in the West Bank became a policy imperative for Israel Galilee and Deputy Prime Minister Yigal Allon. The thrust of settlement was to be oriented around the permanent modification of the first partition state's borders and the creation of a military settlement belt around the strategic Jordan River. These are the origins of the now renowned Allon plan. Three months after the 1967 war, Allon devised a revolutionary plan that advocated what has now become Israeli military doctrine—making the Jordan River the permanent strategic border between Israel and the Arab country (Palestine-Jordan, Jordan-Palestine, or simply Jordan) east of Israel. To ensure total and permanent demilitarization of Israel's eastern boundaries, a complex system of civilian and military collective settlements were established on the West Bank of the Jordan River in what had been Jordanian-occupied territory. To facilitate the military settlements, Galilee also projected the creation of a few central Jewish cities in the West Bank as economic, market, and supply networks. The same settlement doctrine was applied with greater intensity and vigor in the Golan Heights, in Gaza, and northern and northwestern Sinai as well as in the key naval and sea facilities in the southern tip of Sinai and the islands in the Red Sea adjacent to Sinai.

These aspects of settlement were considered to be strictly for security purposes. Yet the separation of security and settlement in Zionism, especially Socialist Zionism, is artificial. Settlement was the fulfillment of the Zionist ideology, placing Jews on agricultural land (redemption); inevitably, this required ensuring their security. To Galilee, the policy of settling the unpopulated part of the occupied territories was an extension of Ben-Gurion's concept of settling unpopulated territories and Tabenkin's concept of strengthening the republic of socialist and pioneer kibbutzim by extending kibbutz settlement into those areas which the Arabs failed to cultivate, settle, improve and develop. For Tabenkin and Galilee, developmental settlement was the essence of dynamic Zionism. "We have concentrated in the past," Galilee said, "on settlement policies, at least in the Western Eretz Israel, with the strong desire to spread and extend our established settlement."[12] Settlement in unpopulated areas beyond the established frontier was the raison d'être of practical (Ben-Gurion) and kibbutz (Tabenkin) Zionism. Given the absence of a hostile mandatory and of serious United States pressure (busy in Vietnam), and the weakness of Arab regimes after 1967, the opportunity to pursue Zionism and settle new empty lands was ideal for persons like Galilee. This, the Zionist challenge, was renewed by the 1967 victory: the borders of the second partition state were to be institutionalized by the same organized, concerted, and rational effort that had characterized Zionism in the past.

Golda Meir's government provided all that was necessary for the establishment of new Jewish settlements in the occupied territories. Their fundamental rationale was Zionist: to settle Jews in empty land, to extend the Jewish majority, and to ensure the safety of the state by extending the border. The concepts of autonomy, self-reliance, skeptical attitudes toward outsiders, and distrust of friend and foe alike, characterized the Meir regime and made it one of the most successful in realizing Zionist ideals in

Israel's brief history. Galilee harnessed the kibbutz movements of Mapai, Ahdut Haavoda, and Mapam to establish kibbutzim in Golan, the West Bank, and Sinai.

Galilee summarized his conception of dynamic Zionism and settlement:

> The venture of settlement and its development, the settling on land, creates a sense of roots, a sense of belongingness that in turn makes the nation in Eretz Israel into a responsible collective defending its homeland [*moledet*]."[13]

There is an element of mysticism in Galilee's vision of settlement, which stems from the concept of the religion of labor and the conquest of land:

> In all we did and said [Ahdut Haavoda and the United Kibbutz movement before the establishment of Israel] the element of uncertainty had its most positive impact. Uncertainty is an element of power. When I delve into the history of Zionism I reach the conclusion that not a small element of Zionism was conceived from dreams, feelings, and sentiments. And what I do not hesitate to say in this consciousness and mysticism is that they are derivative from the historical sources of Jewish people: the Bible, modern Hebrew literature, and the lessons of our own history. All that we have to do now is to learn from the powerful sources of our aspirations and wishes but not in contradiction to political reality and to limitations which we are not allowed to ignore.[14]

This is a clear pronouncement of Yishuv-type kibbutz Zionism. In his ten-year tenure as chief of settlements, Galilee took advantage of the historical circumstances to regenerate the ideology of conquest of land, carrying out his program under tolerable strains of great power pressure and continuous but successful Arab-Israeli wars. Yet, in the case of the West Bank, an Arab-populated area, Galilee, Meir, Allon and the most determined maximalists of the Israel Labor Party remained loyal to Ben-Gurion and the legacy of movement in the Yishuv era—no annexation, no settlement in dense Arab-populated areas of Palestine. When it came to the solution of Israel's eastern borders, the Allon plan and Labor party doctrine was directed toward an eventual restoration of Jordanian sovereignty over the West Bank. The Allon plan, Galilee's settlement policy and Moshe Dayan's open bridges to Jordan were designed to extend Jewish land at the frontier *and* to ensure Jordan as its eastern neighbor by maintaining Jordanian, not Palestinian, political influence on the West Bank. Maximalists inside and outside the party opposed any form of Palestinian self-determination tolerated by the moderates. Their opposition to an independent Palestinian state stemmed from their unalterable commitment to dynamic Zionism and Israel's secure frontiers. The lessons of the Yishuv and two decades of the State of Israel militated against any Labor party solution that would deprive Jordan of sovereignty over the West Bank. Israel would restore Jordanian sovereignty and with Jordan would reassure the security of the Jordan River for both countries.

Dayan's pragmatic "open bridges" policy was inspired by dynamic Zionism and the search for security.[15] The idea of open bridges, i.e., of leaving the West Bank and Gaza as much as possible on their own and of encouraging local self-government and autonomy, was based on the thesis that Jewish-Arab contacts would be imperative for future peace in the area. Thus Israel, as the military authority governing a million non-Israeli Arabs, should create the conditions of peace and Arab-Israeli cooperation on its own terms, without Palestinian sovereignty. The eastern frontiers of Israel would become "no visas, no passports" zones. Dayan left intact all the local government machinery and the Jordanian structure. Even though he advocated freedom for Israelis to purchase *unclaimed* Arab land in the West Bank, the linkage of Palestine to Jordan was an Israeli policy that took cognizance of the Ben-Gurion dictum of partition—Jewish settlements separated from an Arab population center. This policy would change only when Menachem Begin became prime minister.

In the absence of serious international pressure and constraints, Galilee, Meir, and Dayan stretched the doctrines of dynamic Zionism as far as they thought would be politically tolerable. The Labor party refused to draw maps or goals lest the maps be equated with Israel's final negotiating stand before any Arab government had committed itself to negotiations. This "realism" carried Israel into a war of attrition with Nasser between 1968 and 1970 and later led to a politically unfavorable outcome of war in 1973. After 1973, Israel made greater territorial concessions than it had in the golden era of 1967–1973. But success, victory, and activism had created an Israeli diplomatic immobility; this complacency, a product of the arrogance of military success, would be paid for after 1973.

It is not the intent here to speculate on what would have occurred if Israel had made concessions to Nasser at the end of the War of Attrition, or to Anwar al-Sadat in August 1970, or to King Hussein before the 1974 Rabat conference that made the PLO the only Arab instrument to negotiate the future of the Palestinians. The point is that in the post-1967 era Israel remained the ideological captive of its Zionist heritage. Moreover, it was engulfed by the new political forces of LIM, which bolstered the more militant members of Israel's cabinet and Labor party leaders. The government in this period was both the prisoner of a miniscule ideological group and the victim of a larger and older conceptual trap of its own.

The Government Response to the Challenge of 1967: How the Status Quo Was Established

These shifts did not proceed unopposed, and in the new debate over the partition of Israel some of the arguments were reminiscent of those heard in the 1930s; indeed even some of the protagonists were the same. What changed was the context within which the arguments took place. In the 1930s and 1940s the ideological and political debate over partition was mainly conducted within the House of Labor and was more pragmatic and politically realistic, argued within an ideological framework supported by all the structures of Zionists. Now the debate was largely ideological and it was no longer transmitted through the main political structures of Israel. Its terms of reference and purpose were defined by tiny ideological movements at two extremes—LIM and the peace movement—which then spilled into the cabinet, government, Labor, and opposition parties. The government and the Labor collective and elites were themselves now centrist in orientation and nonideological.

The presence of the Land of Israel movement and the peace movement as competing ideological alternatives initially strengthened the government. Considered individually, each might have been expected to have the opposite effect, but the impact of their combined

existence was rather to weaken each other. The Land of Israel
movement. . .which boasted of a broad intellectual base and the
participation of leaders associated with the mainstream. . .was dis-
tressed to find itself defined within a relatively short time as "fanatical"
and "sectarian." The peace movement developed more slowly because
its position was so close to that of a clear majority within the
government. But. . .also found itself successfully defined by the
government as "irresponsible" and "extremist." And precisely because
the perspectives of the peace movement and the government were so
close, the peace movement found itself with less public support than
the Land of Israel movement, which could look upon all Gahal's [the
Herut-Liberal bloc] voters as essentially supporters of the movement.

The government was. . .to brand the movements as irresponsible
extremes so quickly because the very presence of both as competing
ideological alternatives gave the government the tactical benefit of
sheer centrality. . . . In effect. . .the criticism of one group contributed to cancelling out the criticism of the other, and each heightened
the marginality of the opposing movement instead of weakening the
position of the government, whose ability to resist both groups as
impractical extremes [was] enhanced.[16]

In the 1930s the formation of political parties, structures and
movements had been closely linked to ideological aspirations.
Socialist Zionism and Zionist Revisionism were both perceived as
ideological movements before they were perceived as political
organizations. Ideology was a mobilizing force, probably the most
effective system for recruitment of human and other resources in
the formation and institutionalization of the varieties of Zionism.
The institutionalization of Zionism, the political success of Labor
Zionism and the later electoral emergence of Herut, the Begin
party and Revisionism's successor in the new form Likud, were
post-ideological events. The concern shifted to running a state,
winning elections, the welfare of the society, dealing with friends
and foes, dedication to the excellence of Zahal, and above all
political domination. In the 1960s these were no longer ideological
events. Socialist ideology could no longer play the same role it had
in Yishuv times. The instruments of the House of Labor and of the
state were now structures for mobilization, domination, and
control. Socialist ideology became marginal; Zionism became a
concept of the old, of the conservatives of the last generation.
"Don't talk to me of Zionism," meant, "Let's *do*, not incantate."
Ideology, which had been the only language of politics of the

Yishuv and Zionism, was no longer a part of the language of mainstream politics in Israel. To the new generation the primacy of pragmatism, the building of the state, was politics. What cemented the Israeli generations were their contributions to Zahal, to the state, to the modernization of Israel and its economic well-being. The problems of creation, of how to start, where to go from here, no longer seemed relevant in the early 1960s. The post-1967 challenge of LIM and the peace movement—minuscule, seemingly fringe ideological movements—did not at first seem either relevant or politically threatening to the institutionalized political system. Politically they were irrelevant. A faction of LIM which ran in the 1967 election failed to win a single seat in the Knesset; the peace movement won only two seats.

Yet the ideological challenge of LIM and the peace movement to the Labor party was not insignificant. The right and right-of-center of the party wrote, spoke, and behaved like an ideological offshoot of LIM, while the center-left and the left wing sympathized with the peace movement. Galilee, Meir, Dayan, and the party maximalists (maximalist within the context of Labor) never identified themselves with LIM and never established any form of political alliance, not even doctrinal amity. Labor's moderates included Yigal Allon (a new convert), Abba Eban, Arie Eliav, and various Mapam ministers who had close connections with the peace movement. Although LIM was kin to Herut, the latter preserved its autonomy. In fact, Menachem Begin preserved the autonomy of Herut not only from LIM, but from militant religious Gush Emunim, who practically espouse all he has aspired to in his lifelong battle for militant Zionism. The corporate and organizational integrity and autonomy of Zionist political parties and movements, left and right, did not seem the most fertile arena for external penetration. Before 1973, party discipline, authority, and cohesiveness still seemed intact, even while the process of ideological decay and over-institutionalization was in the making. But after 1973, debate in Israel would be conducted along the parameters set by LIM and the peace movement.

The National Security Inner Circle[17]

Israel's political system up to 1973 was highly institutionalized and largely dominated by cohesive ruling groups which also controlled the Labor party, the leading party in the government coalition. Executive power resided with the few who ruled the cabinet, the Labor alignment government, and the national security "kitchen cabinet." The individuals and groups that made national security policy and conducted war could therefore be identified more readily than in most open societies.

Israel, a state under constant military threat since its independence in 1948, has already fought four major wars and maintained one of the most burdensome military budgets in the world—close to 30 percent of its GNP in 1973. Yet the state has no formal legal institutional structure for the making of national security policy. Between 1947 and 1974, national security was conceived and implemented by a small, informal and unofficial body known first as Ben-Gurion's inner circle and later as Golda Meir's kitchen cabinet.[18] Only under Levi Eshkol's reign (1963–1969) did the official cabinet play a significant role in determining national security policy.

No other Israeli governmental agency or institution has had the information, machinery or instruments for designing and implementing the state's security policies. This inner circle monopoly is in part a Ben-Gurion legacy, whereby the minister of defense as supreme commander deals with grand strategy and national security, while the high command executes military policy. The problem with this tradition is that the lines of demarcation of policy by the high command, in particular the relationship between the defense minister and the chief of staff, have never been clearly drawn.

Having institutionalized civilian control, and formalized and depoliticized the Israeli Defense Forces (IDF, or Zahal), Ben-Gurion rarely interfered with military policy. This became the exclusive realm of Zahal's high command. The institutionalization of defense and national security also meant that the IDF high command became the sole arbiter of military policy.[19] The IDF had total freedom of decision-making on such crucial matters as the development and uses of the armed services, their levels of strength, and their weaponry.[20]

Between 1967 and 1974, the national security inner circle was composed of three layers. At the top, national security was the business of Golda Meir, Moshe Dayan, and Israel Galilee. The second level, less cohesive and not always invited to crucial kitchen cabinet meetings, was composed of Deputy Prime Minister Yigal Allon and Justice Yaacov S. Shapira. In defense policy, however, Dayan was preeminent; Meir left it to him to conduct defense policy and policy relating to the occupied territories. In 1971 when Chief of Staff, General Bar-Lev retired and entered politics to become minister of commerce, he also joined the inner security council. On the strategic (third) level, the input of the military was considerable, particularly from General Bar-Lev (until 1971), General David Elazar (1971–1974), and General Aharon Yariv, who was a close associate of Prime Minister Meir, chief of intelligence from 1961 to 1972, and special advisor on combat against terrorism in 1972-1973. All served as ad hoc members of the inner circle. Thus national security policy and military strategy were divided between the political and military inner circle, which became a powerful governing instrument over and beyond its constitutional role. The upper trio's rule was supreme following the formation of the Labor alignment in 1969.

Before the October 1973 war, opposition to the Labor alignment's defense trio was meekly led by Finance Minister Pinhas Sapir, otherwise Meir's most loyal party and government ally and, until his resignation (1974), Israel's economic czar. The opposition of Sapir and Abba Eban was not significant enough to change the national security elite's attitudes and actions. Allon's role was not clear. His ambivalent hawk-dove orientation and his rivalry with Dayan make it difficult to estimate his input to the trio's defense policy. The opposition of Mapam, as part of the Labor alignment, was nil. The power of the trio (who had been bitter rivals before 1969, especially Meir and Dayan) was evident during the 1973 election campaign, when the party platform—better known as the Galilee Document—was modified in favor of policies advocated by Dayan since 1969: to encourage Israeli settlement in the occupied territories and affirm the status quo policy, i.e., reliance on military support from the United States and a militant stance on territories and terrorism.

The members of the inner circle were also the leading politicians of the Labor alignment government. Despite enormous differences in personality and party fractional affiliation, they formed a cohesive, if not coherent, group and worked generally apart from Israel's formal political structures. With the passage of time, national security functions became characterized by conspiracy and a common will of action. The inner circle came to make decisions in relative isolation (even if the issues were debated in the cabinet, the party, and in public); to exhibit such qualities as secrecy, intimacy, and collegiality as well as self-righteousness and self-assurance about taking the right course of action at critical moments; and to engage in political cover-ups.

The inner circle practiced what Irving Janis calls "group-think," a group's high priority for getting along together. Erwin Hargrove says that group-think is characterized, among other attributes, by "excessive risk-taking based on a shared illusion of invulnerability," an ability to block out negative information, a stereotyped view of the enemy, and, above all, a "shared illusion of unanimity."[21]

We must reiterate this mind set of Meir's inner circle. The 1967 war represented the apex of success, the culmination of Labor's political power. In its history, the Labor party had established the pioneer agricultural system and the Histadrut, was first in the formation of Haganah, Palmach, and Zahal, led the way in making the state, its social and economic style and orientation, and organized the 1947–1955 immigration campaign that doubled Israel's population. All had been achieved by two generations, and one—Meir's—saw the experiment all the way from its political inception to the decisive victory over all Israel's foes in June 1967. All these achievements were consummated in 1969 with the creation of the all-inclusive Israel Labor Party and the electoral alignment, the Maarach.

These are cognitive and psychological properties that made the political group at the helm secure, confident, perhaps even arrogant. All the internal and external struggle seemed to have paid off in the establishment of a greater Israel. The leadership was psychologically and intellectually ready for a second partition that would result in an undivided Israel, a secure political and military entity. The mind set of the Meir government was steeped in success despite the enormous adversity. Meir's conspicuous self-righteousness was not without political and realistic foundations. The dream had grown greatly beyond its expected proportions. It was a great and commendable achievement. Thus, the lurking troubles of internal schism, unfavorable world public opinion, the growing challenge of Arab radicalism, the American pressures to return to the old frontier, were dwarfed by the almost eschatological dimensions of the 1967 victory and its fruits. For the Labor party and Israel 1967 was not a war of conquest but the second war of liberation.

Moshe Dayan: The Second Generation

Golda Meir had risen to preeminence among those of the first generation, the Founding Fathers who constituted the real power in the post-1967 Labor government. Moshe Dayan, articulate, active, pragmatist, represented the second generation. As defense minister from 1967 to 1974, Dayan was the most conspicuous and outspoken "second generation" member of the government for the labor and agricultural settlement system in the post-Ben-Gurion era. If Chaim Weizmann characterized the Zionist era before 1937, and David Ben-Gurion from that time to 1967, then Moshe Dayan is probably most representative of the succeeding period. His career was meteoric, dramatic, violent, and often tragic. It spanned most of the history of the Yishuv after 1937, Haganah, Palmach, the wars, Arab-Israeli diplomacy, agricultural settlement, and the political leadership of the Zeirim (youth movement) in Mapai. A portrait of Dayan is both rich and contradictory: a dashing presence, but controversial; arrogant; businesslike; a brilliant soldier and author; courageous; ungrateful; an unreliable political comrade; and a womanizer whose integrity when it came to money was not impeccable. He was charismatic and thought-provoking, continuously challenging yet seemingly inconsistent in his statements and ad hoc writings. Dayan, the quintessential Israeli, physically mutilated in battle and personally without empathy, emerged as the most interesting political innovator between 1967 and 1973.

Dayan was not the choice of the Labor collective in 1967 to become defense minister; Golda Meir, the party's secretary general, fought bitterly against his appointment.[22] Levi Eshkol, then prime minister and defense minister, was not ready to relinquish his defense portfolio. Ahdut Haavoda's opposition to Dayan stemmed from his old ties to the Palmach. Galilee and Ben-Aharon preferred Yigal Allon. But Menachem Begin and Shimon Peres supported him, and in the crisis atmosphere of May 1967 their support, the Zahal high command's lack of confidence in Eskol's military leadership, and organized public protest all combined to catapult Dayan into the defense post. He had been forced on the collective by Nasser's belligerence, and not until Meir's reign began in 1969 was he finally accepted as a colleague, and even then reluctantly. In the end, though, all recognized his political and especially his military talents, his leadership qualities and popular attraction, and the electoral value of his charisma. Dayan was the outspoken maximalist and pragmatic hawk of the Labor party and government between 1967 and 1974.[23]

Dayan begans his long, irreverent odyssey from 1967 to 1973 with a post-war speech echoing LIM. He said:

> We have not abandoned your dream and we have not forgotten your lesson. We have returned to the Mountain, to the cradle of our people, to the inheritance of the Patriarchs, the land of the Judges and the fortress of the Kingdom of the House of David. We have returned to Hebron and Shechem, to Bethlehem and Anatot, to Jericho and the forks of Jordan at Adam Ha'ir.[24]

Writes Rael Jean Isaac:

> In the subsequent months and years Dayan repeatedly associated himself with the government's position of "territories for peace", but increasingly it became apparent that Dayan's definition of negotiable territories was not that of the majority within the government, and more and more Dayan became willing to state his position without the earlier insistence on the personal nature of his views. Rather, Dayan embarked upon an effort to impose his views upon the government. Dayan has frequently been accused in Israel of wavering and inconsistency, of changing his position from month to month, and there is no doubt that it is possible to find contradictory quotations in his speeches. For example, in December 1970, asked if he preferred a larger binational Israel to a smaller one with a Jewish majority, he said he preferred a larger country for defense reasons, "but if it threatens the essence of our Jewish state, then I prefer a smaller one with a Jewish majority." This not only contradicted Dayan's more frequently expressed attitude toward the future of Judea, Samaria and Gaza (where the "demographic threat" was concentrated) but also contradicted the basis upon which Dayan customarily argued, namely the fulfillment of the historic task of Zionism.[25]

Between 1967 and 1973, Moshe Dayan wielded influence far beyond his role as defense minister. To Israel and especially to the international community, Dayan embodied the Israeli victory of 1967, as well as Israel's willpower, determination and stubbornness. His charisma and reputation surpassed that of any single member of the Labor government and its coalition partners. To the Israelis, Dayan symbolized their second liberation since 1948.

He could and did make a considerable contribution to the formation of the second partition state. Although he never subscribed to the LIM maximalist ideology, his political senses told him that the Arabs would not accept the tradeoff of territory for peace.

A collection of Dayan's speeches, essays and statements was significantly entitled, *New Map—Different Relationships*. It is here that we find Dayan's *world view*. In Dayan's new map, the frontier of the second partition state is divided into two basic conceptual structures. One, "secure and guaranteed borders," the other, "facts established in the territories." For Dayan, the frontiers embedded both the hope and the solution for the Arab-Israeli conflict. His was not a simple "Peace for Territories" formula held by Mrs. Meir and the later Rabin government. Peace and territories were deeply linked, and dynamic Zionism dictated that Israel must have the right to settle the territories, including those of the West Bank and Gaza.

In the Golan and Sinai, settlement meant both dynamic Zionism (in Sinai, Dayan planned a port city of 250,000 that he named Yamit) and military security. This was the Ben-Gurion legacy: Jews to settle empty spaces, in deserts. For Ben-Gurion, the Negev had been Israel's southern frontier; for Dayan the frontier was at Sharm el Sheikh, at the tip of the Sinai desert. As he said sometime in 1973, "If we must have peace without Sharm el Sheikh, I prefer Sharm el Sheikh, without peace." He pursued the old Zionist policy and doctrine of settlement and security. In the West Bank, Dayan was concerned with the "nature of peace," not with security, but with facts on the map, with fait accompli. Dayan's concept of "open bridges" meant once more the irradication of frontiers, "no passports, no visas" between the west and east of the Jordan River. In contradiction to Allon, settlement in the West Bank was not to be strategic. Dayan was a skeptic when it came to strategic settlement, arguing that the next strategic problem stems from the first strategic solution, i.e., you build a new "strategic settlement" to defend your former frontier, it now becomes a new frontier to defend.[26]

For Dayan the breaking and dissolution of frontiers was essential. Here he went beyond his mentor, Ben-Gurion, who was frontier-minded and a formalist. He also was more cautious in dealing with the international community. For Ben-Gurion, the Jewish State would create the instruments for peace.

Dayan's concept of peace was more sophisticated, more subtle. Jews and Arabs must live together without barriers between them if peace is to prevail. Ben-Gurion still lived under the shadow of the mighty British Empire, Nazism, and the Holocaust, all without a power center, a state. Dayan, released from these bonds, and head of a victorious liberating army, was not liberating the partitioned state of 1947 but extending the frontier of its successor state. Dayan, in command of a state with a mighty military, exuded greater confidence, less humility and caution than Ben-Gurion. However, he shared with Ben-Gurion the fear of Soviet intervention in the conflict. Like Ben-Gurion, he was pro-American, but he exercised less caution in demonstrating it. Ben-Gurion had been fearful of US-USSR intentions, suspecting they might unite like Assyria-Babylonia and Egypt, the two superpowers of antiquity that crushed ancient Israel several times. Ben-Gurion's policy had been to circumvent the pressure of the superpowers on Israel. Dayan, not oblivious to the mischievous role of the USSR, was nevertheless less sanguine than Ben-Gurion and more daring in his push toward new frontiers for Israel.

In the West Bank, Dayan was determined to establish Israeli law in the territories. The plan was rejected by the government. Dayan did not mean annexation by this, but a strengthening of the military government to "symbolize a change in sovereignty."[27] This was also to be augmented by calling for the establishment of urban centers in Judean and Samarian hills around the Arab towns of Hebron and Nablus. These were to establish Israeli "facts" in the territory. Israel had to "give real content to the borders."[28] To circumvent great power pressure, Dayan refrained from open annexation. In the tradition of Haganah's fortress and tower in the 1930s and Galilee's concept of "One dunam [three acres] at one step, another dunam with the second step," Dayan wrote:

> It is my opinion that in every area we must examine what can be done and what must be done now in order not to waste time and the governmental authority we now possess with the Arabs but even any discussions with them. *In my view, the solution lies in action, not declarations of annexation.* (Emphasis added.)[29]

Dedicated to Arab-Israeli coexistence, Dayan believed that it could come into fruition only under Israeli government rule. Like

Ben-Gurion, he believed that peace with the Arabs could come only after Israel became strong. For Ben-Gurion, peace would be achieved in a strong first partition state. Dayan believed that the second partition state with a new map would create different Arab-Israeli relations accommodating Israel. Pessimistic on peace, he wrote:

> We should regard our role in the administered territories as that of the established government—to plan and implement whatever can be done, without leaving options open for the day of peace—which may be distant.[30]

And in 1972 Dayan said bluntly: "Coexistence of Jews and Arabs is only possible under the protection of the Israeli government and its army. . . .The departure of the government of Israel and its army from the Strip and the West Bank means in fact also debarring Israel from these places." (The official Israeli position was that Jewish settlements were possible in areas that might ultimately be returned, since in a condition of peace there was no reason why Jews could not live under Arab sovereignty.) Dayan urged: "We must persist in implementation of our vision and not be afraid of realizing Zionism, for it is in our hands to build our future." As for the demographic problem, Dayan suggested that the Arabs retain Jordanian citizenship while the territories remained under Israeli sovereignty.[31]

Dyanamic Zionism, Arab-Israeli rapprochement, "facts" in territory, concern for great power intervention, pessimism about peace—all combined to form a strategic concept in the territories that paralleled LIM concepts in many ways even if LIM ideology was far removed from Dayan's outlook. The struggle in Mapai between moderates and maximalists climaxed over the adoption of the party platform for the November 1973 elections. Dayan challenged the Labor party to commit itself openly on Jewish settlement in the West Bank, around Jerusalem, Yamit in Sinai, and other urban centers in the West Bank and Gaza. He achieved partial victory.

Dayan's demands were that the traditional party platform was to be abandoned for the "oral tradition," i.e., stating no specifics on territory but making commitments to the following:

1. That Jewish settlement be open and free to all Israelis without discrimination in the West Bank and Gaza. Jews could buy all the land they wished, if it were for sale.
2. That the military border between Israel and its eastern neighbor be the Jordan River.
3. That the sea port of Yamit be expanded.
4. That Jewish urban and industrial settlement be expanded into the West Bank.

The party resisted accepting all of Dayan's demands. Moderates led by Sapir, Eban, and Allon relentlessly fought Dayan's imposition, but in the end the Galilee Document, the compromise named after its drafter, Israel Galilee, adopted many of Dayan's proposals. Galilee, an ally of Dayan, wrote that the "scope of settlements will be increased," with Israelis buying land or investing in the West Bank to receive tax privileges. On Yamit, the Galilee Document recommended "further study,"[32] but on the most controversial issue of all, the right of Jews to purchase land in Judea and Samaria, Dayan's demands were considerably modified:

> Only in instances in which land is required for constructive purposes—after acquisition is examined from political and security standpoints and after it becomes apparent that it cannot be purchased for the Israel Land Administration (or that the administration is not interested in purchasing it)—will right of purchase be granted to companies and individuals. The committee of ministers will be authorized to decide on granting permission. The Land Administration will also endeavor to acquire land purchased by Jews.[33]

Yet this document still broke all the former rules concerning settlement. License was now given to aspirations that went beyond security; settlement had become a semiofficial government policy. The concepts of territory and Jewish majority were to play once more in the politics of the 1970s, though with the major difference that Israel now faced adamant opposition from the major powers in place of whatever support it had received while in revolt against Britain. This new policy was flatly rejected by Israel's ambiguous ally, the United States.

The Galilee Document and Dayan's doctrine marked a considerable victory for LIM. Although not adopting their maximalist demands, it paved the road to changing the structure of the society and its population, as well as the borders of the second partition state. The challenge from within and without would become pronounced, effective and critical from the October war to the present. For Dayan, settlement was tied to Zionist legitimacy. Israel had been given an historical opportunity to liberate itself after 1967. It should not be missed.

> The question before us is not a question and solution of foreign policy but first and foremost a question of inner will and inner faith, and the answers can only be given by ourselves. First and foremost is the question, "What are we and what do we believe in?"[34]

Thus the opportunity

> . . . also imposed a test—concerning our belief in ourselves and our knowledge of what we want. If we believe and want it, the map of the Land of Israel can be determined by ourselves. If we are prepared for political and military struggle and if we are ready to carry the full burden of the struggle, I believe we can carry it through. It is in our power to withstand military tests and a political struggle, providing we can unite in seeing it the same way, the leadership and the public and the Jewish people.[35]

While the prevailing ideological force, however marginal its political power, was the LIM, and while its influence on the ruling party was considerable, we cannot ignore other forces in an opposite direction. The 1967 war ended for some Israelis the fear of mere survival. The victory was to be exploited for purposes of compromise, peace, and security, and the buttressing of the pre-1967 borders.

THE END OF THE SECOND PARTITIONED STATE: THE COLLAPSE OF THE CONCEPTION AND THE UNWON WAR,

1973–1977

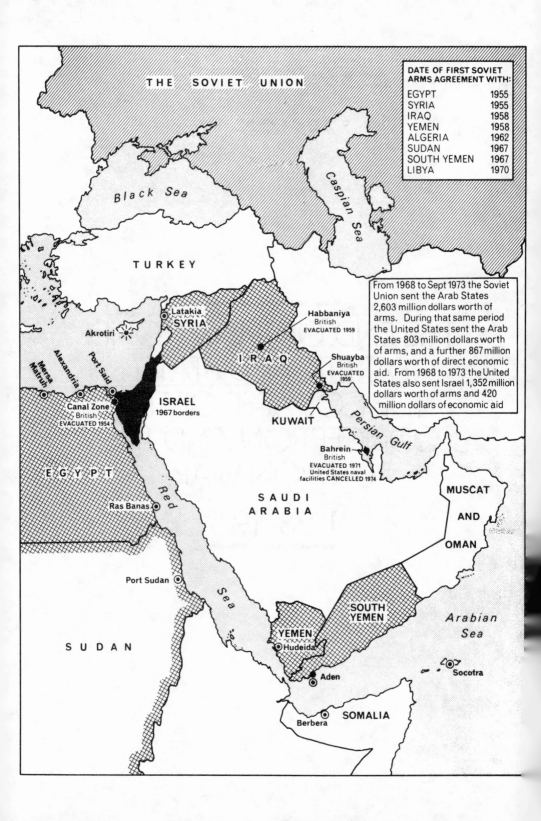

THE SOVIET UNION

DATE OF FIRST SOVIET
ARMS AGREEMENT WITH:

EGYPT	1955
SYRIA	1955
IRAQ	1958
YEMEN	1958
ALGERIA	1962
SUDAN	1967
SOUTH YEMEN	1967
LIBYA	1970

Black Sea

Caspian Sea

TURKEY

From 1968 to Sept 1973 the Soviet
Union sent the Arab States
2,603 million dollars worth of
arms. During that same period
the United States sent the Arab
States 803 million dollars worth
of arms, and a further 867 million
dollars worth of direct economic
aid. From 1968 to 1973 the United
States also sent Israel 1,352 million
dollars worth of arms and 420
million dollars of economic aid

Latakia
SYRIA

Akrotiri

Habbaniya
British
EVACUATED 1959

I R A Q

Shuayba
British
EVACUATED
1959

Alexandria

Mersa
Matrûh

Port Said

Canal Zone
British
EVACUATED 1954

ISRAEL
1967 borders

KUWAIT

Persian Gulf

E G Y P T

Bahrein
British
EVACUATED 1971
United States naval
facilities CANCELLED 1974

Ras Banas

S A U D I
A R A B I A

MUSCAT

Red

AND

Port Sudan

OMAN

Sea

SOUTH
YEMEN

Arabian
Sea

YEMEN

S U D A N

Hudeida

Socotra

Aden

Berbera

SOMALIA

Preface

Ten days following the stunning Six-Day War, Defense Minister Moshe Dayan announced that the new borders were "ideal." In the Labor Zionist tradition "dunam by dunam" (acre after acre) the territorial reaches of the state had certainly widened; but unlike earlier political partitions imposed by foreign imperial powers, the 1967 partition was the first brought about by Israeli military achievement. Dayan, Meir, and Israel Galilee, the leading trio of the 1967–1974 Labor government, now were enabled to establish the "facts" of victory by settling Golan, Sinai, and the West Bank. The Allon plan would combine moral and security purposes and serve as Israel's position when and if direct or indirect negotiations might be expected to resume. Even in 1967 they were aware of the transitional nature of the second partition state; but only after the 1973 war did its borders change.

The second partition state immediately brought forth defenders and challengers. Domestic forces, including the parties, the public and the media, all agreed on issues of security and foreign policy. The national consensus resting on the success of 1967 allowed the decision-makers to dig in and create a national conception that the second partition state was here to stay, and any who challenged it would be rebuffed successfully. The parties were no longer a source for ideological concensus that characterized the political conflict in the Yishuv and during the first partition state. Decision-

makers were no longer seriously divided over security, boundaries, and foreign policy. The informal opposition in the cabinet,
the parties, the public, and the media was rather tame and
relatively silent. The defenders of the second partition state
reigned, supported by public opinion and a national consensus.
The opposition was extremely loyal and was cast voluntarily and
by circumstance into the role of a silent minority. The peace
movement and the Israeli "Palestine State" contingent on the left
and among the intellectuals posed no serious challenge to the
national consensus. But there was a challenge. It did not come
from Britain, as it had in the 1930s, from the United Nations, as
in the 1940s, or from the United States, as in 1956–1957. It came
from the Arabs. In the absence of international political or military
force to modify the second partition state, they went to war in
1973 to change once more the boundaries of Israel.

Israel between 1967 and 1973 was for the first time in its history
in a state of continuous and uninterrupted war—a war of attrition
that culminated in the October 1973 war. Politics since 1973 has
been related to a changed mood created in the aftermath of the
fiasco that year that moved Israel toward accommodation. After
1973 the borders of the second partition state were further
modified, first by United States mediation, then by direct negotiation between Egypt and Israel. Peacemaking, not politics, became
the primary occupation of Israel's decision-makers; they reluctantly but finally began seriously to modify the second partition
state, at least its southern borders. The eastern and northeastern
borders remain roughly those of 1967. Amending and modifying
those borders has been seriously complicated by the emergence of
the Palestine Liberation Organization and by the Palestine nationalist movement that was finally rescued from internal Arab politics
and legitimized by the international community. This period also
marked the end of Labor's long reign and the rise of the
Herut-Likud coalition headed by Menachem Begin, the most
dedicated anti-partition state defender. For Begin, the modification of Israel's eastern frontier was not a security matter but an
historical conception. Begin would not relinquish Judea and
Samaria to Palestinians or anybody else; to him that territory
represented Eretz Israel. Let us see how the journey on the long
road from the "ideal" borders proclaimed by Dayan to the
modification of these borders for the state at peace began.

CHAPTER 8

The Tyranny of the Conception

The tremendous victory in the 1967 war brought Israel something more than military laurels, additional territories, and a redrawing of the Middle East map. It brought with it "the conception"—a mind set that took root in Israeli military and political thinking and stayed there like an ill-fitting house guest right up until October 6, 1973, when Egyptian and Syrian armies moved en masse across the borders. This conception, which was in fact a misconception, colored the thinking of the best military, political, and strategic thinkers in the nation's highest echelons and seeped into the populace as a whole. The swiftness of the 1967 victory and the resultant new borders for Israel, the total collapse of the Arab forces, all helped to form the conception, which centered around what the enemy—the Arabs—could and could not, would and would not do in military and political terms and what the Israelis must and could do in military and political terms. It held that the Arabs could not undo Israel's 1967 achievements by waging another war, could not dictate Israel's strategic choices, and therefore would *have* to accept the 1967 territorial losses as the price for aggression.

Israel's military options and strategic choices also seemed clearcut: the new 1967 borders were ideal and clearly definable, and the IDF could preempt and deny any enemy attempt to reconquer lost territory. It could achieve this by deploying a

228 / ISRAEL: THE PARTITIONED STATE

minimum force and relying on a "foolproof" warning system against enemy attack; only partial mobilization was required to deter the enemy under any circumstance and at any location.

Politically, the conception assumed that no Arab state or combination of Arab states could change the results of the 1967 war through political means, and that indeed, no Arab state or combination of Arab states could or would combine to formulate a political or military strategy that would significantly change the 1967 results. It assumed that time would work against the Arabs, bringing political and internal disintegration, domestic uprising and unrest; the war of attrition (1970–1971) merely demonstrated the exhaustion of the enemy and their inability to combine political and military force. Finally, the conception assumed that no outside force would change the balance of power in favor of the enemy, either politically or militarily.

A whole set of conditions worked to encourage this grand misconception. Israel was united at home, dedicated to preserving the grand achievements of 1967; the country believed that its political and economic system could sustain the expense of defending both the homeland and the occupied territories, and that whatever the conditions of either war or peace, they would be preferable to the military insecurities of the pre-1967 borders.

These were the components of the conception which, after 1967, solidified into diamondlike facets. To Israel's political leaders, military commanders, and citizens it seemed real; if anything, time added to its apparent substance. The men and women who believed in this conception were no dreamers or wishful thinkers. What carried and deepened their faith in it, from the head of state to the cabinet ministers to front-line commanders to the common soldier, was a superior sense of self-assurance—an arrogance—brought about by the stunning success of 1967.

The eventual failure of the conception was caused not by ignorance, but by the unflinching belief that any challenge of any kind would be met successfully under any circumstances. Israel's leaders were blind to the possibility of a serious Arab challenge; they were blind to the possibility of even a partial failure to meet the challenge. There was a kind of hubris in this thinking, a belief in military invincibility. Until the last moment, when Arab forces moved on October 6, 1973, the Israeli military and political establishment was all but paralyzed by the vision of the conception.

Moshe Dayan, characteristically and with little sense of contradiction, had warned several times in 1973 that the Arabs would
never accept the 1967 dictates; at the same time he was reassuring
the people constantly that the IDF would meet any Arab challenge, even while only partially mobilized. And Dayan was
representative of the leadership. When the war came in October
1973, the shock waves that ran through the body politic and the
nation as a whole came not as a result of the war itself, which Zahal
finally and painfully managed to win. The shock was caused by the
exposure of the conception as a false idol. It was not so much what
the Arabs did or did not achieve on the battlefield, but that they
did anything at all. That the Arabs, not the Israelis, took the
initiative, and that preemption did not deter the enemy, amounted
to a strategic defeat for Israel. The Israeli high command, even
after its eventual victory, had to confront the fact that the early
warning system had not worked, that Israeli intelligence had not
proved infallible, and that partial mobilization was not sufficient to
deal with an all-out Arab attack. The conception was false in
military terms and in political terms; it had been built on false
underpinnings. The 1967 achievements had been successfully
challenged, and Israel's strategic choices were much more limited
than originally perceived. Quite suddenly, the 1967 borders were
not "ideal" but fraught with military and political dangers. The
enemy could and did make changes in the territories and boundaries. The toppling of the conception deepened the cracks in the
stability of political authority in Israel.

The Decline of Authority and of Partyism

The highly institutionalized political structure of the Yishuv and
of Israel itself created a momentum of authority that was augmented by its longevity and its uninterrupted success. The relationship between promise and fulfillment was symmetrical. It
began with "Who ever dreamed of a Jewish State in our time?. . ."
which carried with it the heavy political weight of dream-turned-
into-reality, and continued with the spectacular and stunning
military victories of 1956 and 1967. The successful creation and
stabilization of the state of Israel and the military successes that
followed it created an atmosphere of victors and heroes that

colored the political process. It created a symbiotic relationship between success and authority that continued uninterrupted from the early days until 1973.

The uninterrupted cycle of success created an aura of trust between the nation and its political and military leadership. The people completely trusted the military competence of Israel's high command and the political-military judgment of the Labor party's elite. After all, the reasoning went, how could a government composed of Dyan and Allon, the illustrious military leaders, and of the strong and reliable Golda Meir, of the political apparatchik Pinhas Sapir make serious errors?

Even though the 1973 war toppled the conception, the cycle of heroes and victors persisted. Although Dayan was blamed for failing to mobilize Zahal's reserves for war, and although General David Elazar was rebuked and eventually forced to resign, the fact remained that the government, and especially the military, had managed to turn a surprise attack by the Arabs into a military disaster for the Egyptian army and all but total military defeat for Syria. General Ariel Sharon's daring crossing of the Suez Canal between two Egyptian armies had turned the war in the south in favor of Zahal. In Syria, nine out of ten Arab tanks that penetrated through the Golan Heights never returned home.

In spite of these salving and spectacular successes, in 1973 war forced the collapse of the conception and shook the political and military authorities to the core. It brought an end to Labor's political hegemony. The seeds of Labor's vulnerability had been sown as early as 1961 and were apparent in the Lavon affair, but were glossed over by the fruits of the 1956 and 1967 military successes and by the successful uniting of the labor movement.

Israeli politics since 1973 have been characterized by a general decline in historical political institutions and relationships and by the rise of new elites. Since the 1920s the leaders of the Labor political machine, which dominated Israeli politics for four decades, had been recruited mainly from the pioneer Socialist Zionists. Two generations of party leaders can be identified: the pioneers (David Ben-Gurion, Golda Meir, Pinhas Sapir) and their sons (Shimon Peres, Yigal Allon, Yitzhak Rabin, Moshe Dayan, Asher Yadlin, Avraham Offer). After 1967, however, a new meritocracy emerged. This successor generation was different in quality, composed as it was of ex-generals (in the older generation, few generals had joined the political parties), senior bureaucrats and technocrats, and a few university professors and journalists. Its members (then in their forties and fifties) found Yigael Yadin's new party, Dash (Democracy-Change), their natural habitat. This change brought with it the opportunity for new political alignments and coalitions. The creation of Dash in 1977 disrupted the historical coalition—the Labor bloc, the Independent Liberals, and the National Religious party (NRP)—which had governed Israel without a break since Ben-Gurion's first government in 1948. Dash hoped to act as the balance between Labor and Likud (the bourgeois right-wing bloc), as a senior coalition partner. Therefore, like the Free Democrats in West Germany, it would be able to dictate which of the two major parties would serve as the dominant member of a governing coalition. Labor's hegemony had ended; it might be first among equals in a given cabinet, but it now had to practice an unaccustomed accommodation. Although Dash itself failed to act as a balance (and by 1981 became extinct), the days of one-party dominance were over.

Not only was the historical coalition destroyed, but the traditional party blocs were no longer monolithic. The former secretary general of the Labor party, Arie Eliav, split to establish with Uri Avneri the dovish Sheli party. Labor was in a process of decay. The real power of the Labor bloc stemmed from Ben-Gurion's exercise of the neo-Menshevik concept of conquest and domination of economic resources, institutions, and the instruments of public power. Thus since 1920, Labor had dominated and drawn political strength from the Histadrut, or national labor organization. After 1973, however, the Histadrut began to lose its ability to demand discipline from the workers. Following charges of corruption, it found itself unable to bankroll the Labor party any longer. Likud has also experienced serious internal schisms—the defection of General Sharon, the departure of Tamir's Free Center party, and a shaky alliance with its chief partner, the Liberals. In the NRP, the struggle between the party elders and the party's junior and more militant members, who are associated with the orthodox Gush Emunim, is now critical.

The decline of Labor's authority and political leadership, the fragmentation of political parties, and the loss of economic resources mark a revolutionary turn of events in Israel. Although the process of demobilization, the decline of central authority, and the institutional decay of blocs, parties, and groups have not left a political vacuum, uncertainty marked Israeli politics in 1973. Real change took effect only after the 1977 and 1981 elections, but from 1973 onward it was inevitable.

The 1973 Elections: Heroes and Saviors

What were the political conditions before the war and how did the *mehdal* (the misdeed of 1973, as it came to be called) affect the politial realignment in Israel? What would the security and foreign policy perceptions of the new elite be after 1973? To answer these questions, we must begin with the 1973 election, originally scheduled for October. The campaign, which began before the war, was characteristic of the mood of the Israel in which the conception of invincibility reigned supreme. The Labor government went unchallenged on defense and security policies. The campaign revolved instead around Labor's inner power struggles and the challenge of the Likud, the new opposition bloc. But the real, underlying political struggle was between the now adult Israeli-born generation and the generation of their fathers. It was a struggle that cut across party blocs, lines, and movements. The political leaders all had been present at Israel's creation. The Labor party was still led by its founding fathers and its cabinet was composed of veterans like Golda Meir, Pinhas Sapir and Israel Galilee, all veteran Socialist Zionists. The Likud, formerly the Gahal alignment, was dominated by Menachem Begin and his cronies, all of whom dated back to the 1940s. The General Zionist party, Likud's partner, was led by veteran apparatchiks who were all in their late sixties.

The third political bloc in Israel, the religious bloc, also was squarely in the throes of the generational battle, bitterly divided between the old and the young, although in this case the latter had gained a measure of ascendancy by 1973. And if the parties were dominated by the older generation, so was the Histadrut. However, this was not the case with the kibbutz and cooperative movements, where the nonideological technicians and members of the younger generation had taken control. These—essentially a single movement—played a key role in Labor's alignment and its leadership.

Before the 1973 war, Zahal had become the principal source of new political leadership outside the party system. Both Labor and

Likud looked to the IDF for potential candidates, particularly among heroes and veterans of the 1967 war. The IDF had been organized in 1948 and the Palmach as a heroic military force produced a distinguished group of military commanders, and the image that became fixed after the triumphs of the 1956 and 1967 wars. A Zahal commander was the very image of a military superhero: vigorous, straightforward, decisive, aggressive, imaginative, honest, and forthright. The Zahal officer's image, embraced by Ben-Gurion and by the Zionist parties and movements, by international Jewry itself, would inspire Israeli youth and would present to the world the quintessential Israeli. The IDF's retired upper echelon therefore represented an ideal source of potential leadership; they were recruited not to reform political parties but to win elections. In the heroic image of the IDF, the parties would find a gold mine of electoral victories. Whether or not Zahal officers could live up to this incorruptible image seemed politically irrelevant.

Thus, by 1973 the elections were dominated by generals. Curiously enough, although a few generals and juniors officers were punished and singled out for political oblivion, the military was even more in demand after the mehdal. Labor, challenged by Likud, the first serious coalition of the right and center, needed the heroes to enhance its electoral appeal. It asked Yitzhak Rabin, chief of staff in 1967 but a nonparticipant in the 1973 war, to run for the Knesset on the Labor ticket, enticing him with promises of a senior position. Likud also trolled the military waters, landing the hero of the 1973 Egyptian campaign, Ariel Sharon, who became Likud's major political star after Begin.

As a result, the generals gained considerable influence in forming and implementing security policy. In the social-ethnic field, as well as in dealing with problems of health and welfare, the officers had gained considerable experience through their daily contact with recruits. Israeli officers were trained not only as technologists of warfare, but also as human leaders. As junior officers they were in charge of recruits who represented the citizenry of Israel, where conscription is universal between the ages of 18 and 21 for both men and women, and where the reserve army of some 400,000 meets the small (80,000) professional core (in 1973). Officers thus became experts in personal therapy and social welfare, and were trained to pay particular attention to conscripts coming from deprived Afro-Asian Jewish backgrounds, who constituted a sizable number in the recruit intake. The young (40–45) retired military technocratic professional elite were therefore regarded as capable of carrying out political tasks; they were also regarded as catalysts to challenge party nepotism.

Of the public and intellectual elites, the senior Israeli officer enjoyed a reputation of having demonstrated the greatest dedication to the public interest, as well as remarkable personal integrity, courage, and political consciousness. The challenge of the officers was taken seriously by the electorate, which hoped that they would contribute considerably to reforming and rejuvenating Israel's decaying institutionalized political parties. For the Israeli population this was the promise of the war heroes.

Even a successful and promising, well-established and popular political system can and often does demonstrate signs of exhaustion, doubt and insecurity. These are not necessarily altogether unhealthy signs and can, in fact, become functional. The dangers to success are not doubt and insecurity, but arrogance, unwarranted self-confidence, and a firm belief in the continuance of the status quo. In the case of the Labor party and its unmolested rule in Israel, the signs of fatigue and trouble had begun to manifest themselves after 1961. Party and state leadership began to become more rigid, less mobile.

Part of Labor's problem and Israel's as a whole, was that it continued to cling to the old values of volunteerism, unrewarded effort, dedication with little remuneration—values which were good in themselves but could not sustain a developing political system. It was not the formalization of politics as much as its institutionalization which stimulated rigidity and inflexibility and marked the beginning of the end of Israel's particular elan. The beginning of institutionalization also marked the beginning of the decline of authority.

The concept of mamlachtiout had never been clearly inculcated into the system. In Ben-Gurion's time personalism and heroism still prevailed. Even Zahal's relationship to authority was never formally institutionalized; in spite of the growth of a truly professional officer corps, the Yishuv traditions of personalism and partyism prevailed.

However, a state—and a political party in charge of state— cannot act in this heroic fashion. The success of political movements and the successful operation of a state bureaucracy depend not on heroic orientation and practices, but on consensual acts and compromise. Charismatic authority of the kind wielded by Ben-Gurion and Meir can become dysfunctional and disoriented from its original purposes. This is what happened to the Labor elite and its opposition. They became remote from the general Israeli society. They were still living in the context of the Yishuv, a highly idealistic, heroic, but small community. Golda Meir and Menachem Begin had no personal acquaintance with the emerging, changing Israel. The purposes of Zionism and the establishment of an autonomous, stable Jewish state had been fulfilled, but to the political leadership new goals were vague and ill-defined. Only the army officers had day-to-day contact with the general population, and that contact was refracted through the prism of military function, authority and command, hardly the best political conditions to establish contact with the people.

The orientation and political culture of Israel's political leaders, which until 1977 meant Labor, were not successfully transmitted to a nation of post-1948 immigrants. Political subcultures inherited by Jews from non-European cultures continued to prevail. The young immigrant nation had to cope with reconciling Arab-African political culture and the European political orientation and traditions of Israel's ruling Socialist elite. And the new generation was soon to discover the disparity between political leaders' claims of morality, prudence, and heroism and their real behavior.

At the moment when pioneer and frugal values were genuinely needed, the actions of some of the political elite in the Yishuv and Israel were far removed from the ideal model. Political struggles for power became naked and personalist, and there were large scandals involving corruption among the Labor and Histadrut elite in the early and middle 1970s. Labor Minister Avraham Offer committed suicide in connection with an alleged misuse of funds. A candidate for no less than governership of the Bank of Israel, a former secretary general of the Histadrut Health Fund, was found guilty of embezzlement and was imprisoned. Several Mapai and National Religious Party civil servants were found guilty in bank frauds and financial swindles. The politicization of the civil service was endless and the process extended to cultural and social life. This relentless politicization of Israel ironically became politically intolerable. Society, individuals and groups were repelled by and rebelled against the process. The emigration rate matched the rate of immigration and the economic burdens of a perpetually garrisoned state began to manifest themselves. The strain began to show even before the collapse of the conception.

The old leaders had failed to comprehend the generational conflicts created by the coming of age of first-generation Israelis. Changes—demographic, sociological, political, cultural and philosophical—were evident even before 1973. The mehdal and the collapse of the concept opened floodgates for the eventual collapse of the old politics. The shock hit the Labor party and the ruling class most directly. For the first time in its history the Labor leadership was on the defensive and subject to open, at times ferocious, public criticisms. It was unfairly blamed for the conception, which had always been a national delusion, not a party one. The party would eventually face open revolt and a split in its own rank by the desertion of many young, state-trained and intelligence-oriented members who would form the Dash (Democratic Party for Change) group. In the wake of the October war there was widespread and loud criticism of the government, the heroic image, and the heroic leadership of the Labor party. This onslaught on the Meir-Dayan-Galilee regime was unprecedented in the history of Israeli and Yishuv politics. There were cries for Golda Meir's resignation and a trial of Defense Minister Moshe Dayan. A year after the October war, the Meir government did in fact resign, but party chief Pinhas Sapir was not ready for surrender. Sensitive to the challenge of the public outcry, the declining image of the Labor party, and the growth of the Likud, Sapir, bolstered by the presence of 1973 hero General Ariel Sharon, wanted to revitalize Labor and the government by elevating new faces into the public. From the ranks of Zahal came General Yitzhak Rabin, chief of staff of the 1967 victory, ambassador to Washington, and a hero untainted by the 1973 war.

Rabin soon became the candidate that the rank-and-file and the Mapai section of Labor supported for prime minister, but not without challenge. Shimon Peres, the leader of the former Rafi party, and the Ben-Gurionites threw up a vehement and formidable challenge, while Yigal Allon, leader of the Ahdut Haavoda, was pushed by Israel Galilee and the United Kibbutz movement section of Labor. In the end, Rabin was picked by the central committee in spite of the serious opposition from Peres. For the first time in Israeli Labor politics, the party had chosen its candidate openly through the central committee, not by the decision of a select few of the party "politbureau." With the help of Sapir's manipulations, the Labor party won the 1973 election and Rabin was made prime minister.

To pacify the United Labor faction, the leadership was forced to offer Yigal Allon a senior cabinet position as foreign minister, and Shimon Peres took over the next senior position in the cabinet as defense minister. For the first time in the history of Socialist Zionism, the party became headless. The cabinet was led by a member whose roots in the party were not deep and the key ministries were dominated by non-Mapai officers. Again, as in Lavon's time, the defense portfolio was split from the prime minister's. The erosion of authority, the fierce personal struggle between Rabin and Peres, the national malaise that followed in the wake of the 1973 earthquake produced a disunited cabinet which had to contend with American Secretary of State Henry Kissinger's step-by-step diplomacy after the October war. The Israeli team of Rabin, Peres and Allon was a terribly uncomfortable group. As Rabin's former chief in the Palmach, Allon did not accept Rabin's seniority, which created considerable friction between the two. Peres and Rabin continued their rivalry, the former being reluctant to accept the latter's authority. Shimon Peres, although a former deputy defense minister, a Ben-Gurion protégé, and for years the defense ministry director general, did not succeed in dominating the powerful IDF. Having little or no military experience, Peres was lightly regarded by senior IDF commanders and by former Chief of Staff Rabin. Peres thereupon formed a tacit alliance with Chief of Staff General Mordechai Gur. The struggle for power among Rabin, Peres and Allon, especially between the first two, led to a cabinet paralysis. Pinhas Sapir's death in 1975 removed one of the few remaining figures working for unity and further damaged Rabin's authority.

Although the public initially seemed generally satisfied with Rabin, the Rabin government never achieved the wide mandate of trust and confidence that past Labor governments had received. The reasons for this involved the linkage between statism and partyism which had had so much to do with the Labor party's earlier success. To Ben-Gurion, a powerful party was in a position to formalize the institutions and structures of the state. In the final analysis statism was dependent on partyism as much as the party was dependent on the state's bureaucratic power. The relationship between party and state was not dichotomous but in fact symbiotic; one enhanced the power of the other. Ben-Gurion used the

party repeatedly to win major security and foreign policy struggles. The relationship between party and state never weakened
precisely because of Ben-Gurion's continuous struggle with his
antagonists.

Only when the Labor party itself was weakened by its loss of
moral authority did it begin to lose its authority over the state, in
a process that began as early as 1961. Statism lost its momentum
along with the electoral and moral decline of the Labor movement.
Mapai, the center party, wielded more moral and political power
in the state and in society than it did in the united and all-inclusive
Labor party. For Ben-Gurion, Mapai-Histadrut had been the
source of political power. Without it he would no longer have
been in position to create a relatively depoliticalized Zahal. As a
result, each separate political structure became autonomous and
therefore weaker. The collapse of authority was linked to the
political decline of the Labor movement and party. Once the
Labor party ceased to lead and guide the state, and above all to
establish a clear set of realistic conceptions as guidance for policy,
it lost its hegemony and its undisputed authority. The Rabin
government was left without adequate power, authority, and
public support.

CHAPTER 9

Premature Accommodation: The Peace Movement

Some Israeli authors have argued that the 1973 war strength-ened the Land of Israel movement.[1] They assumed that the Israeli military victory would strengthen the hands of the militants. The opposite turned out to be true at least in the short run. LIM was not dead after the war, giving way to a new more militant group called Gush Emunim (The Bloc of the Faithful), composed of religious and militant fanatics. The consequences of the war were sobering in many respects, for the conception was shattered and with it the notion of the infallibility of deterrence.[2]

The peace movement (PM) had equally long and even better established roots in the Yishuv and Israel than did the LIM. While the LIM was strictly a product of the 1967 war, the PM had its roots early in the century, in movements which advocated Jewish-Arab amity, national integration (binationalism), and joint Arab-Jewish fronts against colonialism and imperialism.

The PM derived from several old and established Zionist ideologies and political movements as well as from anti- and non-Zionist ideologies, movements, and persons. The ideas of the PM could be found among the left wing Poale Zion movement in Palestine as far back as 1906.[3] The first Palestine Communist Party (PKP), established in 1919, espoused ideas not dissimilar to some of the PM ideas.[4] The major ideological source, however, for the PM was Left-Socialist Zionism, and the kibbutz and

Hashomer Hatzair movements, which became the Mapam party in 1947. Lehi, the militant movement which split from Begin's Etzel, was also known for its leftist orientation and some of its former members now became some of the most vocal members of the PM. New adherents of the PM included moderates in Mapai and Labor, the academic community, the media, and others of the leftist political culture in Israel.

The peace movement is intensely ideological and its militant wing, like that of LIM, is equally unrealistic and utopian. But while there are few moderates in LIM, the PM mainstream is moderate and institutionalized, especially as represented by the kibbutz and Zionist movements and the Mapam party. While LIM operated independently from its kindred political parties and movements (Rafi, L'Am, Herut, and Zionist Revisionism), the PM had a political and financial power base in the Mapam party and its kibbutz movement. However, the PM, established after 1967, did not gain real effectiveness until after 1973, and even more until the peace treaty with Egypt.

The basic conceptual and ideological doctrines of the peace movement are as follows:

(1) Palestine belongs to Arabs and Jews and should be divided between the two nations.
(2) Jews have no exclusive rights to all of historical Palestine.
(3) Arabs and Jews can live together peacefully.
(4) Neither territory nor nationality dictates Arab-Jewish relations in Palestine/Israel; class and justice are the determining factors.
(5) Militant Zionism and pan-Arabism are reactionary and imperialistic forces.
(6) Imperialistic and local reactionaries created the Arab-Israeli conflict.

The basic ideological premises of the PM, especially the last two, are Marxist revolutionary, antinationalist and anti-imperialist. Their ideological premises are pristine, almost pre-Leninist, cosmopolitan antinationalist orientations.

This is not to say that all PM members or factions believe in Marxist revolutionary ideology. Several in fact relate to the movement only on humanitarian, liberal and pragmatic grounds. But the ideological core of the movement is Marxist, leftist, revolutionary, and has throughout most of its history supported the Soviet Union.

Basically, there have been two trends in the Israeli left: (1) Zionist Poale Zion, the establishmentarian left, Hashomer Hatzair, and the Mapam party, and (2) the anti-Zionist, internationalist, anti-establishmentarian, Poale Zion Smol, the Palestine and Israel Communist parties, Brit Hasmol, Siah, Matzpen, and miniscule fringe coteries.[5] Those of the first orientation consistently attempted to find the most reasonable and acceptable formula for Jewish-Arab political integration and cooperation. In its early history it supported the USSR in a most orthodox fashion, but after the Slansky-Orren affair (a member of Mapam, Mordechai Orren, was arrested with leading Jewish Czech Communists in Prague in 1953)[6] it ended its client relationship with Moscow. The second faction was totally anti-Zionist and always opposed the independent Jewish state unless it became a binational Jewish-Arab state. The Communist party of Israel and Palestine was consistently pro-Soviet and was in fact Soviet-dominated (although a splinter group supported Communist China in the 1960s).[7] It was also well-connected with Arab Marxists and radical Palestinian movements.

In foreign policy, the Zionist or establishment left began as "neutralists" and ended up as anti-Soviet, with ambivalent attitudes on relations with the United States. The Communist and Marxist left, as an instrument of Moscow, was consistently anti-American and anti-imperialist. The Zionist left was ambivalent on relations with the Arab nationalist movement and opposed pan-Arabism while the anti-Zionist left was closely allied with the radical wing of pan-Arabism and Arab nationalism. The Zionist left was dedicated to the Zionist goal of a Jewish majority in an equally and justly partitioned Palestine and Israel, while the anti-Zionist left espoused the dominance of an Arab population in Palestine-Israel.[8]

Although it was ideologically and structurally tied to the historical left of Zionism, the modern peace movement was nevertheless a product of 1967. By then the historical Zionist left, Hashomer Hatzair and Mapam, had become establishmentarian to the core. Mapam joined Mapai in a political and electoral alignment which became the Maarach. Its old revolutionary and Marxist ideologies were, if not entirely dead, shed of their purist Marxist dogmas. Like the old left of Europe and America, Israel's was middle-class and middle-aged, exhausted from half a century of Socialist, Communist and international Socialist struggles as well as from the localized struggles within the Socialist Zionist movement in the diaspora and in Palestine-Israel.

Ben-Gurion's political iron law had been to permanently exclude the left from central Israeli and labor structures and politics. His governments were a Mapai-led coalition excluding the Communists and Herut, the two extreme movements of the left and right. In Ben-Gurion's universe, Hashomer Hatzair and Mapam were Soviet agents in Palestine and Israel, and therefore must be excluded at all costs from the cabinet and Zahal and be relegated to the fringes and margins of Israeli politics. He purged the "leftist" Ahdut Haavoda (hardly a leftist movement even when it joined Hashomer Hatzair to form the Mapam party in 1947). He employed Israeli counterintelligence to spy on the left. Ben-Gurion's policy of excluding the left from Mapai, Histadrut, and the cooperative movement, and his successful imputation of the left as Soviet stooges hurt it badly before 1967. But after 1967 the left was no longer a pariah; the era of Ben-Gurion and Mapai was over.

The young kibbutz generation were neither militants nor ideologues. They were successful pragmatists, technocrats, and nationalists, products of the state and Zahal. The 1967 war, and especially the 1973 October war, created new political space for leftist political action that had not existed previously. The leaders of the peace movement, although primarily from the established left, were now buttressed by the influx of these new kibbutz leftists and pragmatists, who were in rebellion against the petrified ideological confinement of the establishment Kibbutz-Maarach political system. In the peace movement, a movement geared for action, the new kibbutz leftists found a vehicle to their liking.

The left wing of Mapam, the ancients from leftist Poale Zion, independent Marxists, radical liberals, and moderates now found a political platform in the English journal of the left-wing Mapam, the New Outlook magazine. It became the core and the emblem of the peace movement, its center of ideas and action.

The theses and ideas of the peace movement were formalized in the New Outlook. They held that: (1) With Israel now dominant in all of Palestine, the captive Arab Palestine had actually been "liberated" from Jordan. Israel could help establish an independent, friendly, and cooperative Arab Palestine. (2) With pan-

Arabism and Nasserism defeated, new forces in the Arab world would become more moderate and realize that the time for peace and cooperation had arrived. (3) The emergence of the Palestine guerrilla movement after 1967 and that of the PLO as the political spokesman for an independent Palestine would make it easier for Israel to come to terms with united Palestinians. Israel should come to terms not with assorted "reactionary" Arabs such as Jordan's King Hussein, but with an autonomous and genuine Arab Palestine movement. The PLO symbolized the end of reactionary pan-Arabism, and the end of the Arab states' exploitation of Palestinians. As a united and dedicated movement of Palestinian Arabs, the PLO could, should and would become Israel's partner in solving the conflict. The peace movement therefore called for immediate Israeli recognition of the PLO. Some PM leaders actually sought and established contact with moderates among the PLO.

Although the ideological base for the PM is heavily colored by the thinking of Mapam and the left kibbutzim, the movement's most prominent supporters and leaders did not come from the extreme left. One of the influential men in the peace movement was Uri Avnery, editor of the weekly *Haolam Hazeh*. Avnery is now an anti-Zionist, but formerly was a militant Zionist member of Betar (Jabotinsky Youth Movement) and a Canaanite (a super-patriotic Hebraic semitic movement of militants dating back to the 1940s), and was the leading radical member of the Knesset. Today Avnery is one of Israel's most respected journalists, a top-rank investigative reporter.

Another influential PM leader was retired General Mattitayhu Peled, a distinguished military leader who fought to liberate the Golan in 1967 and was probably the best-known and most vocal activist in the peace movement. He is now a leader of the Progressive Arab-Jewish party formed during the 1984 elections, and a new member of the Knesset.

Peled, Avnery, and retired Colonel Meir Pail (a former National Communist) joined with renegade Laborite Arie (Lova) Eliav (formerly Labor's secretary general) to establish Sheli, the first new left party in Israel, which held three seats in the Knesset up to the 1981 elections. The Sheli party, and especially Peled and Eliav, gave luster and respectability to the peace movement. These four joined the movement not as doctrinaire Marxists, leftist

Zionist ideologues, or Soviet stooges, but rather were representatives of Israel's new and pragmatic generation. Peled and Pail
were distinguished soldiers. Eliav was one of the chiefs of Bricha,
which organized illegal immigration to Palestine from 1945 to
1948, was commander of the legendary ship *Exodus*, and was
administrator of Lachish, a model system for successfully integrating the 1948 immigrants into the agricultural settlement system.
Eliav had been the darling of Meir, Eshkol, and Sapir and as
secretary general of Mapai-Labor was a most valued peace movement property.

These men joined the peace movement for nondoctrinaire
reasons. Rather, as one peace movement member writes "There is
another reason why I do not want to hold on to these territories.
I do not want to be a colonist!. . .If we hold on to the territories, we
shall enslave the people living there, since practically all the
inhabitants do not want to live in the State of Israel or in a
protectorate, and they say this even today, while still under the
shock."[9] The peace movement, in fact, succeeded in attracting a
number of nondoctrinaire individuals and groups, including what
we can call "the professors," a group of distinguished social
scientists, historians, and moderate Zionists who were anticolo-
nists and are convinced that the only solution to the Arab-Israeli
conflict is the formation of a moderate, independent Arab Palestine. The professors are not so radical as to advocate a PLO-
controlled Palestine, but some would accept a moderate Palestinian-Jordanian solution. All are firmly opposed to both Labor and
Likud government settlement policies.

I would hardly classify the professors as bona fide PM camp
followers. They were new converts, all of them respected, established and partially active in the moderate wings of Labor. Some
are old-time adherents of the Hebrew University Brith Shalom
movement of the 1930s, then a group of German-Jewish liberal
academics who were opposed to the establishment of a Jewish
state and who believed in "peace and harmony" with Arabs.

The events of 1967, however, revived both the old men and old
orientations. The professors were more vehemently opposed to
the extreme right wing policies of LIM than they were passionately for the peace movement. They were anti-jingoist more than
they were committed to the historical courses of the left movement. For them, peace meant a pragmatic, rational orientation.
The professors felt that Palestine, which was the obstacle to peace,

could now be established since Israel dominates the population and territory from which an independent Palestinian state would be carved. The professors were also concerned about their image abroad. Many of them had served as visiting professors in America and had deep links to liberal American academics, and were worried about the image of Israel in America and Europe as well as their own individual images.[10]

In the sense of being liberal, the professors were part of a larger group that helped to establish and increase the influence of the peace movement after 1973. Prominent political figures became their allies even though they could not be said to be followers. Among them could be counted former foreign minister Abba Eban, Labor's leading moderate. Eban certainly opposed leftist ideologies and any type of radicalism.[11] He represents the Sharett liberal-moderate, pro-American wing of Labor. Eban espouses views identical with the liberal-centrist, non-Marxist portion of the PM. Eban and Yosi Sarid, a young, opportunistic Labor member of the Knesset (who after the 1984 formation of a national unity government split and joined the Citizens Moderate party allied with Labor), would become the only Labor politicians to actively support the peace movement. Sapir, Allon, Yadlin, Bar-Lev and other Labor moderates operated strictly along party lines and stayed away from it.

Other groups were also attracted to the peace movement, including the moderates of the National Religious party and the religious workers' parties. Some were opposed to Zionism for religious reasons, believing that only the Messiah could proclaim redemption. Their commitment to the state was meager although their concern for peace was high. Some even believed in Jewish-Arab social and economic cooperation. None, however, believed in political unity and integration between the Jews and Arabs. Removed from Marxism, radicalism, Zionist nationalism and secularism, the moderate and small orthodox parties had no difficulty in accepting an independent Arab state next to Israel. They were concerned with Jewish survival, not with class or images of self. To them, the land of Israel was holy no matter who owned it. For them, 1967 did not have the religious significance it did for the NRP's militant young nationalists and later for the Gush Emunim. They were never active in the peace movement, but their politics certainly dovetailed with the PM militants.

The most compelling group in the peace movement was made up of latter-day converts who formed the post-1973 Peace Now (Shalom Achshav) movement loosely connected with the dovish wing of the Labor party. Their forerunners were the radical pragmatists and the professors group. The radical pragmatists were concerned with Israel's internal strife and external plight and believed that Israel must rush into a political settlement before the PLO became more radical, the Jewish militants settled more land, and the Americans put greater political pressure on Israel. Above all they were concerned with Israel's image among American liberals and Third World intellectuals. They were nondoctrinaire, nonradical, good middle-class citizens, thinkers set to rescue Israel's moral image from those abroad who were truly committed to deny Israel's right to independence and existence. (Today, support for Peace Now comes primarily from Jewish liberals and academics in the United States. The Sheli party was whipped in the 1981 elections.)

The Marxist wing of the peace movement meanwhile sought a solution through binationalism and an independent Palestine. It held that the road to true socialism both in Israel and Palestine would be paved only after peace, when Israel could finally join the "international progressive forces." The pragmatists, Peled, Eliav and others, sought an Israeli-Palestinian rapprochement. For Eban and the professors the solution was a modified Jordanian-Palestinian state. For the moderate orthodox group, the survival of the people of Israel, not the state of Israel, was at stake.

In spite of its varied and multitudinous makeup, between 1967 and 1973 the peace movement made little inroad into the public life of Israel. The Land of Israel movement dominated the editorials, the streets, and the public already captured by the 1967 mystique and the conception. There was no political space for an organized populist peace movement. It was the 1973 war and the collapse of the conception that paved the way for the peace movement. But even then, the real power and the real initiatives lay with the government, not the movement as such. The political forces that split from Labor after it joined Likud in a national unity government, Mapam (with seven members in the Knesset) and the Peled-Miary Progressive party, today represent the remnant of the peace movement, which was clearly rejected by the majority of Israeli voters in the 1984 elections.

The Protracted Road Toward Peace

It was not the peace movement, but the governments of Israel which initiated and continued the official work of peace and accommodation, and did so little-influenced by the PM. The Labor government of Golda Meir began the negotiations with Egypt. The "Kissinger shuttles" begun in 1973 with Meir continued under Yitzhak Rabin, extending and refining troop separation agreements in the Sinai and Golan Heights. After 1977 the work continued under Menachem Begin, whose government reached a peace treaty with Egypt in March of 1979. If the indirect impact of the LIM on the Begin government was considerable, the influence of the peace movement, despite its varied adherents and followers, was marginal indeed.

The reasons for the basic ineffectualness of the peace movement under both Labor and Likud governments are varied. Israel is a highly institutionalized political system. There is little room or space for action by extrapolitical, extraparliamentary political movements, projects or associations. The most critical issues, which tend to involve foreign policy and national security, always have been resolved by a very small elite shielded by the party and the system from internal (party) and popular criticism and embarrassment.

After 1967 the political leaders of Israel seemed to identify somewhat with LIM, at least partly because LIM goals and policies had their adherents among the ranks of popular generals. The confidence and even the arrogance of the military commanders could be tolerated then, especially in the wake of victory and the rise of the conception. This was not the case with the government's attitude toward the peace movement. Israeli governments, whether left of center (1948–1977) or right of center (1977-) have been categorically antileftist and apprehensive when they perceived and felt pressure from the left. Although the peace movement's most prominent spokesmen were the figures of the center and the left of center such as Eban, Eliav, and the professors, the governments of Eshkol, Meir, Rabin and Begin identified the peace movement with the establishment left, with the Zionist Mapam and the fringe left. The establishment Labor government's antipathy and hostility toward the Zionist left was part of a struggle that went back to the 1920s, when Jewish leaders led Arab workers on May 1, 1921, to riot against Jews in Tel Aviv.[12] The far left has always been identified with Jewish detractors, radical Arabs and Stalinist Russia. The influence of Mapam and especially Hashomer Hatzair on the Labor government was marginal. The Labor government in fact rejected the peace movement.

However, the nonleftist sympathizers of the PM, with their moderate solution to the Palestinian problem, often found a forum with individual members of the Labor party, the cabinet, and the Histadrut. Abba Eban, Pinhas Sapir, Lova (Arie) Eliav (before he joined Sheli) and Avraham Offer often expressed themselves clearly in the spirit of the centrist peace movement, but they failed to modify the positions of those in government who refused to associate with the Marxist-dominated movement. Their impact on foreign policy, even though Eban was foreign minister, was meager. Rabin, as ambassador to Washington, wielded far greater influence with Meir. Sapir's and Allon's fidelity to the party negated their effectiveness as peace advocates. Sapir, for instance, never thought to openly challenge the authority of Meir or Dayan on defense.

The Labor moderates or doves did indeed try to influence the militants in government. But the history of the Labor movement was replete with lessons from the splits of 1942 and 1965, lessons that solidified the need to preserve the unity of the party, Histadrut, and the movement at all cost.

The moderate's lack of impact also had much to do with the organizational structure of the party and the movement. The elitist group of Meir-Dayan-Galilee were not only senior members of the party, but in the party's division of labor they were the security and foreign policy ministers, while Sapir-Offer-Yadlin, also senior party members, were in charge of the bureaucracy and of economic and domestic issues. One group seldom interfered with the other.

Above all, the prime minister, the leader of the party and its authoritative figure, was always more than first among equals. Meir, as a militant influenced and aided by Dayan and Galilee, was never challenged by Sapir. Eban, although foreign minister, was isolated by Meir and Rabin and thus belonged to neither the security nor the domestic group.

The impact of the peace movement on Likud was even more minimal than it was on the Labor party. Begin and his Herut followers and NRP allies considered and treated the peace movement and its members as Soviet and PLO agents. For Likud, the PM was an anathema full of Jewish and non-Zionist traitors. Begin saw the peace movement as an instrument of the PLO and the USSR in the Middle East.

Thus the process of peace has been carried out by the official governments of Israel since 1973 and the ultimate impact of the peace movement has been all but negligible. It was the war, pressures from the United States, and international public opinion that moved Israeli governments finally to begin negotiations over territories. The irony is that the peace movement had little if anything to do with beginning the negotiating process.

Kissinger Diplomacy and Crisis Management: 1973–1975

Between October 1973 and September 1975, United States National Security Advisor and Secretary of State Henry Kissinger accomplished a Middle Eastern diplomatic feat: two Israeli-Egyptian troop separation agreements and one Israeli-Syrian troop separation agreement. Kissinger clearly supported the belligerents without favor and without passion and succeeded in freezing if not deescalating the conflict. This is not the place for a diplomatic history of these tortuous and seemingly endless negotiations but their impact on domestic policies and in turn the impact Israeli politics had on the negotiations are crucial.

The 1973 war certainly called for crisis management. Kissinger harnessed himself to it on the day of attack, October 6, 1973, and a year later the process, which began with negotiations over Suez and the Golan Heights for the disengagement of Egyptian, Syrian and Israeli forces, had resulted in the total withdrawal of Israel from territories occupied in 1973 and in a partial withdrawal from territories occupied in 1967.

To persuade the belligerents into accepting his services Kissinger first had to act as their sympathizer and convince them that he "understood" them, without having any illusions as to the difficulties that faced them. Kissinger, for example, as early as September 26, 1973, told the Arab foreign ministers and ambassadors at the UN: "There are no miracles. . .what is needed is to find ways to turn what is presently unacceptable to you into a situation with which you can live." A prolonged war in the Middle East, he said, would create a high possibility of great power involvement.

To woo the Israelis, Kissinger stated that "the US will not allow the Soviets a victory in the Middle East," and to Egypt he said, "I believe that for the first time in five years we are engaged in a real dialogue with the Arab world." The diplomacy of attrition depends upon the establishment of trust between the mediator and the belligerent party. As Kissinger said, "I think I know the Egyptian position very well, and I have attempted to present it as fairly as I could to the Israeli side on several occasions."

In January, 1974, Terrence Smith of the *New York Times* wrote from Jerusalem on the outlook in Israel during the Egyptian disengagement negotiations: "It is the first time that Israel has placed her faith in something other than her own strength." Kissinger, he said, "has managed to win the confidence and respect of the Israeli authorities. The Israelis are convinced he has played straight with them and fairly represented their views to the other side." Kissinger was seen as the trusted man, the confidant of both adversaries.

By the end of 1974 Henry Kissinger had succeeded in achieving a separation-of-forces agreement and a temporary cease-fire among Israel, Egypt, and Syria. Such an act had been unnecessary in 1967. At that time Israel had won a clear and decisive military victory. The Arab armies had been defeated and Israel's borders extended to their geographically logical limits—the Suez Canal in the south, the Jordan River in the east, and the Golan Heights in the north. The 1967 cease-fire agreement was not guaranteed by the Americans, who evidently had learned from the difficulties they had experienced in keeping their promise to guarantee the 1957 Suez withdrawal agreement.

The aspirations of the belligerents, both immediate and long-range, were utterly asymmetrical. Egypt hoped to exploit the American desire to play a key role in the Middle East negotiations and at the same time to keep a Soviet military option open. Israel hoped for a step-by-step peace arrangement with the Arabs via Kissinger. Meanwhile Kissinger, who had halted a final IDF offensive, hoped to secure a role for America in the affairs of Egypt, which, as the most important Arab country, would carry American influence to the rest of the Arab world.[13] Through

Kissinger, the team of Meir-Dayan-Eban and later Rabin-Peres-Allon achieved a measure of respite for Israel as well as a troop separation agreement supported and defended by the United States. The American economic and military grants that came with the Kissingerian peace helped the government overlook the impending economic crisis. The quadrupling of Zahal in manpower, equipment, and the level of United States aid restored the nation's confidence in its officer corps.

The Kissinger diplomacy had a deep impact and potential for Israeli domestic politics. Kissinger became the central political target of the hawks, and Rabin's weak government, led by three men who neither trusted nor respected one another, failed to pursuade the nation as a whole that Kissinger's mission would be successful. Rabin, Peres, and Allon were by their own doing under continuous strain. Even those who accepted Kissinger's diplomacy doubted the durability of its political value for Israel, although they hoped it would "pacify" the United States so that the latter would continue to support a strong Israel and supply the IDF with up-to-date equipment. At best, Kissinger's diplomacy was perceived as necessary to maintain the American-Israeli entente; it was never viewed as presaging a breakthrough in the Arab-Israeli impasse.

The political decay of the ruling party was not the result of the failure of consensus alone, of course. Neither consensus nor ideological polarization would have made such an impact on the 1977 election if the historically cohesive, ruling Socialist Zionist movement were not being ripped asunder and exposed as infested with corruption at the top. Rabin was a victim of this surge of Israeli "post-Watergate" morality. The bureaucratization of the party's apparatus, the oligarchical and septuagenarian rule over Mapai and the Histadrut (which was certainly firmly installed before 1973) also had its effect. So did the transformation of the Histadrut from an instrument of society or the organized workers into an arm of the party and the state. The absence of functional union differentiation in the Histadrut, its domination of Israel's major industrial and agricultural corporations, and its bureaucratization weakened and distorted the Israeli economic system. Antiquarian egalitarianism, distorted wage and salary structures, featherbedding, the decline of incentives, payment for fictional productivity increases, and unrealistic remuneration—all were by-products of Labor's political consolidation coupled with the political decay of the bureaucracy. They were now challenged by the workers and the middle class, two groups that represented Labor's major constituency.

These factional disputes enhanced the growing political fragmentation, and the general decline (for this was true of the opposition parties as well) contributed to the collapse of authority, the growing political and ideological polarization, and the widening gulf between party and society. Historically, the ruling party had been able to internalize debate, to integrate cleavage, to modify conflict, and to curtail and even to eliminate extremist tendencies. But it was no longer competent to do so. Political struggles now took place between more persons and groups, and their differences were greater than before. Conflict was no longer confined to the meeting rooms of the executive and central committee.

The labor party was weaker than at any time since 1935. It was split down the middle over the struggle between Yitzhak Rabin and Shimon Peres for the premiership. The party was deeply split by generational conflict, by disputes over foreign and security policies, and by the questions concerning the future of negotiations with the Arabs and the Palestinian issue. The time had arrived for changing the guard.

Cleavage: Fragmentation and Polarization, 1973–1977

The October 1973 war further deepened the gulf between hawks and doves and completely disrupted Ben-Gurion's historical consensus. The debacle of October 6 to 8, known as the mehdal (misdeed), brought to the surface the political undercurrents that had existed since 1967. The outward manifestations were a spate of protest movements, the rise of Dash, the personal and political struggle between Rabin and Peres, the emergence of the idealistic, ultranationalist and orthodox Gush Emunim, the radicalization of the NRP, and the rise of Revisionist Zionism as the Likud party became Israel's second most powerful bloc.

Although it is too early to assess fully the impact of the Gush Emunim youth movement or even its prospects for survival, the kind of militant nationalism it represents has always thrived in countries beset by internal troubles and deep-felt frustration.

However, it is not similar in kind to the radical nationalist youth movements in Central Europe in the 1920s that laid the foundations for the rise of fascism. The Gush is a symptom not of real political instability but of the decline of ruling parties and thus of governmental authority. The Gush depends on organizational and financial support from the radical NRP, and it also draws strength from the tacit support of independent and organized hawks and even from some of Labor's hawkish former senior officials. The Gush undoubtedly thrives more from the paralysis of authority, the dissipation of the ruling party's power, and the IDF's reluctance to use force to stop illegal settlement in Arab lands than from its own inner organizational strength.

Ideologically the Gush is messianic in orientation. It is not a descendant of the mystical Sabbatian movement. It is exclusively nationalistic. It is not universalistic as the Sabbatian movement in history was. It believes in Zionist activism and its purpose is to "aid" the supreme powers in accomplishing the concept of redemption fulfilled in settling historical Eretz Israel. The Gush however tore asunder the Zionist wheel. The Gush abandoned the Zionist concept that "Israel lives not isolated from other nations," or that "Israel will be a member of the world of nations." For the Gush, Israel is an isolated nation regionally and internationally.[14]

The tacit backing of public opinion, the government's ill-defined policy over settlement of occupied territories—its failure to distinguish "secure" from "holy" lands and to exert its authority over the limits of settlement and annexation—are other factors that freed the Gush to act. The NRP participated in the government between 1975 and 1976, and its young ministers shielded the Gush from the radical measures that the majority of the Rabin government was ready to take against it.

The disruption of consensus was gradual but steady. It could be observed both in security policy and in domestic social policy. For the first time the workers' councils seriously challenged the Histadrut: rising expectations on the part of the workers led to strikes, and there was a vociferous public outcry against nepotism and creeping Socialist corruption. As a result, the Labor party was in 1977 weaker that at any time since 1935. It was split down the middle over the struggle between Rabin and Peres for the premiership. The struggle over the foreign policy platform on the Palestinian issue, with Moshe Dayan calling for unilateral Israeli administrative withdrawal, demonstrated the deep splits within the party, splits that were not reconciled even after the February 24, 1977, party convention. A party deeply driven by generational conflict, by disputes over foreign and security policies, and by questions concerning the future of negotiations with the Arabs and the Palestinian issue could not lead, even if it remained the senior party in a government coalition. Electoral decline since 1973 cost the party key cabinet positions given to coalition parties and complicated further the conduct of foreign policy.

Yigael Yadin's new party, Dash, inherited the malcontents from the historical Labor constituency. It, too, was deeply split over foreign and security policies, as was demonstrated by the composition of its central committee, elected in the middle of March 1977 and divided between outspoken hawks and doves. It too could not agree on the future of the territories, the creation of a Palestinian state, and the type and style of relations with the United States. In fact, it was united only on domestic reform, the need for political and institutional changes, and the destruction of the established bureaucracy. Its successes stemmed largely from its exploitation of negative feeling against the ruling Labor party, and these very successes enhanced the political cleavages within it. Yadin's party was not a cohesive body any more than Labor, and finally disintegrated in 1981.

There remained little prospect of a new foreign policy consensus being forged after the 1973 elections, given the atmosphere of ideological and political polarization. In discussing Israel's relations with the Arabs it is therefore useful to review the range of opinions of the different political groups on the principal issues at stake between Israel and the Arabs before the 1973 elections.

Negotiations and Territories

The moderates in the Labor alignment (Shimon Peres, Yigal Allon, Chaim Zadok) still adhered to the Kissinger formula of step-by-step diplomacy and were willing to make much more important concessions to Egypt in Sinai than to Syria in the Golan Heights. They rejected package deals.

Yadin's party, composed of both powerful hawks and important doves, did not speak with one voice on the subject of negotiations. It did, however, agree that negotiations should take the form of a Geneva conference. Rather than confronting one united Arab delegation in Geneva, Yadin preferred what he called a "pending" system for negotiations—two-tier negotiations, in which negotiations are conducted separately with Egypt and Syria, with all agreements requiring the approval of both adversaries. The best outcome to be expected from negotiations would be a nonbelligerency, open-borders agreement. In exchange for such an agreement, Israel would make a substantial but incomplete withdrawal from Sinai and the Golan Heights. The Geneva conference would provide an imprimatur for the pending agreement system, not act as a negotiating conference itself. Yadin was adamantly opposed to negotiating with an Arab coalition.

Moshe Dayan opposed step-by-step negotiations. He firmly believed that to deal with an Arab coalition, however ineffective, would be to give up all control of the direction and nature of the negotiations, to the obvious detriment of Israel. He therefore strongly advocated simultaneous negotiations with Syria and Egypt. He opposed Rabin's concept of separating Egypt from Syria.

In 1973, Dayan still agreed with Anwar al-Sadat, Egypt's leader since Nasser's death in 1970, that neither Arabs nor Israelis were really ready for peace and might not be for a decade or more. Dayan therefore suggested an Israeli withdrawal by phases—for assurances of nonbelligerency, minor withdrawals; for an eventual "true peace," major territorial withdrawals. Yigal Allon, the truest devotee of the Kissinger formula, would not insist on a strict Arab nonbelligerency commitment if another accommodating formula could be reached by the United States negotiations.

Dayan hoped for an effective but limited American negotiating stance; he wanted the United States to initiate, promote, and conduct the negotiations, but he did not want to be bound to accept any imposed solution. Yadin concurred with Dayan on this point. Both would restrict the American role to mediation. By contrast, the Labor moderates and their allies sought more active American intervention in negotiations. Peres opted for American military guarantees if Egyptian-Syrian concessions fell short of fulfilling Israel's minimum desire for a state of nonbelligerency, however vaguely defined.

The rigid Likud position was somewhat modified after the party conference in January 1977. Menachem Begin's commitment not to abandon "an inch of territory" was no longer the party's guiding formula. Likud was willing to make territorial concessions in Sinai and the Golan Heights in return for "true peace," and preferred a very restricted mediating role for the United States. The NRP position was strictly circumscribed by its rigid views concerning the future of settlement in the West Bank and the Palestinian question.

The Palestinian Issue

Israelis were bitterly divided on the Palestinian question. It is still the most volatile political issue in Israel. Virtually the only common denominator between hawks and doves is that any Palestinian state must recognize Israel as a sovereign Jewish state. Although many doves distrust the PLO, Labor moderates might have accepted some type of Palestinian-Jordanian solution, including a token PLO representation in the Jordanian delegation to the Geneva conference. The Mapam party, a Labor alignment partner, would have accepted an independent Palestinian state on the West Bank and Gaza if it were not led by the PLO and if it were demilitarized. So would the former Sheli party as well as extreme Labor doves. Yet it is absolutely clear that no government of Israel was able to obtain a majority in the Knesset for a PLO regime on the West Bank of the Jordan River or a demilitarized PLO state.

The NRP and Likud radicals, who favored the annexation and settlement of Judea and Samaria (the Arab West Bank) did not accept any solution to the West Bank question that involved Palestinian rule. Begin considered a PLO Palestinian state a stalking horse for Soviet interventionism. Dayan believed that the formation of a PLO state would make the Middle East a tinder-box because neither Syria nor Jordan really see such an entity dividing them from Israel. He believed that any future Palestinian solution would depend upon a rapprochement between Israel and Egypt and Syria, a prospect that he believed to be far in the future. To Yadin, in contrast, political and socioeconomic reform in Israel itself must take precedence over foreign affairs, including the Palestinian problem. Thus, unlike Rabin and Allon, Yadin was indifferent to the type of regime that was established east of the Jordan River. Yadin was willing to negotiate with a PLO Jordanian state over the future of the West Bank, but he too felt the area must be demilitarized, no matter what regime or state controlled it.

Israel in Transition: 1973–1977

This multiplicity of views, positions, and ideologies reflects the character of the people of Israel and the nature of a democratically oriented state. The views in this wide range are as old as Zionism and basically echo Revisionist and Socialist Zionists historical orientations, now modified by events and circumstances. Yet, although no one abandoned the most cherished commitment—total dedication to a secure, independent, and democratic Jewish state—the divisions within the political and ideological blocs were greater than at any time since the establishment of the Zionist Yishuv in the Palestine of the mandate era.

Israel since 1977 has been a society in transition. In the absence of a cohesive ruling party, no institution has been in a position to modify and integrate cleavages, and certainly not to eliminate them as Ben-Gurion did. But Israeli governments are still highly representative if not authoritative. Internal stability still endures. Political systems do not collapse because consensus is no longer prevalent or because public opinion has become polarized. In fact, it is the existence of cleavage, if it is integrated politically, that guarantees the return of consensus. However, the prolonged failure to integrate cleavage and to institutionalize and modify ideological polarization in Israel is bound to impair the resolution of the Arab-Israeli conflict. Disruption of consensus characterizes the United States, Sweden, the Netherlands, West Germany, and Japan, as well as Israel. But such companionship should not suggest complacency. Rather it should demonstrate the critical political obligation to ensure the stability of a party system, the integration of cleavage, and the reinstitution of national and political consensus, which are imperative for the preservation of the few precious contemporary democratic political systems.

Theodor Herzl in Basil (*Zionist Archives in Jerusalem*)

The Hashomer guard, the first Jewish military organization in Palestine, ca. 1909 (*Zionist Archives in Jerusalem*)

Zeev Jabotinsky in Jewish Legion uniform during World War I (*Zionist Archives in Jerusalem*)

David Ben-Gurion lecturing before a group of Socialist-Zionists, 1928 (*Zionist Archives in Jerusalem*)

Chaim Weizmann testifying before the United Nations on UNSCOP, 1947 (*Zionist Archives in Jerusalem*)

David Ben-Gurion, center, holding the Declaration of the State of Israel (*ZAJ*), May 15, 1948

הכרזת מדינת ישראל

The Haganah ship in Haifa bringing the
first Jewish immigrants to Israel, 1949
(*Zionist Archives in Jerusalem*)

The desert warrior and the
lamb: David Ben-Gurion
in semi-retirement in his
kibbutz, Sdeh-Boker, De-
cember 1954 (*Israel Gov-
ernment Archives*)

Prime Minister Moshe
Sharett in a press conference, 1955 (*Israel Government Archives*)

Defense Minister Moshe Dayan and Chief of Staff Yitzhak Rabin, accompanied by the IDF Front Commander of Jerusalem, triumphantly enter the gate of the Lionsen to the old city of Jerusalem, June 7, 1967 (*Israel Government Archives*)

Prime Minister Levi Eshkol and the Israel Navy, 1967 (*Israel Government Archives*)

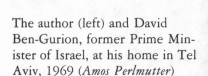

The author (left) and David Ben-Gurion, former Prime Minister of Israel, at his home in Tel Aviv, 1969 (*Amos Perlmutter*)

Ariel Sharon, "King of Israel," after crossing the Canal in 1973

IDF Chief of Staff David Elazar (far left) and Egyptian Defense Minister Gamasi (in white) (*Israel Government Archives*)

Prime Minister Golda Meir and
Defense Minister Moshe Dayan
observing IDF maneuvers in Sinai

Prime Minister Yitzhak Rabin,
1976 *(Israel Government Archives)*

Prime Minister Shimon Peres
(left) and author *(Israel Government Archives)*

Anwar Sadat addresses Israel's Knesset on November 20, 1977. In the middle is Yitzhak Shamir, then president of the Knesset. At right is Ephraim Katzir, then president of Israel (*Israel Government Archives*)

Menachem Begin (right) and Ephraim Katzir, 1978 (*Israel Government Archives*)

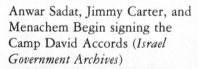

Anwar Sadat, Jimmy Carter, and Menachem Begin signing the Camp David Accords (*Israel Government Archives*)

General Avigdor (Ben-gal), Commander of the Israel Eastern Front during the invasion of Lebanon (*Amos Perlmutter*)

The author (left) and General David Ivry, Chief of the Israel Air Force during the war in Lebanon (*AP*)

IDF in conflict with religious settlers in the West Bank, members of the Gush Emunim (*Israel Government Archives*)

THE THIRD PARTITIONED STATE

STATE

1977–1984

SECTION V
Preface

On May 17, 1977, a seismic political tremor shook Israel, the Middle East and the rest of the world: Menachem Begin, little-known, bespectacled, sporting reams of rhetoric and a weak heart, was elected prime minister of Israel. The tremor which resulted was made up in almost equal parts of trepidation, incredulity, anxiety, and plain astonishment, depending on the vantage point from which the event was perceived.

The man just elected to Israel's highest political post seemed oddly unimpressed by the event. He sounded very much like a man who was accepting his just, if belated, due. He did not even think that his election was the high point of his life. That, according to Begin, had already passed, during Israel's war for independence, when he led the Etzel underground movement.

Begin's victory was the final twist in an election which had already defied belief, an election which was as untypical in its outcome as it was in its conduct.

The initial Labor candidate, reigning Prime Minister Yitzhak Rabin, a war hero and former IDF chief of staff, had been forced to withdraw from the head of the ticket, resigning after a scandal over a foreign bank account he maintained. His successor, Shimon Peres, a Labor party warhorse, was a superb behind-the-scenes manager, but he lacked charisma. Begin had plenty of charisma, but there was serious doubt about his physical survival when he suffered a major heart attack during the middle of the campaign and was rumored to be at death's door.

Begin's victory was typical of his political life; it was an act of willful, dogged survival and perseverance, almost biblical, Joblike in quality. To appreciate the enormity of the event, one has only to imagine that Harold Stassen, after decades of trying, had suddenly been elected president of the United States. Since Israel had gained its independence in 1948 and begun holding elections, Begin had entered every election as the principal and sacrificial opposition to Labor. Routinely, without a ripple, he lost every election. Throughout, he faced some of the giants of Israel's history, most frequently his old political enemy, David Ben-Gurion.

If Begin's victory stunned Israel, it shook and puzzled the rest of the world. To the world at large, Begin seemed to have popped out of some secret and as yet unidentified box, a reactionary anomaly who had "suddenly" and "miraculously" emerged as a major political force. Precious little was known about him, except in terms of shrill clichés. He had been "a terrorist." He engineered the bombing of the King David Hotel in 1947. He was a reactionary, a radical, an extremist, perhaps even a "fascist." Experts around the world feared for the prospects of peace in the Middle East. In Washington, where President Jimmy Carter was moving toward a Palestinian solution in the Middle East, one White House official described Begin's election as "the extreme right wing coalition. . .scoring a clear-cut victory."

In Israel, the Laborites were disappointed, even stunned. There was an air of unreality about a non-Laborite sitting in the prime minister's chair, something that had never happened in Israel's brief thirty-year history as a state. But the Labor stalwarts, from Rabin to Peres, saw the election as a fluke. They went about their usual business, battling for power within the Labor party, while viewing Begin with contempt. They sat back, haggled among themselves, and waited for the collapse of the Begin government, which they felt would not be long in coming. They were wrong. It took six long, hugely eventful and shattering years, and by then, the Labor party was in no shape to challenge Begin or his successor, Yitzhak Shamir. In 1984 it was forced to form a National Unity government with Likud. Shimon Peres was to head this government for the first twenty-five months and then was to be succeeded by Shamir, late in 1986.

The Zionist movement, the governments of the Yishuv, and the first two partition states were composed of similar political coalitions. The early Zionist movement consisted of parties and movements from the left to the right, but by 1933 the right wing, led by Zeev Jabotinsky, split to establish the Revisionist Zionist movement. The left too remained in the movement, except for the Jewish communists, who were always anti-Zionists. The government of Israel between 1949 and 1977 was a continuation of the left-of-center and center coalition that started with modern Zionism and carried through the Yishuv. The Revisionist orientation represented in Israel by Begin's Herut electoral coalition was excluded from rule in both the first and the second partition states. The third partition state marked the first real break with the grand Zionist coalition and certainly with the historical consensus on partition. Begin's first government, 1977–1981, marked a transition, while his second, elected in August 1981, ended the old coalition. The new coalition government dominated by the Herut party was center-right in orientation. The Zionist consensus, upheld by Labor's hegemony, was weakened with the second defeat of the Labor party in 1981. It fell to Begin, followed by Yitzhak Shamir, and Revisionist Zionism to resolve Israel's international and Arab problems. This government was the first in the history of Israel to reject partition and the pragmatist policies allied with the historical evolution of the partition state.

The 1984 National Unity government could not change the deeds of the previous Likud-dominated governments. The 1984 government also is transitional. Although it represents the grandest Zionist coalition of all time, composed of both Likud and Labor, it does so at the expense of both. It is also the least coherent of all Israeli governments. This government can last only if it essentially accepts Likud's or Labor's vision of the future of Israel's borders. This government represents the verdict of a deeply divided Israel. It does not represent a national consensus, which on the whole would be radical and nationalist.

CHAPTER 10

The Begin Era: 1977–1983

Although his Herut party was almost extinct by 1967, the Menachem Begin-Yitzhak Shamir Likud electoral alignment may eventually grow into the major alternative to the Labor party. The 1967 war, as argued earlier, revived old and forgotten debates and postulates. The 1973 war accelerated the debate and demonstrated that the Labor party was in a continuing process of decline.

From 51 Knesset seats in 1973 Labor was reduced to 34 seats in 1977 and could not recapture power with 47 seats in the 1981 Knesset. Meanwhile, Likud grew from 38 seats in 1973 to 44 in 1977, and to 48 in 1981. In 1984, despite the folly in Lebanon and a deep economic crisis, Likud captured 41 seats to Labor's 44—a real decline for the opposition party. Ideologically the circle was complete in 1981. While in the 1930s the Zionists had argued about what kind of autonomy and independence they could win, after 1977 the debate was over how much, if any, autonomy the Palestinians could achieve. Thus 1977 is also the harbinger of a third Palestine state. The Palestinians would fight over what was left of the West Bank territory and the Zionists would hold to the territory of complete Eretz Israel.

The first partition had been the making of the British and the United Nations, together with Socialist Zionism. The second partition was brought about by Nasser. The third partition is in the hands of Revisionist Zionists. The circle is now complete. The

debate over binationalism and Arab-Jewish equality and federalism died long ago. The moderates will accept a secure Israel of
1967 plus minor territorial rectifications. The rejectionists—i.e.,
those who reject the partition of Palestine—will, at least in the
case of Ariel Sharon, offer the Palestinians the East Bank of the
former mandatory, which is now the state of Jordan, with the
remainder of the West Bank to be colonized by Israeli settlers.
The debate is still to be resolved between Labor and Likud in and
out of the new government over what kind of partition should be
made. Labor is willing to partition the West Bank; Likud will
accept once more the original mandatory partition of Palestine as
made by Churchill in 1922. The Arab-Israeli struggle did not end
with Camp David. The Egyptian Sinai was never a part of Palestine
and thus Likud could relinquish it. This is not the case in the
Golan Heights, annexed in December 1980. Although the struggle over partition is no longer connected with life or death for
Israel, it still concerns security, unless the PLO and Arab radicals
modify their aspirations and claims. The struggle over the third
partition state begins with the rise of Begin and Likud to power in
1977, and has not ended yet.

Camp David achieved an Egyptian-Israeli peace treaty, but it
also established a new arrangement for the third partition of
Palestine. This, in essence, was Begin's autonomy concept. For
Begin, 1967 and Camp David were signposts in the direction of
the fulfillment of complete Eretz Israel.[1] The issues, principles,
and opposition concerning the autonomy plan of 1977 were
reminiscent of the debate over partition in the 1930s, but the
differences were substantial. In 1977 an independent, powerful
Jewish state occupied all of historical West Palestine. This government was led by Jabotinsky's, not Ben-Gurion's, heir, who
achieved a crowning success by becoming the first Jewish leader to
establish peace with the most powerful Arab state and leader.
Jewish settlement in the West Bank, begun by Galilee and Dayan
during the Labor administration, was accelerated by the bulldozers
of Ariel (Arik) Sharon. Begin and Sharon established even more
"facts" on the map than Dayan had.

The partition of Palestine was no longer a privy matter of the
imperial Great Britain. Nor could the superpowers (unless combined) really impose a solution on Israel for a new partition of
Palestine. There was a new national consensus *against* any new
partition of the eastern part of the West Bank in Palestine.

Certainly the opposition to an independent or PLO state was clearly registered in the June 1981 and July 1984 elections. The international community, as in the 1930s and 1940s, might influence or even legislate (e.g., the UN 1947 partition or the anti-Zionist Resolution of the 1970s), but it could not impose upon Zionist Israel and the Palestinian Arabs a solution that comes short of either's maximum orientations. Peace with Egypt was achieved because of Begin's willingness to surrender Egyptian territory (Sinai) for real peace, but the Likud governments of 1977 or 1981 were totally unwilling to exchange the West Bank for an insecure peace or, for that matter, to help establish an Arab Palestinian state which is not east of the Jordan River. The 1984 coalition will break if its leader, Shimon Peres, proposes territorial compromises.

The third partition of Palestine is also reminiscent of the 1930s in another way—total rejection by Palestinians as long as the Zionists continue to settle in occupied territory. The differences are that world public opinion is more sympathetic to the Arab Palestine cause than ever; that Israel is now cast in colonial garb, seen as an unregenerate, not very generous expansionist state; that the PLO seemingly is more flexible than Haj Amin al-Hussaini's earlier fanatic organization; and that the PLO is more independent of Arab states and politics than was the Palestinian Arab nationalist movement in the 1930s and 1940s.

Until the summer 1982 war in Lebanon the PLO had substantial international support, not unlike the Zionists in the 1930s. This is gone now even if Palestinian champions in the West have not left the podium or given up their rhetorical, and in some cases cynical, support for the PLO. Yet the fact remains that the Likud electorate and leadership is confident it will establish a third Jewish commonwealth over all Palestine—except for the East Bank, i.e., Jordan—with a weak Arab autonomy in the West Bank and Gaza that is politically and militarily dependent on Israel. These are the Likud goals of the third partitioned state. Labor in decline has lost its primacy and influence in what is now a growing nationalist camp in Israel.

The 1977 election results, known in Israel as the *maapach* (turning about), was an extraordinary event in Israeli politics. After four decades of Labor domination, the party of the political parvenu arrived. The movement ostracized by the organized Yishuv, the leaders of the *porshim* (renegades), Jabotinsky's heir

Menachem Begin and his Herut party and Likud movement took over political power. This stunning upset had not been foreseen by political polls and it shocked both friends and foes of Likud. It was the impossible made real. The 1977 election was supposed to be Begin's swan song, his eighth and last election effort to become prime minister and lead Herut and Gahal-Likud out of the political wilderness into power. It was more than a personal victory for Begin; it was a political victory for Likud. And the rise of the Dash party with fifteen Knesset seats made the Labor alignment defeat even more decisive.

Yet not until the 1981 elections did Menachem Begin become the master of both his coalition and Israel's political system. Although the Likud shared with Labor almost half of Israel's electorate in the 1984 election, the orientation of the government's policy is in the direction of Likud, which now dominates the nation's symbols; that is: no more PLO, Palestine state, or consulting with the United States on what are Israel's principal security needs and deeds. Populism mixed with demagoguery was ushered in by the Begin-Shamir ruling coalition. Begin's popularity initially skyrocketed during the Lebanese war, but the war's consequences foreshadowed his, Sharon's, and possibly Likud's demise by 1984. Despite Begin's undignified withdrawal and Likud's failure to capture the government in 1984, the political trends in the nation demonstrate the ascendancy of Revisionist conceptions of national boundaries and security.[2]

The Rise of Likud

Perhaps it is too early and the times are too unstable for us to gain a proper perspective on the rise and institutionalization of Likud and the decline of the Labor party in Israel, but the two are established and profound political phenomena, dovetailing in historical time. They are political events which, while linked, are also separate and occurred because of identifiable reasons and factors. Likud won at the polls and established itself, and Labor lost and continues to be unable to reassert itself even if today's prime minister, Shimon Peres, is the leader of the Labor party, in spite of often golden political opportunities.

There are basically six factors involved in the rise of Likud and in the slow and continued decline of Labor:

1. Menachem Begin, both as a politician and as a charismatic political leader and statesman.
2. The change in the ideological, social, cultural and political climate in the wake of the watershed 1967 and 1973 wars.
3. The emergence of a new body politic and a nationalist electorate.
4. The demographic transformation of Israel.
5. Changes in the nature of the state and the growth and use of military power.
6. Changes in the regional and international climate and environment.

Menachem Begin has managed to rise above or move around every cliché ascribed to him by his political opposition, his detractors, and foreign observers. He has always been much more than a strident rhetorician, demagogue and fanatic. He proved to be what his Labor party opponents never thought he could be: a rational, political, shrewd statesman, a master politician, and a man willing to compromise. Throughout his political career, beginning with Betar in Poland, through Etzel in the Yishuv, finally to Herut and Likud, he has demonstrated time and time again that, although he may be an extremist in his rhetoric, he is a pragmatist in the task of pursuing his Revisionist Zionist dreams, much in the manner that Labor leaders were pragmatic in pursuing their own dreams and goals. Although he always strove to arrest partition and keep his eye on the dream of Eretz Israel, Begin nevertheless compromised all along the road, beginning with his early career.[3]

With Betar in Poland and with Etzel, Begin was always more influenced by the Revisionist founding father Zeev Jabotinsky than by the extremism of Etzel-Stern and other militants. The radicals were at war with the mandatory and carried this war on actively, but Begin shielded his Betar compatriots from the activist influences of their comrades in Palestine. With Jabotinsky and David Raziel dead (1940; 1941) and Avraham Stern assassinated in 1942, Begin took over as leader of Etzel and draped the mantle of Jabotinsky about himself.[4]

Far from pursuing radical goals, Begin instead called for an end to what he saw as a Jewish civil war, a war that Etzel-Lehi radicals wanted to wage against the Labor-dominated Haganah-Palmach. Begin instead attempted to establish a military and operational alliance among the three Jewish undergrounds, Haganah, Lehi, and Etzel. He was close to concluding an agreement with Haganah commanders Moshe Sneh and Yitzhak Sadeh when David Ben-Gurion got wind of the negotiations and obliterated Begin's plans. Ben-Gurion was simultaneously contemptuous of Begin and shrewd in his dealings with him. He rightfully suspected Begin's intentions, surmising that Begin wanted to play a key role from a real power base in the new state of Israel once the war against the Arabs and the mandatory had been won.[5]

During the *Altalena* affair of 1948, when Ben-Gurion foiled an Etzel operation shipping arms for Etzel in Israel on a ship designed for Jewish immigrants, Begin turned out to be surprisingly and scrupulously careful. Acknowledging defeat, he demonstrated political foresight by completely integrating Etzel into the newly formed IDF rather than establishing it as a separate, elite unit. In the aftermath of the war, although he was still a political symbol of Revisionism, he established Herut and managed to bring an end to official Revisionism by abolishing its organizations and financial resources.[6]

Begin turned his miniscule Herut party into something of a political fortress of radical nationalism within the chambers of the Knesset, displaying his virtuoso skills as a parliamentarian and drawing strength from Israel's democratic and legislative instruments. The effort often seemed futile, with failure after electoral failure as Labor portrayed him as a fanatic, an ideologue, a windbag and zealot, unstable and radical, a grandstanding demagogue.

Yet Begin was indeed a skilled rhetorician in the Zionist tradition, and perhaps one of Zionism's finest. He was also an astute leader with great charisma and something of a coalitional genius, quite deserving to be compared to the skills of Pinhas Sapir and Levi Eshkol, who forged so many Mapai and Labor coalitions. Begin demonstrated that he was not so single-minded as supposed when he helped form the National Unity cabinet by joining a Labor-dominated government as minister without portfolio in 1967, although many referred to him as "minister of no inch of territory." In fact, as his record shows—the record of his coalition with the General Zionists and the Gahal block in the founding of Likud, his overtures to Egypt, and the Egyptian-Israeli peace treaty—Labor's caricature of Begin was not only wrong, but seemed often to work against Labor. The Labor stalwarts had come to believe in their own propaganda.

The second factor to bring about the rise of Likud and have a profound effect on the fortunes of Labor was the almost messianic fervor that gripped Israel in the wake of the stunning 1967 military victory over the Arab armies, a fervor heightened still further by the 1973 war. The 1967 victory was a watershed event in Israel's political history. It not only ended the first partitioned state, but it irrevocably altered the political, cultural and social climate of Israel and the way the country saw itself. Before 1967, the political culture of Israel seemed restrained, defensive, its military posture benign if daring, still reflecting Ben-Gurion's notion of the small, insecure, partitioned state threatened by its neighbors. Victory, and the resultant windfall in territory and change in borders, changed all that. Ben-Gurion may never have limited the idea of borders and territories, but neither had he ever prepared either Labor or the IDF for such a monumental change. After 1967, the forces of a new kind of revisionism were on the march in Israel, bolder, more assertive in nature, filled with an almost religious spirit that often defied pragmatic and rational politics.

Interestingly, Begin was not in the forefront of this change. The essence of Jabotinsky's Revisionism, which Begin espoused, called for revisions in the mandatory and, for Begin, in the United Nations partition, but the spirit of the new, aggressive revisionism went beyond that. The forces of the new revision were not Likud or Herut or even the Land of Israel movement, but the graduates of the National Religious Party youth movement, Bnai-Akiva, who saw in the 1967 victory and in the "miracle" of Israel's survival in the wake of the 1973 war nothing less than an act of God, the moment of redemption. To these activists, to leaders like Geula Cohen of the Herut splinter, the Renaissance party, and to Hanan Porat and the Gush Emunim, it was time to fulfill the dream of Eretz Israel, to regain all of the lands of biblical and historical Israel. Their yearnings and strivings, religous and messianic in nature, sawed away at the cosmopolitan and pragmatic roots of the Labor partition state.[7]

As early as 1967, and continuing into the 1970s, a radical change in demographics had also occurred in Israel, a change involving ethnicity and nationalistic orientations, which Labor was increasingly unable to harness, and which seemed inevitably to drift toward Begin and Likud. Voters were younger, the ruling clique of European Socialist-Labor-Zionist Jews which had ruled

Israel so long was dwindling, and the ranks of the electorate and the body politic were being swelled by non-European Jews from Middle Eastern and African countries, a new, younger breed of Israelis with no love for Arabs, aggressive, wanting to be heard. The new electorate contributed heavily to the swing toward Revisionism. They had little in common with the highly secular nature of the Labor party. Their heroes were Begin and Sharon, because first Begin, then Sharon, had captured the radical-nationalist symbols which the new electorate would respond to.

Begin's electoral victory of 1977, which shocked both Labor and foreign observers, was nothing less than a man and his rhetoric finally finding a home with a newly changed electorate. Although their leader was stricken by a heart attack during the 1977 election, Begin's party nevertheless managed to win 44 seats in the Knesset. If the stunned Labor party thought this was a political fluke, they managed to miss all the political signs. Likud had been on the rise since 1973. The 1977 election solidified its political position, but the 1981 elections, close as they were, institutionalized Likud in the political mainstream. In 1981 Begin literally rose from the ashes, from a 25 percent approval rating in the polls and from another heart attack. He went on, with the considerable political help of Sharon, to squeeze out another stirring electoral triumph, one that signaled the institutionalization of Likud as much as it did the disarray and the declining political fortunes of Labor.[8]

The 1981 elections constituted both a Likud victory and a major Labor defeat; they showed the almost complete depletion of leadership within Labor's ranks. By 1981, and even in 1984, Labor's ideology appears out of step with the times in Israel; its once-glorious ranks are depleted, its ideas seem merely echoes from times gone by. Ben-Gurion, Levi Eshkol, Golda Meir, Moshe Dayan, Yigal Allon, and Pinhas Sapir are all dead. There are no giants to replace them. Yitzhak Rabin is a fine general and perhaps a great chief of staff, but an undeniable failure as a politician and a man who holds petty grudges. Shimon Peres, able and a man with a concern for details, is no great leader and lacks charisma, yet under the Labor-Likud deal he is prime minister for the first twenty-five months of the 1984 government. Labor leaders cried loudly about the desertion of Dash and the heated clash between Ashkenazic and Sephardic Jews, but in reality Labor lost because of a dearth of leadership and because its ideology failed to respond successfully to the changes in Israel's political culture and electorate. Its values still lie with the old partition state. The politics of Israel since 1967 have become the politics of Eretz Israel and Revisionism, and Begin, Sharon and Shamir are its most articulate spokesmen.

Begin: Conceptions and Roots as a Leader[9]

Before examining in detail the two Begin governments and their implications for the history of the partitioned state, it is important to briefly review Begin's roots as a leader of Revisionism and show how the reality clashes with the myths and clichés promulgated about him.

To understand Begin, one must understand to a degree Zeev Jabotinsky, the founder of Revisionist Zionism, Begin's mentor and hero much in the way that Ben-Gurion is Begin's shadow and nemesis. Jabotinsky spoke and wrote in some dozen languages. He wrote poetry in Russian and Italian, translated Poe's *The Raven* into Hebrew, and was Zionism's most articulate, passionate, brilliant and charismatic speaker. Begin became his emulator. He speaks and writes six languages, and still speaks Hebrew with the slight Polish accent reminiscent of both Jabotinsky and Ben-Gurion. Begin, always conscious of language, makes a relentless effort to speak Hebrew not only meticulously but to mix with it biblical phrases and antiquarian words to such an extent that he sometimes seems like a man from another era. His language and manner of speaking are curiously devoid of modern Sabra (native Israeli) colloquial Hebrew. To hear Begin is to hear the voice of Jabotinsky, and the haunting echoes of the traditional Darshan, who, in Jewish tradition, was a Friday night traveling speaker and moralist who specialized in oratory and who lifted the spirits of ghetto-dwelling people unto the Sabbath. Begin emulates his rabbi in voice, talk, dress, walk, oratory and erudition. Even today, he is still a disciple.

Jabotinsky was a leader in the philosophic and passionate sense, infusing a spirit of revolt among Jewish youths in the East European diaspora. Begin's gifts lie in other directions as a party leader and organizer, a preserver of institutions and organizations. Jabotinsky, a cosmopolitan European, would get carried away by his own oratory, his linguistic internationalism, so much so that it was once said that he would get drunk on his own words. Begin is a much more sober, self-conscious person. Essentially, Jabotinsky was a nineteenth-century liberal in the manner of the other founders of Zionism—Theodor Herzl, Max Simon Nordau, Shmariyauh Levin, Louis Brandeis, and Chaim Weizmann. His faith lay with the ability of the great powers to bestow a charter upon the Jews to create their national home. Jabotinsky had his flaws, one of which was a singular lack of talent for organization and preservation. Although he split from the World Zionist Movement in 1925 to establish the new Revisionist Zionist movement that would eventually challenge Great Britain, he was no Lenin or Ben-Gurion, or even a Begin. In fact, Revisionist Zionism would decline under Jabotinsky, and would come close to disintegration and destruction under its more radical leadership until Begin picked up the reins and almost single-handedly assured its survival. Betar, Jabotinsky's youth movement, was transformed before but especially under Begin. A nationalist youth movement, Betar gave birth to two radical underground terrorist and military organizations, Etzel and Lehi. That was not Jabotinsky's vision.

World War II proved to be disastrous for Etzel and Revisionist leadership. By 1940, Jabotinsky was dead in America. In 1941, while on a mission with the British against a military installation in Iraq, David Raziel, Etzel's commander, was killed. In 1942, the British C.I.D. assassinated the Lehi leader, Avraham Stern. The Revisionist underground had become unglued, leaderless. It was left to Begin to pick up the pieces and put them together again.

Under Avraham Stern, Lehi had turned into an exclusive Hebraic messianic movement. The radical Etzel swallowed Jabotinsky's revisionism after 1940. Under Begin, Etzel, although preserving Jabotinsky's essentials, abandoned its founder's dedication to legal military action and Zionist diplomacy. Begin was a transitional figure between Jabotinsky and the young militant Palestinian Betar-Etzel leadership. Begin saved the Etzel from degeneration into factional rivalries, personal assassination, and turmoil. In this, he demonstrated his skill as politician and party organizer. Not that Begin was a colorless party functionary; he distinguished himself as a leader, an especially trustworthy person, a reliable colleague, and a true comrade. Although he was no original ideologue and at the time displayed little charismatic talent, Begin was—and still is—a cautious, highly disciplined, self-conscious person with a great deal of personal perserverance and political acumen. It was because of his skills as politician and conciliator that he was chosen to head the National Military Organization of Etzel in Palestine, in June 1944.

Begin immediately began to apply his skills as conciliator, mediator, organizer and leader, with his stoic patience and loyalty. He sought to turn Etzel into the successor to Revisionist Zionism and to anoint himself as Jabotinsky's true heir. He never merely perceived himself to be a revolutionary guerrilla heading a paramilitary organization, or even as an underground leader. To achieve stature and legitimacy for Etzel, he set upon what appeared to be a contradictory course. On the one hand, he mounted a vicious guerrilla struggle against Britain, combining open revolt with propaganda, terror, and political skill. He hanged British sergeants in revenge for the hanging of Etzel people, he broke into Acre prison to release Etzel prisoners, he planned and executed the King David Hotel bombing, but at the same time he advocated Etzel conciliation with the Haganah, Lehi, and even with Britain if the British would leave Palestine. Begin was a prototype, one of the early leaders of a modern national liberation force, who turned a group of romantic bandits and gangsters into a political military organization.

Even as he attempted conciliation with Haganah-Palmach, he continually clashed with that group and with the overlords of the Mapai, especially Ben-Gurion. Haganah members were arresting and molesting Etzel and Lehi members and contributing information to British counterintelligence services, but Begin never completely severed his ties to them. During this hunting season (the Sezon), Begin refused to retaliate against the Haganah: "There will be no war of Jew against Jew," he proclaimed. During the *Altalena* affair Begin was to show considerable restraint, even if awry judgment and a remarkable sense of survival. It was a political struggle as much as anything, and as usual the struggle was with Ben-Gurion, who would not brook the rise of a serious challenge to his and Labor's power.

The *Altalena* affair, or as Ben-Gurion preferred to call it, "The Affair of the Sacred Howitzer," was a landmark in the history of fledgling Israel, and helped determine the future of not only Begin, Etzel and Herut, but Ben-Gurion as well. In 1948, Etzel bought a ship called the *Altalena* (Zeev Jabotinsky's pen name) in the U.S. Officially intended to transport Jewish immigrants from Europe and America, Etzel meant to use it to transport fighters and arms. Ben-Gurion saw this as a challenge to Israeli stability and to both the power of the Yishuv and himself. Even with Arab armies on the march, Ben-Gurion made a critical, hard, decision to destroy the ship so as to disarm Begin and Etzel. Ben-Gurion saw it as a way of avoiding civil war between the right and the left, and of avoiding dissension in the post-war years. He destroyed the ship and in the process managed to malign and brand Begin even more as a radical and irresponsible leader. Yet it was Begin who gave in, who acted responsibly by merging the cadres of Etzel with the Palmach and Haganah. Though henceforth he was always in the opposition, he nevertheless put the interests of Israel above his own political fortunes, which were not to reach fulfillment until decades later.

Begin: Alternative to the Partitioned State[10]

Menachem Begin's Herut party, which consistently won some 20 percent of the electoral vote, did not exactly receive a roaring national mandate on security and foreign policy. Begin and his party had been rejected by the electorate for over thirty years and eight elections, and the majority of the nation was not enthusiastic about Begin's ringing cries for *Shlemut Hamoledet* (the complete land), which, echoing the language of the Land of Israel movement, meant some form of Judean and Samarian annexation.

Begin and Likud had become the political beneficiaries of the decline of Labor, the rise of Dash (Democratic Party for Change), and Israel's disgust with the corrupt practices of Labor. In addition, the hawkish elite within Labor had joined Likud. This included L'Am, the remnant of the Ben-Gurion party, and, most significantly, Moshe Dayan. In addition, the National Religious Party had been taken over by the militants, and Gush Emunim, a scion of the movement, added to the fire. The election, in the end, was as much a Likud victory as it was a case of the nation rising in protest against the Labor policy, against the failure of the conception, and against the mehdal of 1973.

Menachem Begin is the Last Mohican of the grand old Zionist generation born in the diaspora. Confounding some expectations, he assumed office as if he were a born statesman rather than a guerrilla. His authoritative political style, coupled with strict regard for the forms of legal and constitutional processes, had not been seen in Israel since Ben-Gurion retired in 1963. Like Ben-Gurion he was autocratic, patriarchal, and charismatic, the leader of both his Herut party and the right-wing coalition government bloc, Likud—the National Religious Party (NRP); Yigael Yadin's center reformist party, the Democratic Movement for Change (DMC) (who joined the Likud Coalition in November 1977); and assorted Orthodox religious parties. On the personal level he was more relaxed, less tense than Ben-Gurion, and courteous, pleasant and open where Ben-Gurion was not.

Begin, again like Ben-Gurion, was a Herzelian Zionist. Theodor Herzl regarded Zionism as essentially a political movement for the territorial settlement of the Jews and considered the Zionist Congress he organized in 1897 as the instrument to proclaim the Jewish aim of establishing a state. This political solution to the Jewish problem required that the great powers bestow on the Jews a political charter over a territory destined to become their independent state. This political Zionism—diplomacy with the great powers over the establishment of a Jewish state—was the Herzelian legacy that held overwhelming appeal for both Ben-Gurion and Begin.

Here the similarity between Ben-Gurion and Begin ends. The real chasm between the two is wide. They were deeply divided on strategy to achieve Jewish political and territorial independence. Ben-Gurion represented the mainstream of political Zionist thought. Both he and former President Chaim Weizmann aspired to establish a state populated, if possible, only by Jews. Thus, although Ben-Gurion was a territorialist, for him practical Zionism meant the settlement—urban and rural—by Jews of those mandated areas of Palestine that were either sparsely or not at all populated by Arabs. In the case of the two major Jewish urban centers, Jerusalem and Haifa, where a mixed Arab-Jewish population existed, Jewish numerical, social, economic, and political hegemony over the Arabs was tenable.

The models of the practical Zionists were actually Tel Aviv, a new and strictly Jewish city, and the agricultural collective and cooperative settlements. Ben-Gurion and the Socialist Zionists conceived of these agricultural settlements as being exclusively Jewish. Their idea was the "conquest of the soil," i.e., of empty or sparsely populated areas of land, by settlement, and the creation of an autonomous Jewish working force in the Jewish sector of Palestine. Population and sovereignty were seen as related variables. Jewish hegemony would be established over territory that was not occupied by Arabs and was therefore suitable for Jewish settlement; a Jewish autonomous state would be carved out of the historical and mandated Palestine that was now settled by Jews. Therefore, Ben-Gurion adhered to the concept of the partition of Palestine into distinct and separate Jewish and Arab states. Proclaiming the Jewish Commonwealth in 1942, Ben-Gurion clearly accepted the ideal of the divisibility of Palestine.

Menachem Begin, the most dedicated disciple of Zeev Jabotinsky's Revisionist Zionism, conceived of the future and the structure of the Jewish state in different strategic, ideological and political terms. For Begin, the territorial and political integrity of Palestine was indivisible. Jabotinsky himself tolerated British rule over Palestine only as long as the British did not subscribe to the partition of Palestine; his Revisionist Zionism had as its goal the eventual political domination of Zionism over the whole of mandatory Palestine, which at the time included Transjordan, today's Jordan. Revisionism in fact was born when Transjordan was eliminated from the original British Palestine mandate.

For Begin, the problem of the composition of the population in the Jewish state was secondary to a concern with its territory. He preferred a Jewish majority over all of formerly western Palestine, but in its absence he claimed the political indivisibility of the territory between the Mediterranean and the Jordan River, the right to its settlement by Jews, and the eventual establishment of Jewish hegemony and political domination over all those parts of western Palestine truncated by the 1947 UN partition into separate Jewish and Arab states.

The Foreign Policy of the Likud Coalition: Begin Strategy and Dayan Tactics, 1977–1979[11]

The political implications for the resolution of conflict on Begin's terms were profound. When Begin or his government spoke of Jewish settlement on the West Bank, it conformed with his vision of an independent Jewish sovereign polity destined to dominate historical Palestine. The matter of settlement for Begin was not just tactical, but strategic and fundamental. In approaching the issue of the West Bank, the reality of the present irredentist claims to Judea and Samaria on the part of the Israeli government must be understood: they preclude the formation of a Palestinian state.

The Dayan-Begin relationship was of great importance in view of the fact that Dayan would eventually become Begin's key, and probably only, foreign advisor. Although a Ben-Gurion disciple, a product of Labor Zionism, Palmach, and the agricultural cooperative settlement, Dayan had a hawkish pragmatism that appealed to Begin, the ideological and historical militant. During the National Unity government (1967–1970), Dayan and Begin forged a special and enduring relationship, and even before the 1977 elections, Begin offered Dayan a key cabinet position if he joined Likud. Dayan's integration was a historic achievement. Begin now possessed Ben-Gurion's disciple, Labor's most brilliant and controversial figure, the Israeli with the greatest international reputation, and, above all, a tactician of security. Dayan also commanded considerable support among the NRP young militants.

Because he was a maximalist, Begin, not unlike his Arab rivals, preferred grand solutions to the intractable Arab-Israeli conflict. His strategy was basically two-pronged: opposition to the Kissinger step-by-step approach and opposition to the creation of any form of an independent Palestinian state in the West Bank. Step-by-step withdrawal, Begin felt, would portray Israel to the world in an unfavorable light. It is a mode that portrays Israel as intransigent and uncompromising. Above all, since United States leverage on Israel was greater than on the Arabs, this kind of diplomatic strategy would create unnecessary friction between Israel and America. Therefore Begin preferred a grand solution.

Here an insight into the Begin-Dayan relationship is crucial to understanding Israel's new strategy. Dayan recognized Israel's security imperatives on the Jordan River rather than the historical claims of the Zionist Revisionists. He also knew, however, that he could differ only to a certain degree with Begin. Although there was no formal or informal, tacit or clandestine "deal" between Begin and Dayan, there was a mutual understanding that Dayan, as chief negotiator for Israel, had to have some flexibility at his disposal. And he would use it, though stopping short of violating Begin's real commitments. Dayan was known to be loyal to his superiors. He was a soldier who precisely understood the nature of authority, as well as a politician who recognized the limits of his political influence. Thus, Dayan designed a fallback strategy both on procedure and substance, by which he hoped to assure continuing momentum for negotiations.

Dayan was the one who persuaded Begin that if Israel gave up Sinai, Sadat would be ready to negotiate. Then he was able to tell Sadat's emissary in Morocco of Begin's willingness to relinquish Sinai for peace with Egypt.[12] As soon as Sadat came to Jerusalem, in October 1977, the Begin-Dayan strategy aimed at achieving the best possible outcome despite conditions of duress, such as American political pressure and Arab threats to resort to war. Because Dayan did not view as realistic the convening of a Geneva conference to achieve a final peace between Israel and all the Arabs, his strategy was based on what he felt could realistically be achieved. Dayan was more attuned to process than to grand conference, and that is precisely how he envisioned the construction of peace—as a long and arduous process. Neither Arabs nor Israelis, he believed, are ready to dismantle instantly several decades of hostility, mistrust, and misperception. Dayan also doubted the political legitimacy of Arab regimes, their rulers' authority, and their political longevity. Thus, he preferred short-term arrangements. This was his position for the negotiations with Sadat.

Concerning the PLO, Dayan's position complemented Begin's. He totally rejected negotiating with the PLO, even if it were willing to amend its charter or accept United Nations Resolution 242 that called for the withdrawal of occupying forces and for security arrangements in the Middle East. For Dayan, as for Begin, the PLO stood for the political and physical annihilation of Israel. His reason for refusing to negotiate with an independent PLO delegation was that the purpose of such negotiations would be to establish, eventually, a PLO state in the West Bank and Gaza, which Dayan would not accept on any condition. He favored negotiating with Jordan on the future of the Palestinian population of the West Bank, so they might be granted greater social and economic autonomy. Like Begin, Dayan absolutely rejected the political autonomy or sovereignty of the Palestinians in the West Bank or elsewhere in western Palestine, but he did not object to non-PLO, nonofficial Palestinian members in a Jordanian delegation. Strategically, however, the security of the West Bank would be strictly Israeli; the Jordan River would be Israel's *security* border. Politically, then, Dayan somewhat modified Begin's concept of total domination over western Palestine. The foreign minister conceived of territory as a strategic security asset, not as the essence of political-ideological Revisionist Zionist dogma.

In light of Begin's dedication to territorial goals, his public claim that he was willing to negotiate on everything was open to question. When he called for an overall settlement based on the Camp David accords, he meant that he would not surrender the ideological commitment to territorial Zionism and to settlement in the territory—in other words, that he would not accept a Palestinian state. Compromise on this was ideologically and politically untenable for Begin and the Likud party. Full autonomy for Palestinians was as far as Begin would go.

Does this mean that Begin was an unregenerate ideologue and dogmatist? It is important here to realize how meaningful it is that he did delegate authority. Dayan commanded the procedural strategy both inside and outside of actual negotiations. The foreign minister had considerable influence on the Israeli negotiations and Begin gave him some freedom of action. On procedure, then, the Israeli government fostered movement; but on substance there was no deviation from Begin's Revisionist Zionism.

Six months after Begin's election, he and President Anwar al-Sadat of Egypt stood face to face on a red VIP carpet at Ben-Gurion Airport while millions of people around the world and in Israel watched in amazement. There was a warm and uncharacteristic smile on Begin's face. "I am waiting for you, Mr. President," he said, with great warmth and emotion.

After the dapper, elegant Sadat had made a speech to the gathered crowd at the airport, Begin followed with his own words. "We have one wish in our hearts, one wish in our souls," he said. "To bring peace to our people." At the time, it seemed as if Sadat had dropped quite suddenly out of the sky; that was not quite the case. Begin, faced with what he saw as a hostile President Carter, wanted to make peace with a major Arab country. The question was with whom, and how.

Although Begin had repeatedly vowed never to give up an inch of territory, there was some which was negotiable, at least in the view of Moshe Dayan, Begin's foreign minister. Dayan urged on Begin the idea that the Sinai, now starting to blossom with Israeli settlements and occupied by Israeli troops, nevertheless could be a bargaining chip with which to finesse the West Bank issue.

Feelers were sent out in the Arab world, to the King of Morocco. Dayan met with Sadat's advisor Dr. Muhammed Tahumi, passing the word that the Israelis and Begin would be willing to talk on peace and on Sinai. Sadat was interested. He did not exactly admire Begin, being suspicious of what he saw as an erratic nature, but he was impressed with his strength. Still, there was no official movement. It took American President Jimmy Carter to pave the road toward Jerusalem.

Carter's quest for an overall settlement in the Middle East, his much heralded Geneva Conference which would include the PLO and the Soviet Union, finally drove Sadat over the edge and toward his dramatic initiative. Both Sadat and Begin were aghast at Carter's move.

Jerusalem was a starting point, a startling moment in history, from which Camp David would eventually emerge. Sadat had made it clear he wanted to settle the Palestinian issue, Sinai or no Sinai. Begin thought he could hedge the issue, obfuscate it. Both men would take two steps forward in their meetings in Egypt and Israel, then be pulled back by hard-line, conservative advisors. Begin was being tugged in two directions, by the moderate Moshe Dayan and Ezer Weizman, by the hard-line Moshe Arens and Yitzhak Shamir.

There were separate visits to Washington by Begin and Sadat. Begin both impressed and exasperated Carter. He would not move an inch initially on the West Bank. "There will never be a Palestine state," he told Carter, who, one observer recalled, was "mad as hell." But he was also impressed by Begin's religious sincerity and called him "a man of principle." That feeling would not spill over to Camp David, where at times Carter conjectured out loud that Begin was on the brink of madness.

In the Washington meetings, Begin also showed his surprising capacity for the small human touch and his continued obsession with Jabotinsky.

In a private meeting with National Security Advisor Zbigniew Brzezinski, Begin presented the Polish-born Brzezinski with some documents which related to his father's underground activities during World War II. Brzezinski was touched; they talked for hours about Jabotinsky and his influence on Begin.

Camp David was a tortuous process out of which emerged the eventual Israeli-Egyptian peace treaty entailing the return of the Sinai. The West Bank was formally swept under a legalistic rug, an insoluble problem for future consideration, to be discussed under the heading of autonomy. What did emerge was a formal Israeli peace treaty with a major Arab country, and the return of territory for peace.

Begin quite literally nearly drove Sadat and Carter up the wall. At one point, Sadat complained loudly that Begin was "a hopeless case. He . . . haggles over every word. He is not ready for peace." Carter felt the same way, especially when the question of settlements in the West Bank came up. Begin would become aroused and emotional, invoking thousands of Israeli dead, blood on the battlefield. "My right eye will fall out, my right hand will fall off before I ever agree to the dismantling of a single Jewish settlement," he vowed to a startled Carter.

Yet, the end result of the talks would be the picture of Israeli soldiers razing Israeli settlements in the Sinai. Begin's eye and arm remained in place.

At Camp David, Begin was still being tugged and pulled, in contradiction to his own image of himself as a born leader. The pulling was being done then by Dayan and Weizman, who would constantly urge accommodation, moderation, and compromise. They kept Begin at the conference table and on course.

The question of settlements was never genuinely settled. Months after Camp David, to everyone's consternation, Begin initiated more Israeli settlements on the West Bank, saying he had only agreed to a three-month moratorium.

That was the stark, legalistic side. Yet in the momentous ceremony of the formal peace treaty signing on the White House lawn on March 27, 1979, Begin would hold himself in check and be eloquent.

Sadat in his speech vowed commitment to the Palestinian cause. Weizman, watching the ceremony and listening to Sadat's remarks, blanched, fearing the worst from Begin's rebuttal. It never came. Begin was warm, kind and gracious, especially when talking about Sadat, and never once referred to the Palestinians or the West Bank.

The overwhelming approval by the Israeli Knesset of the Camp David accords was deceptive, perhaps dangerously so from the standpoint of future United States-Israeli relations. The Knesset's dramatic vote (84 to 19, with 17 members abstaining) to accept the Camp David "framework for peace" did not reflect the real mood of the Israeli people, who have become increasingly suspicious of the peace process and bitterly skeptical of American pressures to take it further. What most Israelis expected from the Camp David summit was a separate peace with Egypt, nothing less and nothing more. They had no intention of making concessions, territorial or philosophical, to anyone who did not enter the bargain struck by Carter, Sadat, and Begin. That remains their position, and no exaggeration of Camp David's significance by its American sponsors will alter that Israeli reality.

Neither the current Israeli government nor the general public is so interested in peace as to pay any price the Arabs ask. The elections of 1981 and 1984 demonstrated the rise of a nationalist electorate. Indeed, the Israelis have never intended to withdraw totally from the Arab territories captured in the 1967 Middle East war. For them, there is a crucial distinction between the Sinai in the south and the territories in the central northeast, which are composed of the biblical Jewish lands of Judea and Samaria. For reasons of both military security and long-standing Zionist philosophy, they (particularly Labor) believe they must maintain control over much of the West Bank for many years to come. No alteration of personnel in the American White House or the State Department will change this fact.

The post-Camp David diplomatic turmoil—and the fundamental differences in the way that the framework was viewed by the United States, Egypt and Israel—has had profound ramifications in Israeli politics. A political system that was already changing dramatically now confronted new bitterness and ironies. Begin, long one of the most uncompromising nationalists in the country, was suddenly accused of making almost traitorous compromises with Sadat, while moderates like Yigal Allon, the conciliatory former foreign minister, was in the position of becoming one of Israel's leading militants. A new and profoundly powerful rejectionist coalition emerged.

The Rejectionist Front in Israel[13]

The Nationalists

The whirlwind of events after Anwar al-Sadat's visit to Jerusalem on November 17, 1977, carried the Middle East toward a final Egyptian-Israeli rapprochement, a resolution of peace concluded after Camp David on March 26, 1979. However, the road to peace was sown with many thorns. The peace treaty did not change Begin's position toward an independent Palestine, and the Camp David accords created an Israeli rejectionist front, a curious coalition that defies historical party alignments.

The greatest irony, of course, was defection from within the prime minister's own party, Herut. Begin—often referred to as the supreme commander by the veterans of Herut and of Etzel, the underground movement he led during the struggle for the establishment of Israel—was defied and attacked by his own party and by long-standing and intimate comrades when he returned from Camp David. Of the twenty-one Herut party members in the Knesset, only eleven voted for the accords. Five who voted against the accords or abstained were leading veterans of the Etzel "fighting family." The Herut party's youth group voted to reject the Camp David accords, and some even suggested that Begin be replaced by Moshe Arens, the leading Herut opponent of the accords.

Begin won the first phase of the struggle within his party. But the fight over the West Bank autonomy plan, over an emerging Palestine, and over Israel's dependence on the United States would further divide what had been a united and totally Begin-dominated party. No Herut leader in the Knesset challenged Begin's party leadership, but the intraparty rift was growing. The Herut party could never survive the creation of an independent Palestinian state in the West Bank and Gaza Strip. In the words of a leading party member, "Begin will not fall on Egypt: he will fall on the future of Judea and Samaria."

The most determined opposition to the Camp David accords came from the L'Am (Nation) party. L'Am had been formed in 1969 by dissident members of the Rafi party—whose membership included Ben-Gurion, Dayan, and former Defense Minister Shimon Peres—when the party rejoined Labor, from which it had split in 1965. L'Am, with only seven members in the Knesset, was a curious but representative creation of Israel's political fragmentation and of the decline of the traditional centralized party system. It joined Likud in the 1973, 1977 and 1981 elections. Four of the L'Am Knesset members, including former Minister of Treasury Yigal Hurwitz, voted against the accords; the other three abstained. Hurwitz resigned from the Likud cabinet over the outcome of Camp David, but returned in 1979 as minister of finance. L'Am played a key role in fighting every aspect of the accords, and rejected any future linkage of the agreements to an overall settlement.

Prior to the Camp David summit meeting, Americans who considered Begin ideologically intransigent were inclined to look to the Labor party for the moderation and pragmatism that has characterized Israeli leadership since the founding of the country. They believed that the Labor party would talk rationally about security and that it would be prepared to exchange territory for peace when the time was right. At least half of its membership was composed of pragmatists, including former Foreign Minister Abba Eban and former Prime Minister Yitzhak Rabin, now defense minister in Labor's Knesset bloc. In addition to Rabin, all Labor ministers in the Peres–Shamir government of 1984 are pragmatists.

But when the accords were presented to the Knesset, the main opposition came not unexpectedly from the United Kibbutz movement and its political arm, the Ahdut Haavoda faction of Labor led by Allon. The magnetic former foreign minister chose to abstain during the vote on the accords because he believed they would inevitably result in the creation of an independent Palestinian state. His position is accepted today by the mainstream of the Labor party, which opposes the concept of a comprehensive settlement for the same reason. Labor advocates Jordanian participation in an eventual solution to the Palestinian problem, Israeli independence from the United States, and American involvement in the efforts to achieve a Middle East peace as a mediator, not a partner. The party also endorses territorial compromises in the Golan Heights and the West Bank on the basis of a piece of land for a piece of peace. The theory underlying this concept is that an incremental approach will in the end reward Israel with some Arab territory.

The Allon plan, devised after the 1967 war, was a formula for such territorial compromise. The plan envisaged Israeli recognition of Jordanian, or even joint Palestinian-Jordanian, sovereignty over the West Bank. But it also entailed the division of the West Bank between Israel and Jordan. Israeli military and other settlements would then eventually be incorporated into Israel proper, or at least shielded permanently by its armed forces. Thus, Allon and Labor were outraged with Begin for "abandoning" the Israeli settlements in the Sinai as the price for peace with Egypt. Allon's criticism of Begin raised considerable doubt that Sadat could ever have come to Israel to meet a Labor government dedicated to this kind of territorial compromise. Both Rabin and the late Prime Minister Golda Meir had, in fact, previously rejected peace feelers from Sadat.

Allon, never a member of LIM, his allies in Ahdut Haavoda, and other prominent Labor leaders asserted that the Labor government's diplomatic strategy was the right one. Opposed to an all-parties Geneva conference and overall settlement, they claimed that a Labor government would not have allowed the territorial erosion they saw in surrender of the Sinai without a proper bargain, which resulted in the disintegration of a comprehensive Israeli settlements policy.

In an interview in Israel's daily *Maariv*, Allon declared that he would "not vote in the Knesset for the peace accords with Egypt if the Knesset will not impose on the government a different concept of the autonomy plan" than that which had emerged. "My conditions for an Arab autonomy in Palestine means total Israeli domination over the Jordan valley, the deserts of Judea and Samaria, the Etzion area [the southern tip of the Negev], and the southern tip of the Gaza." Allon argued that those areas were not populated but were strictly security areas that must be dominated by the IDF.[14]

Allon's views were consistent with Tabenkin and Ahdut Haavoda's territorialist views. There could be no secure Israel without some territorial space as physical and psychological elbow room. For Ahdut Haavoda, the concept of territory was always an ideological, political and military package. There was no real security in a truncated Eretz Israel and there was no real peace in extending Israel proper into a heavily populated Arab territory— the West Bank. There was, however, no political leverage against the Arabs without a territorial buffer, consisting of parts of Sinai and the Jordan Valley. There was no room for political or military maneuvers within the borders of the first partition state. Thus fundamental strategic rejectionism in Israel stemmed from the Tabenkin rather than the Jabotinsky school of Zionism. For Begin, Eretz Israel must extend at least to the Jordan River if not beyond. For Ahdut Haavoda, Eretz Israel is a territorial concept that must include parts of Sinai and the unsettled West Bank. Fundamental political rejectionism was not represented by the fanatic Gush Emunim, a minuscule radical nationalist religious schism group whose political messianism was not grounded in territory, space, or strategy but in the doctrine that the Jews are almighty inheritants of Eretz Israel whose heartland is historical Judea and Samaria. Begin's revisionism, however, converged with Gush in the sense that the borders were biblical and defined by the British mandatory before the truncation in 1922 of Transjordan from historical Eretz Israel.

Peres's and Labor's opposition was not based on ideology or territory but on diplomacy. Peres believed that Israel's bargaining power with the Arab countries and the United States and its image in progressive Western circles were totally undermined by Begin's inconsistencies and Israel's rejectionist front. Israel, he feared, would become a United States dependency, and its requests for defense money and support would be denied by some administration in reaction to what Washington regarded as Israel's expansionist settlement policy. Hence, he concluded that Israeli defense and security needs would be hurt by Begin's arrogant and futile settlement policies. Most important, both Peres and Rabin argued that Begin's West Bank autonomy plan would lead directly to what Begin most fervently opposed—the formation of an independent Palestinian state, possibly leaning toward the Palestine Liberation Organization (PLO).

Labor opposition to the accords differed in many respects from Herut opposition. While the right opposed Israeli withdrawals under any circumstances, Labor was committed to the step-by-step peace process and the territorial approach. Labor firmly believed in an eventual Arab-Israeli peace. It recognized the Palestinian people, and its left wing was willing to accept the establishment of a moderate Palestinian non-PLO state, while its center and right would tolerate a Jordanian-Palestinian state, with seriously favorable Israeli territorial compromise.

In its almost three decades of rule, the Labor party never had to face as great a challenge to the most salient feature of its Hityashvut pioneer settlement doctrine as it did in the aftermath of Camp David. Hityashvut was a dynamic pioneering and colonizing, agrarian cooperative enterprise that had been the very heart of the party which considered itself the quintessence of Zionist humanitarianism, nationalism, and non-Communist democratic socialism.

Attitudes in Israel toward settlement became more stylistic than substantive. Begin, the determined but less than subtle legalist, was willing to have the maps drawn and Israel's frontiers established, though he reserved the right to define crucial terms. The Labor leadership, on the other hand, could do without maps indefinitely, preferring a territory in flux.

Begin's complex views on sovereignty and territorial acquisition were incorporated in his twenty-six-point autonomy plan, incorporated with serious modification into the Egyptian-Israeli peace treaty and the Camp David accords. This plan, to be reviewed by Israel after five years, would set up an interim local Palestinian administration in the West Bank, while Israeli troops would continue to handle defense and security matters in the area. The autonomy plan was designed to ensure Israeli military control over the proposed Palestinian autonomy administration. One significant aspect of the plan was Begin's offer to the local Palestinians— or in his vocabulary "the Palestinian Arabs"—of a choice of accepting Israeli, Jordanian, or Egyptian citizenship. Above all, it stipulated that Israel could continue to settle Palestine and that Israelis would always have free access to the newly established autonomous entity.

To understand Begin's plan, one must go back to his rejection of the Labor party's Allon plan. Begin opposed it because it implied a territorial compromise, a division of the West Bank, and the reestablishment of some Jordanian sovereignty over the Palestinians. He claimed that Jordan annexed the West Bank illegally in the war of 1948, in violation of the Palestine partition plan of November 1947, which assigned it to the Palestinians. According to Begin, the U.N. partition plan, which he otherwise vehemently rejected, was the only legal document concerning the West Bank. Thus, since neither Jordan nor Israel could claim sovereignty over the territory, Begin called for the establishment of self-rule for the Arab inhabitants of the West Bank and Gaza.

This concept of autonomy did not originate with Begin. Its underlying principles had been established by Jabotinsky, who wrote several essays on Palestinian autonomy between 1928 and 1932. Jabotinsky was violently opposed to the arbitrary separation of Transjordan (now the Kingdom of Jordan) from the Palestinian mandate by the British in 1922. By calling for autonomy for Palestine, Jabotinsky hoped that in the absence of any formal territorial division, the Zionist movement could expand its settlements into Transjordan as well as west of the Jordan River. The Jews would then be able to claim all of Palestine by fait accompli.

The foundations of Begin's plan remained Zionist-Revisionist and maximalist, although five decades of a Hashemite kingdom and an independent Jordan had modified his stance on Transjordan. Begin's plan deviated from Jabotinsky's vision by relinquishing now Israel's claim to sovereignty over Judea and Samaria, a restraint insisted upon by Dayan when he joined Begin's Likud government. Begin further modified Jabotinsky's concept when he offered both Jordan and Egypt a role in the West Bank autonomy administration.

Here, another Jabotinsky doctrine is crucial—the distinction between citizenship and nationality. Citizenship is the realization of national identity. The sovereignty of a state is determined by citizenship, not nationality. The Arabs in Palestine comprise a nationality, but they are not citizens of a Palestinian state, which Begin claimed had never existed. Thus the autonomy plan would fulfill Begin's concept of nationality, but would preclude any Palestinian citizenship.

The Israelis at Camp David had no intention of ceasing to enlarge or thicken the settlements in the West Bank. These settlements would contribute to Israel's security because its troops would remain on the Jordan River regardless of the state that emerged at the end of the five-year autonomy plan. Begin, who refused to recognize Palestinian sovereignty over the West Bank and Gaza, wanted to provide Israel with enough maneuvering room to prevent the Palestinian autonomy administration from establishing an independent state. Even Dayan believed that all Israelis had a right to settle and buy land in the areas designated in the autonomy plan, no matter what authority replaced the interim administration.

The Annexationists

Begin, Likud and Israel's entire political system after Camp David were challenged by a group of religious fundamentalists and radical nationalists who went beyond mere rejection of partition. The convergence of secular and fundamentalist rejectionists was accelerated after the Camp David accords were signed in March 1979. For example, the secularist Hatechiyah (Renaissance) party is a Herut splinter which rejected Camp David and converged with the ultranationalist orthodox group Gush Emunim (Bloc of the Faithful), which advocated complete annexation of all of historical Eretz Israel.

Guela Cohen, a Lehi veteran, renewed the Sternist eighteen principles of Hebrew renaissance, a messianic doctrine which advocated the establishment of Eretz Israel within a realm specified in the Bible, "To your heirs I decree this land from the Nile to the Euphrates," and that "Eretz Israel must be conquered by the sword."

The Renaissance party, like its predecessor Lehi, was a movement of intellectuals, poets and militant nationalists. By 1979, it was advocating a militant policy toward settlement of the West Bank.

The Renaissance party had a great deal of success in courting members of the labor establishment like the novelist Moshe Shamir, former IDF chief of staff Raful Eitan, as well as graduates of the NRP youth movement and sons and grandsons of the Labor pioneers. It did extremely well among IDF members in the election of 1984. Today it has five seats in the Knesset, as well as close ties to Herut's youth movement, the Sharon wing of Likud, and the radical members of the NRP.

The Renaissance party is a post-Camp David phenomenon. It defied Begin and the Herut leadership in the past. When Likud hoped to be able to form a narrow government in 1984, Renaissance was its chief partner. Renaissance, however, refused to join in a unity government with Labor and today stands as the chief opposition party to the National Unity government.

It remains a highly successful, articulate, aggressive and modern radical movement, which aspires to become Herut's successor. It symbolizes the end of the Begin-Herut style of Revisionism and stands clearly as a nationalist, radical annexationist movement.

The other school of annexationists comes from the National Religious movement, from within its youth movement, Bnai Akiva (Sons of Akiva, named after the rabbi who inspired a revolt against the Romans in 70 A.D.). This group's orientation is a mixture of biblical fundamentalism and aggressive and militant settlement policies.

Briefly, the new fundamentalism incorporates the following ideas and factors:

1. The Jews are no longer displaced or wandering, but are to be collected with and connected to the land (*Zika Artzit*).

2. Fundamentalism and redemption are exclusively nationalist and anti-universalist.
3. Redemption is a process that is governed by the will of the Higher Authority (*Ha-Ashgaha Ha-Éliona*), to be fulfilled now in the natural laws of Zionist settlement of the Land of Israel.
4. Zionist activism must now focus on the protection of *Shlemut Ha-Moledet* (a phrase meaning the integrity of the land, which is coincidentally not unlike the rhetoric of Begin and Herut).
5. The Messiah and redemption are not utopian. The concept is no longer dependent on the Jewish nation's long-held obligation to repent, once thought to be the precondition for the appearance of the Messiah. Redemption is rather an answer to the call of the Prophet Isaiah to create "a new sky and a new land." Redemption, as espoused by the likes of Geula Cohen, is no longer dependent on repentance or the appearance of the Messiah but rather redemptive deeds are already being done.
6. The signs of redemption are here: the overthrow of foreign rule, the ingathering of Jews, the victory over the Arab armies.
7. It is the duty of all Zionist activists to fulfill the dream of Eretz Israel, to put the theory of redemption into forceful action now.

The fervor of fundamentalists, especially as embodied by Gush, sprang up in once-fertile but now rather sterile intellectual ground. Historical Labor and Revisionist Zionism had become intellectually exhausted, clinging to pragmatic Zionism. Not even Begin was quite in the mainstream of the new Revisionism and in one sense could be included in the bloc of exhausted pragmatic Zionists. Small wonder then that the new activist Zionists, the new Revisionists and the new fundamentalists flourished after 1967, turning into the most vital, aggressive realizers of Zionism's iron law: the settlement of Complete Zion.

A minority in Israel, Gush Emunim and its adherents nevertheless captured the newest, deepest symbols, manipulating messianic symbols almost at will while the opposition had nothing fresh to offer. Not a political party itself, Gush Emunim nevertheless wielded a great deal of influence. Soon, one saw such diverse leaders as Cohen, the militants of Herut-Likud, and the radical leaders of the NRP, Zvulun Hammer, Yehuda Ben Meir and Rabbi Chaim Drukman, along with Ariel Sharon appealing and carrying the new symbolism. Autonomous as a movement, Gush

Emunim supported the aggressive settlement policy of Sharon in Begin's first government and became the nucleus and springboard for the Renaissance party, which won three crucial seats in the 1981 elections and five seats in the 1984 elections.

There is a new revival of Zionism in the land, wearing the mantle of fundamentalism, driven by a single-minded belief in Eretz Israel, thriving in an emotional and intellectual vacuum left by the intellectual bankruptcy of the secularist Labor party and the Revisionist nationalists. It is a kind of Zionism hardly envisioned by the sturdy kibbutzim leaders of years gone by, but is a fundamentalist, activist Zionism that is on the rise. There is no real opposition in sight: the Peace Now movement, while active, has failed to capture the popular imagination, while the left clings to worn-out Labor symbols, foreign ideologies, and Marxism, getting no help from a Europe that is cynical and wary and ultimately hostile or from a United States still emerging from its Vietnam trauma, hesitant and unable to properly wield its influence or understand the rising tide of fundamentalism in Israel for what it is.

The rejectionist front is also representative of the Begin era. Although opposed to Begin's pragmatism, it nevertheless represents a most significant intellectual and political foundation for Begin-Herut-Likud and its ultimate aspiration—*Shlemut Ha-Moledet*, the unity of the land—and total rejection of any sort of partition.

CHAPTER 11

The Second Begin Government: 1981–1983

The Electoral Background

It is important to examine the electoral and political background from which the second Begin government came into being. The June 30, 1981, elections presented a political, electoral, and cultural revolution in Israeli politics and society. The elections signaled the emergence of a new electorate inclined toward radical nationalism and Jewish traditionalism. [I clearly distinguish between Jewish traditionalism of the National Religious Party, which is like a European Christian-Democratic party—modern, democratic, and religious (some are even socialist)—and clericalism, which is reactionary and antimodern. The *Agudat Israel* run by the Grand Sages of the Torah are reminiscent of the Ayatollahs in Iran and the Roman Curia Cardinals of the Catholic Church.]

Begin's coalition government represented a new political alignment of the new political, social and cultural forces replacing the Socialist Zionist center, the old progressive and nationalist alignment composed mainly of Jews of European-American origins. It was the old alignment that dominated Israel from even before the state's creation in 1948. The second Begin government was supported by an electorate even more radical and militant than the government itself expected to be. It was an emerging electorate that was politically aggressive, inflexible on territorial concessions, and militant in its attitude toward the PLO, much more so than the diverse and precarious coalition forged by Prime Minister Menachem Begin.

This electoral-social-cultural coalition had been slowly emerging ever since 1967, even before Likud began its own steady ascendancy in 1973, a year that also marked the beginning of the decline of the Labor party. From the mehdal often called the Yom Kippur War onward, Labor began what appeared to be an irrevocable slide, a slide that did not stop with the 1981 and 1984 elections, although appearances made it seem otherwise. From 51 seats in the Knesset in 1973, Labor slumped to 34 (33 if one subtracts the mercurial Moshe Dayan's seat in 1977). By all appearances, Labor seemed to make something of a comeback in the 1981 elections, picking up 47 seats in the election and narrowly missing gaining an electoral victory. But the apparent 13-seat gain was not a demonstration of resurgence; it actually marked a further decline. Labor should have made gains into the Center Liberal party, which disintegrated in the wake of the new electoral realignment. The 15 seats of the Democratic Party for Change (Dash), which split from Labor in 1977, plus the four or five seats of the centrist parties, should have gone to Labor. The possibilities that existed for a 67-seat Labor coalition did not materialize. Labor never came near that total and, in fact, missed its 1973 high-water mark of 51. The gains that Labor did manage to make came from the Israeli Arab vote, which gave Labor an extra five seats it had not anticipated. The old Labor coalition, however, crumbled and all but disappeared. Labor today continues its political decline; it lost three seats in the 1984 elections. While Begin tried in 1981 to make his coalition work, Labor now is engaged in internecine warfare as its colorless party leader Shimon Peres tries to fend off attacks from within. The seeming unity of Peres's Labor party in 1984 faced the test of the next two years.

On the other hand, Likud's rise is an arrow going straight upward. In 1973, Likud won 38 seats, rose to 44 (and electoral victory) in 1977, and captured a record 48 seats in 1981, a fact that went all but unnoticed in the remarkable closeness of the election. In 1984 it lost seven seats, but five of those went to the

Renaissance party. What some observers did notice, however, was the apparent institutionalization of a two-party system in Israel.[1] This again was actually more an apparent fact than a real one, for in 1984 thirteen parties contending for power won seats in the Knesset. The actual facts lead one to an entirely different picture, one of disproportionate results triumphant. Consider for instance what happened to the splinter parties, the special interest parties, and sub-parties, of which there were at least thirty competing in the elections. The NRP (National Religious Party, Mafdal) actually declined by an astounding 50 percent, from 12 seats in 1971 to only six in the 1981 elections. The NRP lost three seats to its radical splinter party Tami (a strictly ethnic traditionalist-oriented Jewish party), and the rest went (ironically) to Likud and the new Renaissance (Hatechiyah) party headed by superhawk and militant settlement policy advocate, Mrs. Geula Cohen. Yet the NRP, emerging from the ashes of what should have been a shattering electoral defeat, became a crucial coalition power. In fact, had NRP leader Dr. Yoseph Burg decided to join Labor, Labor could have formed a coalition government with the help of the Arab Communist party (which, incidentally, also declined, from six to four seats). To that end, according to some sources, Dr. Burg was even offered the post of prime minister, merely to install a Labor government. Burg could have had a repeat performance in the 1984 elections if he had insisted on becoming premier.

While obviously crucial, the nine seats of the NRP and Tami were not sufficient to help Begin cross the 60-seat coalition mark. At this point, Begin needed the assistance of another small party, Agudat Israel, that wielded inordinate coalition power compared to its electoral pull. Begin appealed to the clerical domestic reactionaries who made up the antidemocratic and anti-Zionist Agudat Israel party, for it held the four seats necessary for Begin to form a coalition and gain the 61-seat Knesset majority. Quite obviously, Begin made a deal with Agudat Israel, a non-Zionist religious covenant. Thus he created what surely looks like a peculiar and potentially dangerous political situation: a coalition of Begin and Defense Minister Ariel Sharon and the ultra-Zionist majority, joined by basically anti-Zionist clerics who were moderate on issues of security and foreign policy. The results were the destruction of Iraq's nuclear reactor, annexation of the Golan, and war in Lebanon.

Demography, Political Culture, and Insider/Outsider Factors

The most significant cultural, social and political shift to occur in the wake of the 1981 elections was the emergence of Israel's Oriental Jews as a powerful factor, as well as the general youthful greening of the electorate.

In the 1981 elections, the Jews who came from the east (Asia, North Africa, and the Middle East), known as Sephardim or Oriental Jews, did not by any means gain a political majority but they did gain political clout and become a serious electoral factor. They were gaining fast on the Ashkenazim (Jews of European-American origins) who still dominated the electorate.

Demographically speaking, in 1981 and today the Ashkenazim comprised 32 percent of the Israeli vote and their Israeli-born children another 18 percent, for a total of a full one-half of the electorate. On the other hand, the Oriental Jews comprised 26 percent of the vote and their children another 15 percent; the remaining 10 percent were Arab-Moslem and Christian voters.[2] What was significant was that the Oriental Jewish vote was on the rise, that an emerging political group was asserting itself electorally and moving in a new direction. Previously, the Oriental Jews had been an incohesive electoral group operating either within Mapai Labor circles or at local party levels. What was also significant was that this growing electoral body was exactly that part of the electorate that responded strongly to Begin and the new government he had formed, and everything he and his government symbolically and politically represented.

What the Oriental Jews and their children responded to was personality, tradition, religion, and radical nationalism. They were more inclined to respond to the aggressive parties of Complete (Eretz) Israel—Herut, Likud, some parts of the NRP, and the Renaissance settler party. They responded to Begin's charisma, to the NRP's religious traditionalism, and to radical Zionism in general. The hero image was vivid for Oriental Jews and thus they responded to the gruff paratrooper image of Ariel Sharon as well as to the intransigent, individualistic outsider image of Begin and Herut. They also were strongly attached to the values of Eretz Israel, and were inclined to be very anti-Arab.

On the other hand, the images and values that the Ashkenazim and their offspring responded to were those of the secular Socialist Jews who identified with the pioneer, the kibbutz, the agricultural worker, the Haganah-Palmach fighter, the founders of Labor and IDF, the old images of David Ben-Gurion, Levi Eshkol and Golda Meir. The Ashkenazim, in short, responded to history and often lived in it, whereas the Sephardim tended to look to the future. They may, in fact, be the future, because one of the most significant facts about the new emerging electorate is that much of it is young.

Thirty percent of the 1981 electorate was between 20 and 29 years old; 21 percent was between the ages of 30 and 39. More sons of the Oriental Jews voted Likud. The youth factor was prevalent everywhere. Over 50 percent of Israel's seven universities voted Likud. All of the student bodies in the universities except for the University of Beersheba were dominated by Likud and the Renaissance party. Thirty percent of the IDF conscripts (ages 18–21) divided their vote between Likud and the Renaissance party. The symbols of a beautiful, justly partitioned and moderate Israel were being replaced by the symbols of Eretz Israel, territorialism, and Jewish nonsecularist traditionalism.

The Oriental Jewish electorate, which was often perceived as the outsider, saw in Begin a similar image of "the outsider" while Labor was seen as the ruling class, "the insider." Naturally, there were elements of class as well as cultural differences between the Ashkenazim and the Oriental Jews. What happened was that Likud became a populist party while Labor was seen as the establishment party.

Foreign and Security Policies
in the Second Begin Government

The second Begin government was the most hawkish government in Israel's history. The ruling quartet—Begin, Defense Minister Ariel Sharon, Foreign Minister Yitzhak Shamir, and Treasury Minister Yoram Aridor—were all hawks in the Herut political tradition and philosophy, supported by National Religious Party radicals, and sustained by the Eretz Israel true-believers in the Renaissance party. The ruling Herut party, the NRP, and Renaissance party formed the base of the second Begin government's foreign policy and security policies. The 1981 elections legitimized Begin's new government and his foreign policy. If his narrow victory was not exactly an overwhelming mandate, it indicated that the electorate would at last allow Begin to fulfill his dream of a Complete Israel.

Some questions remained to be answered about the new government and its capability to carry out its policies, and even about its stability. Would Begin be able to manage and politically control the antisecularist ambitions of the Agudat Israel, which formed a tiny but crucial part of his coalition? Would the Labor party manage to pull itself together to form an effective and critical opposition? What would the nature and scope of United States support be and what strings would be attached to that support? Would Israel's support in Congress and among American Jewry hold up under a constant barrage of adverse world and public opinion? In short, the nature of security and foreign policy directions for Israel very much depended on the strength of the resistance to Begin and his ability to overcome that resistance. He managed very successfully.

What is important to know about the second Begin government is that it was not a new government, that for all practical purposes, it actually had begun its operations in July 1980, when the last member of the cabinet who had any ability to restrain Begin resigned from the government. When the flamboyant Ezer Weizman resigned over the Palestinian autonomy issue, he inadvertently helped give birth to the second Begin government. The electoral victory of 1981 merely formalized and legitimized it.

There was a difference between the second Begin government and the one that existed prior to Weizman's resignation. Weizman was the last of Begin's first cabinet members who continuously defied, modified, or resisted Begin's most stubborn, conservative and intransigent inclinations. The pre-1981, and for that matter, the pre-July 1980 cabinet was composed of powerful, ambitious and charismatic generals, politicians whose roots, if they had any, were not with Herut or Likud ideologues, but lay with Labor. Except for Begin himself, the first cabinet had no Etzel-Herut nucleus. It never really worked successfully as a collective but rather was dominated by Begin's powerful personality. Yet, on the surface, the cabinet when first introduced was both impressive and at times efficient, even though it looked like a political oddity.

Although the cabinet was theoretically part of a Likud government, its strongest members were for all intents and purposes
outsiders. Moshe Dayan, a Labor party renegade, became foreign
minister. Ezer Weizman, who was no Herut veteran despite
having been Begin's campaign manager, became defense minister.
Ariel Sharon, who ran on his own ticket in the elections and was
never a Herut member in spite of having founded Likud, became
agricultural minister, a post that really enabled him to become
chief manager of Begin's West Bank settlement policy. Yigal
Hurwitz, a Ben-Gurionite and Dayanist, became minister of
commerce. In November 1977, Begin added Professor Yigael
Yadin, the leader of the Democratic Movement for Change
(Dash) as deputy prime minister.

All of the individuals in the pre-1981 cabinet were ambitious
and proud, men with glowing political and military reputations.
The cabinet had a distinct military flavor to it, more so than in the
past. In addition to those mentioned, there was also former
Mossad chief General Meir Amit, who became minister of transportation. With Amit's addition, there were two former chiefs of
staff, Yigael Yadin and Moshe Dayan, as well as Weizman, the
former Air Force chief of staff and Sharon, the hero of the 1973
war. The cabinet may not have been ideal politically, but it at first
allowed Begin to accomplish the foreign policy objectives he was
then pursuing. He sent out peace feelers to a legitimate Arab
state, Egypt. Dayan played a key role in fulfilling this goal.

For two years, beginning with Sadat's historic mission to
Jerusalem in July 1977, and culminating in the March 29, 1979,
Camp David agreement, the superstar Begin government demon-
strated its strengths and weaknesses. When it came to negotiating
the Palestinian autonomy part of the Camp David accords,
Dayan's concept of a unilateral Israeli withdrawal of its military
government in the West Bank and Gaza did not sit well with
Begin. He then chose to delegate the negotiating over this issue to
Interior Minister Yoseph Burg, the leader of the conservative
National Religious Party.

Dayan, having failed to persuade Begin of a new approach in
implementing the Palestinian autonomy plan, resigned on October 9, 1979. Ezer Weizman lasted until July 1980, when he
resigned over what amounted to the same issue. Weizman claimed
that Begin's narrow approach to Palestinian autonomy would in
the long run damage the new delicate Egyptian-Israeli relationship

and that Begin's rigid approach to the Palestinian question in general would inhibit deeper and more stable Arab-Israeli relations and would dim the prospects of a real peace. By mid-1980, Amit, Hurwitz, and Tamir had also left the cabinet.

Left with a government that had all the appearances of being in political shambles, Begin replaced Dayan with former Lehi chief of operations and Knesset speaker Yitzhak Shamir, a man more to his ideological liking. For defense minister, Begin picked the man with whom he had the most in common: himself—thus taking a page out of the book of David Ben-Gurion. By late summer 1980, the government and cabinet of strong individuals had changed considerably, leaving only Sharon, who by this time acted as if he was an ideological follower of Begin, and Yigael Yadin, who was now a man without a party, Dash having split up and eventually dissolved.

With the disappearance of the galaxy headed by Dayan and Weizman, there was no more serious opposition within the government to Begin or his foreign policies. The previous cabinet might well have opposed or modified such post-October 1980 decisions as the bombing of the Tammuz II Iraqi nuclear reactor, and almost certainly would have vehemently been opposed to the shocking July 1981 raid on Beirut, a decision that Sharon opposed alone and to no avail.[3]

By October 1980, the second Begin government was in place, headed by Begin, Sharon, and Shamir, and by Israel's most hawkish and political chief of staff ever, General Rafael (Raful) Eitan. The most crucial military and political decisions—the bombing of the Iraqi nuclear reactor, the Syrian missile crisis, relations with America, the 1981 Beirut raid, and responses to PLO operations emanating from Lebanon—were made by this quartet, and future decisions of that nature are also likely to be made by them.

The problem of the Palestine Liberation Organization in Lebanon, which ties into the Syrian missile crisis, is also tied into the lack of Middle East policy on the part of the United States, although militarily it stretched back much further than that. The initial Israeli military offensive against the PLO began several months after the Camp David accords were signed with Egypt and the United States. This particular offensive was designed with the following political and military goals in mind: to preempt PLO guerrilla infiltration into Israel and to destroy, divest, moderate and cripple the PLO's military efforts; to put the PLO on the military defensive; and to pound the PLO artillery locations on the northern front through the combined efforts of air and naval forces. By April 1980, the IDF offensive had forced the PLO into a new strategy, one much more ominous to Israel. With the help of Libya, the PLO developed a regular, nonguerrilla military force consisting of tanks, helicopters, airplanes and heavy equipment. The threat of this new infrastructure forced Israel to move against it with air attacks, an offensive that crowded the PLO into a Syrian corner.[4]

At this point, the United States and the new administration of President Ronald Reagan entered the picture, not quite sure what it was doing in the Middle East. For want of a real Middle East policy, the administration instead sent Secretary of State Alexander Haig to the Middle East to attempt to sell a new American strategy which was ill-conceived and ill-received. This new strategic concept—the Strategic Consensus Doctrine—envisioned cooperation among moderate Arab states and Israel under an American military umbrella as a check against Soviet designs in the area. This concept was greeted with polite interest at best and often with disinterest at Haig's stops along his tour: Israel, Egypt, Jordan, and Saudia Arabia.

Against the background of this weak American idea and of Israel's efforts to cripple the PLO, a major crisis erupted in April 1981, when Syria installed USSR-built antiaircraft missiles in Lebanon. Begin, perhaps by his very nature, immediately formulated a military solution. But a heavy fog on April 30 canceled the planned air raid on the missiles and left the Israeli government with only one choice: diplomacy. At this point, the Reagan administration once again entered the scene in the person of Special Envoy Phillip Habib. The deepening crisis in Lebanon was forcing the United States to almost willy-nilly ad lib a Middle East policy.

Habib, low-keyed but quietly professional and efficient, impressed everyone he dealt with in Syria, Lebanon, and Israel with his indefatigable shuttle diplomacy. Habib's choice was difficult, between an "Israeli peace" option for the Syrian missile crisis, which actually meant a Christian Phalange-Israel-Haddad solution, or an "Arab peace" option," i.e., the use of Saudi Arabian mediation between Israel and Syria, Lebanon, and the PLO. The Syrian-Israeli option was simply not open for Habib. Inducing the

Saudi Arabian royal family to put pressure on Syria meant restraining Israel and relying on Israeli flexibility, peaceful Soviet intentions, Syrian ambitions and the influence of the Saudis. Here Habib totally failed.

Israeli flexibility was not immediately achieved. Even as Habib was conducting his shuttle diplomacy, Begin ordered the ruthless July 17, 1981, bombing of PLO headquarters in Beirut, killing numerous civilians as well as guerrillas and creating a serious uproar in Israel, in world opinion, and in the United States, to the point of becoming an embarrassment for the Reagan administration and undercutting and changing the course of Habib's peace efforts.

The Habib mission now turned from the apparantly stabilized Syrian-Israeli missile crisis into a mission of achieving a precarious cease-fire between Israel and the PLO and moving seriously in the direction of an Arab plan. What evolved was a stalemate waiting to be broken. The Israeli offensive against the PLO was stalled and remained, from the Israeli viewpoint, unfulfilled. The Syrian missiles were, for the most part, still in place in the vital Bekaa Valley and Syrian President Assad had no particular inducement to remove them, having reaped immense political advantages from the crisis, while greatly resenting the de facto Israeli annexation of the Golan in December, 1981.

In 1982 the second Begin government had no serious opposition from the Labor party, which was in political disarray. Likud was strongly supported by the emerging electorate and had no internal political restraining forces on its foreign and security policies. Therefore the single most important force that could have a restraining or modifying influence on the Begin-Sharon government was the United States. However, there were serious problems with the capability of the Reagan administration's ability to put restraints on the Begin government.

The Begin government was inclined to resolve regional conflicts strictly on its own terms. Meanwhile, the Reagan administration perceived Soviet global intentions spilling over into regional conflicts, and failed to be sufficiently concerned with the nature of the inherent regional conflicts. This dichotomy was at the heart of the Reagan administration's inability to put restraints on Israel. Begin, while pursuing his own resolutions of inherent regional conflicts, also appeared in agreement with the United States about Soviet intentions. This was the essence of the strategic alliance agreed upon during Begin's August 1981 meeting with Reagan in the United States. It all but made the United States impotent in preventing Israel and Begin from pursuing their own solutions on such crucial issues as Palestine and the West Bank, autonomy, the PLO, Syria and Lebanon. In effect, the United States was pursuing contradictory goals. It was trying to strengthen and solidify its ties with Israel while at the same time pursuing its strategic consensus policy and a closer relationship with Saudi Arabia and other Arab moderates.

For a while, the Reagan administration, which Begin looked forward to with glee and optimism, appeared to be having difficulties with its relationship with Israel, and particularly with Begin. There were serious strains in the relationships. The Israeli raid on Beirut created a major confrontation with the administration. It could in no way be approved of by the United States as a tactic for dealing with the PLO. The raid on the Iraqi reactor proved another political problem for the Reagan administration, although the general reaction was surprisingly restrained, in spite of the administration's temporary withholding of delivery of F-16 airplanes to Israel. For Israel, the administration's decision to go ahead with the sale of AWACs aircraft to Saudia Arabia most surely was an unwanted development. There was also the question of the pressure Egyptian President Anwar al-Sadat had exerted before his assassination for the Reagan administration to recognize the PLO, an organization that Reagan himself had labeled "terrorist."

The strangely incomplete Habib Arab peace plan for southern Lebanon was another source of serious concern and friction between the Reagan administration and Israel, as was the uncertainty of whether or not the Begin-Sharon superhawks would attempt to continue their offensive against the PLO and thereby possibly drag the Middle East into yet another general war.

The Reagan administration's strategic consensus approach was basically a nonstarter doomed to failure. It was the other side of the Carter-Brzezinski comprehensive settlement approach, which aspired to bring Israel and the Arab states into an overall peace conference. While the comprehensive settlement policy was merely utopian, strategic consensus, which aspired to bring Israel and the Arab states into a common war council designed to protect the Middle East from the Soviets, might ultimately be possible.

The idea and the hope of strategic consensus was that moderate Arab states such as Egypt, Jordan, and Saudi Arabia, along with Israel, would be supplied with the necessary weapons to meet the Soviet challenge. Thus each country, on a bilateral basis, and eventually on a collective basis as something of a Middle East NATO, would be protected by an American-supported anti-Soviet umbrella.

Strategic consensus did fly directly in the face of political, regional and military logic. It was obvious from the start that there could be little in common for Israel with such states as Saudi Arabia, which supplies rejectionist-front states such as Iraq as well as the PLO, both of which have Soviet connections. Historically, such a policy tended to upset the balance of military power, which previously had been based on an Arab-Israeli weapon ratio of 1 : 3. The new concept would have changed this balance in favor of the Arabs. The Arabian peninsula would have become a military arsenal that the United States would not be able to control, just as it could not control events in Iran. Strategic consensus also would have given Ariel Sharon the rationale to go to war against the PLO as part of the war against Soviet-inspired Arab terrorism.

By the middle of 1982 the situation in Lebanon, Palestine, and Syria made possible some assumptions about what could be expected from the second Begin government. The guiding principles of that government were not those of the government that was in place in October 1980, the principles were those of Herut. Some of the following purely Herut maximalist goals were achieved in Begin's second government.

The Palestinian Issue

1. Total rejection of the Palestinian Liberation Organization. No recognition of or negotiation with the PLO, even if the PLO accepted United Nations Resolution 242.
2. Rejection of any form of Palestinian political sovereignty.
3. Destruction of the PLO's military infrastructure in southern Lebanon.
4. Creation of a new environment in the West Bank. Drying up the financial resources (from Arab sources) of the West Bank mayors while actively suppressing the PLO and encouraging the emergence of a moderate Palestinian leadership.

5. Pursuing vigorously the Camp David autonomy plan and ensuring that it would consist of no more than an administrative council on the West Bank.

Egypt

Speeding up the Egyptian-Israeli normalization process and in the same context speeding up the negotiations over autonomy, with a target date of establishing the autonomy structure immediately after total Israeli withdrawal from Egyptian territory.

The Nuclear Issue

Establishing nuclear monopoly or a nuclear free zone while Israel still possesses a nuclear capability in the area.[5]

Given these basic Herut positions, which were Begin's, the regional or global aspirations of the United States involving Israel, Saudi Arabia and the rest of the Middle East could not be fulfilled.

LEBANON: THE DEMISE OF BEGIN

SECTION VI
Preface

Like a figure out of Greek tragedy, Begin at the end of 1983 disappeared into a self-imposed oblivion and exile. For an activist like Begin, this was doubly tragic and ironic. This true-believer in the exclusivity of military power was undone by the greatest war Israel had ever participated in, a war he had helped plan and instigate, along with his ideological associates. The war in Lebanon toppled the Begin myth and spirit, if not the Begin government. Begin's folly led to his inglorious resignation.

It is not the intention of this book to detail or narrate the war in Lebanon. Yet this war resulted in a divided Israel, a nation no longer tied together by a historical consensus which said that wars fought must be necessary wars. The domestic implications of the Lebanon war, more than the near-disaster of the 1973 Yom Kippur War, left the nation leaderless, unfulfilled, and bitterly divided. The story of the war and the country is worth looking at briefly.

Contrary to what media experts may say, Lebanon does not constitute a modern political system. It remains, as it has been, the last remnant of the Ottoman empire, a precarious republic that is really a feudal arrangement among Moslem, Christian, and Druse leaders and their followers.

Israeli leaders knew all this to a degree, but somehow their observations did not stop them from pursuing an alliance with the

Gemayel family Christian Phalange faction, which had, between 1976 and 1984, switched its allegiance from Syria to Israel and back again. What resulted was an Israeli quagmire and a Lebanese tragedy.

The unholy covenant between Ariel Sharon and Bashir Gemayel had only one common purpose: destruction of the Palestine Liberation Organization in Lebanon. From there, each man pursued entirely different goals. Gemayel, with the PLO destroyed, wanted a Christian Phalange government with himself at its head, supported by Israeli military power. Having gained power, however, he would pursue a Lebanese Arab policy, meaning that he would be willing to fight to the last Israeli soldier while making a deal with Saudi Arabia for the establishment of a Christian-Arab Lebanon.[1]

Sharon's goals, in all of their zigzagging, vacillating aspects, were never made clear to the cabinet and perhaps even his own prime minister, Menachem Begin. Sharon seemingly never intended to limit the war to a quick-strike, forty-kilometer operation against the PLO. By manipulating and deceiving Begin and his cabinet, he pursued an Israeli hegemonial ambition in Lebanon, seeking to install Gemayel and impose a Christian-Maronite rule, and de-Arabize Lebanon, competing with Israel.

The consequences of that strategy were disastrous. Gemayel outmaneuvered Sharon, never delivering real military support in the siege of Beirut or any other battle. Except for a few minioperations, the only Phalange "military" operation was the massacre in Palestinian refugee camps at Sabra and Shatila.

United States Secretary of State Alexander Haig, who could be said to be one of the casualties of the Lebanon War, was vague on the Middle East and on Lebanon, but his supposed "green light" to the Begin government played a key role in Israel's conduct of the war. Sharon at least implied to Begin that he had tacit American approval of the operation.

Sharon relentlessly pursued "higher" goals in Lebanon: an opportunity to chastise Syria militarily, and a long-range opportunity to impose an Israeli peace and dominance in Lebanon.[2]

None of these plans materialized. There is no peace in Lebanon; United States policy remained as murky as ever; the Phalange was weakened; Israeli and Syrian troops remained in Lebanon; the arms race between Syria and Israel accelerated; and the so-called Lebanese government remained as weak as ever.

CHAPTER 12

Political Deception and Self-Deception: Israel's Invasion of Lebanon[1]

Menachem Begin saw Israel's foray into Lebanon as the key to Eretz Israel, the fulfillment of the final partition state, the annexation of western Palestine. The idea, as Begin saw it, was to destroy once and for all the Palestine Liberation Organization state-within-a-state in Lebanon. Once the PLO was annihilated, the occupation and eventual integration and annexation of the West Bank could be more rapidly facilitated. The utter destruction of the PLO, to Begin's way of thinking, would bring an end to the option of Palestinian autonomy and statehood. Begin felt that with the PLO eliminated, the resistance of Palestinians in Judea and Samaria would slacken, if not diminish altogether, and that world sympathy for the PLO would rapidly end.

Begin saw Lebanon as a means to an end, and a quick one at that. The operation itself—grandiosely dubbed "The Peace of Galilee" by Begin and "Greater Litani" by more pragmatic IDF officers—was the brainchild of Begin, Chief of Staff Rafael (Raful) Eitan, and Defense Minister Ariel Sharon. Eitan saw it strictly in military terms—a quick, massive, and surgical strike against the PLO in Fatahland (as Israelis called southern Lebanon), extending no further than forty kilometers and involving a minimum number of casualties. There were to be no massive land battles, no huge destruction of property, and no large-scale civilian or Israel Defense Force casualties.

But Ariel Sharon had other ideas. He saw Raful's idea as only a jumping-off point, not an end in itself. In Sharon's mind, there should not have been a forty-kilometer limit; he harbored higher ambitions. He saw the incursion as an opportunity to change the political map of Lebanon by establishing a linkage with the Christian Phalange and its young and charismatic feudal lord, Bashir Gemayel—a linkage which ultimately led not to a pro-Israeli government as Sharon wished, but to the camp gates of Sabra and Shatila. Included as part of Sharon's plan was a strike against Syria and her surface-to-air (SAM) missiles in the Bekaa Valley.

Sharon was helped in his ambitions by Begin's vision of fulfilling the old Revisionist-Jabotinsky dream of Eretz Israel. Begin saw the Lebanon operation as his crowning achievement, and he therefore did not need much persuading. Begin probably envisioned the strike as ensuring that he could be the prime minister who, by destroying the PLO, created a secure and united Eretz Israel. Sharon probably saw himself riding in triumph like some Roman praetor entering Jerusalem, the next king of Israel. So optimistic and united was Israel about the avowed aim of the operation—the destruction of the PLO—that all parties, including Labor, joined in support of it. Members of Likud, the Knesset, Laborites Rabin and Peres were all ready to crush the PLO, all of which gave the operation the appearances of having a loud national consensus behind it, a consensus that quickly proved to be illusory.

It did not happen the way everyone seemed to believe it would, as we know. Israel came unglued in Lebanon, splitting apart at its political seams. Not only did Lebanon remain as divided as ever, but deep divisions began to show in Israel after three years of war. Sharon's reputation and ambitions were all but ruined and Begin resigned a defeated man. By a stroke of luck Sharon somehow managed in the 1984 elections to recover, joining the National Unity government as minister of commerce and trade, and becoming a member of the inner security Cabinet of Ten.

It is not our purpose here to recount a history of the war itself, any more than we did with any of Israel's previous wars. What is important is to detail how Israel, strong, secure, unchallenged as the most powerful military state in the Middle East, became enmeshed in a no-win, debilitating war, and the political consequences of the war for Israel's body politic.

Begin and Sharon: Rhetoric and Action[2]

Any evaluation or consideration of the second Begin government must first include an examination of the relationship between Begin and his minister of defense, the volatile and controversial Ariel Sharon. Nowhere is the nature of that relationship more evident than in the course of the Israeli incursion into Lebanon, a kind of culmination and logical outcome of the Begin-Sharon partnership in action.

The relationship is that of rhetorician to tactician. Begin, with his rhetoric, set policy with a specific goal in mind; Sharon carried out the policy, using tactics that often exceeded the scope of both the rhetoric and the more modest policy. In a very simplistic way, it is almost fair to say that Sharon was Begin's instrument, his executor and bully boy. Begin, a devout believer in the concept of Eretz Israel and a stolid and implacable opponent of any sort of nationalist Palestinian movement, was wedded to Sharon as his perfect instrument, who carried out in ruthless action what lay at the heart of Begin's rhetoric.

The Begin-Sharon relationship dated from the aftermath of the 1973 war. It was not always friendly or amiable, to say the least.

In 1973, Sharon, who liked to have his own way, was very much aware of Begin's authoritarianism, his coolness toward opposition and competition, traits Sharon shared but did not admire in others. At the time, Sharon refused to join Begin's party, Herut, even though the party desperately needed a war hero. Instead, Sharon created the Likud, a right and right-of-center electoral coalition composed of four parties of which Herut was the most important. He hoped Begin's strength would be swallowed up by the Likud bloc. But Begin turned the tables on Sharon, who left the coalition in 1974 out of sheer frustration. In 1977 Sharon formed his own party, a left group called Shlomzion (Peace of Zion). Sharon and his newly formed party were spectacular electoral failures, winning only two seats. But the seats were crucial for Begin's coalition and Sharon was asked to join the government as agriculture minister. In that position he proceeded to carry out Begin's policy of settlements in the West Bank and Gaza with an alacrity that had not been seen before, taking the opportunity to rout Palestinian nationalists and dampen the spirit of their movement. Begin invoked Eretz Israel and "Judea and

Samaria" often in his rhetoric, but it was Sharon who turned the words into action.

Sharon, a tough veteran in dealing with Palestinian nationalism, acted out Begin's dream of Eretz Israel. But Begin still balked at totally embracing the unpredictable Sharon, declining to offer him the defense ministry, which Begin took for himself after the departure of Ezer Weizman. Sharon was keenly disappointed and showed it with some ill-tempered comments (e.g., "I will surround the prime minister's office with tanks!" a threat quoted by Begin himself and reported in the daily, *Haaretz*), but eventually his anger subsided. By then, his growing popularity among the changing Israeli electorate proved invaluable to the politically endangered Begin, who had seen his own popularity slide as fast as the inflation rate rose. With Sharon's considerable help, Begin squeaked by in the 1981 elections. Begin rewarded him with the defense ministry at last, in spite of a hue and cry from the political opposition.

From the beginning, Sharon was the blunt instrument of Begin's most controversial policies, the man who did the dirty work and took the blame if the actions backfired. He ousted Israeli settlers from the Sinai, led the debate over the bombing of the Iraqi nuclear reactor, and purged pro-PLO mayors from the West Bank.

Sharon's War in Lebanon

In spite of all the tragedy, failures and fiascos, the misconceptions, deaths, political and diplomatic mistakes, shattered plans and careers which resulted from the Lebanese war of 1982, it must be made clear that in many respects the war was almost inevitable long before it started. It was not an accidental stumbling into conflagration, but an event planned as a response to long-standing provocation. But the scope of the war, and all the disasters and entanglements which stemmed from it, are an entirely different matter. The start of the war was planned with measured debate by a government which set itself a limited and specific goal in response to what it perceived as an intolerable and continued threat to its national security. The man whose responsibility it was to conduct that war, in order to accomplish his own plans set about to manipulate his own prime minister, the cabinet, and the armed forces, thus extending the scope and duration of the war and its tremendous potential for larger tragedy, political fiasco, and disaster. Just as important, he misled Israel's American allies.[3]

The blame for the Lebanese war does not rest solely with former Israeli Defense Minister Ariel Sharon; understanding the situation and events defies that kind of simplicity. But if there is a single person who bears the lion's share of the responsibility for the war's steady descent into disaster, it is Sharon. His plans led directly to the involvement of Syria in the war, to the tragedy at Sabra and Shatila, to the diplomatic and military entry of the United States into the swamplike arena of Lebanon, and to the final collapse of Menachem Begin. Indirectly his actions led to the disaster that befell the contingent-without-a-mission of United States Marines who died in a bomb attack on their barracks in Beirut.

Without Sharon's attempt to implement his own plans, it can be said with a large degree of certainty that much of what ensued would not have occurred. Once Sharon's plans began to be put into motion, the rest followed with a kind of awesome inevitability. Sharon's actions and plans constituted a kind of hubris that infected all of the participants, most particularly the United States, which could no more control events in Lebanon than could Sharon. The war ran away from Sharon, not coincidentally from almost the moment when American diplomatic efforts and pressure, however misguided, began to make themselves felt. The Reagan administration, like everyone else, got stuck in the Lebanese morass and became a target to be used by all sides—the Israelis, Syrians, PLO, and all the multitudinous warring factions within Lebanon itself.

No government of Israel, whether of Labor or Likud, could for any length of time tolerate the existence of the kind of military infrastructure which the Palestinian Liberation Organization, by the eve of the war, had built up in southern Lebanon. Over a period of seven years the PLO had dug in near the northern Israeli border, from where it effectively shelled Israeli settlements. It dominated all of southern Lebanon, had recently supplied itself to the point where it constituted a military threat to Israel, and was headquartered and entrenched in West Beirut under the umbrella of its Arab patron, Syria, and its big-power patron, the Soviet Union. The question, then, was never whether or not Israel would move against the PLO and into Lebanon. It was a question of when, with how much firepower, and with what goals in mind. That question had engaged both government of Labor's Yitzhak Rabin, and the two governments of Likud's Menachem Begin. The changing response to the question constituted a major shift in Israeli attitudes toward war and its uses.

The answers to the question evolved over a period of over a decade, from 1971 to the eve of the war, and involved five phases. From 1971 to 1975 the PLO buildup in the mountains of Lebanon began and Israel limited itself to retaliatory efforts against PLO actions; 1975–1977 marked the start of the Lebanese civil war and the entry of Syria as an actor on the Lebanese scene; 1977–1978 was a period of increasing Syrian-PLO collusion to gain even greater influence in Lebanon, and of PLO attacks on Israel, coinciding with an expanded retaliatory policy from Israel. From 1979 to 1982 Israel shifted toward the use of war as an instrument of policy. This period coincided with Begin's second election and the departure of the more restrained and Laborite members of Begin's first cabinet and the arrival of Sharon. The final phase was the war itself.

During the first period, 1971 to 1975, the PLO, which had announced itself through significant acts of terrorism as the political and military champion of the Palestinian cause, began to move in small units into the Hermon mountains and other portions of Lebanon, including Beirut itself, from which it would conduct hit-and-run raids against Israel. All of this was accomplished with active assistance and training from Syria, the PLO's most vociferous Arab champion, and the Soviet Union. The Labor government of Yitzhak Rabin was naturally alarmed by this growing development, but did not overreact. Its policy was on the whole one of retaliation and restraint, a defensive act, an attempt to control the level of violence before it had a chance to mushroom into major proportions. This policy had been almost an article of faith with all Labor governments in all previous fights, and it was implemented again. The Israelis attempted to check the growth of the PLO as a military organization by occupying the point of entry to the Hermon mountains and by conducting retaliatory raids designed to weaken the PLO, not destroy it. Thus, the Israel Defense Forces conducted actions such as a raid on the Beirut airport, knocking out twelve Lebanese planes on the ground, and thus it conducted a commando raid into the heart of Beirut, killing three key PLO leaders who had participated in the massacre of Israeli athletes at the 1972 Summer Olympics at Munich.

During the period of 1975–1977, there was a lull in PLO activity against Israel; the civil war in Lebanon had heated up, and Syria had tentatively entered the arena. The Syrian move was cautious. At first President Hafez al-Assad's regime seemed to be helping the Maronite Christians in their battle against the PLO, but then the Syrians switched sides and firmly backed the PLO and the left-wing, anti-Maronite forces, which included renegade Christians, Druses, and a variety of dissident Moslem forces.

By 1977 the PLO, through the guidance and support of the Syrians, had begun to maintain something of a stranglehold on large chunks of Lebanon, especially in the south. The Syrian policy in Lebanon was to divide and conquer, and their support of the repressive PLO helped them maintain a heavy hand on what was basically a puppet Lebanese government. At the same time, the PLO was becoming a more deadly military organization.

Israel, with Begin in power but under the influence of a cabinet that was basically moderate and restraining in tone, still clung to a retaliatory policy. Ezer Weizman and Moshe Dayan both served to restrain Begin's instinct to lash out on a grand scale. The Litani operation of the summer of 1978 to establish a zone of security to be occupied by U.N. forces was launched in reaction to growing PLO military activities and was therefore limited in scope.[4]

But in many ways, the Litani raid foreshadowed the new and coming view of war as an instrument of policy. It was the largest military operation ever mounted against the PLO and it involved the use of tank units, artillery and considerable firepower. Yet it kept to the conventions of a raid because its aims were limited in scope, and it avoided large population areas and cities. It was a quick-strike operation designed to destroy and cripple the PLO's ability to wage war. It was not designed to conquer territory but rather to create a buffer or security zone of seven kilometers. Decidedly preventive in nature, it was meant to keep the PLO out of artillery range, not to get the IDF embroiled in Lebanon. However, for the first time, the IDF acted to some degree with the help of anti-PLO forces within Lebanon, mainly the Christians of the south, and particularly the late Major Saad Hadad, who was to become a feature actor in the events that followed. The IDF itself was leery of working with the Christian Phalange, whom they knew to be reckless, vengeful, undisciplined and unreliable as a military force, but they nevertheless on the whole found them a convenience. In addition, the Shiite Arabs in the south had specifically asked for IDF protection from the PLO.

For the first time Begin, who had basked in the role of peacemaker, ran headlong into sharp United States opposition from President Jimmy Carter, who angrily ordered Begin to halt the operation. A bitter Begin, who had hoped to see the PLO militarily shattered, would later rail that the United States "had saved the PLO," not the last time that Begin and other Israeli leaders would make that accusation. Still, within its limited scope, the Litani operation was something of an immediate success. The PLO had been dealt a sharp setback and Israel had the makings of a tentative security zone. Restraint was still the order of the day, as a jubilant Ezer Weizman welcomed the introduction of a UNIFIL—United Nations Interim Force in Lebanon—presence in the buffer zone to keep the peace.

The period from 1979 to the eve of the 1982 war marked a huge turnabout in Israeli policy and attitudes, in the nature of the PLO-Israeli struggle and events in Lebanon, and in the activities and policies of Syria and the PLO. In Israel there was a marked deterioration of the national consensus, a deterioration that had begun to crack sharply in the wake of the 1973 Yom Kippur War. Also, with the departure of Dayan in 1979, Weizman in 1980, and Yigal Yadin after the 1981 election, there was no one left to restrain Begin's strong inclination, even preference, to find decisive, large-scale military solutions to what he perceived as threats to Israeli security. The Israeli destruction of the Iraqi nuclear reactor and the massive bombing of PLO headquarters in Beirut were the results. With the appointment of Sharon as defense minister after the 1981 elections, Begin not only had no moderate voice in the cabinet to suggest restraint, he had a defense minister who played upon his ego, vanity, and nationalistic fantasies. Sharon knew that Begin would love to have another chance to destroy the PLO, a goal not many Israelis of influence would disagree with. Within the framework of that goal, Sharon envisioned grander plans, and everything that was happening in Lebanon at the time seemed to serve as building blocks for those visions.

The PLO and Syria did not remain idle during the years following the Litani operation. The PLO had finally all but ended its terrorism and for a while toned down its military activities, embarking upon a world-wide diplomatic campaign advocating the legitimization of a Palestinian state, with the PLO as the Palestinians' only political representative. The public relations and diplomatic campaign was effective, drawing support from European countries as well as the Carter administration.

But the PLO, in the wake of the Litani setback, had also begun to rearm itself on a large scale with weapons funneled from Syria and the Soviet Union. Bit by bit, the PLO was becoming a highly entrenched and effective military organization that loomed as a major threat to Israel, especially to its northern settlements. For, by 1982, PLO units equipped with Russian Katyusha rockets had begun mounting large-scale attacks against settlements in Galilee. These attacks were effective; they shook morale in the settlements badly enough to result in a heavy influx of settlers into Haifa. PLO Foreign Minister Farruq Quadami boasted that "the de-Zionization of Israel had begun."

Syria, meanwhile, had succeeded in uniting most of the anti-Christian, antigovernment forces within Lebanon, as well as taking some beginning steps to stir up trouble within the ranks of the PLO, the more radical members of which were rabidly opposed to the PLO's diplomatic efforts. Israel, under Rabin and under the first Begin government, had studiously avoided becoming too closely tied to the Phalange or becoming directly involved in the Lebanese civil war, limiting itself to giving military aid and helping the Phalange to protect themselves. But between 1979 and 1982, Israeli involvement became more direct; there were now Israeli military advisers on the ground with the Phalange.

In response to the closer Phalange-Israeli alliance, the Syrians had decided to install antiaircraft missiles in the Bekaa Valley to prevent Israeli support of the Phalange; this raised the specter of another Syrian-Israeli conflagration. Once again, the United States, through the auspices of Special Envoy Philip Habib, stepped in to defuse the crisis. Begin characteristically did not see this as effective diplomacy, but as meddling. From his viewpoint the United States, just as it had done with the PLO, "saved" the Syrian missiles.

Against this background, Israel made a crucial switch from retaliation to the use of massive military force as an instrument of policy. By the spring of 1982 Begin, Sharon, the cabinet, and the IDF awaited an opportunity to destroy the growing PLO military infrastructure in Lebanon, the state-within-a-state.

Begin viewed the Palestine Liberation Organization as having a Holocaust mentality. He took PLO leader Yasir Arafat's vow to destroy Israel literally, even though the PLO just may have lacked the military means to carry out their vow. Begin's pursuit of the destruction of the PLO led him straight into the waiting arms of Ariel Sharon and the invasion of Lebanon. It also showed that in some respects Begin was a distant leader who was being led by others.

A grand-scale military operation and plan began to take shape with the sole intent of destroying the PLO military state-within-a-state, no small aim in and of itself. There was no full cabinet or IDF contemplation of extending the war into Beirut; if anything, there was a great deal of worry about possible conflict with Syria and no real plan to attack Syrian forces or missiles. There was no thought of combining with Christian forces or of manipulating Lebanese politics. The plan was something of a super-Litani operation, whose chief element would be an armored infantry thrust some forty-five kilometers into Lebanon, across the Litani into the PLO heartland, along with coastal attacks and the shelling of PLO forces near Beirut.[5]

The more the PLO fired rockets at Israeli settlements, the more the PLO infrastructure grew, the more the idea of destruction of the source took on a momentum of its own in Israel. But Begin worried. So did the nervous IDF and its general staff. What, the field commanders and Chief of Staff Raful Eitan asked, would Syria do? Was there a danger of Syrian involvement, or a head-on clash with the Syrians? And then there were the missiles in Bekaa, which more and more were beginning to look like an inviting target.

The debate raged for months. Do we, Eitan and the IDF generals asked, have to deal with the Syrians? The Mossad reassured Begin and the generals that there was no reason for the Syrians to become involved. But still the generals fretted. They looked on the maps and saw the Bekaa Valley bristling with Syrian tanks and missiles.

The debate also concerned itself with the reaction and the possible interference of the United States, factors that could become crucial. Begin especially was extremely nervous about American reaction. He, Sharon, and Foreign Minister Yitzhak Shamir all agreed that the United States would oppose the operation, even if it were limited to the size of the earlier Litani raid. What was needed was to avoid both precipitate U.S. action and U.S. destruction of the surprise element. The Reagan administration could not be allowed to limit and restrain the operation from its beginning. Begin and the cabinet feared that the United States would attempt to get some kind of agreement on the coordination of all the elements operating in Lebanon, and this would confer political legitimacy on the very PLO it was trying to destroy.

The general worry about the United States had a very legitimate base. Under the Carter administration, none too friendly toward Begin and Israel, the United States had moved away from globalism to a regional approach which was pragmatic in concept but ineffectual in execution. Under Reagan, the United States appeared to be executing a sharp turnabout, now conducting foreign policy in terms of the perceived Soviet threat. In the Middle East this led to confusion and policies which the Israelis looked at with incredulity, skepticism and foreboding, particularly Secretary of State Haig's unwieldy and misguided strategic consensus policy, which would somehow wed moderate Arabs and Israel in a united front against Soviet adventures in the Middle East. There was also the American sale of AWACs and F-15 aircraft to Saudi Arabia, and an increasingly intensified thrust toward finding friendly Arab allies. To Israel, all of this was sharply at odds with Reagan's avowed hostility toward the PLO and his repeated pledges of undying support for Israel. In short, the Begin government had reason to worry about United States reaction to the coming operation.

Those worries aside, Begin, the cabinet, the general staff, and the IDF unanimously agreed that the object of the operation, which they knew constituted an invasion, was the destruction of the PLO military infrastructure once and for all—nothing more, nothing less. True, this was Litani doubled and tripled in size, but then, so was the PLO. True, there would be incursions into populated areas. But the goal was clear—destroy the PLO. There would be no entanglements with Lebanese units except on a minimal level, and that would be coordinated through Major Saad Hadad. There would be no meddling in Lebanese politics. Contact with the Syrians was to be avoided unless absolutely necessary. This was a limited operation with specific, limited goals, everyone agreed—everyone, that is, except Ariel Sharon.

Sharon understood Begin's Revisionist Zionist dreams and his plans. He himself cared about Eretz Israel, though not about any sort of ism, and was a man single-minded in the pursuit of power. Throughout his career, Sharon had yearned to be what he was not. As a general, brilliant tactician and war hero, he coveted the position of chief of staff, which he never attained. As a politician with limited success, he coveted the defense ministry. Now, as defense minister, he yearned to be prime minister. After all, he was still a hero to many, he had a huge following, and people all over Israel were already calling him "King of Israel." He was determined to succeed Begin, and the invasion of Lebanon was his gamble to attain that goal.

Sharon's concept of the incursion was much grander than a large-scale Litani operation. He had thought all along that the whole idea of repeating Litani was too limited and unrealistic. Sharon's monumentally ambitious ideas started where Litani ended. The IDF would make a forty-five-kilometer thrust into Lebanon, but it would not be limited to a vertical thrust. It would be a squared thrust, forty-five kilometers *wide* as well as deep, which would bring the IDF directly into contact with Syrian forces in the Bekaa Valley. What Sharon had in mind was control of the strategic Beirut-Damascus road on the outskirts of Beirut, which would allow him to bottle up the PLO forces within Beirut and destroy them piecemeal. Sharon was intending to go straight to the gates of Beirut. If that should entail disciplining the Syrians and, not incidentally, create an opportunity to destroy the SAM missiles, so much the better. It would not, he thought, lead to a general war with Syria.

Sharon had intricate political plans as well. He did not intend to fight in the streets of Beirut. For that, he needed the Phalange, in particular the Gemayel family, whom he had been courting, conferring with and pursuing studiously for months. Sharon saw in the incursion a chance to control the political destiny of Lebanon, to create a government friendly to Israel while allowing a Syrian presence in the north. This was a direct departure from previous policies of avoiding direct involvement with Lebanon's convoluted, fratricidal political struggles and divisions. Sharon saw the operation as a chance to create a Pax Israeliana in Lebanon and to do this he needed a tacit alliance with Bashir Gemayel and his family, whom he could then control.[6]

Sharon's plans—the thrust toward Beirut, the probable clash with the Syrians, and the creation of a pro-Israeli Lebanese government—were intricate and grandiose. Sharon meant to implement his plans as the war progressed, and to do this he had to accomplish several things. He needed to isolate Begin and the cabinet from the military; more important, he needed to minimize or *appear* to minimize the threat of American interference. Up to a point, he accomplished all of these goals by chivying, maneuvering, manipulating, and keeping information from the cabinet, the IDF, and later his supposed ally, the United States.

Sharon's first order of business was to isolate Begin and the cabinet from their military advisers, the IDF's general staff. To do this, he created a small group of some twenty-five officers which became known as the national security unit. It was run by General Avraham (Abrasha) Tamir as a kind of military liaison between the cabinet, the Knesset Committee on Defense and Foreign Affairs, and the IDF. The cabinet by this time was ill-equipped to handle military decisions, since none of them, Begin included, had actual military experience except Sharon and the minister of communication, retired Brigadier General Mordechai Zipori, who was excluded from the smaller "war cabinet." Increasingly, Sharon's was the only military voice of experience Begin was allowed to hear. The IDF command, excluding Chief of Staff Eitan, one of Begin's favorites, had little input into the final decisions, and were, at any rate, obedient to the government. Sharon had succeeded in making himself his own chief of staff, in charge of the war and its execution. As for Eitan, even though he heartily disliked Sharon, their common hatred of the PLO made them tacit allies, even though Eitan disapproved of the Litani-plus operation.

The question of United States reaction was more complex and brought out much of Sharon's cunning. There was no question of letting the United States know of Israel's specific plans. Sharon, at this point, became shrewd and engaged in a subtle battle of wits with Secretary of State Alexander Haig, whom he saw as a pragmatic ideologue. In cabinet meetings Sharon was persuasive. He insisted that the Americans, while publicly denouncing the operation, would secretly and tacitly support it. The cabinet remained skeptical. The key for Sharon was Haig, who Sharon thought was more than likely not averse to the operation, but would not give official United States approval. Sharon had already made Haig aware that an Israeli incursion was a serious possibility.

He was aware that Haig wanted to ensure the *limited scope* of the operation if it could not be prevented.⁷ For Sharon this was tantamount to a green light from Haig, and thus from the United States. At least that is what he continued to tell the cabinet, and more important, Begin. As the cabinet waited to decide on the war, Sharon, in a crucial move, sent IDF Chief of Intelligence, General Yehoshua Saguy, to Washington for another talk with Haig about the operation and United States attitudes. Saguy brought back word in the form Sharon wanted to hear, which is to say that he insinuated that Haig was not indifferent. That was enough for Sharon. "We will persuade Begin," he said at a high-level meeting in the middle of 1982, "as if Haig agrees with the operation." At least one high military officer would later say that Haig never gave the green light. At the very least, Sharon persuaded Begin to hear things that were not really being said.⁸

Sharon handled the IDF generals in a similar manner. Obviously the generals were concerned about Syria, and to that end contingency plans had been drawn up for the case of a military confrontation with Syria. Yet the various contingency plans, which included the thrust toward the Beirut-Damascus road, were never *approved* by the cabinet, nor were many IDF field commanders happy with them, like General Avigdor Ben-Gal, who muttered with contempt at the start of the war, "That bastard Arik [Sharon] is going to Beirut."⁹

To Sharon, control of the Beirut-Damascus road was crucial to his goals. Yet it was obvious to everyone that that would widen the original forty-five-kilometer thrust to seventy kilometers, and would include the conquest of Damur and the Shouf Mountains, as well as IDF encampment on the outskirts of Beirut. Sharon had contingency plans for all of this, plans that never were approved, but rather were rushed forth as events dictated. In effect they were actions approved after the fact, which increasingly left Begin as a rubber stamp who had no control over events or over Sharon.

One of Sharon's chief "contingencies" involved courting Bashir Gemayel and using the Lebanese army. In meetings with the Gemayel family, leaders of the Maronite Christians in Lebanon, Sharon described the scenario as "the opportunity of a lifetime." He pictured a government in which the Gemayel family, with Bashir at their head, would be the dominant factor in Lebanon. There would be no foreign forces in Lebanon, and Israel and Lebanon would coexist in trust and cooperation. Gemayel was interested but skeptical. "You are newcomers in Lebanon," he told Sharon. "I would be the [Christian] leader of a Lebanese state which is still an Arab state."¹⁰ He was cautious. He wanted to do it his way, to keep his Arab option open. But Sharon continued to insist. He wanted Bashir and his forces to take Beirut. Once established, Israel would help him institutionalize his government.

Sharon had a reason to push. Time was running out on his grand plans. The United States had entered the field. Its first reaction to events in Lebanon was to call for a cease-fire. Israel pleaded for coordination. In Washington, Haig knew now that he had been outwitted. Decision-making on Lebanon moved into the White House. Official American reaction and participation occurred in three stages. During the first five days of the war, United States concern centered on an escalation with Syria. This was followed by concern over the enlargement of the operation against the PLO, and finally by concern over the siege of Beirut and the interminable shelling and bombardment of the city.

By June 8, the Syria-Israeli confrontation had become a reality as two Syrian tank battalions were destroyed near Hasybiya, in the southern Bekaa Valley. The missiles there were destroyed, as was a staggering number of Syrian MIG fighter planes in air battles. Now Philip Habib quickly entered the scene as United States mediator. Sharon had not yet controlled the coveted Beirut-Damascus Road when Habib issued the first American call for a cease-fire. He was now in a quandary. He genuinely did not want a major war with Syria, nor did he want to enter Beirut. And the United States was now at his doorstep, with success almost in sight.

Habib insisted that the IDF should withdraw from the outskirts of Beirut. Fearing that the Maronites, with their close ties to the Israelis, would become overly ambitious, he wanted presidential elections and a national unity government that would include a cross section of the various factions within Lebanon. Habib told Bashir Gemayel that he should tiptoe away from the Israeli embrace, mend his fences with Moslem factions, and keep the door open toward negotiations with the Syrians, whom he saw as crucial in achieving a settlement. The Syrians wanted and needed to play a role in the future of Lebanon.

Sharon, feeling the intense pressure of the American presence, kept pressing Gemayel to move into Beirut, but by this time,

Gemayel was moving away from Sharon. All of Sharon's plans were starting to become unglued. His meetings with Habib were acrimonious. In frustration, Sharon invited Walid Jumblatt, the Druse leader who was openly hostile to the Gemayels, for a conference in Jerusalem. More serious, he tightened the siege of Beirut and intensified the bombardment of Palestinian positions.

When this happened, the Syrians, who had been the object of intense negotiations by Habib, felt rebuffed and betrayed by the Americans. Hafez al-Assad turned to the Russians to replenish his military forces, and quelled a near-revolt by his restive and humiliated officers. He accused Habib of having no control over the Israelis, noting that they remained on the Beirut-Damascus road and showed no signs of leaving, United States pressure or not.

For Sharon, the game was beginning to fall apart. The siege was not bringing about a satisfactory conclusion. He was reacting to events and to United States diplomatic efforts, not to his own plan. Even Begin and the cabinet were becoming restive. The Israeli consensus was now coming apart at the seams, with public demonstrations against the war taking place.

Habib, meanwhile, pushed hard. He bluntly told Gemayel that he must, when and if elected, form a broad national unity government and maintain relations with Syria. At the same time, Habib began to negotiate with Yasir Arafat and the PLO. Arafat mistrusted the Israelis, and he especially mistrusted the Christian Phalangists now ready to move into West Beirut. At first he was skeptical of a United States offer to evacuate the PLO and its forces, but his choices were limited. Habib made the same offer to Sharon, in somewhat stronger terms, telling him that the siege was "counterproductive."

Habib's offer led directly to the first appearance of United States Marines. Their mission: protect the PLO evacuation from Beirut, which allowed the PLO to convey to the world the impression that they had somehow managed a victory, which in fact they had not. In addition, the marines were to protect the PLO evacuation of Palestinian refugee camps in Lebanon.

The final act of what many called "Arik's War" was about to be played out. When Bashir Gemayel died at the hands of assassins, Sharon told the new United States envoy, Morris Draper, that there were left-wing, radical forces in the Shouf mountains and in Beirut. He would, he told Draper, as if asking for approval, move

Israeli forces into West Beirut "to keep the peace" in the wake of the assassination. In fact, Sharon may have already given the order for Israeli forces to move. In the sense that he did not voice his disapproval, Draper appeared to acquiesce, which Sharon, as in the case of Haig's oblique nondisapproval, took to be tacit approval.

It was the last time that Sharon would control events to any degree in Lebanon. The massacre of refugees by Phalangists in camps at Sabra and Shatila would follow, and from that, the return of the United States Marines, this time to protect the Palestinian population in West Beirut as well as a tottering Amin Gemayel government. The later developments—bickering over the Reagan peace plan; Arafat's abortive peace mission and his expulsion from Syria; a fake and useless Lebanese-Israeli peace treaty; the Israeli Commission of Inquiry; the firing of Sharon; the steady decline and final resignation of Begin; and increased involvement of American marines—all these were further links in a horrifying chain of events. The chain had begun with the entrenchment of the PLO in Lebanon, but Ariel Sharon forged it as surely as anyone, carrying with him his country, his prime minister, and the United States. The death of nearly 260 marines, 75 Arabs and 56 Frenchmen was, in that context, only another link in the chain, and surely not the last one.

More than anything else, it was the furor over the massacre of Palestinians by Christian Phalange militia personnel in the camps at Sabra and Shatila after the assassination of Gemayel that would eventually break Begin. Begin responded to the news and the world outrage in characteristic fashion: he withdrew into a shell of defiance.

Responding to charges that the Israelis were at least in part responsible for the massacre, Begin called the accusation a "blood libel." "Goyim kill Goyim," he complained, "and they blame the Jews." Not once did he express any sympathy, horror, shock or condolences for the victims, many of them women and children.

Sabra-Shatila would not go away. After first refusing to appoint a special committee of inquiry to investigate the massacre, Begin backed down under pressure from members of his own cabinet. The result was devastating for Begin and his government. The verdict attacked Begin himself, and laid prime responsibility on Sharon.

"For two days," the commission found, "he [Begin] showed absolutely no interest in the camps. . . . His lack of involvement casts him a certain degree of responsibility."

Begin refused to believe so. He was also torn in his feelings toward Sharon. By this time he knew that Sharon had led him down the garden path, and the garden was turning into a Gethsemane. But he could not bring himself to sack an old ally. Sharon, much against his will, finally submitted his resignation and Begin shunted him into the post of minister without portfolio.

By that time, Begin had begun to stop caring. It was a long, drawn-out process that built steadily over the summer. Few people saw him and those that did were shocked by his frail appearance. A scheduled trip to the United States was canceled. Israeli soldiers were dying daily in Lebanon. Begin missed his wife and companion, who had died at the time of Shatila. He stopped making public appearances. Finally, came the abrupt, unadorned announcement of his resignation. Finally came silence.

CHAPTER 13

A Greek Tragedy: The Disappearance of Begin[1]

It was in the middle of September 1983 that Menachem Begin, after a summer in which he had been remarkably reclusive and silent, bluntly announced that he would resign. His Likud coalition partners and long-time cronies from the underground days pleaded with him to change his mind. Israeli politicians were skeptical. But Begin stuck to his decision and to his isolation. On September 13, Begin's cabinet secretary, Dan Meridor, stoically and unceremoniously delivered Begin's handwritten and signed resignation to President Chaim Herzog.

Begin's resignation, an event with thunderous political reverberations, was conducted in almost complete silence. It was as if Begin were willing himself to disappear. There were no emotional television appearances, no political rallies. Begin remained in silent seclusion, reportedly disheartened, depressed, ill and frail. There were rumors that he did not shave, that he saw no one, that he did not venture out of his house. He had turned into smoke. After seven years of tumult and shouting, during a reign which was loudly punctuated by events which rocked the Middle East, Begin became politically mute.

What had happened? Certainly, Begin was ill, and he appeared tired and worn out. He was depressed and still in the depths of grief over the death of his wife Aliza, the one person in the world he trusted completely. To those of his colleagues who saw him in the months prior to his resignation, it was obvious that Begin's fire had cooled. The visionary flame which had propelled him in the past had begun to dim.

It was also obvious that Begin's depression was reflected in Israel. The economy was worsening every day and was headed toward disaster. Lebanon was becoming a quagmire that swallowed Israel's youth, its resolve, and its confidence. Every week brought word of Israeli casualties, a debilitating process that pecked away at the nation's and the prime minister's morale. The harsh findings of the commission of inquiry into the Sabra-Shatila massacre in Beirut had tarred everyone—from Begin to Defense Minister Ariel Sharon, to Shamir, to the generals—with a layer of shame. The country as a whole was restive, moribund, and more divided than it had ever been. For Begin, the days of glory when he shaped history with decisive, defiant acts, were over.

His seven-year reign had been eventful. Only six months after he was elected, Begin had stood face to face in Jerusalem with Egyptian President Anwar al-Sadat at the start of a process that would culminate in the Egyptian-Israeli peace treaty and the Camp David agreement. For both Begin and Sadat this was a monumentally courageous political act, an act of statesmen who went ahead in spite of heated opposition from their political allies and enemies at home. In many ways, it was not untypical of Begin, a most unusual politician and prime minister who made it a habit to defy convention and common practice. In the end, however, Begin's most cherished dream remained unfulfilled. Even with the signing of the Egyptian-Israeli peace treaty, a major achievement by any statesman's standards, Begin had bigger dreams. Shortly after the treaty signing, he was asked how he wanted to be remembered in history. His reply was revealing: "I want to be remembered as the man who set the borders of Eretz Israel for all eternity," he said. He wanted the West Bank (Judea and Samaria) and Gaza incorporated into Israel, a vision that allowed no room for an independent Palestinian state. Given the cumulative impact of Israeli settlements in the West Bank, Begin's vision might yet become a reality, but not in his lifetime.[2]

Still, the achievements during his tenure, negative and positive, are impressive:

- Two stunning electoral victories over the entrenched Labor party.

- The realignment of the Israeli electorate.
- The forging of the Egyptian-Israeli peace treaty and the Camp David accords.
- The return of the Sinai to Egypt and the dismantling of Israeli settlements there.
- The crippling of the PLO.
- The bombing of the Iraqi nuclear reactor.
- The invasion of Lebanon.

In the aftermath of all that, how does one assess the man?

Begin had all the earmarks of a potentially great man. He suffered from living in a time of great men. Throughout his life he was haunted by the image of two giants. One, Zeev Jabotinsky, was his mentor. The other, David Ben-Gurion, was his principal antagonist. Begin often despised Ben-Gurion, always respected him and just as often emulated and imitated him. Deep in his heart, as he related to his intimates, Begin never quite measured up to either man and the long shadows they threw even after their deaths.

The odd quality about this curious form of hero worship is that Begin is so startlingly different from both Jabotinsky and Ben-Gurion.

Jabotinsky, as we already know, was the patron saint and founder of Revisionist Zionism. This movement, the exact opposite and rival of Ben-Gurion's pragmatic Socialist Zionist movement, sought to create not only a Jewish state, but a state which encompassed Judea and Samaria, Eretz Israel, the Land of Israel, which includes today's West Bank and Gaza and what is today Jordan. The rhetoric of Revisionist Zionism had a Biblical strain to it, and still does. It tended to ignore the entire existence of the Arab question. With Begin at its head, it challenged and rose up against the British presence in Palestine.

Jabotinsky was a Renaissance man, an intellectual and an indefatigable and charismatic speaker of immense gifts. When Begin, then a leader of Betar, a Revisionist Zionist youth movement in Poland, first met Jabotinsky, he was enthralled. He had found his leader and mentor, but it must have seemed a little like staring in awe at a distant mountaintop.

Jabotinsky was indeed distant, a vain man who would never stoop to informality with his subordinates. He quite naturally treated his followers as enlisted soldiers in a cause. The relationship was that of disciple looking up to master, and Jabotinsky never let Begin forget it.

The Revisionist Zionist movement was personally created by Jabotinsky. By the time Begin had become high commissioner of Betar in Poland, the movement was coming apart, its more radical members urging military action against the British.

Jabotinsky, however, still retained the imperious power with which he could chastise the presumptuous rebels in 1939. At a Betar executive committee meeting in Warsaw, in September 1938, Jabotinsky had almost casually dismissed the idea that Betar and Revisionism should turn into a military organization.

"Mr. Begin," he said, "please be seated and be silent. Our movement will not tolerate terror or military formations which are neither legal nor legitimate."[3]

This was a sharp and cold rebuke and it must have stung Begin, who revered his mentor and would always do so. Begin was nothing if not loyal. He resurrected the leaderless Etzel, Revisionism's underground group in Palestine, during World War II after Jabotinsky died in exile in the United States in 1940. He kept the faith all along.

In the 1960s Begin succeeded in having Jabotinsky's body interred in Israel near Mt. Herzl. On the eve of the 1967 war, when Begin had joined a National Unity government, the first thing he did was to stride up Mt. Herzl. Standing over Jabotinsky's grave, like the constant and dutiful Betar soldier that he was, he proudly made his report:

"Sir," he reportedly said, "Head of Betar, we have come to inform you that one of your followers is now serving as a minister in the government of Israel."

Ben-Gurion was always Begin's and Revisionism's main antagonist. He repeatedly thwarted every early effort by Revisionist forces to establish themselves in Palestine, resorting to propaganda, political maneuvering and suppression. In the 1940s, he helped tarnish Begin's Etzel forces with the taint of terrorism and murder and ordered his own forces to cooperate with the British in hunting down Etzel members. During the war for independence, he ordered the sinking of the supply ship *Altalena,* which was carrying arms for Begin's Etzel underground members. Begin, refusing to risk a Jewish civil war, backed down.

Ben-Gurion would treat Begin with undisguised contempt.[4] In all the time that Begin served in the Knesset, the burly Ben-

Gurion would refer to him as "that member of the Knesset sitting next to M. K. Menachem Bader," (Bader was Begin's deputy).

Although Ben-Gurion loathed Begin, Begin secretly admired Ben-Gurion. Begin saw Ben-Gurion's achievements as milestones to be surpassed. If Ben-Gurion was the founder of the state, Begin would be the man who brought peace to Israel, the man who would achieve Israel's final security and reclaim Eretz Israel.

The differences between Begin and Ben-Gurion and a generation of Israeli leaders are nevertheless sharp. Begin was something new, or rather, old in Israeli history and politics, a classic Diaspora Jew. Ben-Gurion and his followers were present in Palestine at the creation and stayed there like a steady metronome, their feelings, doings, and plans voluminously recorded in official and private documents and books. Begin, who did not come to Palestine until the mid-1940s, left few literary traces. Material on Begin as a young man is very difficult to find, it also is difficult to find clues in his writings. With Begin, there is hardly any intimate written material at all. It is as if the man had almost no private life.

There is an eloquent reticence in the record that does exist, for such a publicly vivid man. There are few, if any, letters. Begin wrote two semi-autobiographical books—*White Nights* and *The Revolt*—but both are bombastic, laced with rhetoric and propaganda, and curiously devoid of introspection.

To reconstruct Begin, one must look to the times in which he lived. The route is speculative and intriguing. Begin's ideas and emotions were forged in Betar and its political culture, against the backdrop of Polish anti-Semitism in the 1920s and 1930s. He is a product of the underground groups and the ideas of Herzl and Jabotinsky. Except for small details, Begin's world view has changed little since then.

We can conjecture that the young Begin, schooled by his learned and deeply religious father, was well-educated, somewhat bookish, intelligent, overly sensitive, and probably something of a political romantic. A reconstruction of his childhood would reveal the seeds of his adult rhetoric. He was steeped in the Jewish-Hebraic language, in images from the Bible. Laid out on his father's table was an ever-present map of Eretz Israel.

Begin represents the classic diaspora European Jew. The concerns of European Jewry were Begin's concerns, especially the indelible effect of the Holocaust, which Begin experienced first hand. He lost most of his family to the Nazi slaughter. He narrowly escaped the war. He was imprisoned in the Russian Gulag before finally making his way to Palestine as a member of the Polish army.

It is the Holocaust that is Begin's principal metaphor, his source of moral outrage and justification for action. When invoking the memory of the Holocaust, Begin is entirely sincere, entirely impassioned, and entirely haunted. The history of the Jews for Begin is clear; it is the diaspora history of the blackjack, the pogrom, the extermination camp. As a member of the Knesset in the 1950s, Begin was so violent in his opposition to the acceptance of German reparations that he very nearly caused full-scale riots outside the building during the debate. In Begin's mind the Holocaust became a metaphor for the sufferings of Jews in history, and he used the metaphor often, especially when responding to criticism and opposition.

There is a kind of moral outrage in Begin's Holocaust utterings that is contradictory. At their best, they are eloquent, a stirring reminder of events the world would rather forget. At their worst, they sound shrill, paranoid, and unforgivably insensitive, as when Begin, railing against the world outcry over Shatila, seemed completely oblivious to the horror of the event, saying: "Goyim kill Goyim and they blame the Jews."

A contradictory nature also is evident in Begin's attitude toward the Arabs. As a statesman, he worked hard to forge a close and basically successful personal relationship with Anwar al-Sadat. Camp David showed Begin had vision, that he could be pragmatic. Yet, when Begin considered the Arab world as a whole, he saw the enemy. For a man who could speak eloquently about Jewish suffering, he was curiously indifferent to the sufferings of others, especially Arabs. When several West Bank mayors were severely wounded by bombs, Begin remained detached and indifferent, although he did not go so far as to condone the bombings. He remained profoundly ignorant of Arab customs, culture and aspirations. He saw only one thing: that they represented a threat to Israel.

Begin was above all a man who dealt in symbols. He was a superb propagandist, as he demonstrated in his strategy as Etzel commander in the undergound's battle against the British.

The flogging of British military personnel, the Acre prison raid, the bombing of the King David Hotel, and the hanging of the British sergeants were all highly symbolic acts. The flogging humiliated the British and stung their pride. The hangings were an act of revenge which was purely biblical in nature (an eye for an eye). The hotel bombing struck at the heart of British authority in Palestine. The Acre raid was an effective display of Jewish courage and military prowess.

The 1944–1947 struggle against the British, when Begin led Etzel, was his first real, very brief, time of impact on Israeli history. He would not have significant impact again until his first election as Prime Minister in 1977.

The history of Israel and Zionism stretches across five distinct eras. It begins with the blooming of Zionism in Europe in the late 1800s. The second era spans the accumulation of Zionist power in Palestine from 1917 to 1941. The third and briefest is the era of fighting Zionism, which can be dated from 1941 to 1947. The fourth era involves the creation of the state of Israel, the fight for independence, and the consolidation of power and statehood, from 1947 to 1973. The fifth and final era involved the state of Israel's ensuring its security, when it emerged as an assertive and dominant military power in the Middle East. What is remarkable about Begin is that he figures so briefly in the span of Israel's history. Although he first emerged in the era of fighting Zionism, in which he played an undeniably crucial role, he did not appear again with any real impact until 1977.

After three decades of events and developments in Israel, by 1977 the time was ripe for the ascension of Menachem Begin. He had found his constituency among the Sephardic Jews who now made up a large proportion of the Israeli voting population. They had flocked from African Moslem countries to Israel in huge numbers in the 1950s. In countries like Morocco, Libya, Algeria, and Tunisia, they had been an oppressed minority who worked as tradesmen, merchants, caterers and small businessmen. They were not affluent, but they did not live in abject poverty, either. What they lacked was political rights and what they suffered was discrimination and the mistrust of their Arab rulers. They were, in spite of their economic health, outsiders.

In Israel, they became part of a Jewish nation but they were still outsiders. Not only that: they were economically, and politically, deprived. The only jobs open to them were as common laborers, construction workers, and agricultural workers. The ruling Ashkenazi Jews, those with European cultural roots, and Labor party political roots, mistrusted and often misused them. The

Labor party courted the Sephardim only as voters. Secure in their political power, party members treated the newcomers with cultural contempt. In many ways the Sephardim were like the blacks in the United States who would consistently vote for the Democratic party because there was no place else to go.

Menachem Begin finally gave the Sephardim someplace else to go. Although Begin was a European, they saw a reflection of themselves in the leader of the Herut party. Begin, too, was an outsider, treated with contempt by the Laborites. Like the Sephardim, he believed in Eretz Israel and was at heart hostile to the Arabs. Begin had suffered European anti-Semitism, the Sephardim had suffered Arab anti-Semitism. The Sephardim helped Begin gain an impressive electoral victory in 1981. They responded to his biblical exhortations, for they shared his conservative views and his antipathy toward the Arabs.

When Menachem Begin resigned on September 4, 1983, no one, except perhaps Menachem Begin himself, had forced him to resign. If anything, the politically beleaguered Herut-Likud party stalwarts, fearful of electoral disaster, pleaded with him to stay on. Begin turned a deaf ear to the cries of his old cronies.

It is probably fair to say that Begin, an avid student of Scripture, saw the handwriting on the wall. He was, by the time of his resignation, an embittered, unfulfilled man whose legacy was ashes and turmoil.

The truth of the matter is that Begin left Israel, the nation, in a state of confusion, and as shaky and battered as it has been in a long time. One has to go back to the perilous early days of the Yom Kippur War of 1973 to find a time when the country's morale was as badly shaken as it was when Begin turned in his resignation.

Begin's dream of forging a permanent Eretz Israel and of dousing the chances of a Palestinian state is decidedly unfulfilled. The third partition state is ongoing. East Palestine, the West Bank—or Judea and Samaria as Begin likes to refer to it—is far from fully and permanently settled, let alone annexed. The war in Lebanon may have eradicated the PLO as a military and political force, but the aspirations of the Palestinians, on the West Bank and all over the Arab world, are very much alive. The idea of making a Palestinian state on the West Bank a reality remains in place.

The nation of Israel is as divided as it has been in its brief and tumultuous history. It is divided over Eretz Israel, settlements, the economy. The IDF, Israel's military shield, is still in place, and as professional and effective as ever, but the national confidence in military solutions for political problems has been badly shaken. Lebanon has cast a pall over the usually natural Israeli confidence. Menachem Begin's legacy, aside from the Egyptian-Israeli peace treaty and Camp David, is a legacy of failure.

POSTSCRIPT

The 1984 Election

The results of the 1984 election were a vivid, if confusing, demonstration of the trends we have analyzed and examined since 1967, and which accelerated after 1973.

The Labor party continued its decline by standing still and by being unable to decisively unseat a Likud government that was harnessed to the grandiose and divisive failures of Begin and Sharon in Lebanon, the lackluster leadership of Begin's successor Yitzhak Shamir, and a spiraling inflation.

In spite of the fact that Likud appeared to lose ground, it continued the process of its own institutionalization simply by not going under. It demonstrated again, in spite of the absence of a leader of the stature of Begin, that it spoke for the Israeli populist voices, which it had begun to do in 1980 and even before that. It showed that it was the party in command of the political and cultural symbols of modern Israel while Labor still clung to pre-1967 symbols which had lost their effectiveness and their hold on the popular imagination.

The election proved the validity and popularity of the values and ideology of the Land of Israel movement in the emergence of a radical religious nationalism accompanied by a dramatic change in the political elite that developed from the 1950s influx of immigrant Arab Jews from Moslem countries in Africa and Asia.

The electorate is now younger, more aggressive, and more traditionally Jewish; it is less elitist, less secular, and less European.

The emerging populism so evidenced by the 1984 results has made serious inroads, perhaps fatal ones, into the pioneer spirit that dominated social and political culture until 1967. Labor still hangs on to the forgotten legacy of Socialist Zionism, a legacy that is almost unknown to a much younger and militant generation of voters. Labor has remained unchanged, while Likud, once espousing traditional Revisionist causes and values, has changed with the times. It has become a populist party. It has a steady center in Herut, but the predominant ideological values come from LIM, bringing with it a combination of radical religious values and militancy toward territorial expansion. The Land of Israel movement rejects compromises on territory; it rejects the whole idea of the partitioned state which was a product of Labor; it rejects diplomacy and moderation as instruments of territorial development and national policy. Likud rejects the idea of Israel as a state defending its frontiers, but prefers to exploit Israel's military strength.

Although Likud lost Knesset seats (from 47 down to 41) and percentage points of the vote (from 37.1 to 31.9) in the 1984 election, it was nevertheless strengthened by the Renaissance party, which went from three seats to five. Labor barely outdistanced Likud and also lost strength, declining from 47 seats to 44, although it too had support from such small and diverse parties as Shinui, Ratz, and Ezer Weizman's miniparty Yahad, for an additional nine seats.

Significantly, neither major party could form a government, thus resulting in a political phenomenon which had not occurred since 1967—a National Unity government, consisting of the two major political parties, Labor and Likud, supported by a religious bloc of thirteen seats.

In fact, the failure of the two major parties saw a significant shift occur. While both major parties appeared to decline, many of the smaller parties gained strength at the expense of both Likud and Labor. Fifteen parties gained seats in the Knesset, the most since 1949, and five more minor parties than in the outgoing Knesset. The proliferation and variety of parties shows a state of Israel in flux and transition. The election indicates the stability and perhaps

even the rise of Likud-Renaissance and the continued decline of
Labor, but it also shows an Israel searching for new values and new
faces.

Another major trend demonstrated by the 1984 election is the
increasing importance of the Oriental (i.e., African/Asian-origin)
Jewish vote, the vote of the Sephardim. In all Knesset elections
from 1949 to 1969, Oriental and European Jews tended to vote
pretty much along the same lines, with Labor garnering around
50% of the Oriental vote and Likud a predictable and steady 25%.
But the elections of 1977, 1981 and 1984 demonstrated a totally
different distribution of the Oriental Jewish vote. In 1977, Labor
and its affiliates received only 24.6% of the Oriental vote, a
crushing defeat indeed, for these voters comprise just under 50%
of the total electorate. Labor's share of this vote declined to
22.5% in 1981, and 21.8% in 1984. By contrast, Likud-plus-
Renaissance captured 51% of the Oriental Jewish vote in 1977
and 57.5% in 1981. In the 1984 elections it dropped slightly, to
55.5%—the 2% went to the party of extremist Meir Kahane. But
the trend would seem clear: the Sephardic vote is on the verge of
becoming Israel's dominant electoral and political factor, and
Likud is the party to which it is predominantly loyal.

The trend has also transformed the religious bloc. Before 1973,
the religious parties were not affected by Sephardic-Ashkenazi
divisions. But beginning with the Tami revolt of 1981, and the
emergence of the Sephardic-orthodox party, Shas, a rejection of
Ashkenazi political leadership of the religious parties was clearly
in evidence.

The National Unity government led by Shimon Peres of the
Labor party that resulted in 1984 is clearly considered to be
something of a caretaker government. It represents an Israel in
transition and a clear message from the voters, who refused to give
either major party a mandate. The government is not ready to
reject the concept of a partitioned state, but it has also been told
to delay any final settlement of its eastern borders, meaning that
there will be no drastic movement on the West Bank issue. Any
mandate in foreign policy was restricted to a strategy for Israeli
withdrawal from Lebanon, and a tacit troop separation arrangement with Syria. But on the issue of the frontiers of Eretz Israel,
the future of Palestine, the new government is paralyzed, with no
real authority to go beyond what was agreed at Camp David.

In a way, the Israeli electorate settled the issue of frontiers for the time being. Israel seems settled into a period of domestic concerns and regaining some economic stability, an issue which neither Likud nor Labor has tackled successfully over the past two decades.

EPILOGUE

Whither the Partitioned State?

The Zionist ideologues and pamphleteers and their various "philosophers" conceived the establishment of a Jewish hegemony in historical Eretz Israel. The realities of Palestine always were that it was predominantly populated by Arabs and that Jewish sovereignty depended heavily on great-power imperial designs and good will, and on regional and international politics. These split the Zionist movement into two camps, "moderates" and "militants."

The moderates sought to establish a Jewish Commonwealth by guarded means and depended on the combination of good will and political interests of the great powers. The militants, not totally indifferent to international power politics, wanted to establish a maximalist Jewish state. Neither achieved their ideal aspirations, but both sought pragmatic ways to find ideal solutions.

Each group wanted a Jewish state with a Jewish majority, but could not find mutually acceptable borders. The moderates were willing to live with internationally-arranged borders, while the militants challenged such arrangements. The Arab factor was also crucial in deepening the split between these two pragmatic Zionist camps. The moderates sought an accommodation with the Arabs, proposing a multitude of schemes and arrangements to satisfy the two nations, though never at the expense of a Jewish state and Jewish hegemony over that state. Some of the maximalists ignored the Arabs, while others were convinced that superior Jewish political and military power would dictate Arab-Jewish relations.

The two schools, although split, did not live in isolation from one another. During the Yishuv period their antagonism was high. In Israel, especially after 1967, individuals and groups sometimes moved from one camp to the other. And the extreme fringes of both the right- and left-wing Zionist movements had an impact on moderate Zionists. The supermaximalists sought a Jewish state with boundaries that approximated biblical Israel. The minimalists were willing to integrate politically with Palestinian Arabs at the expense of a Jewish state. Both were still Zionists, even if some minimalists claimed to be non-Zionists. The issues of territories, boundaries and sovereignty were always resolved by a combination of diplomacy and violence, never to the satisfaction of the extremists on either side. The 1979 Egyptian-Israeli peace treaty marked the triumph of moderate Zionism.

Yet, the problems confronting the Israel of the 1980s are beyond Zionism. Security with Egypt was institutionalized in a peace treaty. The process may be extended to Syria and Jordan, and a satisfactory solution for the Palestinian problem may become possible, but hopes so far have been chimeric. Israel also faces serious domestic, political, economic and authority problems which go far beyond Zionism, territories, borders, and international diplomacy.

The boundaries of the third partition state have not as yet been finally established. Jewish hegemony and sovereignty in Palestine have been achieved, as has the security of the state. The Zionist enterprise, according to some, has been fulfilled; for others it has not. If Israel was meant to be a home of refuge, it did become one for some Jews. If it was meant to become the concentration of the Jewish "spiritual" elite (Achad Ha'am), it did not. And if it was meant to be the country to dump poor Jews into, paid for by rich Jews, in some ways that is what it has become.

For the Zionist majority, represented by the three major political blocs in Israel, the task of immigration and settlement has not been fulfilled. The momentum of immigration and settlement has been restrained, but not by the Zionists. More Jews prefer to live in affluent liberal countries—those from countries of oppression are not flocking to Israel. The borders of Israel, even if settled, do not meet the basic aspirations of Zionism, i.e., immigration, settlement, and safe frontiers. It is wrong to assume that immigration and settlement will result in Israel changing its priorities. Historically, the frontiers of Israel were—and they continue to be—essential to the legitimacy of the Jewish state and the Zionist enterprise. The Zionists came to settle in their historical homeland and establish a Jewish Commonwealth. They never drew its frontiers. The boundaries from the Balfour Declaration onward were set by negotiation and violence between the Zionists, the governing powers, and the neighboring Arabs. The Zionists have not defined their final frontiers and will not do so until they are legitimized as a state by the Arabs, who as yet fail to accept them. To Israelis, nonacceptance is tantamount to insecurity. Arab rejectionism is complemented by militant settlement of the West Bank. The third partition state is not final.

Security is not defined by frontiers alone (except for the maximalists), and it has not been achieved by force or for that matter by negotiations. Security is also a political-psychological factor; it is the true barrier between Arabs and Jews, Israelis and Palestinians. The media's notion that Begin was a religious fundamentalist is erroneous. Begin once again was a territorial and maximalist Zionist. Neither Jabotinsky's Revisionist movement nor Begin and Shamir's Herut party had ever claimed *Shlemut Hamoledet*—the unity of the land—on anything but a secular political basis. Before 1977, Begin never identified himself with the extremist wing of the Gush Emunim. He reluctantly and symbolically supported them, since in his view there were no other Zionists willing to settle Judea and Samaria except for the purely border-security conscious kibbutzim established by Dayan and Galilee and Labor before 1977.

Settlement is a secular political issue that cuts across political movements, ideologies and persons in Israel. Only the fringe makes religious claims to the land. Immigration to establish settlements continues to remain a secular security purpose and raison d'être for all Zionists. Zionism in Israel was established by secular Zionists, socialist and otherwise. The religious Zionist is a latecomer to the settlement beyond the frontier of the first partition state. In Ben-Gurion's days, there were no religious Zionist maximalists. In fact, the National Religious Party was dominated by moderates and by strict adherence to the 1949 frontiers. Nonsecular Zionist militants are a product of the second partition state.

Until Israel is legitimized by all Arabs and the Camp David process expands, as it should, to encompass all Arab confrontation states and the Palestinians, Jewish militants, both secular and orthodox, will attempt to preserve as much of the frontiers of the third partition state as possible. But the frontiers of the partition state and their final acceptance depend more on Arab good will than on Jewish moderates and radicals, or even the great powers. The latter can help define the frontiers only if the Arabs agree to go along with them.

Notes

Sources are identified by author/editor and full title when first cited; abbreviated titles are used in subsequent citations. Publication data for books and scholarly journals are given in the bibliography; publication data for newspapers and popular periodicals are included in these notes, not in the bibliography.

Chapter 1, Why a Jewish State? An Overview

1. For the best study on the origins of Zionism, see David Vital, *The Origins of Zionism*, especially pp. 3–22.
2. Stefan Zweig, "König der Juden," *Theodor Herzl*, Meyer W. Weisgal, ed., p. 26, quoted in Vital, *Origins of Zionism*. There is no modern biography of Herzl; the classic work is Alex Bain, *Theodor Herzl*. The best source for the person and his ideas are Herzl's diaries, of which there is a short version, *The Diaries of Theodor Herzl*, edited and translated by Marvin Lowenthal. There is a very good analysis of Herzl and the "Jew's State" in Vital, *Origins of Zionism*, Chs. 9–13. On Herzl's youth, see Andrew Handler, *Dori: The Life and Times of Theodor Herzl in Budapest (1860–1878)*. On Herzl and the Austro-Hungarian empire, see Carl E. Shorske, *Fin de Siecle Vienna: Politics and Culture*, pp. 146–175, and William M. Johnson, *The Austrian Mind*, pp. 357–361. John W. Boyer, *Political Radicalism in Late Imperial Vienna*, pp. 70–76, 90–97, deals with the anti-Semitism of Karl Lueger (1844–1910) and

challenges several of Shorske's theses. See also Walter Z. Laqueur, *A History of Zionism*, a brief summary of the men and the ideas of the movement.

The number of monographs and studies of early Zionism, its ideas, and its leaders is considerable. Among those to be consulted are: Alter Druyanov, *Ktavim Le-Toldot Hibbat Zion Ve-Yeshuv Eretz Israel (Works in the History of the Lovers of Zion and the Settlement of Israel)*; Shulamit Laskov, *Bilu*; David Vital, *The Origins of Zionism: The Formative Years*; Yigal Elam, *Mavo Le-Zionot Acheret (An Introduction to another Zionist History)*; and [Shazar Center] *Ideological and Political Zionism*.

3. Michael Bar Zohar, *Ben-Gurion: A Political Biography*, v. 1, p. 323.
4. There is no serious complete modern biography of Chaim Weizmann. Yehudah Reinhertz is preparing a multi-volume biography whose first volume was published in 1985. The standard work is *Trial and Error: The Autobiography of Chaim Weizmann*, written with the help of Maurice Samuel. The Weizmann Historical Center has already published several volumes of his letters and papers in Hebrew; twenty-three volumes, edited by Meyer W. Weisgal, have been published in the U.S. See also the following monographs and essays: Evyatar Friesel, *Zionist Policy After the Balfour Declaration, 1917–1922*; Yoseph Gorni, *Partnership and Conflict*; Yoseph Gorni and G. Yogev, eds., *A Statesman in Times of Crisis: Chaim Weizmann and the Zionist Movement, 1900–1948*; and Menachem Kedem, *Chaim Weizmann in World War II*.
5. Gorni and Yogev, *Statesman in Times of Crisis*.
6. On Blanche Dougdale, see Norman A. Rose, ed., *Baffy: The Diaries of Blanche Dougdale*.
7. On the Balfour Declaration and British Palestine policy during World War I, see Leonard Stein, *The Balfour Declaration*, and Isaiah Friedman, *The Question of Palestine, 1914–1918*.
8. The most comprehensive, lucid, and economical study of the British policy in Palestine is Michael J. Cohen, *Palestine: Retreat from the Mandate; The Making of British Policy, 1936–1945*.
9. The most comprehensive biography of David Ben-Gurion is M. Bar Zohar, *Ben-Gurion*. The journalist-turned-historian, Shabtai Teveth, is now writing what is going to be the longest biography of Ben-Gurion, *The Zealot David*, of which two volumes have appeared. Ben-Gurion kept extensive diaries from 1916 to 1963; they are at the Ben-Gurion Institute, Sdeh Boker (the University of Beersheba). They are as yet largely unpublished except for three volumes relating to 1947–1949 which reveal Ben-Gurion the war leader in his daily operations. His letters are now being published; three volumes have already appeared. Ben-Gurion's articles and essays are scattered in various labor periodicals, diaries, and collected works. The most interesting are: *We and Our Neighbors*, on his attitude toward the Arabs; *Mishmarot (Watches)*, on diplomacy and Arab terrorism; *When Israel Fights; History of Israel's War of Liberation*, on the war and the state; and five volumes of collected works, *Dvarim*. Other Ben-Gurion works include *Zichronot (Memoirs)*, and *From Class to Nation (Memaamad L'Am)*, on Socialist Zionists in Palestine.
10. M. Bar Zohar, *Ben-Gurion*, p. 325.

11. Ibid., p. 324.
12. Ibid., p. 325.
13. See Yaacov Shavit, "Zeev Jabotinsky," *Dream and Realization: Philosophy and Practice in Zionism,* Y. Padan, ed., pp. 124–127.
14. Ibid., p. 125.
15. See Ch. 2, note 5, below. Also see "Sir Herbert Samuel and the Government of Palestine," Elie Kedourie, *The Chatham House Version and Other Middle-Eastern Studies,* pp. 52–81.
16. Gabriel Sheffer, "British Colonial Policymaking Toward Palestine (1929–1939)," *Middle Eastern Studies,* Oct. 1978, pp. 10, 308–309.
17. Yehoshua Porath, *The Emergence of the Palestinian Arab Nationalist Movement: 1918–1929,* v. 1, pp. 303–303.
18. Eliahu Eilat, "The Rise of Haji Amin al-Hussaini," *Maariv,* 30 Apr. 1967. Muhammad Amin al-Hussaini, *Haqaiq an Qadiyat Filastin (Truths Regarding the Palestine Problem).* George Antonious, *The Arab Awakening.* Y. Porath, *Emergence,* v. 1, pp. 184–207.
19. For a comprehensive description and analysis of the evolution and consequence of the revolt, see Yehoshua Porath, *The Palestinian Arab Nationalist Movement, 1929–1939: From Riots to Rebellion,* pp. 233–273, 301.
    See also Yehuda Slutsky, ed., *Sepher Toldot Ha-Haganah (History of the Haganah,* v. 3, pts. 1, 2, 3; Yehuda Bauer, *Diplomacy and Underground in Zionism, 1939–1945;* and Amos Perlmutter, *Military and Politics in Israel.*
20. J. C. Hurewitz, *The Struggle for Palestine.* The document itself was published as the Palestine Royal Commission *Report.*
    Nathaniel Katzburg, *From Partition to White Paper,* p. 7.
21. Neil Caplan, *Britain, Zionism and the Arabs 1917–1925,* pp. 5–7, 13.

Chapter 2, Battle Over Partition: The Arab Challenge and the Jewish Response

1. For one of the finest collections on this topic, see Samuel Ettinger et al., eds., *Zionism and the Arab Question,* a collection of essays in Hebrew. See also Yoseph Gorni, "Four Early Attitudes Toward the Arab Question," *Dream and Realization: Philosophy and Practice in Zionism,* Y. Padan, ed., pp. 55–72.
2. See S. Ettinger's introduction to *Zionism and the Arab Question,* p. 7.
3. For the definitive study of pre-Zionist Arab attitudes toward Zionism, see Neville Mandel, *The Arabs and Zionism Before World War I,* pp. 223–231.
4. Ibid., p. 231. The points made earlier are a summary of Mandel's research.
5. The most comprehensive, balanced study based on primary sources and objective detailed narrative and analysis of the evolution, growth, and early demise of Palestinian Arab nationalism are two volumes by Yehosua Porath, *The Emergence of the Palestinian Arab Nationalist Movement, 1918–1929,* and *The Palestinian Arab Nationalist Movement, 1929–1939: From Riots to Rebellion.* The ideas here are borrowed from the first of these two books.
6. Porath, *Emergence of Palestinian Arab Nationalist Movement,* p. 31.

7. Ibid., p. 30.

8. Ibid., p. 31.

9. Ibid., p. 36.

10. On Gordon's religion of labor see Amos Perlmutter, "A. D. Gordon: A Socialist Zionist Ideologue," *Middle Eastern Studies*, Jan. 1979. See also Eleizer Schweid, *A. D. Gordon: The Man and His Deeds.*

11. All quotations are from Gordon, in Perlmutter, "A.D. Gordon."

12. Most of the following was borrowed from Gorni, "Four Early Attitudes."

13. For an elaborate analysis of these schools, see Gorni, "Four Early Attitudes." I owe much to Gorni for delineating so clearly the boundaries between and within the Zionist-Arab orientations.

14. Gorni, "Four Early Attitudes," pp. 58–60.

15. Ibid., pp. 60–64.

16. Ibid., p. 61.

17. Ibid., p. 62. The literature on Ahdut Haavoda is impressive. See, for example, Yoseph Gorni, *Ahdut Haavoda, 1919–1930: The Ideological Principles and the Political System;* Amos Perlmutter, "Ideology and Organization: Socialist Zionist Parties, 1897–1957"; Dan Horowitz and Moshe Lissak, *Origins of the Israeli Polity;* Yonathan Shapiro, *The Organization of Power: Historical Ahdut Haavoda.*

18. Quoted in Gorni, "Four Early Attitudes," p. 62.

19. For an analysis of Socialist Zionist attitudes toward Arabs, see Yoseph Gorni, "Zionist Socialism and the Arab Question." *Middle Eastern Studies,* Jan. 1977. Also see Perlmutter, "Ideology and Organization," pp. 130–176; David Ben-Gurion, *We and Our Neighbors;* and Yitzhak Tabenkin, *Works,* v. 2, pp. 31–49.

20. See Anita Shapira, *Futile Struggle: The Jewish Labor Controversy, 1929–1939,* p. 23. Also see Gorni, "Zionist Socialism," p. 50.

21. A. Shapira, *Futile Struggle,* pp. 11–44, 345–352.

22. Tabenkin quoted in Gorni, "Zionist Socialism," p. 51, also see p. 53; and see Shapira, *Futile Struggle,* p. 25.

23. Ben-Gurion quoted in Shapira, *Futile Struggle,* p. 25.

24. Ibid., p. 26.

25. For these ideas, see Shapira, *Futile Struggle,* pp. 345–357. Also see E. Friesel, *Zionist Policy After the Balfour Declaration,* pp. 45–46.

26. David Ben-Gurion, *We and Our Neighbors,* quoted in Gorni, "Four Early Attitudes," p. 63.

27. Ibid., p. 47. Also see Yosef Luntz, "Diplomatic Contacts Between the Zionist Movement and the Arab National Movement at the Close of the First World War," *The New East,* v. 11 (1972), pp. 212–224. And see E. Friesel, *Zionist Policy After Balfour,* pp. 49–55.

28. G. Antonious, *The Arab Awakening,* pp. 218–280. On the Jewish view of how the Weizmann-Faisal agreement failed, see Luntz, "Diplomatic Contacts." For a total revision of Anglo-Arab post-World War I policies, see Elie Kedourie, *In the Anglo-Arab Labyrinth.*

29. Avraham Sela, "Conversations and Contacts Between Zionist and Palestinian Arab Leaders, 1933–1939," *Hamizrah Hehadash (The New East),* v. 22, (1972) p. 404.

30. For an excellent analysis and interpretation of this period and especially of the various schemes and men connected with partition, see Shmuel Dotan, *The Struggle for Eretz Israel.*

31. For an analysis and debate over the plan, see the thorough study of Ben-Gurion's plan in Yaacov Goldstein, *On the Road to Hegemony: The Formation of Mapai Policy, 1930–1936,* pp. 70–95.

32. Elkana Margalit, "The Debate over Partition in the Labor Movement," *Zionism,* v. 4, pp. 183–258.

33. Some of these ideas are borrowed from Y. Goldstein, *On the Road to Hegemony,* pp. 61–63.

34. On Katznelson's attitude toward partition, see A. Perlmutter, "Ideology and Organization," pp. 172–180.

35. H. P. Thornton, *Imperialism in the Twentieth Century,* p. 120.

36. Elie Kedourie, *The Chatham House Version.*

37. Eli Sha'altiel, "David Ben-Gurion and Partition, 1937," *The Jerusalem Quarterly,* Winter 1979, p. 38; for greater detail on Zionist division, see pp. 39–40. See also, M. Cohen, *Palestine: Retreat from the Mandate,* and Y. Gorni, *Partnership and Conflict.*

38. For an analysis of the different schools and positions on partition, see Shmuel Dotan, *The Partition Controversy in the Mandate Period,* pp. 113–138.

39. E. Sha'altiel, "David Ben-Gurion and Partition," pp. 40–41.

40. Ibid., p. 45.

41. Ibid., p. 40.

42. Ibid., p. 39.

43. See S. Dotan, *The Partition Controversy,* pp. 138–153.

44. Y. Goldstein, *On the Road to Hegemony,* pp. 70–95.

45. Ibid.

46. Ibid., pp. 140–149.

47. Ibid., p. 142.

48. Ibid., p. 143.

49. See Shavit, "Zeev Jabotinsky."

50. Yaacov Shavit, *Revisionism in Zionism,* p. 36.

51. Ibid., p. 41.

52. Ibid.

53. See my elaborate analysis of Tabenkin in "Ideology and Organization," pp. 159–175.

54. Ibid.

55. On Tabenkin, see his *Works.* See also Yosi Rabinovitz, ed., *On Tabenkin,* and Perlmutter, "Ideology and Organization," pp. 159–175.

56. See Amos Perlmutter, "Berl Katznelson and the Theory and Practice of Revolutionary Constructivism," *Middle Eastern Studies,* Jan. 1977, pp. 71–89. In the same journal see also Yoseph Gorni, "Zionist Socialism and the Arab Question," pp. 50–70.

57. E. Sha'altiel, "David Ben-Gurion and Partition," p. 41.

58. Y. Goldstein, *On the Road to Hegemony.*

59. E. Sha'altiel, "David Ben-Gurion and Partition."

60. Ibid., p. 39. For a comprehensive analysis and explanation of the growth of labor and its newly acquired power, see Perlmutter, "Ideology and Organization," pp. 155–189. See also Y. Gorni, *Ahdut Haavoda*, pp. 265–314, and Y. Shapiro, *The Organization of Power*, pp. 47–91. For extensive analysis of David Ben-Gurion's attitude on partition, see Perlmutter, "Ideology and Organization," and E. Sha'altiel, "David Ben-Gurion and Partition," pp. 39–42. Ben-Gurion's speech in 1937, which contains the essence of his views, is found in *The Jerusalem Quarterly*, Winter 1979, pp. 42–59. Also see M. Bar Zohar, *Ben-Gurion*, v. 1, pp. 349–368, and M. Cohen, *Palestine: Retreat from the Mandate*, pp. 128–139. The role of Jewish military in the Yishuv is found in Perlmutter, *Military and Politics in Israel*, and in Meir Pail, "The Transformation of the Concept of the High Command from the Haganah to Zahal."

61. E. Sha'altiel, "David Ben-Gurion and Partition," pp. 40–41.

62. See also my complete analysis of the reasons for Ben-Gurion's options for Jewish statehood in "Ideology and Organization," pp. 150–168. I wrote this over two decades ago, before his archives were opened. Available to scholars after his death in 1973, the archives corroborate my early thesis. See also: E. Sha'altiel, "David Ben-Gurion and Partition," pp. 38–42; M. Bar Zohar, *Ben-Gurion*, v.3; and Slutsky, *Sepher Toldot Ha-Haganah*, v.3, pt.1, pp. 20–38.

63. E. Sha'altiel, "David Ben-Gurion and Partition," pp. 38–42.

64. M. Cohen, *Palestine: Retreat from the Mandate*, p. 37.

65. This is not the place to delve into details of the political and military struggle between the Yishuv, its political and military groups, and the mandatory, or into the struggle within and among the Yishuv parties and their undergrounds. For information, see: Y. Bauer, *Diplomacy and Underground*; David Niv, *History of Irgun Zvai Leumi, The Campaigns of Etzel;* [Lehi], *Lohamei Herut Israel (Fighters for the Freedom of Israel)* [collected papers]; and Natan Friedman-Yellin, *History of Lehi*.

66. The most detailed and authoritative analysis of the partition struggle is found in Nathaniel Katzburg, *The Palestine Problem in British Policy, 1940–1945*, p. 12. See also two works of Gabriel Cohen: *The British Cabinet and Palestine: April–July 1943*, and *Churchill and Palestine: 1939–1942*.

Chapter 3, The Jewish Struggle Against the Mandatory

1. A truly comprehensive work on the period has not been written yet, but several books, most in Hebrew, provide extremely useful synopses. Shmuel Dotan, *The Struggle for Eretz Israel*, is an excellent overview and analysis of 1928–1948 politics and diplomacy. Yehoshua Porath and Yaacov Shavit, eds., *The British Mandate and the Jewish National Home*, in the series *The History of Eretz Israel*, covers the political, diplomatic, military, social, economic, cultural, and educational aspects of the period, written by Israel's

best scholars. The writings of David Ben-Gurion, Chaim Weizmann, Zeev Jabotinsky, Yitzhak Tabenkin, Moshe Sharett (Shertok), and other authors mentioned in the notes for chapters 1 and 2 also should be consulted.

The most comprehensive and as yet unsurpassed, although partisan, account is the history of Haganah project in Hebrew, sponsored by the Ministry of Defense and Haganah Archives. The last three volumes, *Sepher Toldot Ha-Haganah*, are indispensable for scholars and the interested reader. Most of the work has been written by the historian Yehuda Slutsky with the help of others; he had at his disposal oral and formerly undisclosed written material. Under pressure from Menachem Begin, sections on Etzel-Lehi were included which on the whole are fair. Political pressure used by Begin as Minister without Portfolio (1967–1970) in Mrs. Golda Meir's government (1967–1974) caused a change of publishers, from the Ministry of Defense to the Labor publishing house, Am Oved, thus ending the claim of the history project to being published under the auspices of the state and therefore being authoritative, and also thus leaving the editors the discretion of their pro-Haganah point of view. The Revisionist Etzel challenge to the Haganah history is David Niv, *History of Irgun Zvai Leumi*, a history of Etzel beginning in 1931 and ending in 1946. The material is mainly based on the Jabotinsky archives in Tel Aviv. Unfortunately Niv's writing and editing are not as comprehensive and as scholarly as that in the pro-Haganah history, but this is our most comprehensive written source on Etzel. See also Yigal Elam, *Haganah, the Zionist Way to Power*, and Meir Pail, *The Emergence of Zahal*, a partisan book. For Menachem Begin on Etzel, see his *The Revolt*. See also, especially for the Etzel in America, Yitshaq Ben-Ami, *Years of Wrath, Days of Glory; Memoirs from the Irgun*. Yaacov Shavit, *Sezon (The Hunting Season)*, is the authoritative study of the Sezon. For a good summary including all Etzel operations, see the short but concise Pesach Gany, *The Irgun Zvai Leumi (Etzel)*. See also the many sources listed in Ch. 4, note 1, below.

Yaacov Amrami (Yoel), former (1945–1947) Etzel chief of operations, has produced a superior annotated bibliography on the revolutionary right in Palestine, *A Practical Bibliography: Nili, Habiryonim, Etzel, Lehi*. This is an essential work for students of radical Zionism and its underground organizations. Another useful tool is Eliahu Stern, ed., *Chronology of the History of the New Yishuv in Eretz Israel, 1936–1947*, a superb selection of most relevant data. The works of Menachem Begin, which include his speeches and the Etzel street pamphlets and underground wall posters of the Revolt period, are collected in his *Ktavim (Works)*. Stern-Lehi collected works, articles, posters, and editorials are found in [Lehi], *Lohamei Herut Israel*. Etzel paper publications and posters are collected in [Etzel], *Hametzuda* (1932–1933) and [Etzel], *Herut* (1942–1948). On the Palmach the definitive book is Zrubavel Gilad, ed., *Book of the Palmach*. The work includes history, operations, and Palmach literature; the summary of events by Yigal Allon is superb.

2. "The White Paper Document," in *The Middle East and North Africa in World Politics*: J. C. Hurewitz, ed., pp. 531–538.

3. Ibid., p. 537.

4. M. Bar Zohar, *Ben-Gurion*, v.1, p. 397.

5. On Churchill and the White Paper, see G. Cohen, *Churchill and Palestine*.

6. On Betar, the most comprehensive anthology (no extensive book has yet been written) is Chaim Ben-Yerucham, ed., *Sepher Betar (The Book of Betar)*. Despite its partisan approach, like the *Book of the Palmach* this is a most valuable source, edited with care and comprehensiveness.

7. On Tabenkin, see Ch. 2, notes 53 and 55, above.

8. On the Haganah, see note 1, above. Most of the material here is taken from v. 3, pts. 1 and 2 of the *History*. See also Perlmutter, *Military and Politics in Israel*.

9. On Hashomer, see [Hashomer] *Sepher Hashomer*, and Perlmutter, *Military and Politics*, pp. 22–24.

10. On Sadeh, see Gilad, *Book of the Palmach*, and Yitzhak Sadeh, *What Did the Palmach Innovate?*

11. A. Perlmutter, *Military and Politics*, pp. 3–32.

12. On Etzel-Lehi, see note 1, above.

13. D. Niv, *History of Irgun Zvai Leumi*, v. 2, pp. 74–94, and v. 3, pp. 52–60; see v. 3, pp. 34–43 for the split with Stern. See also Shlomo Lev-Ami (Levi), *By Struggle and By Revolt*, pp. 143–151, 236–293; Natan Friedman-Yellin, *History of Lehi*, pp. 57–71; and Y. Slutsky, *History of Haganah*, v. 3, pt. 1, pp. 66–67, 494–519.

14. Slutsky, *History of Haganah*, v. 3, pt. 1, pp. 487–493.

15. M. Bar Zohar, *Ben-Gurion.*, v.1, p. 398.

16. C. Ben-Yerucham, *Sepher Betar*.

17. Weizmann to Halifax, quoted in M. Cohen, *Palestine: Retreat from the Mandate*, p. 133.

18. See Gilad, *Book of the Palmach*, v. 1; Perlmutter, *Military and Politics*, pp. 32–48; and Bauer, *Diplomacy and Underground*, pp. 95–130.

19. Perlmutter, *Military and Politics*, p. 37.

20. For Zionist diplomacy, see Ch. 4, note 1, below.

21. On the death of Raziel, see Slutzky, *History of Haganah*, v. 3, pt. 1, pp. 481–482, and see D. Niv, *Irgun Zvai Leumi*, v. 3, pp. 67–76.

22. On Stern, see notes 1, 12, 13 above. See also Yoseph Nedava, *Avraham Stern-Yair: Creator of Lehi's Underground*, pp. 34–38. And see Yoseph Heller, *Stern and Lehi*, unpublished ms.

23. On the principles of the Renaissance, see [Lehi], *Lohamei Herut Israel*, v. 1, p. 495.

24. Ibid.

25. On Lehi and Nazi-Fascist contacts, see Perlmutter, *Military and Politics*, p. 45. Other information from interviews with Natan Friedman-Yellin and Yitzhak Shamir, Tel Aviv, summer 1966. See also Lev-Ami, *By Struggle*, p. 148.

26. Yigal Allon, in Z. Gilad, *Book of Palmach*, quoted in Perlmutter, *Military and Politics*, pp. 38–39.

27. Slutsky, *History of Haganah*, v. 3, pt. 1. pp. 374–469.

28. Monty N. Penkower, *The Jews Were Expendable*, pp. 56–87. The most comprehensive study is Yoav Gelber, *Struggle in Europe*. See also Bernard Wasserstein, *Britain and the Jews of Europe, 1939–1945*, pp. 40–80.

29. Amikam Nachmani, "Generals at Bay in Post-War Palestine," *The Journal of Strategic Studies*, v. 6, no. 4, Dec. 1983, pp. 66–83.
30. Ibid., p. 66.
31. Ibid., p. 82.
32. On Begin, see note 1, above.
33. Interview with Mrs. Ben-Eliezer and Shmuel Katz, Tel Aviv, July 1983.
34. On the King David Hotel attack, see the authoritative Thurston Clarke, *By Blood and Fire*. For the Etzel account, see Niv, *Irgun Zvai Leumi*, v. 4, pp. 273–288. For the Haganah version, see Slutsky, *History of Haganah*, v. 2, pp. 898–902. Also see Lev-Ami, (Levi), *By Struggle*, pp. 310–317. Levi was a senior Etzel commander.
35. Interviews with Menachem Begin: summer 1970, October 1973, June 1977, and Summer 1979, 1981, 1983.
36. Interviews, as note 35.
37. On the Sezon, see the authoritative Shavit, *Sezon*; Niv, *Irgun Zvai Leumi*, v. 4, pp. 96–114; Lev-Ami, *By Struggle*, pp. 239–258; and Slutsky, *History of Haganah*, v. 3, pt. 1, pp. 520–543.
38. Weizmann letter in Slutsky, *History of Haganah*, v. 3, pt. 2, p. 1189.
39. Michael J. Cohen, *Palestine and the Great Powers, 1939–1948*, p. 73.
40. M. Begin, *The Revolt*, p. 27. For the complete Begin declaration, "There will be no Jewish civil war," see his *In the Underground*, pp. 169–172.
41. See notes 1 and 34, above.
42. Begin, *In the Underground*, p. 21; for the whole declaration, see pp. 21–25.
43. Interviews; see note 35, above.
44. For complete texts and analysis of the Ben-Gurion-Sneh exchange, see Y. Elam, *Haganah, Zionist Way to Power*, pp. 331–349.
45. Interview with Amichai Paglin, summer 1977.
46. M. Begin, *The Revolt*, pp. 245, 247.

Chapter 4, Anglo-American Rivalry and the Final Partition of Palestine

1. The most significant writings explaining the reasons for the end of British rule in Palestine and the emergence of Israel are cited here in two categories: (A) Zionist, British, Arab, and American participants and apologists, and (B) the few reliable historians and political scientists who have examined the events with various degrees of immediacy or hindsight.

A. Actors and Apologists

Zionists of the mainstream and Labor

Chaim Weizmann; see Ch. I, note 4, above.
David Ben-Gurion; see Ch. I, note 9, above.
Moshe Sharett (Shertok), *Political Diary*, and *Personal Diary*.
David Horowitz, *State in the Making*.
Eliahu Eilat, *The Struggle for Statehood*. The most detailed analysis by the first Israeli ambassador to Washington.

Nahum Goldmann, *Sixty Years of Jewish Life.*

Bernard (Dov) Joseph, *British Rule in Palestine.*

Zionists of the radical right

Zeev Jabotinsky, *Works.* See especially vols. 1–5, dealing with politics, statehood (*Toward Statehood*), and the essence of Revisionism. *The Storm* is directed against the left. *Nation and Society* presents socioeconomic theories of Revisionism. A collection of Jabotinsky essays, *The Jewish War Front,* [*The Jew and the War*] was published in English in 1940.

Menachem Begin, *The Revolt.*

Yaacov Meridor, *Long Road to Freedom.*

Shmuel Katz, *Days of Fire.*

Natan Friedman-Yellin and others; see Ch. 2, note 66, above.

British

Alan Bullock, *Ernest Bevin: Foreign Secretary, 1945–1961.*

R. H. S. Crossman, *Palestine Mission, A Personal Record.*

CMD 6808: Report on the Anglo-American Commission on Palestine.

Elizabeth Monroe, "Mr. Bevin's 'Arab Policy'," *Middle East Affairs* No. 2, A. Houraini, ed.; *Britain's Moment in the Middle East.*

Norman A. Rose, ed., *Baffy: The Diaries of Blanche Dougdale;* and *Gentile Zionists.*

Kenneth Harris, *Attlee.*

Harry St. John Bridger Philby, *Arabian Jubilee.*

John Marlow, *Rebellion in Palestine;* and *The Seat of Pilate: An Account of the Palestine Mandate.*

George Kirk, *Survey of International Affairs, 1936–1946: The Middle East in the War.*

Malcolm MacDonald, *Titans and Others.*

G. W. Rendel, *The Sword and the Olive.*

Anthony Eden, *Memoirs,* v. 3.

Arab

George Antonius, *The Arab Awakening.*

Abdullah ibn-Hussain, *Memoirs.* Abdullah was Emir of Transjordan (1921–1946), and King of Jordan (1946–1951).

The literature in Arabic on Zionism, Palestine, and Anglo-Arab-Jewish relations is staggering, but not readily available in English-speaking countries.

American

James M. Burns, *Roosevelt: Soldier of Freedom, 1940–1945.* Section on President Franklin D. Roosevelt and the Saudis.

Bartley Crum, *Behind the Silken Curtain.* Crum was a pro-Zionist member of the Anglo-American Commission.

James Forrestal, *Diary.* The first U.S. Secretary of Defense, Forrestal was the leading anti-Zionist American statesman.

Harry S. Truman, *Memoirs,* v. 2.

Evan M. Wilson, *Decision on Palestine.* Wilson, American Minister and Consul General in Jerusalem in the 1940s, was an Arabist with a strong anti-Israel bias.

B. Political Scientists and Historians

(Jewish, Arab, British, American, and other works of analysis, interpretation, and scholarly investigation.)

The Jewish Agency, *The Jewish Case Before the Anglo-American Committee of Inquiry*. Statements and memoranda.

The most comprehensive survey on Palestine to 1945 is ESCO Foundation, *Palestine: A Study of Jewish, Arab and British Policies in the Middle East, 1939–1945*. J. C. Hurewitz, *The Struggle for Palestine*, although outdated is still a very good reference book. The modern analysis of Palestine policy is contained in two works of Michael J. Cohen: *Palestine: Retreat from the Mandate, 1936–1945*, and *Palestine and the Great Powers, 1945–1948*.

John Snetsinger, *Truman, the Jewish Vote, and the Creation of Israel*, is the chief proponent of the connection between the Jewish-American vote and Truman. Amikam Nachmani, *The Anglo-American Commission and British-American Rivalry*, challenges the Snetsinger thesis, arguing that the American policy on Palestine was part of its successful efforts to replace Britain in the Middle East. Nachmani also challenges the claim of Elizabeth Monroe's "Bevin's 'Arab Policy' " that Britain was ready to withdraw. Kenneth Ray Bains, *The March to Zion*, is a poor argument on U.S. failure to work with the world community to find a peaceful solution to Palestine. Amitzur Ilan, *America, Britain, and Palestine, 1938–1947* (Hebrew), believes in the "miraculous" American policy, while Britain entered a vicious circle in her Palestine policy. Zvi Ganin, *Truman, American Jewry, and Israel, 1945–1948*, is a balanced analysis of Zionists' conflicts in the U.S., the rise of militants led by Rabbi Abba Hillel Silver, and how they and the White House staff worked to help Truman overcome a U.S. bureaucracy adamantly opposed to partition and Zionism. See also the excellent debate between Israeli scholars on the British decision to evacuate Palestine, *Katedra*, v. 14, Apr. 1980, pp. 140–193. The participants were Michael J. Cohen, Amitzur Ilan, Yisrael Kollat, Gabriel Cohen, and Yoseph Heller. The latter challenges the American, British, and Israeli explanations for the British departure from Palestine. He argues that Zionist policies failed, the British were confused, and the American involuntary involvement came as a result of the U.S. refugee policy that antagonized Britain. See Heller, "Neither Masada nor Vichy: Diplomacy and Resistance in Zionist Politics, 1945–1947," *International History Review* III Oct. 1981, pp. 540–563. Heller argues that the Sternists had no influence over the British and that the Jews were lucky that Britain was in decline; otherwise the British would have done to Zionists what they did to the Arabs in 1936–1939. See also: Heller, "Anglo-American Commission of Inquiry on Palestine, 1945–1946: The Zionist Reaction Reconsidered;" *Zionism and Arabism in Palestine and Israel*, Kedourie and Haim, eds., pp. 137–170; and the essays by Ilan and Roi in the same collection. See Amikam Nachmani, "Generals at Bay in Post-War Palestine." Yehuda Bauer, *From Diplomacy to Resistance*, argues that the Holocaust played a key role in the creation of Israel. This is challenged by Heller, Nachmani, and myself. He confuses the U.S. refugee problem in Anglo-American relations and the Holocaust as the major reason for final British withdrawal, i.e., the creation of Israel. Roger Louis, *The British*

Empire and the Middle East, 1945–1951, came out after I had finished this book. It will become the classic account of the foreign policy of the British Labor government in the Middle East; see especially the section on Palestine, pp. 381–572.

2. Montgomery, "Bevin's 'Arab Policy'," p. 75.
3. Nachmani, *Anglo-American Commission*, pp. 1–33.
4. See Nachmani, Heller, Ilan.
5. Heller, "Neither Masada," pp. 540–542.
6. Ganin, *Truman, American Jewry, and Israel;* on Biltmore, pp. 10–11, 117, 124; on Ben-Gurion and Biltmore, pp. 1–15.
7. Heller, "Neither Masada," pp. 544–549; M. Cohen, *Palestine and Great Powers*, pp. 135–183.
8. Bauer, *From Diplomacy to Resistance.*
9. Quoted in Heller, *op cit.*, p. 544.
10. Nachmani, *Anglo-American Commission*, pp. 23–33.
11. Ibid., pp. 22
12. Ibid., p. 15.
13. Ibid.
14. Ibid., pp. 31–32.
15. Ibid., pp. 31–33.
16. Quoted in Ganin, *Truman, American Jewry, and Israel*, p. 78.
17. M. Cohen, *Palestine and Great Powers*, pp. 96–135.
18. Ibid., pp. 136–170; Heller, "Neither Masada," pp. 159–165.
19. Ibid.
20. M. Cohen, *Palestine and Great Powers*, pp. 141–149.
21. Nachmani, *Anglo-American Commission*, p. 33.
22. Ibid.
23. Ibid.
24. See the American sources cited in note 1 above, especially Wilson and Forrestal.

Chapter 5, Partyism vs. Statism

1. S. N. Eisenstadt was the first to identify the transformation, but he failed to take account of its nonfunctional behavior; see his *Israeli Society*.
2. For a more informed and analytical understanding of the transformation, see D. Horowitz and M. Lissak, *Origins of the Israeli Polity: Palestine Under the Mandate.*
3. These ideas have been distilled from Horowitz and Lissak, *Origins of the Israeli Polity*, pp. 272–275. The Histadrut was a unique institution in the annals of labor and trade union movements. It was divided into two major functional and structural divisions, one a bona fide trade union (but unique in that members voted as individuals to the parent organization, not to a

union which would then forward a single consensus vote), and the other, called the Workers' Society, a holding company of the labor movement's voluntary socioeconomic institutions and structures. Most important of these were the agricultural cooperative, the kibbutz movement, the Health Fund (Sick Fund), and *all* the agricultural producing and distribution companies. Histadrut also dominated the major industrial and settlement enclaves of the state of Israel, as well as the Israeli armament industries. For an analysis of Histadrut, see Perlmutter, "Ideology and Organization."

4. Horowitz and Lissak, *From Yishuv*; Yonatan Shapiro, *The Formative Years of the Israeli Labor Party: The Organization of Power, 1919–1930;* Gorni, *Ahdut Haavoda*; M. J. Aronoff, *Power and Ritual in the Israel Labor Party.*

5. For the scope and level of the institutionalization, see S. P. Huntington, *Political Order in Changing Societies.*

6. For some of these ideas, see C. S. Liebman and E. Don-Yehia, *Civic Religion in Israel.*

7. Quoted in Gorni, *Ahdut Haavoda,* p. 61.

8. Ibid.

9. For detailed analysis, see Perlmutter, "Ideology and Organization," pp. 169–179; and see D. Ben-Gurion, *From Class to Nation.*

10. Perlmutter, "Berl Katznelson," pp. 78–80; Gorni, *Ahdut Haavoda,* pp. 181–208.

11. Quoted in Gorni, *Ahdut Haavoda,* pp. 174–175, 202–203.

12. Ben-Gurion, "On the Histadrut and the Parties," *Kuntres,* 201, p. 3.

13. Ben-Gurion, *Ktavim (Works),* v. 3, and *Zichronot (Memoirs),* v. 2, pp. 11–25.

14. Aronoff, *Power and Ritual,* pp. 1–5.

15. See Chapter I.

16. Aronoff, *Power and Ritual,* pp. 20–21.

17. Aronoff, *Power and Ritual,* p. 21.

18. Shapiro, *Formative Years of Israeli Labor,* pp. 23–91.

19. See Perlmutter, *Military and Politics.*

20. The Health Fund organized by Histadrut in 1920 became one of the most powerful political-economic weapons. Since voting in Histadrut was not by unions as groups but by all members as individuals, the latter paid dues directly to the Fund, which gave it a measure of financial and political control over 30% of Israel's population. Not until 1980 did Israel have a national health program.

21. See Chapter I.

22. On the politics of partition, see Sharett, *Political Diary.* The history of partition has not yet been fully covered, studied, or analyzed; I know of no comprehensive study of the subject. See also Eliahu Eilat, *On the Road to Independence.*

23. For the Israeli interpretation, see in addition to note 22: Ben-Gurion, *The History of Israel's War of Liberation;* Chaim Weizmann, *Trial and Error;* and Abba Eban, *An Autobiography.* For the Arab interpretation the apologetic literature is monumental. See King Abdullah, *Memoirs,* and Sir Alan Kirkbride, *From the Wings.*

24. Perlmutter, *Military and Politics,* pp. 55–57.

25. See Moshe Dayan, "Israel's Security Borders," *Foreign Affairs,* July 1955.
26. Still the best analysis of Ben-Gurion and Zahal is found in Perlmutter, *Military and Politics.* See also Horowitz and Luttwak, *The Israeli Army*; and see Yoram Peri, "Retired Army Officers and Politics: The Case of IDF."
27. Related to me by Rabin. See also Yitzhak Rabin, *Memoirs,* v. 1. pp. 85–88.
28. See Horowitz and Lissak, *Origins of Israeli Polity,* pp. 277–280.
29. The revisionist version of the *Altalena* story clearly demonstrates the political rather than the statist nature of the struggle. See Shlomo Nakdimon, *Altalena.* For a weak and unconvincing rebuttal see Uri Brenner, *Altalena.* See also Shmuel Katz, *Days of Fire.*
30. Bracha Habas, *Only in His Generation.*
31. Ben-Gurion, *We and Our Neighbors.* See also Shapiro, *Formative Years of Israeli Labor Party,* pp. 45–68, and see Shabtai Tevet, *The Zealotry of David,* pp. 90–110.
32. In Ettinger, *Zionism and the Arab Question,* p. 135.
33. The ideas on the evolution of Sharett's views on the Arab question can be seen in Sheffer, "New Analysis," pp. 135–143. Also see Sharett, *Political Diary.*
34. Quoted in Sheffer, "New Analysis," p. 136.
35. Shertok (Sharett) to Ben-Gurion, 1921, quoted in Sheffer, p. 136.
36. Michael Brecher, *Decisions in Israel's Foreign Policy.*
37. Sheffer, "New Analysis," p. 140. D. Ben-Gurion, *When Israel Fights,* a collection of articles, 1947–1950.
38. Ben-Gurion, quoted in Sheffer, "New Analysis," p. 140.
39. For extensive analysis of the Arab-Israeli conflict, see Nadav Safran, *From War to War: The Arab-Israeli Confrontation 1948–1967.*
40. Townsend Hoopes, *The Devil and John Foster Dulles.*
41. This story is still incomplete. Ben-Gurion mythmakers would not tolerate anyone but Ben-Gurion being regarded as the only farsighted statesman. Thus the "courageous" Ben-Gurion fearlessly proclaimed the state while the "weakling" Sharett of course oscillated. On the role of Sharett in the proclamation of the state, see Sheffer, "New Analysis," pp. 144–145.
42. Sharett, *Personal Diary,* v. 2, pp. 873–874.
43. Sharett, *Political Diary,* entry for 11/16/1956, quoted in Sheffer, "New Analysis," p. 142.
44. Ibid. p. 145.
45. Quoted by Sharett, *Personal Diary,* pp. 874–876.
46. As yet no book has added as much to the analysis of Ben-Gurion and Zahal as did my *Military and Politics.*
47. Quoted in M. Bar Zohar, *Ben-Gurion,* v. 4, p. 1,139.
48. Most of these ideas were written by me in 1967–1968, but I have modified some of my theses, especially concerning the relationship between Zahal and Ben-Gurion; see my *Military and Politics,* pp. 54–68. I am grateful to Yoram Peri of Israel for challenging some of my theses in his *Israel's Army and Politics.*
49. See Perlmutter, *Military and Politics,* pp. 81–82.
50. See Michael Handel, *Israel's Political-Military Doctrine,* pp. 16–20.

51. Quoted in Bar Zohar, *Ben-Gurion*, v. 3, p. 1,139.
52. M. Handel, *Israel's Political-Military Doctrine*, and Uri Milstein, *The Paratroopers: 101*. General Raphael Eitan, Chief of Staff (1977–1982), and Mota Gur, former Chief of Staff (1974–1977), were graduates of the Ben-Gurion–Dayan–Sharon paratrooper command.

Chapter 6, The Lavon Affair and Its Consequences

1. Sharett, *Personal Diary*, v. 3, p. 654.
2. Meir Pail, "The Transformation of the Concept of the High Command from the Haganah to Zahal." Slutsky, *Sepher Toldot Ha-Haganah*, v. 3, pt. 2, pp. 20–47.
3. On Palmach see Bauer, *Diplomacy and the Underground*, and see Yigal Allon, "Deeds and Determination," in Gilad, *Book of the Palmach*.
4. Quoted in Bar Zohar, *Ben-Gurion*, v. 2, p. 799.
5. Quoted in Allon, "Deeds and Determination," *Book of the Palmach*, v. 1, pp. 35–39.
6. On the controversy and the committee, see Bar Zohar, *Ben-Gurion*, pp. 807–810.
7. See Ch. 5, note 23, above.
8. On American policy in the Middle East, see: U.S. Department of State, *Israel: 1948*; John Snetsinger, *Truman, the Jewish Vote, and the Creation of Israel*; John Badeau, *The American Approach to the Arab World*; Chaim Weizmann, *Trial and Error*; John C. Campbell, *Defense of the Middle East*; Nadav Safran, *Israel: The Embattled Ally*; Amitzur Ilan, *America, Britain, and Palestine*; Zvi Ganin, *Truman, American Jewry, and Israel*; and for the view of the Near Eastern Department of the U.S. State Department, Evan Wilson, *Decision on Palestine*.
9. Most of the documentation—letters, Cabinet and intelligence papers, and the like—is still stored in the Ben-Gurion archives in Sdeh Boker. The Ministry of Defense Historical Section, which handles the Ben-Gurion correspondence of 1953–1957, is open only to a select few, notably the official biographers (whose works are cited elsewhere). However, I made private inquiries, with significant results, in the summer of 1979 concerning a number of topics: Israel-American relations; Ben-Gurion–Nasser relations with reference to Anderson's mission between the two men in 1955; the fiasco and the Lavon-Dayan conflict; the Israel-French connection; and the road to Sinai 1956 and its aftermath. The memorialist and biographical literature should be consulted with care and suspicion not as to its veracity, but with a concern primarily for what is missing. The recent autobiographies of Meir, Dayan, Eban, and Rabin are books mainly for money-making publicity purposes. Not all are candid or reflective biographies; some are self-serving. Bar Zohar's biography of Ben-Gurion lacks deep intellectual and analytical perspective; it is most readable, but a lightweight work.

However his access to Ben-Gurion's archives and his working with Ben-Gurion on the book make it so far the best official biography. The footnotes and source list are indeed impressive. Certainly nothing can surpass as yet Moshe Sharett's candid, reflective, elegant, sad, and heartbreaking makeshift autobiography, *Personal Diary*. Shimon Peres avoids writing an autobiography; he prefers to write on other leaders and on events in which he participated. The world press of the time is no guide or help because it was completely shielded from crucial events. The 1960–1961 Hebrew press should be consulted.

10. See my partial and incomplete, but still relevant, analysis of U.S. policy in that period, "The Fiasco of Anglo-American Middle East Policy," in Michael Curtis, *People and Politics in the Middle East*, pp. 220–250. And see my "Sources of Instability in the Middle East," *Orbis*, 1968. Also see Hoopes, *Devil and John Foster Dulles*.

11. Quoted in Bar Zohar, *Ben-Gurion*, v. 2, p. 1,136.

12. In my view the most recent and so far the best book on Nasser and Nasserism is P. J. Vatikiotis, *Nasser and His Generation*; the footnotes are a gold mine for the researcher. See also Vatikiotis, *The Egyptian Army in Politics*. For biographies of Nasser, I recommend Anthony Nutting, *Nasser*; Robert Stephens, *Nasser*; and Lewis Awad, *Revolution and the Disaster*. On the ideology, see Nissim Rejwan, *Nasserist Ideology, Its Exponents and Critics*; and Gamal Abdul Nasser, *The Philosophy of the Revolution*. On Nasser and the Soviets, see M. H. Haikal, *The Sphinx and the Commissar*. On Nasser's regime, see Amos Perlmutter, *Egypt: The Praetorian State*; and see R. Baker, *Egypt's Uncertain Revolution Under Nasser and Sadat*. This is not an exhaustive list.

13. Vatikiotis, *Nasser and His Generation*, p. 225.

14. Ibid., p. 233.

15. Ibid., p. 249.

16. On Nasser and Ben-Gurion, see Bar Zohar, *Ben-Gurion*, v. 3, pp. 1,100–1,150. To analyze the Israeli perception of Nasser, the best piece is Yitzhak Oron, "The Nationalist Myth in Contemporary Egypt," *The Near East*, 39, 1960, pp. 153–177. Oron, a key member of the Israeli intelligence community and a leading Arabist, was close to the key decision-makers at the time and influenced them considerably. He was influenced by reading the Nasserite propaganda literature of the time, *Ikhtarna Lak* (*We Present to You the People*). See Perlmutter, *Egypt: Praetorian State*, pp. 65–77.

17. Vatikiotis, *Nasser*, p. 251.

18. Sharett, *Personal Diary*, v. 3, p. 682.

19. The real issue revolved around the veracity of Lavon and his intelligence chief, Colonel Benyamin Jibly. Both denied responsibility for "giving the order" for the Egyptian operation; both accused the other; and both clearly lied (about two different fiascos) before the blue-ribbon committee of inquiry appointed by Sharett and headed by General Dori, first IDF Chief of Staff.

20. The Dori-Olshan report is found in Sharett's *Personal Diary*, v. 3.

21. In fact Lavon twice confessed that in July 1954 he instructed Jibly to activate the units in Egypt against British targets in order, he hoped, to delay British

evacuation from the Suez. The most conclusive evidence is furnished by the most recent and comprehensive study of the affair: Haggai Eshed, *Who Gave the Order?—The Lavon Affair*. See also my *Military and Politics,* chapters 4–7 and p. 99, for a bibliography of the affair with a completeness second only to Eshed's. I am convinced by Eshed's evidence of Lavon's complicity, even if Eshed is clearly and openly a Ben-Gurion partisan. In fact, his book was written with the help and in defense of Ben-Gurion. For other Ben-Gurionites on Lavon, see Bar Zohar, *Ben-Gurion,* v. 2, pp. 1,040–1,065, and v. 3, pp. 1,471–1,518.

22. For several months in 1960–1961 I was with Lavon and his allies in a Tel Aviv cafe at least three times a week. At the same time I personally knew Peres, with whom I have worked closely. In 1968 I spent several months with Ben-Gurion in Tel Aviv and Sdeh Boker. These are my impressions and interpretations, corroborated by some of the partisan literature cited earlier. I have also received help from the Ministry of Defense Historical Section and from the Ben-Gurion archives in Sdeh Boker. In 1981 and 1982 I checked more of Ben-Gurion's documents, especially his diaries.

23. See Eshed, *Who Gave the Order?*, pp. 38–41. On Haganah intelligence, see Pail, "Evolution of High Command," and Slutsky, *Sepher Toldot Ha-Haganah,* v. 3, pt. 2.

24. Told to author by Generals Yigael Yadin and Moshe Dayan.

25. The analysis is based on Sharett, *Personal Diary,* v. 5, pp. 1,243–1,276; Bar Zohar, Ben-Gurion, v. 3, pp. 1,150–1,170; Moshe Dayan, *Avney Derech (Memoirs)*; and Abba Eban, *An Autobiography.*

26. Sharett, *Personal Diary,* v. 5, p. 1,253.

27. Ibid., pp. 1,272–1,276.

28. Ibid., p. 1,265.

29. Ibid., v. 3, pp. 681–684.

30. Dayan, *Diary of Sinai Campaign,* p. 17.

31. See Ben-Gurion, *Zichronot (Memoirs),* v. 2; Bar Zohar, *Ben-Gurion,* v. 3, pp. 1,158–1,161.

32. Quoted in Bar Zohar, *Ben-Gurion,* p. 1,159.

33. Ibid., p. 1,165, based on Ben-Gurion's personal diary.

34. The best study of the Israeli-French connection is still Bar Zohar, *Bridge Over the Mediterranean.* The Suez literature "renaissance" is ongoing. See also Anthony Eden, *Full Circle*; Kenneth Love, *Suez, The Twice-Fought War*; Selwyn Lloyd, *Suez 1965: A Personal Account*; Chester Cooper, *Britain's Last Roar, Suez 1956.* A fascinating analysis of the Suez fiasco is given by Elie Kedourie, "The Entanglements of the Suez," *Times Literary Supplement,* 30 Nov. 1969, pp. 67–70. Last, and certainly not least, is Donald Neff, *Warriros at Suez.*

35. For the story of the French connection from the Israeli side, in addition to Bar Zohar, *Bridge Over Mediterranean,* see: Dayan, *Avney Derech*; Ben-Gurion, *Zichronot*; and Shimon Peres, *David's Sling.*

36. Sharett to author, Tel Aviv, 1961.

37. See Eshed, *Who Gave the Order?*

38. Sharett, *Personal Diary,* v. 3, p. 682.

39. Quoted in Eshed, *Who Gave?,* p. 190.

40. Ibid., pp. 192–242: details of the Lavon campaign and his methods.
41. Ibid.
42. Ibid.
43. Ibid.
44. Ibid.

Chapter 7, Neo-Zionism: The Land of Israel Movement and the Rise of Political and Territorial Militancy

1. Quoted in Rael Jean Isaac, *Israel Divided: Ideological Politics in the Jewish State*, p. 84. This work presents the finest and most elaborate analysis of both the Land of Israel movement and the peace movement. Some of my analysis of the LIM is based on this meticulous and innovative study.
2. Quoted ibid., p. 66.
3. Ibid.
4. Tabenkin, *Works*. See also the analysis of Tabenkin in Ch. 2 and in Perlmutter, "Ideology and Organization."
5. Quoted in Isaac, *Israel Divided*, p. 104.
6. Ibid., p. 109.
7. Aronoff, *Power and Ritual in Israel Labor Party*, pp. 33–34.
8. Interview with Allon, Jerusalem, Summer 1966.
9. See Aronoff, *Power and Ritual*, pp. 21–27, and see Medding, *Mapai in Israel*, pp. 298–302.
10. Ibid., p. 28.
11. Interview with Israel Galilee, in *Davar Hashavua*, 5 Oct. 1977, p. 26.
12. Ibid., p. 28.
13. Ibid., p. 13.
14. Ibid.
15. On Dayan's open bridges policy, see his *New Map—Different Relationships*; see also Amos Perlmutter, "Dayan Open Bridges," *The New Middle East*, May 1970.
16. Isaac, *Israel Divided*, pp. 197–198.
17. On the position and attitudinal behavior of some members of the national security inner council, see Michael Brecher, *The Foreign Policy System of Israel: Settings, Images, Process*. Also see Shabtai Teveth, *Moshe Dayan*, and Yuval Elizur and Elizahu Salpeter, *The Establishment*. On Dayan's military doctrine see Michael Handel, *Israel's Political-Military Doctrines*, and Dayan, *Diary of the Sinai Campaign*. On the institutionalization of the security function, see Brecher, and see Pail, "Transformation of Concept of High Command." For an evaluation of Israeli military and security relations, see Perlmutter, *Military and Politics in Israel*; see also Zeev Schiff, *Earthquake in October*.
18. The "Kitchen cabinet" was a composite of Rafi party members and defense loyalists.

19. This point was missed by the Agranat Committee. The Agranat Committe was set up by the government under strong public pressure to determine the reasons for the unpreparedness of the Israeli armed forces and the initial setback during the October 1973 war. In putting the onus of responsibility for the lack of preparedness and alertness on the Chief of Staff, General David Elazar, the committee based its conclusions on the argument that the IDF high command had enormous powers in the field of military doctrine and strategy. The committee's full interim report was published in Hebrew as *The Agranat Report*, 2 Apr. 1974. An English summary appeared in the *New York Times* the following day, and parts of the report were carried in Hebrew in *Maariv*, 4 Apr. 1974. The *Final Report* appeared the following year; see note 20, below.

20. See Samuel P. Huntington, *The Common Defense*, p. 4; Matitayuh Peled, "On the Brink," *Maariv*, 16 May 1976, p. 176; and Amos Perlmutter, "The Relationship between IDF and the Civilian Authorities," *Maariv*, 19 Dec. 1969. My view contradicts the Agranat Committee interim report. The committee argued that the "defense minister was never intended to be a super chief of staff. Nor is the defense minister ipso facto a sort of supreme commander." (*New York Times*, 3 Apr. 1974, p. 12.) Therefore the committee placed direct responsibility for the mehdal (misdeed) on General Elazar, the Chief of Staff. The Agranat *Final Report* of March 1975 deals with some of my later arguments but again shirks making political judgments.

Military strategy, particularly in a state under constant military threat, is not the only concern of officers today. In Israel as elsewhere, the military plays a part in the formation of national security policy. Thus, after Ben-Gurion resigned in 1963, the IDF chief of staff began to wield considerable influence in this area. The IDF high command no longer remained a simple instrument for the implementation of defense policy. Nevertheless, under Eshkol the defense minister and the cabinet made security policy; the prime minister never succeeded in establishing the kind of supremacy Ben-Gurion had over security affairs. He was primarily a finance minister and became dependent on the military—especially Chief of Staff General Yitzhak Rabin—for advice on military policy.

21. Erwin C. Hargrove, *The Power of the Modern Presidency*, p. 140.

22. On the formation of the 1967 National Unity Government, see Shlomo Nakdimon, *Zero Hour*.

23. The best books on Moshe Dayan are his own; most are autobiographical. See his *Diary of the Sinai Campaign, Avney Derech (Memoirs; Autobiography)*, and *New Map—Different Relationships*; see also Teveth, *Moshe Dayan*. On the Dayan of 1967–1973, see *Avney Derech*, ch. 5.

24. Isaac., *Israel Divided*, p. 135.

25. Ibid.

26. Meetings with Dayan at his home in Zahala, July 1973.

27–32. Dayan, *New Map*. pp. 35, 35, 37, 38, 38, 39.

33. Isaac, p. 239.

34. Quoted in *Isaac, Israel Divided*, p. 240.

35. Ibid.

Chapter 8, The Tyranny of the Conception

[No notes.]

Chapter 9, Premature Accommodation: The Peace Movement .

1. See Amnon Rubenstein, "The Israelis: No More Doves," *New York Times Magazine*, 21 Oct. 1973.
2. Deterrence means "working on the psychology of the enemy so that he will not decide to attack." The Israeli model of deterrence is clearly distinguished from the nuclear model in the sense that the latter means, among other things, the deployment of nuclear forces capable of inflicting "unacceptable damage" on the enemy in a second-strike attack. The Israeli concept was based primarily on the deployment of superior conventional forces; little attention was given to the "unacceptable levels of damage" the Arabs might be prepared politically and psychologically to suffer. Based on a preponderance of military power, Israeli deterrence failed because its military power was not sufficient to discourage the combined Egyptian and Syrian forces from initiating an attack, even though the Arabs did not expect to win an all-out war. Israeli policy-makers failed to perceive the willingness of the Egyptian and Syrian leaders to accept high levels of damage in order to change a political status quo that the government of Israel seemed unprepared to alter.
3. Moshe Erem, *Left Poale Zion*.
4. See Walter Laquer, *Communism and Nationalism in the Middle East*. Although out-dated, mostly inaccurate, and sloppy, it is still the best chronological description of the PKP and Jewish Communism in Palestine. The best study of the Zionist Left is Elkana Margalit, *Anatomy of the Left*.
5. Elkana Margalit, *Hashomer Hatzair: From a Youth Movement to Revolutionary Marxism*; Laquer, *Nationalism and Communism*; D. Israeli, *Mapam-PKP-Maki: History of the Israeli Communist Party*; Perlmutter, "Ideology and Organization."
6. See *Commentary*, October 1953.
7. See Yaacov Landau and Moshe Czudnowski, *The Israel Communist Party*.
8. On the anti-Zionist Left see Rober Wistrich, ed., *The Left Against Zion*.
9. Isaac, *Israel Divided*, p. 100.
10. See Professor Yaacov Talmon's articles in *Maariv* in 1969–1970.
11. Abba Eban, "Review of I. F. Stone," *Washington Post*, May 21, 1979.
12. Laqueur, *Nationalism and Communism*, p. 76.
13. Henry A. Kissinger, *Years of Upheaval*, pp. 614–666.
14. On the Gush see the formidable even if unfriendly analysis by Zvi Raanan, *Gush Emunim*.

Chapter 10, The Begin Era: 1977–1983

1. The literature on Camp David is surprisingly small. The perspective is still narrow, especially as reflected in the memoirs of President Carter, Secretary of State Cyrus Vance, and National Security Adviser Zbigniew Brzezinski, all written between 1981 and 1982, and all dealing extensively with the American side of the negotiations as well as American Middle East policy. Moshe Dayan's last book, *Breakthrough,* based on his own foreign office official documents, reveals some of the story. Yoel Marcus in *Camp David* tells some of the intimate relations involved in the meetings and negotiations there. Based in large part on Dayan's records, it is a reasonable book but weak on analysis. See also Ezer Weizman, *The Battle for Peace,* on his relations with Sadat and problems with Begin.

   I have myself covered the whole negotiation period, from the Sadat trip to Jerusalem to the Accords signing. I had access to Begin, Dayan, and Weizman, and spent considerable time with each of them between 1977 and 1984. I also met Sadat on a few occasions in 1977, 1978, and 1979.

   Among the Israelis and the Egyptians, I had considerable access to and secured interesting information from General Avraham Tamir, head of IDF national security under Begin, Weizman, and Sharon. Osama al-Baz, advisor to Presidents Sadat and Mubarek, was helpful, as was Butrus-Ghali, Egyptian Minister of State for Foreign Affairs. I am grateful to Ambassador Tahsin Bashir for introducing me to senior Egyptian generals who shall remain unnamed. IDF Generals Avigdor (Yanush) Ben-Gal, Dan Shomron, and the late Yekutiel (Kuti) Adam were of immense help. So were some of Dr. Brzezinski's advisors. U.S. Ambassador to Israel Samuel Lewis has always been a good source of knowledge and perspicacity, along with former ambassador to Egypt Herman Eilts. However, the story of Camp David remains incomplete.

2. For an analysis of Begin and Revisionism, see my forthcoming book, *The Times and Life of Menachem Begin.*

3. On Begin's early career, see the two authorized biographies: Aviezer Golan and Shlomo Nakdimon, *Begin,* and Eitan Haber, *Menachem Begin: The Legend and the Man.* Both are somewhat self-serving and incomplete. See also Begin's *In the Underground.* These books are poor in actual information and suspect in accuracy. More is missing than can be found in them, except for a book of Begin's collated writings and speeches. Eric Silver's *Begin* is disappointing; the author failed to do his research, and he repeats the errors and claims of most other books on Begin.

4. On Etzel's splinters and struggles, see Shavit, *Sezon,* as well as Niv, *History of Irgun Zvai Leumi,* v. 3, pp. 34–77. This relationship is also covered in my forthcoming *Times and Life of Begin.* See also note 1, Ch. 3, above.

5. See Slutsky, *Sepher Toldot Ha-Haganah,* v. 3, pt. 2, pp. 1,540–1,559.

6. On the *Altalena* affair see two versions, both in Hebrew: Shlomo Nakdimon's *Altalena,* taking Etzel's point of view but also comprehensive, and Uri Brenner's *Altalena,* presenting the Haganah-Palmach point of view,

but mainly concentrating on the military role of the Haganah in the war against Etzel.

7. On Gush Emunim, not much has been written. The only reliable works are Raanan, *Gush Emunim,* and Danny Rubinstein, *On the Lord's Side: Gush Emunim.*

8. On the 1977 and 1981 elections, see notes 1 and 2, Ch. 11, below.

9. See note 2, above.

10. This section is distilled—but also made considerably more detailed—from my "Begin Strategy and Dayan Tactics," *Foreign Affairs,* Jan. 1978, pp. 358–372.

11. Ibid.

12. Based on extensive interviews and conversations with Dayan.

13. Based on interviews with leading rejectionists Yigal Allon, Israel Galilee, Moshe Arens, Geula Cohen, Rabbi Chaim Druckman, Hannan Porat, and Rabbi Moshe Levinger.

14. Yigal Allon, *Maariv,* 26 July 1979, and his essay, "A National Tragedy," in his book *Communicating Vessels,* pp. 192–200.

Chapter 11, The Second Begin Government: 1981–1983

1. These analyses are based on:

   Howard Penniman, ed., *Israel After the Polls: The Knesset Election of 1977.*
   Yair Kotler, "The 1977 Turnabout Is Not Singular," *Maariv,* 10 July 1981.
   Professor Shevah Weis, "1981 Election: What Do the Results Tell?" *Yediot Aharonot,* 2 July 1981, and four articles on the elections in *Haaretz,* 6, 8, 9, and 10 July 1981.
   Hanoch Smith, "The Rise of Likud Not Only Due to Bombing of the Reactor," *Maariv,* 19 June 1981.
   Charles Hoffman, "Analyzing the Oriental Vote," *Jerusalem Post,* 19 June 1981.
   Eli Tavor, "Who Are You, the Israeli Voter?" *Yediot Aharonot,* 20 June 1981.

2. Amnon Barzilai, "Turnover or Continuity," *Haaretz,* 20 June 1981, and "The Turnabout and the Labor Party," *Haaretz,* 10 July 1981.
   Uzi Benziman, "Beyond the Bullet's Dust," *Haaretz,* 10 July 1981.

3. Amos Perlmutter, "Begin Strategy and Dayan Tactics," *Foreign Affairs,* Jan. 1978.
   Moshe Dayan, *Breakthrough,* pp. 303–321.
   Ezer Weizman, *The Battle for Peace.*
   Uzi Benziman, "Balance Sheet of an Escalation," *Haaretz,* 21 July 1981.
   Amiram Nir, "Take Time to Think," *Yediot Aharonot,* 20 July 1981.
   Leslie Gelb, "War and Peace in the Mideast," *New York Times,* 23 May 1981.
   Zeev Schiff, two articles on the Syrian missile crisis, *Haaretz,* 2 and 8 June 1981, and "Hitting in the Heart of Beirut," *Haaretz,* 20 July 1981.

Bernard Gwertzman, "Not Much Time to Cool Crisis," *New York Times,* 10 May 1981.

David Hirst, "Israel Juggles Everlasting Crisis," *The Guardian,* 10 August 1981.

David Lennon, "Why Begin Is Risking War Over Lebanon," *Financial Times,* 14 May 1981.

William Clairborne, "Arab Solution to Crisis," *Washington Post,* 22 May 1981.

David Ignatius, "Lebanon Crisis Likely to Force Reagan to Decide on Policy for Middle East," *Wall Street Journal,* 15 May 1981.

"The Syrian Missile Crisis," *The New Republic,* 16 May 1981.

4. Yoram Hamizrahi, "Is This the War?" *Haaretz,* 22 July 1981.

Hagai Eshed, "The Israeli Target in Lebanon—Quick Action," *Davar,* 20 July 1981.

"Raful Recommended—Begin Decided," *Maariv,* 21 July 1981.

5. Amos Perlmutter, "The Israeli Raid on Iraq," *Strategic Review,* Winter 1982, pp. 34–43.

Zeev Schiff, "Preventing Strikes: 1967 and 1981," *Haaretz,* 16 June 1981.

"Bombing of Reactor: The Arab Reaction," *Haaretz,* 15 July 1981.

"Big Brother in Washington," *Haaretz,* 15 July 1981.

"Ministers vs. Experts," *Haaretz,* 17 July 1981.

"The Begin Doctrine," *Haaretz,* 19 July 1981.

Shlomo Nakdimon, "The Bombing of Iraq—A Chronology of Events," *Yediot Aharonot,* 22 June 1981.

Uzi Benziman, "Atomic Election," *Haaretz,* 12 June 1981.

Section V, Preface

1. In an interview with Gemayal's former chief ally, Camille Chamoun on July 23, 1982, in Beirut, he told me that before a Christian dominating government could be established in Lebanon, Israel must win its war against Syria and the PLO. "Do you mean that?" I asked, "Doesn't it mean that you will fight to the last Israeli soldier to win Maronite domination?" He retorted, "You said so," but he never denied my question. When I related the story to Prime Minister Begin two days later in Jerusalem, his answer was, "Don't you worry, we shall make peace with a Christian Lebanon."

2. For the definitive analysis of Sharon's goals and purposes in Lebanon, see Zeev Schiff and Ehud Ya'ari, *Israel's Lebanon War,* (New York: Simon and Schuster), 1984, particularly, pp. 31–44, "The Grand Design."

Chapter 12, Political Deception and Self-Deception: Israel's Invasion of Lebanon

1. This chapter is based on several sources. In June of 1982, in the midst of the Lebanese war, I was invited by General Avigdor (Yanush) Ben-Gal, commander of the IDF in the battle over the Bekaa Valley, to his headquarters,

and witnessed the struggle against the Syrians in the first two weeks of the war. From there I traveled to Beirut and met with major Lebanese political figures, including the late Bashir Gemayal, former Lebanese president Camille Chamoun, Druze leader Walid Jumblatt, and other key Christian, Druze, and Moslem leaders in Eastern and Western Beirut.

Second, I had long conversations with key Israeli political figures on Lebanon, including Shimon Peres, the late Moshe Dayan and Yigal Allon, Yitzhak Rabin, Mota Gur, Abba Eban, Chaim Herzog, Michael Bar Zohar, Gad Yaacobi, Tamar Shoham of the Labor Party, and Begin, Shamir, Ezer Weizman, Sharon, Moshe Arens, Yaacov Meridor, Yitchak Modai, Ehud Olmert, Yoseph Rom, Yehiel Kadishai, Mati Schmuelevitz of Likud, Dr. Yoseph Burg, Zvulun Hammer, Yehuda Ben Meir of the NRP, and Ammon Rubinstein of the liberal party, Shinui. I also had long and extensive conversations with several key and senior IDF officers including former Chiefs of Staff Mota Gur and Raful Eitan, Generals Herzl Shaffir, Yanush Ben-Gal, David Ivry, Uri Simchoni, Dan Shomron, and the late Kuti Adam.

In addition, General Avraham Tamir (Abrasha), an old friend and veteran, confided much detailed information to me. I also had the sagacious help of the doyen of Israeli defense correspondents, Zeev Schiff of the leading Israeli daily, *Haaretz,* whose information and assistance were invaluable. I feel there is no writer today who knows better the subject of the Lebanese struggle as it evolved from 1976.

Several of the points and ideas made in this chapter can be found in my article "Begin's Rhetorics and Sharon's Tactics," *Foreign Affairs,* Fall 1982, and in Zeev Schiff and Ehud Ya'ari, *Israel's Lebanon War.*

2. The following is distilled from my "Begin's Rhetorics," *Foreign Affairs,* Fall 1982, pp. 67–71.

3. For analysis of how Sharon manipulated his prime minister and government see Schiff-Ya'ari op. cit., pp. 37–44. See also Perlmutter "The Begin," *Foreign Affairs,* p. 73. On Sharon's manipulation of Washington and particularly Secretary Haig, see Schiff-Ya'ari ibid., pp. 63, 65–67, 151–152, 156–157.

General Yanush Ben-Gal, Commander of the Eastern front that fought the Syrians, related to me in detail how Sharon planned the Syrian campaign as early as March 1982 and what role he and General Ben-Gal played in the planning. At the time I was invited to stay in General Ben-Gal's Var during the war against Syria and personally witnessed Sharon's unauthorized war against Syria. See my article "Glimpses of War," *Encounter,* Nov. 1982.

4. On Israel's war against the PLO, see Schiff and Ya'ari, *Israel's Lebanon War,* Ch. 8, pp. 103–182. Also see Itamar Rabinovich, *The War for Lebanon,* 1970–1983, pp. 34–43, 51–56, 59, 85–87, 135–137, 138–152.

5. Interviews with cabinet members, Dr. Yoseph Burg, General Mordechai Zipori, Yitchak Berman, who were opposed to a large-scale operation and only approved a cabinet decision to operationalize the Small Pines plan, i.e., 40 kilometers' incursion into Lebanon. Generals Simhoni, Saguy, Drori, and Ben-Gal related to me the High Command's *opposition* to moving north, i.e., to Beirut, and their lack of contingency plans for a Beirut operation. See also Schiff-Ya'ari op. cit., pp. 40–41.

6. Schiff and Ya'ari, *Israel's Lebanon War*, pp. 21–40.
7. Contrary to Schiff's "Green Light," Sharon's national security advisor, General Avraham Tamir, argued that Haig wanted to control the unruly Sharon. The source is General Tamir himself, who was in charge of negotiations with the United States for Sharon in 1981–1982. I have personally examined the minutes which were available with General Tamir.
8. Conversation with Avraham Tamir, Sharon's former national security advisor, Washington D.C., Fall 1984.
9. See my "Letter from Lebanon," *Encounter*, Nov. 1982.
10. Bashir Gemayel to Ariel Sharon, in minutes obtained from General Tamir. See also Schiff and Ya'ari, *Israel's Lebanon War*, pp. 21–40.

Chapter 13, A Greek Tragedy: The Disappearance of Begin

1. Most of the literature on Begin's political/governmental demise is speculative. I did interview Begin in August 1983 before and after the elections. He seemed in a reflective mood: sad, filled with a sense of unfair contemporary judgment, waiting for history to correct the picture. For Israeli press reports and quick summations, see a series by Teddy Preuss in *Davar*, October-November 1983, collected in T. Preuss, *Begin: His Regime* (Hebrew). Also see:

   Eitan Haber, a Begin stalwart, "Begin To Those Who Do Not Know," *Yediot Aharonot*, 5 June 1983.

   Gidon Levy, interview with Professor Saul Friedlander, "Begin," *Haaretz* magazine, 1 Sept. 1983, pp. 5–7.

   Yoel Marcus, "The National Poorman," *Haaretz*, 15 June 1983.

   Gideon Reicher, "A Sad and Sorry Man," *Maariv*, 7 Sept. 1983.

   Menachem Begin, "My Policy in Connection with My Illness," *Haaretz*, 4 Dec. 1981.

   Allen Shapiro, "Begin's Disability," *Jerusalem Post*, 28 Dec. 1984.

   David Shipler, "Begin's Era in Israeli Politics: A Period of Historic Change," *New York Times*, 10 Sept. 1983.

   "Begin Quits," *Washington Post*, 10 Sept. 1983.
2. Interview with Begin in his office in Jerusalem, 13 July 1984.
3. "Menachem Begin versus Jabotinsky": *Betar High Commission in Rumania, Proceedings, Third Betar World Congress* [Warsaw, 10–11 Sept. 1938], pp. 60–62.
4. Interviews with Ben-Gurion at Tel Aviv and Sdeh Boker, summer 1970.

Bibliography

Books and articles in scholarly journals cited in the chapter notes are listed here by author/editor. Works for which no author/editor is identified are listed by sponsoring organization or by key subject in square brackets (e.g., [Etzel]). Except for signed pieces by major figures (e.g., Menachem Begin), articles in newspapers and popular periodicals are not listed here; the citations in the notes give publication data for such sources.

Abdullah ibn-Hussain ['Abd Allah Ibn Hussain]. *Memoirs.* Philip G. Graves, ed.; G. Khuri, trans. Philadelphia: American Philosophical Society; London: Cape, 1951.

Agranat Committee. *The Agranat Report* [Interim]. Jerusalem: April 1974. 33 pp., mimeo.

——— *Final Report.* Jerusalem: March 1975.

al-Hussaini: see Hussaini.

Allon, Yigal. *Communicating Vessels* (Hebrew). Tel Aviv: Hakibbutz Hameuchad, 1980.

——— "Deeds and Determination." *Book of the Palmach,* Z. Gilad, ed.

——— *Curtain of Sand* (Hebrew). Tel Aviv: Hakibbutz Hameuchad, 1962.

Ami: see Ben-Ami; Lev-Ami.

Amrami (Yoel), Yaacov. *A Practical Bibliography: Nili, Habiryonim, Etzel, Lehi* (Hebrew). Tel Aviv: Hadar, 1975.

Antonious, George. *The Arab Awakening.* (London: Hamish Hamilton, 1938.) Bowling Green Station, NY: Gordon Press, 1976.

Aronoff, Michael J. *Power and Ritual in the Israel Labor Party.* Amsterdam: Van Gorcum, 1977.

Awad, Lewis. *Revolution and the Disaster* (Arabic). Cairo: 1971.

Badeau, John. *The American Approach to the Arab World*. New York: Harper and Row, 1978.

Bein, Alex. *Theodor Herzl*. Philadelphia: 1941.

Bain, Kenneth Ray. *The March to Zion: United States Policy and the Founding of Israel*. College Station, Texas: Texas A & M University Press, 1979.

Baker, Raymond W. *Egypt's Uncertain Revolution Under Nasser and Sadat*. Cambridge, Mass: Harvard University Press, 1978.

Bar Zohar, Michael. *Ben-Gurion: A Political Biography* (Hebrew). 3 vols. Tel Aviv: Am Oved, 1971–1975.

—— *Ben-Gurion, A Biography*. Peretz Kidron, trans. New York: Delacorte, 1978.

—— *Bridge Over the Mediterranean: French-Israel Relations, 1947–1963* (Hebrew). Tel Aviv: Am Hassefer, 1964.

Bauer, Yehuda. *Diplomacy and Underground in Zionism, 1939–1945* (Hebrew). Tel Aviv: Sifriat Poalim, 1966.

—— *From Diplomacy to Resistance: A History of Jewish Palestine 1939–1945*. Philadelphia: 1970. Trans. by Alton M. Winters. New York: Atheneum, 1973.

Begin, Menachem. *In the Underground (Ba-Machteret): Writings and Documents* (Hebrew). Vol. 1 of *Ktavim*; see below.

—— *Ktavim (Works)* (Hebrew). 3rd. ed., 3 vols. in 2. Tel Aviv: Hadar, 1978.

—— "My Policy in Connection with My Illness." *Haaretz*, 4 Dec. 1981.

—— *The Revolt* (Hebrew). Tel Aviv: Steimatzky, 1951; New York: Dell; reprint, New York: Nash, 1977.

—— *White Nights*, Steimatzky, Tel Aviv, 1977 (Hebrew) Tel-Aviv: Karni, 1953.

Ben-Ami, Yitshaq. *Years of Wrath, Days of Glory: Memoirs from the Irgun*. New York: Robert Speller and Son: 1983.

Ben-Gurion, David. *War Diaries* (Hebrew). 3 vols. Tel Aviv: Maarachot, 1983.

—— *Dvarim* (Hebrew). [Collected works] 5 vols. Tel Aviv: Mapai, 1953.

—— *From Class to Nation (Memaamad L'Am)* (Hebrew). Tel Aviv: [Ayanot, 1956] Am Oved, 1974.

—— *The History of Israel's War of Liberation* (Hebrew). Tel Aviv: Maarachot, 1959.

—— *Ktavim (Works)* (Hebrew). 5 vols. Tel Aviv: Mapai, 1963.

—— *Letters* (Hebrew). 3 vols. Tel Aviv: Am Oved, University of Tel Aviv, 1971, 1972, 1976.

—— *Mishmarot (Watches)* (Hebrew). Tel Aviv: Mapai, 1935.

—— "On the Histadrut and the Parties." *Kuntres* [quarterly] 201, Tel-Aviv, 1924.

—— *We and Our Neighbors* (Hebrew). Tel Aviv: Mapai, 1931.

—— *When Israel Fights* (Hebrew). 5 vols. Tel Aviv: Mapai, 1949.

—— *Zichronot (Memoirs)* (Hebrew). 2 vols. Tel Aviv: Am Oved, 1971, 1972.

Ben-Yerucham, Chaim, ed. *Sepher Betar (The Book of Betar): History and Sources*. 3 vols. Tel Aviv: Special Committee on Publication of Betar Books, Jabotinsky Institute, 1969, 1973, 1978.

Betar High Commission in Rumania: *Proceedings, Third Betar World Congress* [Warsaw, September 1938]. Bucharest: Rumania, 11–16 October, 1938.

Boyer, John W. *Political Radicalism in Late Imperial Vienna.* Chicago: University of Chicago Press, 1981.

Brecher, Michael. *The Foreign Policy System of Israel: Setting, Images, Process.* New Haven: Yale University Press, 1972.

———— *Decisions in Israel's Foreign Policy.* New Haven: Yale University Press, 1975.

Brenner, Uri. *Altalena* (Hebrew). Tel Aviv: Hakibbutz Hameuchad, 1978.

Bullock, Alan. *Ernest Bevin: Foreign Secretary, 1945–1961.* Vol. 3 of *The Life and Times of Ernest Bevin.* London: Heinemann, 1984.

Burns, James M. *Roosevelt: Soldier of Freedom, 1940–1945.* New York: Harcourt Brace, 1970.

Campbell, John C. *Defense of the Middle East.* New York: Praeger, 1950.

Caplan, Neil. *Britain, Zionism, and the Arabs, 1917–1925.* London: Frank Cass, 1966.

———— *Palestine Jewry and the Arab Question.* London: Frank Cass, 1978.

Clarke, Thurston. *By Blood and Fire.* New York: G. P. Putnam, 1981.

CMD [Colonial Memorandum Draft] *6808: Report on the Anglo-American Commission on Palestine.* London: 1946.

Cohen, Gabriel. *The British Cabinet and Palestine: April-July 1943* (Hebrew). Tel Aviv: University of Tel Aviv, 1976.

———— *Churchill and Palestine: 1939–1942* (Hebrew; English summary). Jerusalem: Yad Ben-Zvi, 1976.

Cohen, Michael J. *Palestine and the Great Powers, 1945–1948.* Princeton: Princeton University Press, 1982.

———— *Palestine: Retreat from the Mandate; The Making of British Policy, 1936–1945.* London: Paul Elek, 1978.

Cooper, Chester. *Britain's Last Roar, Suez 1956.* New York: Harper & Row, 1977.

Crossman, Richard Howard Stafford. *Palestine Mission, A Personal Record.* London and New York: Harper & Row, 1947.

Crum, Bartley. *Behind the Silken Curtain: A Personal Account of Anglo-American Diplomacy in Palestine and the Middle East.* (New York: 1947.) Reprint, Port Washington, NY: Kennikat, 1969.

Curtis, Michael, ed. *People and Politics in the Middle East.* New Brunswick, NJ: Transaction, 1971.

Dayan, Moshe. *Avney Derech (Memoirs)* (Hebrew). In English: *Autobiography.* London: Weidenfeld, 1975.

———— *Breakthrough.* New York: Knopf, 1981.

———— *Diary of the Sinai Campaign (Yoman Sinai).* (New York: Harper and Row, 1966.) Reprint, Westport, Conn.: Greenwood, 1979.

———— "Israel's Security Borders." *Foreign Affairs,* July 1955.

———— *New Map—Different Relationships (Mapah Khadasha—Yachasim Acherim)* (Hebrew). Tel-Aviv, Maariv, 1969.

Department of State: see U.S. Department of State.

Dotan, Shmuel. *The Partition Controversy in the Mandate Period* (Hebrew). Jerusalem: Yad Ben-Zvi, 1979.

———— *The Struggle for Eretz Israel* (Hebrew). Tel Aviv: Ministry of Defense, 1981.

Druyanov, Alter. *Ktavim Le-Toldot Hibbat Zion Ve-haYeshuv Eretz Israel (Works in the History of the Lovers of Zion and the Settlement of Israel)* (Hebrew). 3 vols. Odessa: Omanut, 1919.

Eban, Abba. *An Autobiography.* New York: Random House, 1977.

—— "Review of I. F. Stone." *Washington Post,* 1979.

Eden, Anthony. *Full Circle: The Memoirs of Anthony Eden.* Boston: Houghton Mifflin, 1960.

—— *Facing the Dictators: The Memoirs of Anthony Eden.* Boston: Houghton Mifflin, 1962.

Eilat, Eliahu. *On the Road to Independence* (Hebrew). Tel Aviv: Am Oved, 1978.

—— "The Rise of Haji Amin al-Hussaini." *Maariv,* 30 Apr., 1967.

—— *The Struggle for Statehood* (Hebrew). 3 vols. Tel Aviv, Am Oved, 1979, 1982, 1983.

Eisenstadt, S. N. *Israeli Society.* New York: Basic Books, 1968.

Elam, Yigal. *Haganah, the Zionist Way to Power* (Hebrew). Tel Aviv: Zmora, 1979.

—— *An Introduction to Zionist History* (Hebrew). Tel Aviv: Levin Epstein, n.d. [1975?].

Elizur, Yuval, and Elizahu Salpeter. *The Establishment* (Hebrew). Tel Aviv: Levin Epstein, 1973.

Erem, Moshe. *Left Poale Zion* (Hebrew). Merchavia: Hakibbutz Haartzi, 1975.

ESCO Foundation. *Palestine: A Study of Jewish, Arab, and British Policies in the Middle East, 1939–1945.* 2 vols. (New Haven: Yale University Press, 1947.) Reprint, Millwood, NY: Kraus Reprint.

Eshed, Haggai. "The Israeli Target in Lebanon—Quick Action." *Davar,* 20 July 1981.

—— *Who Gave the Order?—The Lavon Affair* (Hebrew). Tel Aviv: Yediot Aharonot, 1979.

Ettinger, Samuel, et al., eds. *Zionism and the Arab Question* (Hebrew). Jerusalem: Shazar Center, 1979.

[Etzel] *Hametzuda* (1932–1933) (Hebrew). *Herut* (1942–1948) (Hebrew). Tel Aviv: Hadar and Jabotinsky Institute, 1978.

Forrestal, James. *The Forrestal Diaries.* Walter Millis, ed. New York: Viking, 1951.

Friedman, Isaiah. *The Question of Palestine, 1914–1918.* London: Routledge and Kegan Paul, 1973.

Friedman-Yellin, Natan. *History of Lehi* (Hebrew). Tel Aviv: Hadar, 1976.

Friesel, Evyatar. *Zionist Policy After the Balfour Declaration, 1917–1922* (Hebrew). Tel Aviv: Hakibbutz Hameuchad University of Tel Aviv, 1977.

Ganin, Zvi. *Truman, American Jewry, and Israel, 1945–1948.* New York; Holmes and Meier, 1979.

Gany, Pesach. *The Irgun Zvai Leumi (Etzel)* (Hebrew). Tel Aviv: Jabotinsky Institute, 1983.

Gelber, Yoav. *Struggle in Europe* (Hebrew). Vol. 3 of *History of the Jewish Volunteer Movement in World War II.* Jerusalem: Yad Ben-Zvi, 1983.

Gilad, Zrubavel, ed. *Book of the Palmach (Sepher Ha Palmach)* (Hebrew). 2 vols. Tel Aviv: Hakibbutz Hameuchad, 1957.

Golan, Aviezer, and Shlomo Nakdimon. *Begin* (Hebrew). Tel Aviv: Edanim, 1978.

Goldmann, Nachum. *Sixty Years of Jewish Life, The Autobiography of Nachum Goldmann*. Helen Sebba, trans. New York: Holt, Rinehart, Winston, 1969.

Goldstein, Yaacov. *On the Road to Hegemony: The Formation of Mapai Policy, 1930–1936* (Hebrew). Tel Aviv: Am Oved, 1980.

Gorni, Yoseph. *Ahdut Haavoda, 1919–1930: The Ideological Principles and the Political System* (Hebrew). Tel Aviv: University of Tel Aviv, 1973.

——— "Four Early Attitudes Toward the Arab Question." *Dream and Realization*, Y. Padan, ed.

——— *Partnership and Conflict* (Hebrew). Tel Aviv: University of Tel Aviv, 1966.

——— "Zionist Socialism and the Arab Question." *Middle Eastern Studies*, Jan. 1977.

Gorni, Yoseph, and G. Yogev, eds. *A Statesman in Times of Crisis: Chaim Weizmann and the Zionist Movement, 1900–1948* (Hebrew). Tel Aviv: University of Tel Aviv, 1977.

Gurion: see Ben-Gurion.

Habas, Bracha. *Only in His Generation* (Hebrew). Tel Aviv: Davar, 1948.

Haber, Eitan. *Menachem Begin: The Legend and the Man*. New York: Delacorte/Dell, 1978/1979.

——— "Begin to Those Who Do Not Know." *Yediot Aharonot*, 5 June 1983.

Haikal, M. H. *The Sphinx and the Commissar*. New York: Harper and Row, 1978.

Hametzuda: see [Etzel].

Handel, Michael. *Israel's Political-Military Doctrines*. Cambridge, Mass.: Harvard University, Center for International Affairs Occasional Papers, No. 30, August, 1973.

Handler, Andrew. *Dori: The Life and Times of Theodor Herzl in Budapest (1860–1878)*. Tuscaloosa: University of Alabama Press, 1983.

Hargrove, Erwin C. *The Power of the Modern Presidency*. Philadelphia: Temple University Press, 1974.

Harris, Kenneth. *Attlee*. London: Weidenfeld and Nicolson, 1982.

[Hashomer] *Sepher Hashomer (The Book of Hashomer)* (Hebrew). Tel Aviv: Mapai, 1936.

Heller, Yoseph. "Anglo-American Commission of Inquiry on Palestine, 1945–1946: The Zionist Reaction Reconsidered." *Zionism and Arabism*, Kedourie and Haim, eds.

——— "Neither Masada nor Vichy: Diplomacy and Resistance in Zionist Politics, 1945–1947." *International History Review* III, Oct. 1981.

——— *Stern and Lehi* (Hebrew). Jerusalem: forthcoming.

Herut: see [Etzel].

Herzl, Theodor. *The Diaries of Theodor Herzl*. Marvin Lowenthal, ed. and trans. (New York: Grosset, Dunlap, 1956; Dial, 1962) Reprint Magnolia, Mass.: Peter Smith.

Hoopes, Townsend. *The Devil and John Foster Dulles*. New York: Harper, 1972.

Horowitz, Dan, and Moshe Lissak. *Origins of the Israeli Polity: Palestine Under the Mandate* (Hebrew). (Tel Aviv: Am Oved, 1977.) English edition, Charles Hoffman, trans. Chicago: University of Chicago Press, 1978.

Horowitz, Dan, and Edward Luttwak. *The Israeli Army*. Cambridge, Mass.: Abt Associates, 1976.

Horowitz, David. *State in the Making*. Julian Meltzer, trans. New York, Knopf, 1953.

Hourani, Albert Habib, ed. *Middle East Affairs*, No. 2. Oxford: Oxford University Press, 1961.

Huntington, Samuel P. *The Common Defense*. New York: Columbia University Press, 1961.

———— *Political Order in Changing Societies*. New Haven: Yale University Press, 1969.

Hurewitz, J. C., ed. *The Middle East and North Africa in World Politics, A Documentary Record: British-French Supremacy, 1914–1945*. 2nd rev. ed. New Haven: Yale University Press, 1979.

———— *The Struggle for Palestine*. (New York: Norton, 1950). Reprints, Westport, Conn.: Greenwood, 1968; New York: Schocken, 1976.

al-Hussaini, Muhammad Amin. *Haqaiq an Qadiyat Filastin (Truths Regarding the Palestine Problem)* (Arabic). Cairo: Dar al-Islam, 1954.

Ilan, Amitzur. *America, Britain, and Palestine* (Hebrew). Jerusalem: Yad Ben-Zvi, 1979.

Isaac, Rael Jean. *Israel Divided: Ideological Politics in the Jewish State*. Baltimore: Johns Hopkins University Press, 1976.

Israeli, D. *Mapam–PKP–Maki: History of the Israeli Communist Party* (Hebrew). Tel Aviv: Am Oved, 1953.

Jabotinsky, Zeev (Vladimir). *The Jewish War Front*. London: Allen & Unwin, 1940. [*The Jew and the War*. New York: 1940] Reprint, Westport, Conn.: Greenwood, 1975.

———— *Works (Ktavim)* (Hebrew). 18 vols. Tel Aviv: Eri Jabotinsky Pub. House, 1953–). Individual volumes include *Toward Statehood* (1959), *The Storm* (1959), *Nation and Society* (1959).

Jewish Agency for Israel/Jewish Agency for Palestine. *The Jewish Case Before the Anglo-American Committee of Inquiry, Palestine* (Jerusalem: Jewish Agency, 1947.) Reprint of 1936 ed.: *Memorandum Submitted to the Palestine Royal Commission on Behalf of the Jewish Agency for Palestine*. Westport, Conn.: Greenwood, 1975.

Johnson, William M. *The Austrian Mind*. Berkeley: University of California Press, 1972.

Joseph, Bernard (Dov). *British Rule in Palestine*. Washington: The Jewish Agency, 1948.

Katz, Shmuel. *Days of Fire* (Hebrew). Tel Aviv: Hadar, 1966.

Katzburg, Nathaniel. *From Partition to White Paper* (Hebrew; English abstract). Jerusalem: Yad Ben-Zvi, 1974.

———— *The Palestine Problem in British Policy, 1940–1945* (Hebrew; English abstract). Jerusalem: Yad Ben-Zvi, 1977.

Kedem, Menachem. *Chaim Weizmann in World War II* (Hebrew). Tel Aviv: Maariv, 1983.

Kedourie, Elie. *The Chatham House Version and Other Middle-Eastern Studies*. New York: Praeger, 1970.

—— "The Entanglements of the Suez." London: *Times Literary Supplement,* 30 Nov. 1979.

—— *In the Anglo-Arab Labyrinth.* Cambridge: Cambridge University Press, 1976.

Kedourie, Elie, and Sylvia Haim, eds. *Zionism and Arabism in Palestine and Israel.* London: Frank Cass, 1982.

Kirk, George. *Survey of International Affairs, 1936–1946: The Middle East in the War.* London: Oxford University Press, 1952.

Kirkbride, (Sir) Alan. *From the Wings.* London: Frank Cass, 1972.

Landau, Yaacov, and Moshe Czudnowski. *The Israel Communist Party.* Stanford: Hoover Institution Press, Stanford University, 1965.

Laqueur, Walter Z. *A History of Zionism.* (New York: Holt, Rinehart and Winston, 1972.) New York: Schocken, 1976.

—— *Communism and Nationalism in the Middle East.* 3rd ed., with a postscript. London: Routledge & Kegan Paul, 1961.

Laskov, Shulamit. *Bilu* (Hebrew). Jerusalem: Yad Ben-Zvi, 1980.

[Lehi] *Lohamei Herut Israel (Fighters for the Freedom of Israel)* (Hebrew). [Collected papers.] 2 vols. Tel Aviv: private publication, 1958.

Lev-Ami (Levi), Shlomo. *By Struggle and by Revolt* (Hebrew). Tel Aviv: Ministry of Defense, 1979.

Liebman, C. S., and E. Don-Yehia. *Civic Religion in Israel.* Berkeley: University of California Press, 1983.

Lloyd, Selwyn. *Suez 1956: A Personal Account.* London: Cape, 1978.

Louis, Roger William. *The British Empire and the Middle East, 1945–1951.* Oxford: Clarendon Press, 1984.

Love, Kenneth. *Suez, The Twice-Fought War.* New York: McGraw-Hill, 1969.

Lowenthal, Alan, ed.: see Herzl.

Luntz, Yosef. "Diplomatic Contacts between the Zionist Movement and the Arab National Movement at the Close of the First World War." *Hamizrah Hehadash (The New East)* (Hebrew), v. 11, 1972.

MacDonald, Malcolm. *Titans and Others.* London: MacMillan, 1972.

Mandel, Neville. *The Arabs and Zionism Before World War I.* Berkeley: University of California Press, 1976.

Margalit, Elkana. *Anatomy of the Left* (Hebrew). Jerusalem: Y. L. Peretz, 1976.

—— "The Debate Over Partition in the Labor Movement." *Zionism* (Hebrew). Tel Aviv: University of Tel Aviv, Hakibbutz Hameuchad, 1975.

—— *Hashomer Hatzair: From a Youth Movement to Revolutionary Marxism* (Hebrew). Tel Aviv: University of Tel Aviv, 1971.

Marlowe, John. *The Seat of Pilate: An Account of the Palestine Mandate.* London: Cresset, 1959.

—— *Rebellion in Palestine.* London: Cresset, 1946.

Marcus, Yoel. *Camp David* (Hebrew). Jerusalem: Schocken, 1980.

Medding, Peter. *Mapai in Israel.* Cambridge, Mass.: Harvard University Press, 1972.

Meridor, Yaacov. *Long Road to Freedom.* Tel Aviv: private publication, 1968.

Milstein, Uri. *The Paratroopers: 101* (Hebrew). Tel Aviv: private publication, 1970.

Monroe, Elizabeth. *Britain's Moment in the Middle East, 1914–1971.* 2nd, new and rev. ed. Baltimore: Johns Hopkins University Press, 1981.

—— "Mr. Bevin's 'Arab Policy'." Middle East Affairs, No. 2, A. Hourani, ed.

Nachmani, Amikam. *The Anglo-American Commission and British-American Rivalry.* London: Frank Cass, forthcoming.

—— "Generals at Bay in Post-War Palestine." *Journal of Strategic Studies,* v. 4, n. 4, Dec., 1983.

Nakdimon, Shlomo. *Altalena* (Hebrew). Jerusalem: Edanim, 1978.

—— *Zero Hour* (Hebrew). Tel Aviv: Yediot Aharonot, 1967.

Nakdimon, Shlomo and A. Golan: See Golan.

Nasser, Gamal Abdul. *Egypt's Liberation: The Philosophy of the Revolution.* Washington: Public Affairs, 1955.

Nedava, Yoseph. *Avraham Stern-Yair: Creator of Lehi's Underground* (Hebrew). Haifa: University of Haifa, Dept. of Political Science, 1980.

Neff, Donald. *Warriors at Suez.* New York: Simon and Schuster, 1981.

Niv, David. *History of Irgun Zvai Leumi: The Campaigns of Etzel* (Hebrew). 6 vols. Tel Aviv: Klausner Institute, 1969–1977.

Nutting, Anthony. *Nasser.* New York: Dutton, 1972.

Oron, Yitzhak. "The Nationalist Myth in Contemporary Egypt." *Hamizrah Henadash (The Near East)* (Hebrew) 39, 1960.

Padan, Yehiam, ed. *Dream and Realization: Philosophy and Practice in Zionism* (Hebrew). Tel Aviv: Ministry of Defense, 1979.

Pail, Meir. *The Emergence of Zahal* (Hebrew). Tel Aviv: Zmora, 1979.

—— "The Transformation of the Concept of the High Command from the Haganah to Zahal." M.A. thesis, History Department, University of Tel Aviv, 1970.

Palestine Royal Commission. *Report.* London: His Majesty's Stationery Office, 1937.

Penkower, Monty W. *The Jews Were Expendable.* Urbana and Chicago University of Illinois Press, 1983.

Penniman, Howard, ed. *Israel After the Polls: The Knesset Election of 1977.* Washington: American Enterprise Institute, 1979.

Peres, Shimon. *David's Sling* (Hebrew). Tel Aviv: Am Oved, 1972.

Peri, Yoram. *Israel's Army and Politics.* Cambridge: Cambridge University Press, 1982.

—— "Retired Army Officers and Politics: The Case of IDF." Ph.D. dissertation. Sociology Dept., London School of Economics, 1980.

Perlmutter, Amos. "A. D. Gordon: A Socialist Zionist Ideologue." *Middle Eastern Studies,* Jan. 1979.

—— "Begin's Rhetorics and Sharon's Tactics." *Foreign Affairs,* Fall 1982.

—— "The Begin Strategy and the Dayan Tactics." *Foreign Affairs,* Jan. 1978.

—— "Berl Katznelson and the Theory and Practice of Revolutionary Constructivism." *Middle Eastern Studies,* Jan. 1977.

—— "Dayan Open Bridges." *The New Middle East,* May 1970.

—— *Egypt: The Praetorian State.* New Brunswick, NJ: Transaction, 1974.

—— "The Fiasco of Anglo-American Middle East Policy." *People and Politics in the Middle East,* M. Curtis, ed.

———— "Ideology and Organization: Socialist Zionist Parties, 1897–1957." Ph.D. dissertation. Political Science Dept., University of California, Berkeley, 1957.

———— "The Israeli Raid on Iraq." *Strategic Review,* Winter 1982.

———— "Letter from Lebanon." *Encounter,* Nov. 1982.

———— *Military and Politics in Israel.* London: Frank Cass, 1969.

———— *Politics and the Military in Israel: 1967–1977.* London: Frank Cass, 1978.

———— "Sources of Instability in the Middle East." *Orbis,* v. 12, n. 2, Summer 1968.

———— *The Times and Life of Menachem Begin.* Forthcoming. 1986.

Philby, Harry St. John Bridger. *Arabian Jubilee.* New York: Day, 1953.

Porath, Yehosua. *The Emergence of the Palestinian Arab Nationalist Movement, 1918–1929.* London: Frank Cass, 1975.

———— *The Palestinian Arab Nationalist Movement, 1929–1939: From Riots to Rebellion.* London: Frank Cass, 1977.

Porath, Yehosua, and Yaacov Shavit, eds. *The British Mandate and the Jewish National Home* (Hebrew). Tel Aviv: Ketter, 1982.

Preuss, Teddy. *Begin: His Regime* (Hebrew). Jerusalem: Keter Publishing House, 1984.

Raanan, Zvi. *Gush Emunim* (Hebrew). Tel Aviv: Sifriat Poalim, 1980.

Rabin, Yitzhak. *Memoirs* (Hebrew). Tel Aviv: Maariv, 1979.

Rabinovich, Itamar. *The War for Lebanon, 1970–1983.* Ithaca, NY: Cornell University Press, 1984.

Rabinovitz, Yosi, ed. *On Tabenkin* (Hebrew). Tel Aviv: Hakibbutz Hameuchad, 1982.

Rejwan, Nissim. *Nasserist Ideology, Its Exponents and Critics.* New Brunswick, NJ: Transaction, 1974.

Rendel, G. W. *The Sword and the Olive.* London: Hamish Hamilton, 1957.

Rose, Norman A., ed. *Baffy: The Diaries of Blanche Dougdale.* London: Valentine Mitchell, 1973.

———— *Gentile Zionists.* London: Frank Cass, 1973.

Rubinstein, Danny. *On the Lord's Side: Gush Emunim* (Hebrew). Tel Aviv: Hakibbutz Hameuchad, 1982.

Sadeh, Yitzhak. *What Did the Palmach Innovate?* (Hebrew). Merhavia: Sifriat Poalim, 1950.

Safran, Nadav. *From War to War: The Arab-Israeli Confrontation, 1948–1967.* New York: Pegasus, 1968.

———— *Israel: The Embattled Ally.* Cambridge, Mass.: Harvard University Press, 1978.

Schiff, Zeev. *Earthquake in October* (Hebrew). Tel Aviv: Zmora, 1974.

Schiff, Zeev, and Ehud Ya'ari. *Israel's Lebanon War.* New York: Simon and Schuster, 1984.

Schweid, Eleizer. *A. D. Gordon: The Man and His Deeds* (Hebrew). Tel Aviv: Am Oved, 1975.

Sela, Avraham. "Conversations and Contacts between Zionist and Palestinian Arab Leaders, 1933–1939." *Hamizrah Hehadash (The New East)* (Hebrew), v.22, 1972.

Sha'atiel, Eli. "David Ben-Gurion and Partition, 1937." *The Jerusalem Quarterly,* Winter 1979.

Shapira, Anita. *Futile Struggle: The Jewish Labor Controversy, 1929–1939* (Hebrew). Tel Aviv: Hakibbutz Hameuchad, 1977.

Shapiro, Yonatan. *The Formative Years of the Israeli Labour Party: The Organization of Power, 1919–1930*. Los Angles and London: Sage, 1976.

—— *The Organization of Power: Historical Ahdut Haavoda* (Hebrew). Tel Aviv: Am Oved, 1975.

Sharett (Shertok), Moshe. *Personal Diary* (Hebrew). 8 vols. Tel Aviv: Maariv, 1980.

—— *Political Diary* (Hebrew). 5 vols. Tel Aviv: Am Oved, 1970–1976.

Shavit, Yaacov. *Revisionism in Zionism* (Hebrew). Tel Aviv: Maariv, 1978.

—— *Sezon (The Hunting Season)* (Hebrew). Tel Aviv: Hadar, 1976.

Sharit, Yaacov, and Y. Porath: see Porath.

[Shazar Center] *Ideological and Political Zionism.* Jerusalem: Shazar Center, 1978.

Sheffer, Gabriel. "British Colonial Policymaking Toward Palestine (1929–1939)." *Middle Eastern Studies,* Oct. 1978.

—— "Comprehensive Solution vs. Conflict Resolution in the Arab-Israeli conflict: New Analysis on Moshe Sharett and David Ben-Gurion's Confrontation." In Ettinger Samuel et al, eds. *Zionism and the Arab Question.*

Shorske, Carl E. *Fin de Siecle Vienna: Politics and Culture.* New York: Knopf, 1979.

Silver, Eric. *Begin.* London: Weidenfeld and Nicolson, 1983.

Slutsky, Yehuda, ed. *Sepher Toldot Ha-Haganah (History of the Haganah),* vol. III, parts I, II, III, (Hebrew). Tel Aviv: Am Oved, 1972–1974.

Snetsinger, John. *Truman, the Jewish Vote, and the Creation of Israel.* Stanford, CA: Hoover Institution Press, Stanford University, 1974.

Stein, Leonard. *The Balfour Declaration.* New York: Simon and Schuster, 1961.

Stephens, Robert. *Nasser.* New York: Simon and Schuster, 1981.

Stern, Eliahu, ed., *Chronology of the History of the New Yishuv in Eretz Israel, 1936–1947* (Hebrew). Jerusalem: Yad Ben-Zvi, 1974.

Tabenkin, Yitzhak. *Works (Ktavim)* (Hebrew). 5 vols. Tel Aviv: Hakibbutz Hameuchad, 1973–1975.

Teveth, Shabtai. *Moshe Dayan.* Boston: Houghton Mifflin, 1973.

—— *The Zealot David* (Biography of Ben-Gurion). 2 vols. Jerusalem and Tel Aviv: Schocken, 1976, 1980.

Thornton, H. P. *Imperialism in the Twentieth Century.* Minneapolis: University of Minnesota Press, 1971.

Truman, Harry S. *Memoirs.* 2 vols. Garden City, NY: Doubleday, 1956.

United States Department of State. *Foreign Relations of the United States 1948,* vol. 5, Part 2, *The Near East: Israel,* Washington D.C., 1976.

Vatikiotis, P. J. *The Egyptian Army in Politics: Pattern for New Nations.* (Bloomington: Indiana University Press, 1957). Reprint, Westport, Conn.: Greenwood, 1975.

—— *Nasser and His Generation.* New York: St. Martin's, 1978.

Vital, David. *The Origins of Zionism.* Oxford: Oxford University Press, 1975.

—— *The Origins of Zionism: The Formative Years.* Oxford: Clarendon Press, 1982.

Wasserstein, Bernard. *Britain and the Jews of Europe, 1939–1945.* Oxford: Clarendon Press, 1979.

Weisgal, Meyer W., ed. *Theodore Herzl.* (New York: 1929.) Reprint, Westport, Conn.: Hyperion, 1976.

———— see Weizmann, Chaim.

Weizman, Ezer. *The Battle for Peace.* New York: Bantam, 1981.

Weizmann, Chaim. *Letters and Papers of Chaim Weizmann,* Meyer W. Weisgal, ed. 9 vols. New Brunswick, NJ: Rutgers State University, 1978.

———— *Trial and Error: The Autobiography of Chaim Weizmann.* (New York: Harper & Row, 1949.) Reprint, Westport, Conn.: Greenwood, 1972.

Wilson, Evan M. *Decision on Palestine.* Stanford, CA: Hoover Institution Press, Stanford University, 1979.

Wistrich, Robert, ed. *The Left Against Zion.* London: Valentine Mitchell, 1979.

Yellin: see Friedman-Yellin.

Yerucham: see Ben-Yerucham.

Yogev, G., and Y. Gorni: see Gorni.

Zohar: see Bar Zohar.

Glossary

Ahdut Ha-Avoda United Labor Party. Formed as a coalition of Poale Zion and other minor Socialist Zionist parties in Eretz Israel in 1919. Joined Histadrut in 1920. Merged with Hapoel Hatzair in 1929 to form the Mapai party. Faction B, which split from Mapai in 1942, assumed the old name Ahdut Ha-Avoda. In 1954, when split from Mapam, this group assumed the name Ha-Tnu'ah Le-Ahdut Ha-Avoda.

Am Lochem Fighting nation. The Jewish Resistance movement established in 1944.

Ashkenazim Jews of European origin.

Avoda Israel Labor Party. Formed in 1968.

Betar Zeev Jabotinsky's youth movement. Established in Lithuania and Poland in the middle 1920s, its goal was to train Jews in military science: It became the major source of recruitment for the undergrounds of Etzel and Lehi.

Bnai Akiva The nationalist religious youth movement. Established in the 1930s in Palestine, it has become the source of recruitment for the militant nationalist religious Gush Emunim movement.

Camp David Accords On September 26, 1979, Egyptian President Anwar al-Sadat and Israeli Prime Minister Menachem Begin signed a peace treaty between their two countries that had been worked out in a final series of meetings arranged by United States President Jimmy Carter at Camp David, Maryland. The treaty consisted of two major agreements, or accords. Accord A deals with Egypt–Israel relations, accord B with autonomy for the Palestinians residing in the West Bank and Gaza.

Dash Democratic Party for Change. An electoral coalition and party established in the 1977 elections, led by Professor Yigael Yadin. It joined Begin's cabinet in 1977 and then split: By the 1981 election it had dissolved.

Eretz Israel Literally, the Land of Israel. Also British Palestine. Eretz Israel is the all-inclusive name for Zionist territorial aspirations.

Etzel Irgun Zvai Leumi. National Military Organization. Established in 1931 as a schism from the Haganah by Avraham Tehomi. Since 1937 Etzel led by David Raziel and Avraham Stern, Betar's military underground. Between 1944–1948 was led by Menachem Begin's Revolt.

Gahal Herut General Zionist parliament, any electoral bloc between 1965–1973 when Likud was established and incorporated Gahal.

Gush Emunim Group of the Faithful. The ultraradical religious movement. Advocates settlement and annexation of the West Bank and Gaza.

Haganah Defense. Jewish underground in Palestine, led and organized by the labor movement. Begun as an organization in 1921. Forerunner of the IDF.

Ha-Kibbutz Ha-Meuchad United Kibbutz movement. Ahdut Ha-Avoda Kibbutz movement. Established in 1927.

Ha-Mosad The Institute. Haganah and Israel's special intelligence services.

Hapoel Hatzair The Young Laborer. The Palestinian Socialist Zionist party. Non-Marxist: Founded in 1905 in Petah Tiqvah. Merged with Ahdut ha-Avoda in 1929 to make the Mapai party.

Hashomer The Watchman. Jewish self-protection organization established in 1909.

Hashomer Hatzair Young Guard. Marxist Zionist youth movement. Established in 1927.

Hatechiyah Renaissance. The radical nationalist faction that split from Likud in opposition to the Camp David Accords: Led by Geula Cohen, a Lehi veteran. An ultraradical, Ashkenazi-led party closely allied with Ariel Sharon, it advocates annexation of all territories occupied in 1967. Gained five seats in the 11th Knesset elections, 1984.

Havlagah Containment. The passivist resistance policy advocated by moderate elements in Zionism and by the Yishuv.

Hehalutz The Pioneer. The movement of pioneers for Palestine founded by Yoseph Trumpeldor in 1918.

Herut Freedom party. A Revisionist party. Legal successor since 1948 to the National Military Organization (see Irgun Zrai Leumi), a group encompassing all splinters of Zionist Revisionist military structures: led by Menachem Begin, former commander of NMO: since 1973 the leading party of the Likud coalition.

Histadrut Literally, "Organization." The General Federation of Jewish Labor in Eretz Israel, founded in 1921.

Homa U-migdal Fortress and Tower. Defense settlement system during the 1936–1939 Arab Revolt.

Irgun Zvai Leumi *See* Etzel.

Israel Defense Force (IDF) *See* Zahal.

Kibbutz (*pl. Kibbutzim*) Collective. An organization of workers on a communal basis.

Knesset Israeli Parliament: Established in 1949.

Labor Party Mifleget Ha-Avoda. The party founded in 1968 when Mapai, Rafi, and Mapam merged into one party, and since 1965 its electoral coalition Maarach.

L'Am To the Nation. A nationalist splinter of Mapai.

Land of Israel Movement (LIM) The post–1967 movement of radical nationalists, maximalists, and annexationists. Its most influential ideologue was Yitzhak Tabenkin, founder of Ahdut ha-Avoda and Ha-Kibbutz Ha-Meuchad.

Lehi Abbreviation for Lochamei Herut Israel (Israel Freedom Fighters), a Revisionist underground movement engaged in personal terrorism. Established by Avraham Stern in 1940: after Stern's assassination, led by a trio including Natan Friedman-Yellin, Dr. Israel Shayeb, and Yitzhak Shamir (who was Prime Minister in 1983–84). This group was dissolved at the 2nd Knesset elections in 1951.

Likud The coalition of all nationalist forces organized by Ariel Sharon in 1973: composed of Herut, liberals (Gahal), L'Am, and minor militant nationalist groups. Became the leading bloc in the 1977 and 1981 governments, and the partner of Labor in the 1984 government.

Maarach The Alignment. The parliamentary party and electoral alliance of Mapai, Ahdut ha-Avoda, and Rafi formed in 1965.

Mafdal Abbreviation for Miflagah Datit Leumit (National Religious Party). In coalition with Mapai since 1948. Played a key role in the appointment of Moshe Dayan as Defense Minister in 1967. Joined Likud coalition governments in 1977, 1981, and national unity government in 1984.

Mamlachtiout Statism. The concept of institutionalization and formalization of Yishuv's volunteer political organization in the newly formed Israel.

Mapai Abbreviation for Mifleget Poale Eretz Israel (Israel's Labor Party). Formed when Hapoel Hatzair united with Ahdut ha-Avoda in 1929. Social-democratic in orientation.

Mapam Abbreviation for Mifleget Poalim Meuchedet (United Labor Party). Formed when Hashomer Hatzair united with Ha-Tnu'ah Le-Ahdut ha-Avoda in 1948. Marxist in orientation.

Moshav Small holders cooperative settlement.

Moshava A privately owned agricultural settlement.

Nahal Abbreviation for Noar Halutzi Lohem (Fighting Youth Movement). Zahal's special military-agricultural pioneer unit: Established in 1949.

National Religious Party (NRP) See Mafdal

Palmach Abbreviation for Plugot Ha-Machatz (Haganah Shock Platoons). Established in 1941, these units served as the elite of the Haganah. They were dissolved in 1949 when Zahal was organized as the army of the State of Israel.

Poale Zion Workers of Zion. The first Socialist Zionist party in the diaspora: Marxist in orientation. In the early days of the twentieth century, Poale Zion groups were scattered without any organizational unity in various Russian towns.

Rafi Mapai splinter group—the Ben-Gurion–Dayan–Peres faction—formed in 1965. Dissolved in 1968 and joined Maarach to make Israel Labor Party.

Revisionist Party Zeev (Vladimir) Jabotinsky's splinter group from the World Zionist Movement. A Zionist nationalistic party whose platforms call for the annexation of the East Jordan territory. Founded in 1925 in Paris: Formed the New Zionist Organization in 1933.

Sepharadim Jews from Oriental-Arab countries.

Shay Sherut Yediot, Haganah's political intelligence service: Part of Ha-Mosad.

Shinui Change. A small party of liberals and anti-annexationists: Split from Dash in 1979. Member of the National Unity government of 1984.

Shlemut Ha-Moledet The Unity of the Land. The ideological concept of Begin and ultranationalists that calls for a complete Eretz Israel and annexation of Judea and Samaria.

Yishuv Community, settlement. Up to the second immigration wave (1905), Yishuv refers to the baronial farmer settlement (1880s), antagonistic to Zionism and to the Socialist Zionists. Since the change in Palestine with the increase of Zionist immigrations, the term applies to the growing constructive Zionist community in Eretz Israel.

Zahal Abbreviation for Zva Ha-Haganah Le-Israel (Israel Defense Force—IDF). Army of the State of Israel, established in May 15, 1948, and under the Defense Service Act of March 1949.

Index

War of 1967, (*Cont.*):
  political fragmentation and, 192
Wars of Independence of 1947–49,
  123, 130
Weizman, Ezer, 300–301
Weizmann, Chaim, 58–59, 69–73,
  78–79, 111, 115, 117
  profile of, 14–16, 24
  split from Ben-Gurion, 69–73
  Zionist movement and, 22–27, 30,
  32–34
West Bank, settlement of, 205–6
  See also Camp David.
White Paper, 12, 54–55, 75–81
  Jewish immigration and, 77–78, 80
  Jewish reaction to, 78–81
  land sales, restrictions, 77–78
  policy statement of, 75–77
  Revisionists' reaction to, 87
  Socialists' reaction to, 86–87
Wingate, Orde, 84
Wise, Stephen, 108, 111
World War II
  beginnings of, 78
  Haganah, British training of, 90, 93
  Jewish-Anglo cooperation, 89–91,
  93
  Jewish-Anglo discord, 93–96
  Jews in Allied forces, 88
  refugee boats, 94
World Zionist Congress, Uganda is-
  sue, 22
World Zionist Organization, 17, 21,
  24

"X Committee," 103

Yadin, Yigael, 231, 254–55, 301
Yariv, Aharon, 213
Yishuv, 5, 12, 45
  post-partition position, 129–31
  role after partition, 124–26

Zahal, 143–45
  1973 elections and, 232–33
  Ben-Gurion and, 143–45, 159–60,
  168–69
  Dayan's leadership, 169
Zeirim, 138
  defeat of, 1942, 140–41
  prominent members of, 138–39
Zionism
  aims of movement, 43–44
  early history of, 11–13, 28–37
  early leaders, 14–37
  eras of, 337
  ideology versus institutionalization,
  210–11
  mamlachtiout and, 135
  partition concept, 1946, 111–20
  partition controversy, 1937, 56–60
  Revisionist Zionism, 12, 23
  revolutionary constructivism, 43
  Socialist Zionism, 12, 23
  White Paper, reactions to, 78–80
  See also Revisionist Zionism; Socialist Zionism; United Kibbutz
  movement.